Women in the
American Revolution

Women in the American Revolution

Gender, Politics, and the Domestic World

EDITED BY BARBARA B. OBERG

University of Virginia Press

CHARLOTTESVILLE AND LONDON

University of Virginia Press
© 2019 by the Rector and Visitors of the University of Virginia
All rights reserved
Printed in the United States of America on acid-free paper

First published 2019

9 8 7 6 5 4 3 2

Library of Congress Cataloging-in-Publication Data

Names: Oberg, Barbara, editor.
Title: Women in the American Revolution : gender, politics, and the domestic world /
    edited by Barbara B. Oberg.
Description: Charlottesville : University of Virginia Press, 2019. | Includes
    ibliographical references and index.
Identifiers: LCCN 2018054112 | ISBN 9780813942599 (cloth : alk. paper) |
    ISBN 9780813942605 (ebook)
Subjects: LCSH: United States—History—Revolution, 1775–1783—Women. | United
    States—History—Revolution, 1775–1783—Biography. | Women—United States—
    Social conditions—18th century. | Women—Political activity—United States—
    History—18th century.
Classification: LCC E276 .w66 2019 | DDC 973.3082—dc23
LC record available at https://lccn.loc.gov/2018054112

Cover art: Detail of *Mrs. Schuyler Burning Her Wheat Fields on the Approach of the
    British,* Emanuel Gottlieb Leutze, 1852, oil on canvas. (Los Angeles County Muse-
    um of Art, Bicentennial gift of Mr. and Mrs. J. M. Schaaf, Mr. and Mrs. William D.
    Witherspoon, Mr. and Mrs. Charles C. Shoemaker, and Jo Ann and Julian Ganz, Jr.
    [M.76.91])

To Pauline Alice Maier, 1938–2013,
and to
C. Dallett Hemphill, 1959–2015
Jan Ellen Lewis, 1949–2018
Scholars, Teachers, Mentors

Contents

Preface

As Rosemarie Zagarri asks in the Introduction, "What did the American Revolution mean to—and for—women?" Over the past several decades, the subject of the role and status of women during the War for Independence has attained its rightful place in the study of early American history. At a time of significant disruptions in daily life and radically changed expectations of what a woman's place in a marriage, the household, and the community "ought" to be, American women were called on to perform a variety of tasks and assume multiple roles. They showed patriotism by supporting boycotts of British goods and encouraging manufacturing at home; they raised funds to feed and clothe the troops; and they took over the management of the farm or family business to keep the household running smoothly in the absence of men. Some traveled with the army in supporting roles. Others remained loyal to the British crown, weakening or destroying their relations with family members, friends, and neighbors. Women wrote poetry, novels, plays, and essays. They exchanged letters with husbands away in battle, relatives, and friends. Some kept a journal or diary in which they recorded the routine of daily life in wartime, and some wrote more intimately, sharing the emotional turmoil in which they lived. These records, public and private, yield poignant and little-known stories that allow us to rethink the world that women inhabited during a time of political and economic upheaval, social change, and armed conflict that we have long referred to as "the era of the American Revolution." It is an era that will never cease to demand our attention. As Sheila Skemp observes in the Afterword, "Anthologies produce at least as many questions as they do answers, thus preparing the way for new and exciting perspectives." This is what we have set out to do.

Women in the American Revolution: Gender, Politics, and the Domestic World had its origins in June 2014, when a group of early American historians met in Williamsburg, Virginia, to share their work and suggest how it might add to and reshape our understanding of the revolutionary era. We began by posing a series of questions: What was the state of the field and how had it changed over the preceding decades? What questions had been answered and what required additional exploration? Where was the study of "the era of the American Revolution" headed? The conference and now this volume will, we hope, take another step toward resolving some questions and, just as important, give us new and challenging ones to consider.

Barbara B. Oberg

Acknowledgments

This conference was convened under the auspices of the National Society of the Sons of the American Revolution (SAR), led by the energetic and dedicated past President General Joseph W. Dooley. Colin W. Campbell, president of the Colonial Williamsburg Foundation, and Karin Wulf, director of the Omohundro Institute of Early American History and Culture at the College of William and Mary, provided wisdom and moral support throughout. Kate Haulman, associate professor of history at American University, opened the conference and suggested the issues that would be raised. Rosemarie Zagarri closed the proceedings with broad and perceptive comments that highlighted the contributions of each paper.

The generous support of the following organizations and individuals also helped to make the conference possible: the George Washington Endowment Fund of the National Society of the SAR; the George Knight-Kenneth C. Patty Memorial Trust Fund of the Virginia Society of the SAR; the George Mason Chapter and the George Washington Chapter, both of the Virginia Society of the SAR; George Washington's Mount Vernon; Arlington Blue Top Cabs; the WinSet Group, LLC; the California Society SAR Ladies Auxiliary; Constance Barker; Cynthia Bigbee; Janet Brown; J. Thomas Burch, Jr.; Karen A. Carlson; Marilyn Chilton; Karen Dodd; Karen and Jim Faulkinbury; Mr. and Mrs. John H. Franklin Jr.; Un Hui Yi Fosdyck; Joseph R. Godfrey, Ph.D.; Lisa Gregory; Barbara Magerkurth; S. John Massoud; Eugene D. Melvin; Samuel C. Powell, Ph.D.; and Timothy E. Ward. Leslie S. Noble, Stephanie Saulnier Lally, and Michele Derosa provided valuable and patient assistance in arranging lodging, meals, and meeting space at Colonial Williamsburg. Manav Kapur, a graduate student in history at Princeton University, played a crucial role in readying the manuscript for submission. We offer our thanks to all of these people.

Women in the
American Revolution

Introduction

ROSEMARIE ZAGARRI

What did the American Revolution mean to—and for—women? Only within the past half-century has this question come to be considered a valid and important topic of scholarly inquiry. Among previous generations of historians, the American Revolution was assumed to be by, for, and about men—usually white men, who were often of elite status. These were, after all, the individuals who led the armies, fought the battles, and gathered in legislative assemblies to create a new government for the country. Changes within the field of history, however, have challenged the conventional narrative. With the development of social history in the 1970s, women's history in the 1980s, and gender history in the 1990s, scholars and nonscholars alike have come to realize that one cannot fully understand the American Revolution without understanding women's participation in, and contributions to, the revolutionary movement. Yet not all women supported the revolutionary cause. Like some men, certain women remained loyal to the Crown. In addition, it has become clear that those on the margins of the Revolution, including lower-class white women, enslaved women, free black women, and Native American women, should have a place in accounts of the period. Willingly or not, these groups often found themselves swept up in the revolutionary maelstrom.[1]

Women played an integral role in all phases of the revolutionary process: in the prerevolutionary movement to resist British policies, in the struggles during the War for Independence, and afterward, in efforts to build a new nation. Nonetheless, after decades of scholarship on this topic, there is still no consensus on a critical question: did the Revolution benefit women or actually reinforce traditional gender roles? For white women, much of the attention thus far has been on their political or legal status, which, at least on the surface, did not change much. The doctrine of coverture, which declared women legally subordinate to their husbands or fathers, persisted. Married women could not own property, make contracts, or sue (or be sued) in court. Women did not win the vote (except briefly in New Jersey); nor could they hold public office. They remained legally invisible.[2]

Yet other historians, who have looked beyond formal legal and political institutions, have discovered whole new realms of women's revolutionary experiences and ideas. The coming of the Revolution encouraged women's interest in, and involvement with politics. Women participated in boycotts against Britain, protested British policies, and suffered under the travails of war. In this process, women's role was politicized, producing a construct that the historian Linda Kerber has called "republican motherhood." Even as wives and mothers women could make sacrifices for the public good and promote the revolutionary cause. They could influence their husbands and sons, encouraging them to become virtuous citizens of the republic. Women might also become interested in political ideas. As "female politicians," they now felt free to express their views in public writings or in private salons. Women, it is clear, exerted a profound, though largely indirect, impact on the country's political life.

Consequent to the Revolution, scholars have tracked the ripple effects of the Revolution throughout American society and politics. To tutor their children, women gained greater access to education; female literacy soared. More women discovered opportunities to participate in public life, directly and indirectly. Their activities in charitable societies, benevolent movements, and social reform activities reshaped civil society. In more intimate realms, the Revolution stimulated the rise of companionate marriage, a politicization of women's fashions, the increasing ease of friendship between the sexes, and a long-term decline in women's marital fertility. Not all changes, however, were positive. After a few decades of social and political experimentation, a backlash against women's broader social and political roles ensued. By the 1820s, there was greater scrutiny of women: harsher policing of women's sexuality, increasing antagonism toward "female politicians," and a hardening of traditional gender roles through the emergence of separate spheres ideology and the rise of biological essentialism.[3]

The essays in this collection approach the study of the American Revolution with a specific intent: to examine what the Revolution meant to—and for—many different American women. Yet in addressing this issue, the volume does not pretend to be comprehensive or complete. Although there is some attention to the experience of Native American and African American women, the majority of the women discussed are white, and many are elite.[4] Nonetheless, all of the essays attempt to recover the diversity of women's actual experiences. Some women were staunch patriots; others were fervid loyalists. Some found that the Revolution created new opportunities for them to write, to market goods, or to find a new kind of independence in the world. Others saw their lives diminished—their property confiscated, their businesses failing, or their sense of security shattered. Some women acted on their political beliefs; many others simply tried to find a way to keep their lives intact as armies occupied their region, trampled their fields, or stole their farm animals. To their dismay, many women found that their marriages faltered, failed, or had to be renegotiated under the stresses of war.

The central focus, then, is on lived experiences rather than on abstract ideology or high-minded principles. Although certain elite white women wrote highly intellectual tracts about the American Revolution—most notably, Abigail Adams, Judith Sargent Murray, and Mercy Otis Warren—most women at the time did not approach the Revolution from this perspective.[5] Cognizant of this fact, these essays highlight other factors—age, educational background, marital status, social class, race, and region—that had a profound but widely divergent set of effects on women's experiences of revolution. By providing a broad sample of women's lives, the volume hopes to provide scholars with a wider empirical basis from which to theorize about changing conceptions of masculinity, femininity, and heteronormativity.

The volume also suggests the limits of generalization: there proves to be no single "woman's experience" during the Revolution. Although some women used their femininity to achieve certain desired outcomes, the precise ways in which women deployed "gendered power," as Martha King calls it, varied immensely. The African American poet Phillis Wheatley, for example, used neoclassical imagery in her poetry, according to David Waldstreicher, to articulate her radical ideas through a coded language. Still others, such as enslaved midwives and Iroquois women, lived in the shadows of the war, reacting only when it directly touched their lives. Yet women of all races often faced deep personal loss through separation from their loved ones, forced migration, or the final separation, death. Collectively, then, the essays assert a critical point: just as there was no single experience of the American Revolution for men, women also witnessed the Revolution in many diverse ways.[6]

Historians who wish to recover women's lives during the revolutionary era face many more challenges than historians writing about white men. Although women constituted half of the population, they typically did not leave behind nearly as many written documents as men did, partly because women were not as literate as men and partly because women's writings often were not thought worth saving. Because women did not vote, serve in public office, or lead armies, their works were typically regarded as ephemeral or unimportant; such records were often discarded or destroyed.

In fact, women sometimes collaborated in the destruction of their own works. In the case of the Washingtons, for example, Martha Washington burned her private correspondence with her husband, George, to prevent prying eyes from glimpsing the intimate details of their marriage. In the case of Mary Willing Byrd, the bias of male historians almost led to her erasure from the printed public record. A political leader from an old Virginia family, William Byrd III nearly drove his estate into bankruptcy and committed suicide in 1777. Mary Willing Byrd lived another thirty-seven years and thrived, rescuing the estate for their children. Nonetheless, documentary editors printed a series of edited volumes containing the works of William Byrd I, II, and III. They did not include Mary Willing Byrd's extensive correspondence, dating to the three-plus decades after Byrd III's death. Fortunately, because of the family's elite status, many of Mary's letters and papers were preserved in the archives, even when they were not deemed worthy of publication. Such accidental survivals help make women's history of the revolutionary era challenging but possible.[7]

The historians in this volume have used new or underused sources and asked new questions of traditional sources. Some have focused on women who lived in the shadows of their better-known husbands, such as the wives of male loyalists or the spouses of revolutionary leaders such as Richard Stockton and George Washington. Because of these women's relationships with prominent men, their papers tend to be better preserved than the writings of those whose husbands lived in complete obscurity. Ami Pflugrad-Jackisch used archived probate records and legal documents to uncover Mary Willing Byrd's extraordinary life. Looking at the Boston Massacre, Serena Zabin examines unpublished church records, muster rolls, account books, and other sources to reveal the dense web of intimate ties and neighborly relations that existed between British Regulars and Boston women prior to the momentous clash that occurred on March 5, 1770. Sara Collini and Maeve Kane use other kinds of records—account books, estate records, and claims for wartime losses—to provide revealing insights into the lives of Indian women and African American women during the Revolution. Phillis Wheatley represents the unique case of a woman who was both black and enslaved but whose words were actually published during her lifetime, thus preserving a rich trove of writings from her own pen.

To provide greater coherence, the volume is divided into three thematic parts: "Economic Relationships," "Political Identities," and "Marriage and the Family." Each highlights a particular aspect of women's revolutionary experience. Yet the parts are not mutually exclusive; essays may speak to the themes in more than one part. Larger themes cut across parts and provide fodder for further analysis.

The essays on economic relationships in Part I reveal the many ways in which the revolutionary crisis both tore apart women's economic lives and enabled—or compelled—women to reshape their own economic prospects. Sara Collini's "The Labors of Enslaved Midwives in Revolutionary Virginia" brings to light an underground economy among enslaved midwives that persisted before, during, and after the American Revolution. African American midwives, Collini explains, performed important duties within the plantation economy: delivering babies, caring for new mothers, and providing general healthcare to the enslaved population. The women learned their skills by apprenticing themselves to other midwives, who might be black or white, male or female, enslaved or free. Their work sometimes required that they leave their home plantation and travel to other places. In doing so, they experienced a kind of geographic mobility that few other enslaved women could. Slave owners, recognizing the women's expertise and abilities, sometimes even compensated their enslaved midwives for their services.

The Revolution, Collini argues, did not radically disrupt the midwives' daily lives or alter the nature of their contributions. Yet after the Revolution, the internal contradictions of the women's labor became more apparent. With the impending closure of the international slave trade, slave owners in Virginia realized that their slaves might be even more valuable as commodities. They could be sold for cash to the Deep South. This changed the meaning of the enslaved midwives' work. By facilitating the growth of a healthy slave population, the midwives were actually enriching their owners at the expense of fellow slaves who were sold as chattel. Like Phillis Wheatley, enslaved midwives found that the American Revolution heightened rather than resolved the contradiction between slavery and freedom.

Kaylan M. Stevenson's discussion of milliners and mantuamakers in colonial Williamsburg is another case in point. During the 1760s, a number of unmarried women emigrated from England to Virginia in the belief that they could use their contacts in London to become successful merchants in the colony's capital. Aware that wealthy Virginians hoped to keep pace with their European counterparts, they imported a variety of hats, gloves, wigs, fans, jewelry, and silks to sell in their own shops. At the same time, they carefully assessed the realities of the economic environment in which they found themselves.

The most successful of these merchants, Stevenson shows, timed their orders to reach Williamsburg during meetings of the Virginia legislature, a period of peak demand. They skillfully advertised their goods to appeal to Virginians' desire for conspicuous consumption. Most important, they stoutly insisted that customers pay in cash rather than through credit, the typical practice in cash-poor colonial Virginia. Nonetheless, as hostilities with Britain intensified, the women found their situation increasingly untenable. Unwilling and unable to participate in the boycott of British goods, and faced with a declining demand for luxury items, the women—one by one—closed up shop and returned to England. Politics destroyed their economic dreams. Rather than victims, however, the women made their own choices about how and where their futures would unfold.

In contrast, a Philadelphia woman found that the upheavals of the revolutionary crisis presented her with new economic opportunities that might not have existed in more settled times. Elizabeth Dickinson Weed, according to Susan Hanket Brandt, found her calling as an apothecary, a seller of medicines and pharmaceutical potions of all sorts. Having learned the medicinal arts from her second husband, she successfully maintained the business after his death in 1777. Not only did her business survive; it actually thrived. Significantly, she made a number of bold economic decisions. First, she kept the apothecary shop open throughout the war, even while British troops occupied Philadelphia. Although this action raised suspicion about her loyalties, both patriots and redcoats needed her products. In 1779, Weed married a man who had served with the American military, thus quelling rumors about her suspect loyalties.

Weed did not rest on her first husband's laurels. She fiercely protected his secret pharmaceutical recipes from competitors and actively promoted her products, advertising their effectiveness and uniqueness. Perhaps even more important, Weed knew how to preserve her economic assets through legal means. When a huckster began selling "Weed's Syrup" as his own concoction, she denounced him publicly and sued him in court. Moreover, she fought to keep what she had earned within her immediate family. Weed succeeded in displacing her stepson (Dr. Weed's son from a previous marriage) as the owner of the building that housed the apothecary shop. In her will, she actually left the building and the business not to her second husband or stepson but to her own biological son. Unlike many women who floundered during the war, Weed excelled at discovering "entrepreneurial strategies" for maintaining her economic independence. Significantly, America's political independence facilitated Weed's ability to attain personal economic independence.

The essays in Part II shift the focus from economics to explore the precise way in which individual women who were related to political figures understood their political identities. The experience of Indians during the American Revolution was, not surprisingly, radically different from that of white Americans. Although their degree of participation varied, most of the tribes that made up the Iroquois nations supported Britain in its conflict with the new United States. In each case, however, Indian women came in for particular kinds of attack and abuse. They were, according to Maeve Kane, the objects of both real and symbolic political violence.

Whether symbolic or actual, the violence served to undermine women's role and status within the Iroquois communities. For example, among the wartime claims for loss filed by these tribes, more than one-third came from women. Marauding American soldiers particularly targeted trade goods owned by women to be plundered or destroyed. European commodities such as gowns, jewelry, and gloves endowed Indian women with a kind of "civilized" status. By confiscating such objects, Americans symbolically stripped Indian women of their claim to civility. At the same time, American soldiers often attacked the fruits of the women's labor with a singular fury and destructiveness. In Captain John Sullivan's attack on the Seneca, soldiers torched the houses they knew to be associated with women and burned the crops they knew women had cultivated in violation of Euro-American gender roles. Moreover, American soldiers sometimes grotesquely mutilated and desecrated women's dead bodies in a calculated show of gendered power. Finally, American negotiators failed to acknowledge women's political and diplomatic importance in peace negotiations. They failed to offer women ceremonial gifts and deliberately marginalized their participation. The Revolution, then, represented an assault on Iroquois women's labor, status, and public position—an attack from which it was very hard to recover.

For Annis Boudinot Stockton, according to Martha J. King, a desire to restore the family's public reputation drove her to a fervid assertion of her patriotic identity. Stockton's husband, Richard, had served in the Second Continental Congress from New Jersey. Although a political moderate, he chose to support the revolutionary cause and sign the Declaration of Independence. On November 30, 1776, however, the British captured Stockton. Two months later he was released. It soon emerged, however, that under duress, Stockton had retracted his signature on the Declaration and signed a pledge eschewing future involvement in the war. Although Stockton did not face public censure, his loyalties were now suspect.

Annis realized that the burden of the family's reputation rested on her shoulders—or more accurately, with her pen. Already a published poet, she quickly wrote a series of poems over the next several years on patriotic themes that enthusiastically voiced the family's allegiance to the American cause. When Pennsylvania women collected money for Washington's troops, Annis eagerly joined the effort. After Richard died in 1781, Annis continued to defend his name and rehabilitate the family's reputation. Even after the war's end, she continued to publish writings with patriotic themes. "I am no politician," she insisted, "but I *feel* that I am a patriot, and glory in that sensation."

Ironically, Richard Stockton's misfortune during the American Revolution provided Annis with the opening she needed to enter the public arena and to fully express her American identity. She declared her patriotism publicly, through her writings. Perhaps even more important, she could make her own decisions about the family's enslaved laborers. In his will Richard had given his widow permission to free as many slaves as she wished. Subsequently, she liberated at least one—and probably more—of the slaves. Unlike Mary Willing Byrd, who used slaves for her own gain, Stockton chose freedom for the enslaved.

Although celebrated rather than attacked, even the quintessential elite white woman, Martha Washington, experienced changes in her sense of political identity as a result of the American Revolution. Overshadowed by her famous husband, Martha Washington has seldom been regarded as a political actor in her own right. Yet as Mary V. Thompson shows, Martha, in her own, understated way, made distinctive contributions to the revolutionary cause. In response to her husband's request, Martha left the comfort of Mount Vernon every year during the war and traveled to be with the general at the army's winter encampments. She ended up spending more than half the war years with him at various locations. Her experiences during these inconvenient and at times dangerous sojourns created an opportunity for Martha to ease her way into a larger public role.

Like other generals' wives, Martha provided secretarial assistance, emotional support, and sociability for her husband and his military circle between seasons of battle. Even more important, instead of remaining within the confines of their winter quarters, Martha ventured out among the troops, nursing the wounded and boosting morale. She became a popular and beloved figure among the soldiers. Over time, she began to engage in more overt political activity. When a group of Quaker women came to make a special request of her husband, she facilitated their meeting. When Native American visitors arrived at camp, she became an unofficial diplomatic mediator. When Esther de Berdt Reed's Ladies Association came to Virginia, she donated $20,000 of her own money to support the troops. In response, the country embraced her. During her journeys to and from the winter encampments, citizens along the way showered her with gifts, praise, and testimonial dinners. Surprised at her own popularity, she remarked that she was being treated "as if I Had Been a Very Great Somebody." Despite her modesty, Martha's actions reveal how much the war had changed her. Forced by circumstances to push against the boundaries of a traditional feminine role, Martha had come to embrace a new, more highly political identity.

By way of contrast, David Waldstreicher takes a new look at Phillis Wheatley, a black enslaved female poet whose life could not have been more different from that of Martha Washington. In his strikingly revisionist reading of Wheatley's life and work, Waldstreicher shows that Wheatley's poems may have conveyed a far subtler understanding of the Revolution than critics have acknowledged. According to Waldstreicher, Wheatley's deployment of neoclassical forms and imagery revealed more than a mastery of the typical poetic genre of the day. Rather, in Wheatley's hands neoclassicism enabled her to provide a coded language through which she pointed to the underlying contradiction of the American Revolution—that is, that white people fought to preserve their own freedom while at the same time enslaving black people. References to ancient history and literature could be read as describing her own background as an African and as a slave.

To many Americans, Wheatley's classical references would have had an unmistakable meaning. Coming from both a woman and a slave, Wheatley's message, Waldstreicher says, possessed incredible power, magnifying her abolitionist message. Wheatley's poems, then, both reflected and created what Waldstreichercalls the "Wheatleyan moment."

In the volume's third and final part, the authors explore the aspects of womanhood that are most often associated with women at the time: marriage and family life. As violence and destruction entered the domestic realm, it often altered, reshaped, or severed marital relationships and family ties. If the French Revolution should be construed, according to Lynn Hunt, as a "family romance,"[8] then the American Revolution can be understood as a family divorce. In such families, the American Revolution was literally a civil war.

As Ami Pflugrad-Jackisch tells us, the American Revolution transformed Mary Willing Byrd from a shy plantation mistress into an independent economic dynamo. In 1777, Mary's husband, the eminent William Byrd III, committed suicide, leaving Mary a widow with eight young children and an estate on the verge of bankruptcy. As the war ravaged the Virginia countryside, Mary attempted to rebuild the estate by growing crops, buying slaves, selling land, and trading goods to all comers. Yet because it was wartime, her activities landed her in trouble. She was accused of trading with the enemy and indicted for treason. Although not legally convicted, she spent many months trying to convince her neighbors and friends that she was in fact a true patriot and a good American who would never betray her country.

What becomes clear from Pflugrad-Jackisch's essay, however, is that Mary actually put the restoration of her family's economic fortunes above any and all political loyalties. She was, in a sense, the surrogate patriarch. Stepping into her dead husband's place, she acted as the family's primary caretaker, property owner, and slaveholder. In these roles, she was forceful and assertive, assuming that she had the same kind of rights as any property-holding male citizen. This was particularly true as she attempted to obtain compensation for property lost or destroyed during the war. Not only did she seek compensation for trampled crops and stolen cattle; she also relentlessly pursued the return of slaves who had run away to join the British. At the end of the war, Byrd sought help from the highest British authorities in America. Writing to Sir Guy Carleton in New York, shortly before he left the country, she informed him, "I have lost 49 of my people [i.e., slaves], 3 fine Horses and two fine Ferry Boats." Horses, boats, and enslaved people—all were lost in the Revolution, and all, it seemed, existed on the same plane in Mary's mind.

Ultimately, Byrd succeeded in restoring her family's fortune and leaving a substantial legacy for her children. By her sheer force of intellect and will, she turned the twin tragedies of her husband's death and the upheavals of war into an advantage. She attained economic independence. Yet the authority she assumed had all the weaknesses of male patriarchy in a slave society. As Pflugrad-Jackish observes, "her mastery over her dependents," including slaves and children, created "her status as property owner." Ironically, Byrd proved to be as capable as any American man of depriving African Americans of their freedom while pursuing her own right to liberty.

Moving northward, Serena R. Zabin's essay provides a new perspective on the Boston Massacre. The story of the Boston Massacre has usually been told as an encounter between men: a violent clash between the town's patriotic young males against the king's arrogant troops who so forcefully imposed their presence in the city. According to Zabin, however, women played a crucial, though hitherto overlooked, role in this tale. After two regiments of British Regulars arrived in Boston in late 1768, they were not, she explains, universally regarded as intruders or treated as hostile strangers. Billeted in the town and living amid ordinary Bostonians, these soldiers came to be integrated into local churches, neighborhoods, and communities. The British and the Americans became friends, neighbors, and even spouses. More than one thousand Boston women married British soldiers, with whom they had children and for whom other Bostonians became godparents.

These marriages did not represent political betrayal. Before the massacre, inhabitants of the British colonies considered themselves British. A woman's marriage to a British soldier "did not," Zabin notes, "automatically either proclaim or create a family's partisan loyalties" as pro-British. Instead, she insists, we must acknowledge that the situation in Boston involved real people whose personal relationships were often complex and messy. At the same time, it is clear that these intimate bonds did affect the political calculus of Boston's leaders. The Sons of Liberty and others who were always suspicious of the standing army in their midst and concerned about the influence of these marriages on people's potential loyalties.

After the clash of March 5, 1770, the issue came to a head. With the withdrawal of the troops from the city proper, husbands and wives had to make wrenching decisions about the fate of their marriages. There was no clear pattern in their choices: some women stayed with their spouses while others chose to separate. What was clear, however, was that the Boston Massacre involved women as well as men, families as well as individuals, communities rather than just institutions. As a result, according to Zabin, Bostonians "came to understand that the fight against Great Britain was truly, literally, a family argument."

The fracturing of families, however, was not unique to supporters of the revolutionary cause. As Kimberly Nath shows, loyalist women faced even more extreme situations than the wives of American soldiers. After independence, ordinary women and men in Pennsylvania were forced to declare their allegiance publicly to either Britain or America. Although women were usually presumed to follow their husband's political sentiments, the American Revolution created a rare opening in which the state acknowledged the possibility that women might assert a separate political identity, differing from that of their husbands. In Philadelphia (and elsewhere), some couples who remained loyal to the Crown sought to exploit this situation to their own advantage. Certain husbands chose to leave the country to protect themselves from reprisals. The wife remained behind and was charged with protecting protect the family's property from confiscation. At times this strategy worked. While the women served as "proxy heads of households," their allegiance was not questioned, and the family's estate was spared. At other times, however, as in the case of the suspected loyalist Grace Galloway, the wife was physically carried out of her abode and the property was forfeited.

The fact of separation created another point at which women had to assert control over their own futures. To what lengths would a woman go to be reunited with her husband? The outcomes differed immensely from case to case. For some wives, life without their husbands seemed impossible. Mustering all of their financial and personal resources, they and their children left America in a desperate quest to achieve family reunification. For example, Susanna Marshall fled Philadelphia in June 1776 to search for her loyalist spouse. After sailing to Virginia and failing to find him there, she chartered a schooner to sail to the West Indies, where he reportedly had resettled. Although briefly diverted to St. Augustine, she was eventually allowed to depart for England. Once in the motherland, she discovered, to her dismay, that her husband had died. Now she faced a bleak future alone, as a lonely widow in a foreign country, without any visible means of support. However, some women found different fates as a result of separation.

With time, distance, and the progress of the war, these women came to accept—and even embrace—their independent status. Not only did they not seek to be reunited with their husbands; they created entirely new lives for themselves and their children. War, then, strained or broke certain marriages, loyalist and patriot alike. Yet, as Nath emphasizes, personal character was as important as political ideology in determining the outcome.

The growing sense of personal independence among women raises questions about how the institution of marriage itself weathered the American Revolution. In her close analysis of the marriage of Deborah Norris and George Logan, C. Dallett Hemphill provides some clues. Marrying in 1781 at the tail end of the War for Independence, Deborah and George both came from distinguished Pennsylvania Quaker families. Well-educated, charming, and attractive, Deborah entered marriage imbued with a belief in Quaker mutuality and revolutionary egalitarianism. George, though trained as a physician, saw himself primarily as a political leader and statesman. Yet according to Hemphill, George was a "bumbler," prone to making political gaffes that embarrassed himself and his country. How, then, did the more savvy and perceptive Deborah manage to preserve her marriage, as well as maintain her dignity?

The answer, according to Hemphill, was to practice a skill found among many women of the post-revolutionary generation: the art of self-subordination. Over the years, she explains, Deborah developed a variety of strategies that allowed her to fulfill her wifely duties yet also maintain a genuine affection for her husband. Like Annis Boudinot Stockton of New Jersey, who also suffered from a husband who made serious political mistakes, Deborah would become her husband's biggest public defender. At the same time, Deborah increasingly protected herself by separating herself from her husband. She pursued her own, independent projects in reading and writing. She refused to accompany her husband to the nation's capital after he was elected to Congress. Turning inward, she increasingly withdrew into the confines of their comfortable home, Stenton, rather than risk public embarrassment.

Finally, after bravely nursing George through his final illness and death in 1821, Deborah decided to compose a memoir in honor of her husband's memory. Significantly, according to Hemphill, her work constructed an image of George Logan that was more imaginary than real—a portrait as she would like him to have been rather than as he actually was. In this act of homage, Deborah engaged in her final act of "self-subordination" to her husband. Through mutuality and deference, Deborah had been able to integrate traditional forms of patriarchy with revolutionary-era egalitarianism into an apparently congenial union. Thus, although the American Revolution did not succeed in overturning the customary norms associated with marriage, it did introduce a new sense of women's equality that substantially changed the intimate power dynamics between husband and wife.

While these essays focus on women, they raise a larger question: to what extent did men and women share experiences of revolutionary upheaval? For both men and women, the American Revolution was a time of profound dislocation, an experience of fracture that destabilized or reshaped almost every aspect of their lives. Both sexes felt the effects of war on the home front and within their family lives. Yet there were also profound differences between the sexes. Marital status determined the range of choices for women much more than it did for men. Deborah Logan, for example, was expected to echo her husband's political allegiance. A married woman with children, such as Susanna Marshall, might feel compelled to follow her husband to England or the Caribbean to secure a means of support. After the Boston Massacre, Massachusetts women who had married British soldiers faced a terrible choice: abandon their marriages or their birth families. Single women, such as the Williamsburg mantuamakers, by contrast, could choose to return to Britain when they decided not to support the resistance against the mother country. When Elizabeth Dickinson Weed, the Philadelphia apothecary, knew that her loyalties were suspect, she could choose to marry a man who had served in the American army, thus absolving herself of suspicion. Thus, while the very instability of the revolutionary milieu shook up traditional gender roles in new and unexpected ways, women's marital status continued to exercise a disproportionate effect on their revolutionary experiences in ways that it never did for men.

In the end, placing women at the center of our understanding of the American Revolution is not just about the recovery of individual women's stories from the past. A more comprehensive understanding of women's experiences actually changes the nature of the revolutionary narrative itself. Instead of a movement primarily about achieving equality, preserving natural rights, or promoting representative government, the Revolution becomes much more about people, their diverse choices, and the human costs of war. It shows how the upheavals of war created openings in which gender roles might shift—sometimes temporarily and sometimes permanently—and how even Indians and enslaved women could glimpse the creation of new possibilities, and the foreclosing of others. The Revolution was first and foremost a story about individuals and communities and their relationships to the political worlds in which they lived. This new emphasis makes the American Revolution both incredibly more accessible but also infinitely more troubling and complex. Yet only by fully integrating women's stories into the standard narrative of the country's revolutionary origins can we come to terms with the Revolution's capacious meaning and ever deepening significance.

Notes

1. Although scattered works on women during the era of the American Revolution appeared earlier in the twentieth century, the current wave of scholarship traces its origins to Linda K. Kerber, *Women of the Republic: Intellect and Ideology in Revolutionary America* (Chapel Hill: University of North Carolina Press, 1980), and Mary Beth Norton, *Liberty's Daughters: The Revolutionary Experience of American Women, 1750–1800* (Boston: Little Brown, 1980). In 1989, a volume appeared representing the state of the field at that time: Ronald Hoffman and Peter J. Albert, eds., *Women in the Age of the American Revolution* (Charlottesville: University of Virginia Press, 1989). For more recent historiographical overviews of the field, see Susan Branson, "From Daughters of Liberty to Women of the Republic: American Women in the Era of the American Revolution," in *The Practice of U.S. Women's History: Narratives, Intersections, and Dialogues* (New Brunswick, NJ: Rutgers University Press, 2007), 50–66; Jennifer Manion, "Historic Heteroessentialism and Other Orderings in Early America," *Signs* 34, no. 4 (Summer 2009): 981–1003; Terri L. Snyder, "Refiguring Women in Early American History," *William and Mary Quarterly* 69, no. 3 (July 2012): 421–50. For good synthetic overviews of the period, see Joan R. Gundersen, *To Be Useful to the World: Women in Revolutionary America, 1740–1790* (New York: Twayne, 1996); Carol Berkin, *Revolutionary Mothers: Women in the Struggle for America's Independence* (New York: Alfred A. Knopf, 2005).

2. The classic article making the case against the American Revolution as an agent of change for women is Joan Hoff Wilson, "Illusion of Change: Women and the Revolution," in *The American Revolution: Explorations in the History of American Radicalism,* ed. Alfred F. Young (DeKalb: Northern Illinois University Press, 1976), 383–95. For other works on women, see Marylynn Salmon, *Women and the Law of Property in Early America* (Chapel Hill: University of North Carolina Press, 1986); Pauline Schloesser, *The Fair Sex: White Women and Racial Patriarchy in the Early American Republic* (New York: New York University Press, 2002); Elizabeth Maddock Dillon, *The Gender of Freedom: Fictions of Liberalism and the Literary Public Sphere* (Stanford, CA: Stanford University Press, 2004).

3. For examples of works that discuss these issues, see Linda Kerber, "The Republican Mother: Women and the Enlightenment—An American Perspective," *American Quarterly* 28, no. 2 (Summer 1976): 187–205; Jan Lewis, "The Republican Wife: Virtue and Seduction in the Early Republic," *William and Mary Quarterly* 44, no. 4 (October 1987): 689–721; Nancy F. Cott, *Bonds of Womanhood: "Woman's Sphere" in New England, 1780–1835* (New Haven, CT: Yale University Press, 1977); Mary Kelley, *Learning to Stand and Speak: Women, Education, and Public Life in America's Republic* (Chapel Hill: University of North Carolina Press, 2006); Carolyn Eastman, *A Nation of Speechifiers: Making an American Public after the American Revolution* (Chicago: University of Chicago Press, 2009); Cynthia A. Kierner, *Beyond the Household: Women's Place in the Early South, 1700–1835* (Ithaca, NY: Cornell University Press, 1998); Ellen Hartigan-O'Connor, *Ties That Buy: Women and Commerce in Revolutionary America* (Philadelphia: University of Pennsylvania Press, 2011); Kate Haulman,

The Politics of Fashion in Eighteenth-Century America (Chapel Hill: University of North Carolina Press, 2011); Clare A. Lyons, *Sex among the Rabble: An Intimate History of Gender and Power in the Age of Revolution, Philadelphia 1730–1830* (Chapel Hill: University of North Carolina Press, 2006); Susan E. Klepp, *Revolutionary Conceptions: Women, Fertility, and Family Limitation in America, 1760–1820* (Chapel Hill: University of North Carolina Press, 2009); Cassandra A. Good, *Founding Friendships: Friendships between Men and Women in the Early American Republic* (Oxford: Oxford University Press, 2015); Rosemarie Zagarri, *Revolutionary Backlash: Women and Politics in the Early American Republic* (Philadelphia: University of Pennsylvania Press, 2007).

4. For a discussion of the historiography concerning nonwhite women in this era, see Manion, "Historic Heteroessentialism and Other Orderings in Early America"; Snyder, "Refiguring Women in Early American History." For an excellent recent volume focusing on the experience of nonwhite women in early North America and beyond, see Thomas A. Foster, *Women in Early America* (New York: New York University Press, 2015). For a biography of an enslaved woman of this era, see Erica Armstrong Dunbar, *Never Caught: The Washingtons' Relentless Pursuit of their Runaway Slave, Ona Judge* (New York: Simon and Schuster, 2017).

5. See, e.g., Edith Gelles, *Portia: The World of Abigail Adams* (Bloomington: Indiana University Press, 1992); Woody Holton, *Abigail Adams* (New York: Free Press, 2009); Rosemarie Zagarri, *A Woman's Dilemma: Mercy Otis Warren and the American Revolution,* 2d ed. (West Sussex, UK: John Wiley and Sons, 2015); Sheila L. Skemp, *First Lady of Letters: Judith Sargent Murry and the Struggle for Female Independence* (Philadelphia: University of Pennsylvania Press, 2009).

6. For an excellent survey of the historiography of the American Revolution relating to men as well as women, see Alfred F. Young and Gregory Nobles, *Whose American Revolution Was It? Historians Interpret the Founding* (New York: New York University Press, 2011).

7. For Martha Washington's burning of George's papers, see Joseph E. Field, ed., *"Worthy Partner": The Papers of Martha Washington* (Westport, CT: Greenwood, 1994), xxxi. While William Byrd III's papers were published, Mary Willing Byrd's were not: see Marion Tinling, ed., *The Correspondence of the Three William Byrds of Westover, Virginia, 1684–1776,* 2 vols. (Charlottesville: University Press of Virginia, 1977). I thank Ami Pflugrad-Jackisch for telling me about the omission of Mary Willing Byrd's papers.

8. Lynn Hunt, *The Family Romance of the French Revolution* (Berkeley: University of California Press, 1992).

PART I

Economic Relationships

The Labors of Enslaved Midwives in Revolutionary Virginia

SARA COLLINI

During the summer of 1794, an enslaved woman named Kate petitioned George Washington with an unusual request. She wished to become a paid midwife "[to] serve the negro women (as a Grany) on [his] estate." Washington received word of this appeal from one of his overseers, an enslaved man named Will who was also Kate's husband, while he was home during his second term as president of the United States. Although Washington was accustomed to managing his eight thousand-acre Mount Vernon estate in addition to leading the new nation, this was a vitally important application. Kate not only wanted to serve the plantation as midwife; she also requested monetary payment for her skills. According to Washington, she "intimat[ed] that she was full as well qualified for this purpose as those into whose hands it was entrusted and to whom [Washington] was paying twelve or £15 a year." Washington admitted that he could think of no reason "why she should not be so," so he directed his farm manager to "commit this business to her, if thereupon [he] shall be satisfied of her qualifications."[1]

Kate's request occupies only a few lines within the vast archival holdings of the Washington papers, and the brevity with which Washington discussed the "application . . . made to [him] by Kate at Muddy Hole" belies the significance of that exchange.[2] It is uncommon that the limited choices of women enslaved in eighteenth-century America are preserved, and even then they are almost always mediated through the voice of the slaveholder. These fragments of information are found within plantation accounts and reports, slave owners' and overseers' correspondence, and diaries of those who exercised enormous power. Weaving these archival pieces together reveals both the significance of childbirth in an expanding slave society and the complicated narratives of choice and agency for the women enslaved within it.

For enslaved African Americans, the era of the American Revolution was a period of both continuity and change, of radical disruption and of persistence and tradition. Lord Dunmore's Proclamation in 1775 offered enslaved men in Virginia the possibility of freedom if they took up arms for the British; thousands responded. Even more important, more than twenty thousand enslaved people in the South took advantage of the dislocations of war to run away from their masters. Both Washington and Thomas Jefferson had enslaved people claim their freedom by running away during the Revolution.[3] Yet for many enslaved people, the Revolution did not radically alter the rhythms and patterns of their daily lives. Hundreds of thousands of enslaved women and men lived and worked in the young United States during this turning point in American slavery. This included enslaved midwives.

Yet the Revolution did put a new premium on enslaved bodies. While slavery was integral to the development of the British North American colonies, the significant political and economic changes wrought by the American Revolution further entwined slavery in the fabric of the nation. Virginia, along with several other states, banned the transatlantic slave trade in 1778. Because no foreign source of slaves was legally available, plantation owners' financial interests in enslaved women's reproductive health began to rise. Enslaved women—and the children they produced—formed the core of the entire plantation system, a major economic engine for the new nation.[4] Kate, a woman who herself gave birth to at least four newly enslaved children, boldly petitioned her owner not only to facilitate and contribute to that process but also to control her labor as a slave. She demanded monetary compensation for her services.

This essay explores the important, yet paradoxical, work of enslaved midwives in the late eighteenth century, using Washington's Mount Vernon and other Virginia and Chesapeake plantations as examples.[5] Throughout the revolutionary and postrevolutionary eras, enslaved midwives continued their work through a variety of methods. In addition to nurturing African American families and communities by helping to bring new children into the world, enslaved midwives shared knowledge across complex social spaces, reinforced connections between plantations and communities through their movements, and even developed unique economic relationships with their owners by petitioning for, and receiving, compensation for their labor. After the American Revolution, slave owners increasingly incorporated enslaved midwives into the plantation's economic regime.

Paradoxically, although such acknowledgment affirmed the women's importance, as well as their agency, enslaved midwives' actions inadvertently contributed to the growth of the slave system. By successfully birthing enslaved African Americans, midwives helped increase the numbers of slaves owned by white masters. For the slave-owning population, the birth of enslaved children represented an increase in their property, wealth, and laboring population. Thus, for enslaved midwives, the legacy of the American Revolution was a double-edged sword.

Midwives of the eighteenth century practiced in a world of varied racial and social contexts. Enslaved women, free African American women, white women, and male physicians all practiced midwifery during this time, often on the same plantations and in the same urban areas. The majority of practitioners of this skill were older women, as the birthing of children existed as a common social experience that took place in domestic spaces.[6] It was among the skills in which women could independently contribute to their family economies.[7] By the turn of the nineteenth century, however, childbirth had become more medicalized. Male physicians began to intrude on the birthing process, presenting themselves as "man-midwives." Their supposedly superior expertise would earn supplemental income for themselves.[8]

Midwives learned their skills in a variety of ways. Through the transatlantic circulation of people and medicinal knowledge, many white midwives and male physicians acquired access to formal training. White women and physicians often gained certificates of practice from reputable, practicing doctors or attended medical school in Europe. In 1764, Benjamin Catton, a self-proclaimed surgeon and man-midwife, noted in the *Virginia Gazette* that he had attended the hospital in London, where he "gave particular attention to the study of MIDWIFERY." He also indicated that he had received a certificate in this skill "from under the hand of one of the most eminent for that art in London."[9] Julia Hughes advertised in Norfolk, Virginia, in 1773 that she had just arrived from the West Indies, "where she has practiced for a Number of Years with great Success."[10] She traveled back to the British Caribbean after the Revolution and advertised her midwifery services in the *St. George's Chronicle and Grenada Gazette,* including a "Certificate of a Medical Gentleman of eminence."[11]

For enslaved women, the spaces of the plantation environment and the social and legal confines of the slave system severely constricted their access to formal training. Yet enslaved midwives gained medical knowledge and skills that enabled them to foster reputations as figures of authority. Enslaved midwives trained through observing white practitioners, including female midwives and male physicians, in addition to other African American midwives. Thus, they cultivated local networks of care and shared knowledge that often transcended social and racial divisions.[12] The work these enslaved midwives performed reflected a form of personal agency and included them within a wider network of medical knowledge circulating throughout the Atlantic world.

Enslaved women often learned skills from white midwives within the plantation environment. For example, on William Ennalls's land on Maryland's Eastern Shore in 1771, Ann Smith delivered babies for two enslaved women, Phoebe and Dinah. The following year, Ennalls paid "Negro Phoebe for serving as a midwife to Ama," her fellow enslaved woman, and paid Ann Smith for "coming to her," or assisting Phoebe in her midwifery work. In 1773, Ennalls compensated Ann Smith for "serving as midwife to Jons wife some time since 10/ & for assisting Ama in labour lately 5/ pd [paid] Phoebe for delivg [delivering] Ama 5/." Finally, on February 7, 1774, Ennalls "pd [paid] Phoebe for servg [serving] this summer as midwife to Liddy 7/6 & to Jons Dinah last night 7/6 is 15/."[13] From these payments, it is possible to see that Phoebe, an enslaved woman, started serving as the midwife on the plantation soon after her own childbirthing experience with the white midwife Ann Smith—all amid the chaos of the American Revolution. Less than one year after Smith delivered Phoebe's child, Phoebe began acting as midwife, with Smith assisting and possibly supervising her. Phoebe apparently learned her midwifery skills from Smith, indicating a crucial connection between white and black women, free and enslaved. Within three years, Phoebe independently delivered children for Liddy and Dinah on William Ennalls's plantation. Enslaved women in the eighteenth-century Chesapeake could surpass racial perimeters on the plantation to gain training and practice in midwifery work.

Kate at Muddy Hole, mentioned in the beginning of the essay, most likely learned midwifery through a white practitioner, as well. Susanna Bishop delivered the majority of enslaved children on the Mount Vernon estate until after the Revolution in 1785. She lived on Muddy Hole farm, where her husband, Thomas Bishop, served as the overseer during the 1760s. Kate also lived and worked on Muddy Hole farm from at least 1760 until Washington's death in 1799.[14] In fact, Susanna Bishop delivered at least three of Kate's four known children between 1767 and 1773.[15] It is highly probable that Kate learned midwifery and nursing skills from Susanna Bishop over this period, perhaps starting in those intimate moments of childbirth.

Enslaved midwives also trained by observing and assisting other enslaved midwives. This exchange of knowledge and skills was often intergenerational. Alce, an enslaved woman at the same Muddy Hole farm at Mount Vernon, attended a woman in childbirth in July 1790.[16] This "attending" meant that she helped wash the infant, nurture both mother and child, and prepared herbal remedies.[17] Alce probably learned these skills through her mother, as the woman most likely to have been her mother at Muddy Hole was Kate, the midwife.[18] It does not seem accidental that Alce named her first child Kate. This chain of learning, remarkably seen on one farm over twenty-five years, indicates the cross-racial and intergenerational exchange of medical knowledge and skills.

Free African American midwives also trained enslaved midwives. Betty Armfield, a free black midwife who rented land from 1782 to 1813 on Carter's Grove in York County, Virginia, probably taught the neighboring enslaved women on the plantation.[19] She was practicing midwifery since at least 1763, when she was paid 10 shillings for delivering a "Negro woman" from the York County orphan's accounts.[20] She may have shared her knowledge with the surrounding women or performed her skills as part of her rent payments.[21]

As in other places in North America, childbirth was a communal occasion, when women came to the laboring woman's house to offer aid, comfort, and support. In their respective communities, both enslaved and white women came together in the event of birth. Yet the skills midwives learned during their training went well beyond the delivery of a child. The practice of midwifery at this time encompassed many other aspects of women's health. It involved preparing the mother for birth, labor, and delivery, as well as cleaning the newborn and providing postpartum care to the mother.[22] Midwives also supported mothers in the event of miscarriage and infant death. Occasionally they played a part in the complex personal and legal matters concerning abortion and infanticide. Mothers, children, and midwives were together involved in these intimate and often dangerous experiences.

At a time of significant infant and maternal mortality, female midwives occupied a unique and powerful role at the crossroads of birth and death.[23] Slave owners employed midwives because of their skill in navigating these precarious conditions. For example, from the ledgers and cash memoranda that George Washington assiduously kept throughout his tenure at Mount Vernon, it is clear that he employed at least fifteen midwives from 1754 to 1799 to ensure the health of the mothers and children enslaved on his estate.[24] These midwives were both male and female, free and enslaved. Susanna Bishop, the white woman married to an overseer employed by Washington, delivered approximately ninety-seven babies between 1763 and 1785.[25]

In addition to white midwives, at least eight enslaved women at Washington's plantations attended to women in childbirth between 1790 and 1798.[26] In May 1797, Daphney at Union Farm remained in childbed for four weeks. Two other enslaved women, Grace and Sabine, attended her for six days each during the first week of her labor.[27] Lynna at Dogue Run farm gave birth to a son during the week of February 16, 1793. Matilda, another enslaved woman at Dogue Run who was also Lynna's mother, attended Lynna for eight days over the next few weeks, as did Moll, an elderly woman on the same farm.[28] Lynna "had a remarkable bad breast after her Lying in."[29] Matilda and Moll, both enslaved, together acted as the midwives to Lynna and nursed her while she experienced what was probably mastitis, an infection of mammary tissue that results in inflammation, swelling, and soreness.[30] The farm manager reporting the incident to Washington wrote, "Docr Craik has attended her."[31] Only after several weeks did the farm manager call in the male physician to attend to this infection.

In addition to birthing the child, midwifery entailed many other skills, such as providing postpartum care for the mother and handling the complications of delivery, including miscarriages and infections. In November 1777, Washington paid Susanna Bishop 10 shillings for "attend[ing] Mill Judah in a Miscarriage."[32] On Francis Taylor's Midland Plantation in Orange County, Virginia, an enslaved midwife named Granny Venus assisted another enslaved woman, Hannah, through a complicated delivery. On March 20, 1799, Francis Taylor had Frank, one of his enslaved men, travel to his Aunt Taylor's nearby estate to fetch Venus. Hannah, who worked on Midland plantation, was having "several convulsion fits" while in labor. Venus delivered Hannah of a girl that evening. Hannah continued to experience convulsion fits, and Venus stayed with her through the night. Hannah's fits became so severe that Francis Taylor called on his brother, Dr. Charles Taylor, around midnight, who "directed sundry things for her." Venus traveled back to her owner's estate the next afternoon.[33] These convulsion fits were probably eclampsia, or postpartum seizures.[34]

Childbirth at this time was often fatal. In the summer of 1794, an enslaved woman named Jenny died in childbirth at Mount Vernon. The farm manager wrote to George Washington, "We have Lost the Girl Jinney at Dogue run she died Last Wednesday Evening in Labour she Could not be delivered of her child, Doctor Craick was sent for as soon as I had Notice of her Situation but altho he was with her 2 days and a night he Could not deliver her."[35] The Dogue Run farm report for that week noted, "By Sickness Jinney 3 days & died In child Bed"—that is, Jenny was sick for at least three days before she died in childbirth. An enslaved woman named Charlotte, who lived at Mansion House farm at Mount Vernon, attended a sick woman for three days during that week, who may have been Jenny.[36] Although Washington's physician, Dr. James Craik, stayed with Jenny for two days and one night, even he could not deliver the child. Both mother and child died in childbirth.

In addition to aiding delivery, midwives were healthcare workers, healers of a variety of ailments.[37] For example, Grace, an enslaved woman at Mount Vernon, cared for parturient women and children. She assisted the enslaved woman Daphney during childbirth in 1797 and nursed the sick at Union Farm and her own children multiple times in Washington's farm reports throughout the 1790s. Sixteen women across the estate possessed skills in nursing, according to the plantation work reports. Midwives conveyed knowledge to one another, creating a wide network for circulating medical knowledge between and among plantations.

Midwives could even be involved in medical procedures on plantations. One striking example is that of Kate at Muddy Hole, the same enslaved woman who petitioned George Washington to become the Mount Vernon midwife. In the winter of 1799, Kate was paid 25 cents to "by [buy] Scissors to cut the Tongues of Young Children."[38] Every so often, the lingual frenulum, a small membrane that fastens the underside of the tongue to the bottom of the mouth, is too small or tight. This condition, known as ankyloglossia or tongue-tie, impedes infants' ability to breastfeed and receive vital nutrients.[39] If not remedied, tongue-tie often results in death. In the eighteenth century, tongue-tie was corrected through frenotomy, a procedure to cut the lingual frenulum with scissors or one's fingernail.[40]

The procedure was known throughout the eighteenth century. Washington, in fact, was familiar with a book on midwifery owned by Daniel Parke Custis, *The Accomplisht Midwife, Treating of the Diseases of Women with Child, and in Child-Bed,* by François Mauriceau.[41] This work, originally published in 1673, discussed the use of scissors or a small fork to cut the tongues of infants. The author warned mothers not to create ulcers of the mouth by "[tearing] this thread with your Nails," and advised them to call a "chirurgeon," or physician. Due to the delicate nature of the lingual frenulum, Mauriceau directed that only physicians should perform the procedure, which they would carry out "with sharp Scissers, cutting at the point, being careful not to cut the proper Ligament of the Tongue."[42]

At Washington's plantations, both trained physicians and African American midwives performed frenotomies. In October 1797, Washington paid Dr. James Craik of Alexandria 2 shillings and 6 pence for "Cutting the Frenum of a N [negro] child's Tongue."[43] Dr. Craik, the Washingtons' personal physician, was educated at the University of Edinburgh and had practiced medicine in the West Indies.[44] He performed the same frenotomy procedure in May the following year.[45] As noted, Kate obtained scissors to perform the procedure just months after Dr. Craik's last recorded frenotomy. Kate probably was present at the time the procedures were performed, learned through observation, and was able to help the women and children enslaved at Mount Vernon. Thus, midwives became known as healthcare practitioners, not just as those who deliver babies. Kate contributed to the transmission of medical knowledge at Mount Vernon and, through her association with Dr. Craik, participated in the transatlantic field of health and healing work.

For all practitioners, practicing midwifery required travel away from one's home base. Midwives journeyed to wherever parturient women lived to deliver babies. Free midwives traveled regularly among urban areas, rural plantations, and small towns in the course of their practice. Sarah Lester of York County, known locally as Granny Lester, for example, traveled to Carter's Grove and Kingsmill plantations from her home at least four times to deliver enslaved women. She also delivered babies, both enslaved and free, in her local neighborhood.[46]

At Mount Vernon, the white midwives whom Washington employed assisted several enslaved women in childbirth across all five farms of the estate. One entry in the ledger for August 6, 1783, reveals that Susanna Bishop delivered five women across every farm of the estate: "To Mrs Bishop for Diliverg Sarah of Md [Muddy] Hole Lucy of D. [Dogue] Run, Betty of the Ferry L. [Lame] Alice H. [Home] House & Suky in the Neck." In September 1785, Darcus Parker delivered six women across three of the five farms: "To Mrs Parker for Diliverg Lucy & Betty @ the Ferry. Amy & Dorchus at M. Hole, and Charity and Silla @ Dogue Run @ 10/."[47]

Physicians also traveled to the birthing woman when they were called in to assist. Dr. Craik traveled to Mount Vernon at least twice for that purpose, and many other physicians traveled to perform midwifery skills.[48] Some large plantations in this period had rooms or entire buildings set up purposely to serve as hospitals, such as Landon Carter's Sabine Hall. Most healthcare, including childbirth, however, was performed in the sick or expectant person's home or cabin.[49]

Historians often point to the jobs and skills that required travel and afforded some freedom of movement for enslaved people—a group that included wagoners, boaters, personal valets, and postilions, among others. These were jobs held exclusively by men. Women were less likely to be mobile across plantations and the wider landscape. The historian Stephanie Camp has argued that this restriction on mobility was part of a "geography of containment" that enslaved people were forced to work in and around to exert their own agency.[50] Anthony Kaye, in his study of antebellum Mississippi, maintains that enslaved women's movements across plantations connected neighborhoods but were also sites of struggle. He argues that labor performed by enslaved women, such as nursing, could foster social and kinship connections among enslaved people in the neighborhood, but the gendered division of plantation labor limited them in those connective roles.[51] The historian Sharla Fett has studied African American midwives in the antebellum South specifically and argues that they also exercised unusual geographic mobility.[52]

For enslaved women, midwifery was one of the few skills that allowed them to leave their home plantations and move freely between and among neighboring plantations. The geographic mobility entailed in midwifery allowed women to connect with other communities of enslaved people, nurturing kinship ties and sustaining social networks. This movement also expanded economic connections between plantations. Nell, a woman enslaved by the Mason family at Gunston Hall along the Potomac River, connected three plantation economies and groups of people through her work as a midwife. In the winter of 1790, Nell was called on to assist an enslaved woman named Leah who went into labor at Martin Cockburn's nearby Springfield estate. Nell successfully delivered Leah of her child on February 21, and Cockburn paid her 12 shillings. Later that year Nell helped Hagar, another enslaved woman at the Springfield estate, give birth to a daughter and earned 12 shillings and 4 pence.[53]

Nell's reputation as a skillful midwife circulated throughout the wider Northern Neck neighborhood. George Washington paid "Negro woman of Thoms. Mason" 12 shillings for delivering Sall at River Farm during the heat of summer in 1796.[54] Nell continued to help the pregnant enslaved women at Mount Vernon for two more years, traversing the tidewater landscape in all four seasons to perform this skill. In 1798, Washington paid "Negroe Nell Mrs. Masons" a lump sum of $10 for assisting Sall, Bett, and Alsey at River Farm, Caroline at Mansion House, and Grace at Union Farm.[55]

In Orange County, Virginia, Granny Venus traveled at least four times to Colonel Francis Taylor's Midland Plantation from 1788 to 1799. She belonged to his aunt, Jane Taylor, who lived on neighboring land. On March 3, 1788, he recorded in his diary that Venus had stayed with Milly, one of his enslaved women, overnight and delivered her of a boy the next morning. On April 27, 1795, Venus delivered Sary, belonging to Francis Taylor's father, of a boy. A couple of years later, Venus delivered Sary again in the middle of the night of a son. As mentioned previously, in March 1799 Francis Taylor had Frank, one of his enslaved men, travel to Aunt Taylor's estate to fetch Venus to assist an enslaved woman who was experiencing eclampsia. Venus cared for the mother all night and traveled back to her owner's estate the next morning.[56]

One midwife could assist multiple plantations, and multiple enslaved midwives could work within one geographic area. Jane, an enslaved woman belonging to Penelope Manley French of Fairfax County, traveled to Mount Vernon to assist enslaved women in childbirth. On February 20, 1776, she delivered Jane at Dogue Run, and on April 28, 1783, she delivered Doll at Ferry Plantation of a child.[57] Mrs. French lived at Rose Hill, which was about three miles northeast of Mount Vernon.[58] She traveled between plantations to act as midwife on multiple occasions, connecting those communities of people along the way. The frequency of movement reinforced social connections among African American women on plantations scattered throughout the Chesapeake region and strengthened the economic ties among those plantations.

Midwifery was regarded as a valuable skill that necessitated specialized knowledge and a certain kind of expertise. For free midwives, this, of course, meant they were compensated for their labor. The standard monetary payment for midwives was approximately 6–10 shillings per birth. At Mount Vernon, George Washington compensated each free white midwife an average of 10 shillings per delivery, except Dr. Craik, who was paid £1 for each of his known two deliveries.[59] In April 1778, Washington paid Susanna Bishop 20 shillings for "[Laying] Betty at the Ferry of two children." Betty at Ferry Plantation (later Union Farm) gave birth to twins, and Washington paid Susanna Bishop 10 shillings per child.[60]

Surprisingly, even enslaved midwives were paid. In February 1776, Washington paid the enslaved woman Jane, who belonged to Penelope French, for delivering one of his enslaved women at Dogue Run farm. In April 1783, Washington paid "Mrs Frenches Negroe Woman" for delivering Doll at Ferry Plantation. Washington paid 10 shillings for each delivery, and they were both recorded in the cash accounts.[61] The payments went directly to the enslaved woman, because they were not recorded in their respective owners' accounts. In October 1798, Washington paid Nell from Gunston Hall for assisting five of his enslaved women. He paid Nell $2 per delivery, amounting to a total payment of $10.[62] Williams Ennalls, across the Potomac in Maryland, paid his enslaved woman Phoebe cash for her services as a midwife at 7 shillings and 6 pence per delivery.[63]

Some slave owners even kept separate accounts for midwives in their plantation ledgers. In Westmoreland County, Virginia, George Washington's nephew William Augustine Washington kept a plantation account book from 1776 to 1792. "Old Pegg the Granny" had her own designated account of debits and credits. In Washington's account with "Old Pegg the Granny" from 1784–87, Pegg delivered seventeen enslaved women on William Washington's plantation. That labor was valued at 10 shillings per delivery on the credit side of the account, and the total earnings for that three-year period amounted to £8.10.0. On the debit side, Washington recorded the corresponding payments he made to Pegg for her services, including bushels of wheat and credit on his account at the nearby Mattox Bridge and Leeds stores. These payments reflected the local economy and indicate that Pegg probably purchased items at these stores with her earnings.[64] William Washington's account with Pegg demonstrates that enslaved women held crucial roles in the business of childbirth and that they could claim economic space for themselves within the institution of slavery.

Compensating enslaved midwives reflected the unique and complex economic relationship between master and slave, particularly with regard to slave bodies. Masters considered enslaved people property that could increase their wealth. Enslaved women thus represented chattel property that could increase financial holdings through both productive labor as well as through the capacity for reproduction.[65] Midwifery work promoted good care for enslaved mothers and infants at the same time that it expanded and reinforced slavery. Slave owners needed these practitioners to ensure the health of their reproducing enslaved women and the health of newborn infants, who expanded the labor force.[66] Midwives were also expected to ensure that enslaved women returned to work in timely manner following childbirth.

Slave owners' management of enslaved women in childbirth reflected their dual interest in the productive and reproductive abilities of their bodies. Washington, in fact, instructed his farm overseers to turn in a weekly report accounting for the labor performed on each of the five farms. At the end of each report, the overseer listed sick laborers and enslaved women in childbed, along with the accounting of stock. Reports indicated that most parturient women were given an average of four to six weeks off from field or domestic work.[67] Between January 1797 and December 1798, the most consecutively documented farm reports, at least thirty-five women were pregnant across the estate. This means that for that two-year period, approximately 24 percent of the labor force was in childbed.[68]

From Washington's perspective, the time taken to birth and care for newborn infants directly amounted to labor lost for several enslaved women. The farm reports in April 1797 for Muddy Hole farm documented three women — Darcus, Letty, and Amie — in childbed. Washington calculated the worth of labor by multiplying the number of workers by the six days they were expected to work during the week. At Muddy Hole for the week of April 8, 1797, fourteen "hands" equaled eighty-four days of labor. Darcus, Letty, and Amie were listed as being in childbed for that entire week, which equated to eighteen days not working. To Washington, those three women in childbirth represented a 21 percent loss of labor for that single week. All three women remained in childbed for four successive weeks.[69] They were constantly unable to work within his plantation economy.

Richard Corbin wrote to his farm manager in Virginia in 1759 that "the breeding wenches more particularly you must instruct the overseers to be kind and indulgent to, and not force them when with child upon any service or hardship that will be injurious to them."[70] Using the word "breeding" to refer to pregnant enslaved women indicates that Corbin regarded them as increasing his property. Joseph Ball, uncle to George Washington, was an absentee planter in England, and he wrote in the 1740s to his farm manager, Joseph Chinn, about the management of his Virginia estate near the Rappahannock River. The direction of healthcare was a primary concern. He wrote, "If any of the Negroes should be Sick, let them ly by a Good fire; and have Fresh Meat & broth; and blood, and vomit them, as you shall think proper. . . . I would have no Doctor, unless in very Violent Cases: They Generally do more harm than Good."[71] Ball explicitly directed Chinn to not employ doctors because he believed they inflicted more harm to enslaved bodies than they did care.

Ball also specifically discussed the management of women in childbirth. He instructed his plantation manager to "let the Breeding Wenches have Baby Cloths; for which you may tear up old Sheets, or any other old Linen . . . and let them have Good Midwives; and what is necessary. Register all the Negro Children that Shall be born. And also keep an account of their ages among my Papers."[72] Ball expressed the need to use midwives for his enslaved women in labor, but he also assigned the word "breeding," indicating that he, too, saw enslaved women as valuable reproducers. The use of midwives was directly related to the management of his enslaved laborers and the increase in his property through the registration of their births.

Many slave owners considered the time their enslaved women were in childbed a loss in valuable labor. As Landon Carter noted in 1758, the corn at his Mangorike quarter farm would have been finished sooner if not for the "one big bellyed woman that has seemed to be near her time about 2 months."[73] In 1770, he complained about two women feigning pregnancy. Sarah "worked none last year pretending to be with Child and this she was full 11 months before she was brought to bed," and Carter assured himself that he would "break her of that trick." Another enslaved woman named Wilmot at Fork quarter "always pretended to be too heavy [with child] to work and it cost me 12 months before I broke her."[74] Carter also complained of enslaved women taking what he thought was too much time from fieldwork to nurse their infant children. He stated, "Last year the suckling wenches told the overseers that I allowed them to go in five times about that business; for which I had some of them whipt and reduced it."[75] Landon Carter directly equated the time his enslaved women were pregnant and nursing to time lost in productive labor on his plantations, even using corporal punishment to enforce this business practice.

Compensating enslaved midwives could include labor exploitation in other ways. Many slave owners significantly decreased the value of elderly enslaved people they thought could no longer do fieldwork.[76] This included enslaved midwives. Kate at Muddy Hole farm was considered an old woman, and in 1797, Washington petitioned Fairfax County for a tax exemption on sixteen older enslaved people at Mount Vernon, including Kate.[77] Yet in February 1799, she was involved in remedying tongue-tie in infants.[78] As an enslaved woman, she was clearly still providing valuable care, but Washington deemed her too old to be financially productive on his plantation. Landon Carter wrote in his diary that he allowed his "old midwife" and her husband to "live quite retired" after he decided they could no longer contribute productively to the plantation economy. Sukey, the enslaved midwife, most likely continued to deliver babies or at least act in some other form of caregiving.[79] While being an enslaved midwife was a valuable skill, it was also a way for a slave owner to extract work out of elderly enslaved people they deemed not fit to work the land for their economic benefit.[80]

Midwifery skills were so valuable in protecting property interests and securing profits that slave owners often paid midwives regardless of servitude status, which placed enslaved women in this nebulous space of volitional, yet additional, labor under slavery. It was a service performed not just as extra labor on Sundays or holidays but whenever and wherever a woman went into labor. The compensation for that medical skill specific to enslaved women represented a different economic relationship that carried certain expectations. It was not a discrete exchange. Paying enslaved midwives was a unique and valuable service that owners used to protect their chattel property.[81]

Given the anomalous place of enslaved midwives in the slave system, did the American Revolution change their role or status in any significant ways? Put simply in terms of practice, the answer is, "no." Midwifery among enslaved women in Virginia remained much the same after the American Revolution as it had been before. Enslaved midwives continued to cultivate intricate social and interracial networks of shared medical knowledge. They sustained this knowledge through local, transatlantic, and intergenerational exchanges. Enslaved midwives traversed landscapes to nurture mothers and infants and strengthened the bonds of community within and among plantations.[82]

What did change, however, was the larger political and economic context, which, in turn, altered the larger significance of the enslaved midwife's role. Although white people had long regarded enslaved people as property, following the American Revolution slave owners' interest in protecting their chattel significantly increased. In fact, for Virginians in particular, slave bodies themselves became much more valuable. In 1778, Virginia, along with several other states, banned the transatlantic slave trade. This ban continued through the American Revolution. Surprisingly, slave owners in Virginia actually did not perceive the ban as financially inhibitive. The state's enslaved population was already increasing through reproduction. The economy was transitioning to the cultivation of wheat and other grains, which did not require as much labor. Instead of needing more slaves, they started to have a surplus of slaves.[83]

After the ratification of the Constitution in 1789, it was clear that the ban on the international slave trade might become permanent for the entire country. As early as 1808, Congress might pass a law that completely prohibited the transatlantic slave trade. Moreover, due to westward expansion and the growth of the cotton staple, the value of enslaved people as commodities began to increase. These political and economic changes heightened the demand for slave bodies.[84] Especially in Virginia, slave owners increasingly realized that their enslaved people represented not only labor but also capital: commodities that could be sold to the Deep South for cash. The domestic slave trade—the "second middle passage"—created new incentives to encourage slave births and nurture the health of the existing slave population. Midwives were essential to this process.

Examining midwifery at Mount Vernon and other Virginia and Chesapeake plantations during the revolutionary and postrevolutionary eras illuminates the multiple roles of enslaved midwives within their plantation communities. Midwifery necessitated a shared knowledge of childbirth and a network of care that extended beyond gender roles, servitude status, and racial boundaries. The geographic mobility that the skill required enabled women to connect communities of enslaved people, as well as plantation economies. In this context, an enslaved midwife's labor represented not only an economic transaction on different levels, but also multiple avenues for social and cultural exchange and interaction.

Although midwifery was a business practice to slaveholders, enslaved women exercised personal agency through this skill and claimed their own economic space within the slave system. They earned money and goods for their services. Kate at Mount Vernon even demanded compensation for her skills by petitioning George Washington for payment. Slave owners, in turn, recognized that enslaved midwives possessed specialized knowledge in medical matters, especially women's and children's health. In paying them, owners acknowledged the women's status and authority in these arenas.

After the American Revolution, however, slave owners increasingly valued slave bodies not only for their labor but also for the capital they might bring. The more slaves they possessed, the more they could profit from the expanding domestic slave trade. To slaveholders, then, enslaved midwives represented a cost-effective way to manage enslaved people's health and protect their chattel property.

Enslaved midwives thus occupied a unique, but paradoxical, space during the era of the American Revolution. The work they performed both supported enslaved mothers, children, and communities and, at the same time, expanded the institution of slavery. In helping to bring new enslaved children into the world and caring for their mothers, enslaved midwives increased the master's property and ensured the growth and expansion of the slave population. Ironically, enslaved midwives unwittingly contributed to the continuing existence of the very institution that held them in bondage.

Notes

1. George Washington to William Pearce, August 17, 1794, in Presidential Series (September 24, 1788–September 30, 1794), vol. 16 (May 1–September 30, 1794), in *The Papers of George Washington Digital Edition*, ed. Theodore J. Crackel (Charlottesville: University of Virginia Press, 2008–18), 574.

2. Washington to Pearce, 574. Muddy Hole was one of five farms that made up Washington's Mount Vernon estate.

3. Sylvia R. Frey, *Water from the Rock: Black Resistance in a Revolutionary Age* (Princeton, NJ: Princeton University Press, 1991); Cassandra Pybus, *Epic Journeys of Freedom: Runaway Slaves of the American Revolution and Their Global Quest for Liberty* (Boston: Beacon, 2006); Cassandra Pybus, "Jefferson's Faulty Math: The Question of Slave Defections in the American Revolution," *William and Mary Quarterly* 62, no. 2 (2005): 243–64.

4. Jennifer L. Morgan, *Laboring Women: Reproduction and Gender in New World Slavery* (Philadelphia: University of Pennsylvania Press, 2004). As Jennifer Morgan argues, the development of racial slavery and political economy of the British colonies were dependent on the reproductive capacity of enslaved women. See also Katherine Paugh, "The Politics of Childbearing in the British Caribbean and the Atlantic World during the Age of Abolition, 1776–1838," *Past and Present* 221, no. 1 (November 2013): 119–60.

5. Sharla M. Fett, "Consciousness and Calling: African American Midwives at Work in the Antebellum South," in *New Studies in the History of American Slavery* (Athens: University of Georgia Press, 2006), 65–86. As Fett argues, enslaved midwives in the antebellum period continued to work in this contradictory space. This essay builds on those arguments.

6. Richard W. Wertz and Dorothy C. Wertz, *Lying-In: A History of Childbirth in America* (New York: Schocken, 1979), 1–26; Catherine M. Scholten, *Childbearing in American Society: 1650–1850* (New York: New York University Press, 1985), 22–30; Judith Walzer Leavitt, *Brought to Bed: Childbearing in America, 1750 to 1950* (New York: Oxford University Press, 1986), 36–38; Laurel Thatcher Ulrich, *A Midwife's Tale: The Life of Martha Ballard, Based on Her Diary, 1785–1812* (New York: Knopf, 1990; reprint, New York: Vintage, 1991), 12, 61, 66; Deborah Gray White, *Ar'n't I a Woman?: Female Slaves in the Plantation South* (New York: W. W. Norton, 1985), 115–17.

7. Ulrich, *A Midwife's Tale*, 75–83.

8. Deborah Kuhn McGregor, *From Midwives to Medicine: The Birth of American Gynecology* (New Brunswick, NJ: Rutgers University Press, 1998); Jane B. Donegan, *Women and Men Midwives: Medicine, Morality and Misogyny in Early America* (Westport, CT: Greenwood Press, 1978).

9. Benjamin Catton, "Lately Imported," *Virginia Gazette,* March 16, 1764, Accessible Archives.

10. Julia Hughes, "Norfolk, December 10, 1773. Mrs. Hughes, Midwife," *Virginia Gazette,* December 16, 1773, Accessible Archives.

11. Julia Hughes, "The Subscriber Begs Leave Again," *St. George's Chronicle and Grenada Gazette,* April 19, 1799, Caribbean Newspapers, 1718–1876, America's Historical Newspapers, NewsBank/Readex.

12. Fett, "Consciousness and Calling," 75–78. As Fett shows, enslaved midwives' work continued to cross social and racial boundaries throughout the era of enslavement, although with added tension due to the professionalization of obstetrics and gynecology in the antebellum period.

13. William Ennalls, "William Ennalls Notebook, 1771–1774," Manuscript Division, Library of Congress, Washington, DC; Philip D. Morgan, *Slave Counterpoint: Black Culture in the Eighteenth-Century Chesapeake and Lowcountry* (Chapel Hill: University of North Carolina Press, 1998), 325.

14. George Washington, Memorandum List of Tithables and Taxable Land and Property, June 16, 1766, in Colonial Series (July 7, 1748–June 15, 1775), vol. 7 (January 1, 1761–June 15, 1767), in Crackel, *The Papers of George Washington Digital Edition,* 442–43; George Washington, Memorandum List of Tithables, May 1760, in Colonial Series (July 7, 1748–June 15, 1775), vol. 6 (September 4, 1758–December 26, 1760), in Crackel, *The Papers of George Washington Digital Edition,* 428. George Washington, Negroes Belonging to George Washington in His Own Right and by Marriage, June 1799, in Retirement Series (March 4, 1797–December 13, 1799), in Crackel, *The Papers of George Washington Digital Edition,* 531. Accessed through the Mount Vernon Slavery Database, Mount Vernon Ladies Association, 2016 (hereafter, MVSD).

15. George Washington, Thomas Bishop Account, July 8, 1767, in General Ledger A, 1750–72, 247; George Washington, Cash Account, July 6, 1769, in General Ledger A, 1750–72, 292; George Washington, Thomas Bishop Account, July 1773, in General Ledger B, 1772–93, 33, all in *George Washington Papers, Series 5, Financial Papers,* Manuscript Division, Library of Congress. Mount Vernon holds digitally transcribed copies.

16. George Augustine Washington, Farm Report, July 10, 1790, in *George Washington Papers, Series 4, General Correspondence,* Manuscripts Division, Library of Congress, Washington, DC. Accessed through MVSD.

17. Marie Jenkins Schwartz, *Birthing a Slave: Motherhood and Medicine in the Antebellum South* (Cambridge, MA: Harvard University Press, 2006), 189–91.

18. Washington, Memorandum List of Tithables, 428.

19. Lorena S. Walsh, *From Calabar to Carter's Grove: The History of a Virginia Slave Community* (Charlottesville: University of Virginia Press, 1997), 132, 173–75.

20. "Elizabeth Armfield," York County Records Project Biographical File, 1980, John D. Rockefeller Jr. Library, Colonial Williamsburg Foundation, Williamsburg, VA.

21. Walsh, *From Calabar to Carter's Grove,* 132, 173–75. The historian Lorena Walsh notes that the payments to midwives and physicians for childbirth expenses decreased in the plantation records after the Revolutionary War. She argues this negative evidence indicates that enslaved women were delivering their own and that they were not paid for this labor, or, at least, the payments went unrecorded.

22. Schwartz, *Birthing a Slave*; Sharla M. Fett, *Working Cures: Healing, Health, and Power on Southern Slave Plantations* (Chapel Hill: University of North Carolina Press, 2002), 111–25; Fett, "Consciousness and Calling," 69.

23. Susan E. Klepp, *Revolutionary Conceptions: Women, Fertility, and Family Limitation in America, 1760–1820*, (Chapel Hill: University of North Carolina Press, 2009), 21–55. Infant and maternal mortality rates varied across colonies and states, often based on class and servitude status.

24. Washington, Cash Account, General Ledger A; George Washington, Cash Account, General Ledger B, 1772–93, both in *George Washington Papers, Series 5, Financial Papers*; George Washington, Cash Account, General Ledger C, 1790–99, Morristown National Historic Park, Morristown, NJ. Mount Vernon holds a digitally transcribed copy.

25. Calculated from querying childbirth events in the MVSD.

26. These are the years that the farm reports for Mount Vernon were the best documented, as the Revolution ended. It is highly probable that the enslaved women at Mount Vernon cultivated social and kinship relationships through health and healing work long before the American Revolution began.

27. James Anderson, Farm Report, May 13, 1797, Morristown National Historic Park, MVSD.

28. Anthony Whitting, Farm Reports, February 16, 1793, March 23, 1793, Mount Vernon Reference Book 9-F, Mount Vernon Ladies Association, Fred W. Smith National Library for the Study of George Washington, MVSD. See also Mary V. Thompson, "'They Appear to Live Comfortable Together': Private Lives of the Mount Vernon Slaves," in *Slavery at the Home of George Washington*, ed. Philip J. Schwarz (Mount Vernon, VA: Mount Vernon Ladies Association, 2001), 84–85.

29. Anthony Whitting to George Washington, March 27, 1793, in Presidential Series (September 24, 1788–September 30, 1794), vol. 12 (January 16, 1793—May 31, 1793), in Crackel, *The Papers of George Washington Digital Edition*, 386.

30. Whitting, Farm Reports, February 16, 1793, March 23, 1793.

31. Whitting to Washington, 386.

32. Lund Washington, Account Book, 1772–86, November 27, 1777, 66, Manuscript Collection, Mount Vernon Ladies Association, Fred W. Smith National Library for the Study of George Washington, MVSD.

33. Francis Taylor, "Diaries, 1786–1799," Accession 35049, Personal Papers Collection, The Library of Virginia.

34. Schwartz, *Birthing a Slave*, 122–23.

35. William Pearce to George Washington, August 31, 1794, in Presidential Series (September 24, 1788–September 30, 1794), vol. 16 (May 1–September 30, 1794), in Crackel, *The Papers of George Washington Digital Edition*, 621.

36. William Pearce, Farm Report, August 30, 1794, in *George Washington Papers, Series 4: General Correspondence*.

37. Fett, "Consciousness and Calling," 69.

38. James Anderson and Tobias Lear, Mount Vernon Distillery and Fishery Ledger, 1799–1801, February 6, 1799, JJ1-JJ2, 40, Manuscript Collection, Mount Vernon Ladies Association, Fred W. Smith National Library for the Study of George Washington. Digital transcription by Mount Vernon Ladies Association. Special thanks to Mary Thompson, Mount Vernon's research historian, for pointing to this reference, and to Molly Kerr.

39. Mayo Clinic, "Tongue-Tie (Ankyloglossia)," *Mayo Clinic Diseases and Conditions*, May 16, 2012, http://www.mayoclinic.org/diseases-conditions/tongue-tie/basics/definition/CON-20035410.

40. François Mauriceau, *The Accomplisht Midwife, Treating of the Diseases of Women with Child, and in Child-Bed. As Also, the Best Direction How to Help Them in Natural and Unnatural Labours With Fit Remedies for the Several Indispositions of New-Born Babes . . . Written in French*, trans. Hugh Chamberlen (London: John Darby, 1673), 386–88, HathiTrust Digital Library.

41. George Washington, Appendix D: Inventory of Books in the Estate, 1759, in Colonial Series (July 7, 1748–June 15, 1775), vol. 6 (September 4, 1758–December 26, 1760), in Crackel, *The Papers of George Washington Digital Edition*, 289; Mauriceau, *The Accomplist Midwife*.

42. Mauriceau, *The Accomplisht Midwife*, 386–88.

43. James Craik, Receipted Bill: [Dr.] James Craik to His Excy Geo[rge] Washington, August 25, 1797–January 22, 1799, Washington Collection, Mount Vernon Ladies Association, Fred W. Smith National Library for the Study of George Washington.

44. Adam D. Shprintzen, "James Craik," *Digital Encyclopedia of George Washington*, accessed June 3, 2017, http://www.mountvernon.org/digital-encyclopedia/article/james-craik.

45. Craik, Receipted Bill.

46. Walsh, *From Calabar to Carter's Grove*, 174.

47. Washington, General Ledger B, August 6, 1783, 173 and September 28, 1785, 189.

48. Craik, Receipted Bill.

49. Landon Carter, *The Diary of Colonel Landon Carter of Sabine Hall, 1752–1778*, ed. Jack P. Greene, Virginia Historical Society Documents, vols. 4–5 (Charlottesville: University Press of Virginia, 1965), 662. In Richard Dunn's *A Tale of Two Plantations*, the Mesopotamia plantation in the Caribbean sugar islands had a maternity room, a centralized location in which the white midwife delivered enslaved women, but that was the exception during this period: Richard S. Dunn, *A Tale of Two Plantations: Slave Life and Labor in Jamaica and Virginia* (Cambridge, MA: Harvard University Press, 2014), 161–62.

50. Stephanie M. H. Camp, *Closer to Freedom: Enslaved Women and Everyday Resistance in the Plantation South*, (Chapel Hill: University of North Carolina Press, 2004).

51. Anthony E. Kaye, *Joining Places: Slave Neighborhoods in the Old South* (Chapel Hill: University of North Carolina Press, 2007), 80–118.

52. Fett, "Consciousness and Calling," 72–73.

53. Martin Cockburn, Ledger, 1790, Typescript copy provided by Gunston Hall Library and Archives; Martin Cockburn Papers, 1765–1818, Manuscript Division, Library of Congress.

54. William Pearce, Mount Vernon Account Book, 1794–97, July 25, 1796, 85, in *George Washington Papers, Series 5, Financial Papers*.

55. James Anderson, Manager Ledger, 1797–98, October 11, 1798, 187; James Anderson, Farm Reports, January–February 1797, *Mount Vernon Farm Accounts*, vol. 1, 1797, Mount Vernon Ladies Association, Fred W. Smith National Library for the Study of George Washington; James Anderson, Farm Reports, January, February,

April, and November 1798, *Mount Vernon Farm Accounts*, vol.2, 1798, Mount Vernon Ladies Association, Fred W. Smith National Library for the Study of George Washington.

56. Taylor, "Diaries, 1786–1799."

57. Washington, Account Book, 1772–86, February 20, 1776, 51, April 28, 1784, 121.

58. It is possible that Jane lived there, but the French family also held land adjacent to the Dogue Run and Ferry Plantation land at Mount Vernon. Jane could have been living there, and she would have just traveled a small distance to deliver both of those women: George Washington, diary entry dated January 9, 1773, in Diaries (March 11, 1748–December 13, 1799), vol. 3 (January 1, 1771–November 5, 1781), in Crackel, *The Papers of George Washington Digital Edition*, 155; George Washington to Lund Washington, August 15, 1778, in Revolutionary War Series (June 16, 1775–December 31, 1783 [in progress]), vol. 16 (July–September 14, 1778), in Crackel, *The Papers of George Washington Digital Edition*, 315–17.

59. Craik, Receipted Bill.

60. Washington, Account Book, 1772–86, April 18, 1778, 73.

61. Ibid., February 20, 1776, 51, April 28, 1784, 121.

62. Anderson, Manager Ledger, 1797–98, 187.

63. Ennalls, "William Ennalls Notebook, 1771–1774."

64. William Augustine Washington, Account Book, 1776–1792, Manuscript Division, Library of Congress, Washington, DC; Ulrich, *A Midwife's Tale*, 197–200. The historian Laurel Ulrich discusses the fees that white midwives, such as Martha Ballard in Maine, charged and earned for delivering babies. Though the average charge was 6 shillings per delivery, customers also paid her in household goods. Payments to midwives in eighteenth-century New England included items such as sugar, butter, shingles, and textiles. These payments, both cash and nonmonetary, indicated the local economy and industry of the surrounding communities.

65. Morgan, *Laboring Women*.

66. Fett, "Consciousness and Calling," 67–72.

67. Most white women refrained from domestic labor for that same amount of time: Wertz and Wertz, *Lying-In*, 4.

68. Washington, "Negroes Belonging to George Washington in His Own Right and by Marriage." This number represents the enslaved people able to contribute productively to the plantation economy, according to Washington. This number therefore excludes children and those deemed "passed labor.".

69. James Anderson, Farm Reports, April 8, 1797, April 15, 1797, April 22, 1797, April 29, 1797, Morristown National Historical Park, MVSD.

70. Richard Corbin Papers, 1746–1825, John D. Rockefeller Jr. Library.

71. Joseph Ball to Joseph Chinn at Morattico, February 14, 1743, transcript 92, Joseph Ball Letterbook, 1744–59, John D. Rockefeller Jr. Library.

72. Ball to Chinn.

73. Carter, *The Diary of Colonel Landon Carter of Sabine Hall*, 204.

74. Ibid., 372.

75. Ibid., 496.

76. Fett, *Working Cures*, 125–34.

77. George Washington, "Tax Exemptions for 16 Slaves at Mount Vernon," October 16, 1797, Fairfax County Minute Book, 1797–98, pp. G–H, MVSD.

78. Anderson, Manager Ledger, 1797–98.

79. Carter, *The Diary of Colonel Landon Carter of Sabine Hall*, 840.

80. Fett, "Consciousness and Calling" 69.

81. Ibid. Fett argues that in the late antebellum period, midwifery for enslaved women represented a further exploitation of labor and wages. The majority of slave owners would take the midwife's payments or a percentage of those payments for themselves, since they legally owned their bodies and their labor.

82. Schwartz, *Birthing a Slave*, 146–53; Fett, "Consciousness and Calling"; Fett, *Working Cures*, 111–41; White, *Ar'n't I a Woman?* 111, 119–41.

83. Damian Alan Pargas, *The Quarters and the Fields: Slave Families in the Non-Cotton South* (Gainesville: University Press of Florida, 2010), 13–21.

84. Adam Rothman, *Slave Country: American Expansion and the Origins of the Deep South* (Cambridge, MA: Harvard University Press, 2007); Edward E. Baptist, *The Half Has Never Been Told: Slavery and the Making of American Capitalism* (New York: Basic, 2014); Daina Ramey Berry, *The Price for Their Pound of Flesh: The Value of the Enslaved, from Womb to Grave, in the Building of a Nation* (Boston: Beacon, 2017); Sven Beckert and Seth Rockman, eds., *Slavery's Capitalism: A New History of American Economic Development* (Philadelphia: University of Pennsylvania Press, 2016).

"Until Liberty of Importation Is Allowed"

Milliners and Mantuamakers in
the Chesapeake on the Eve of Revolution

KAYLAN M. STEVENSON

On April 18, 1766, Catherine Rathell introduced herself to Virginia society with an advertisement in Purdie and Dixon's *Virginia Gazette*. Identifying herself as a "Milliner," she announced that she was "Lately arrived from *London*" and was in possession of a "large assortment of European and other Goods, suitable for Ladies and Gentlemen," which she would be pleased to sell "very cheap" at her store in Fredericksburg.[1] Sometime the previous year, she had arrived in Virginia, a single woman, alone, armed only with her skills as a milliner, her carefully chosen cargo of millinery wares, and a letter of introduction to Robert Carter, a prominent member of the Governor's Council. John Morton Jordan, a London merchant, described Rathell to Carter as a "Person of very good Character and Family," but, "meeting with misfortunes," Jordan explained, Rathell had determined to set off for "Virginia with a view of setting up a Milliners Shop."[2] Her advertisement certainly marked an auspicious beginning. Rathell was the first milliner in Virginia to identify not only her goods but herself, the purveyor of fashion, as direct from London—an exceptional enticement if ever there was one in a colony where, one outsider had observed, "Fashion reign[ed] . . . with despotic sway."[3] Yet, only nine short years later, almost to the day, she placed what was to be her final notice to her customers. In Pinkney's *Virginia Gazette*, April 20, 1775, she declared her intention to go "to England as soon as I can dispose of my goods." She did not plan to return "until liberty of importation is allowed."[4] Rathell found her carefully constructed means of support in direct collision with the cause of American liberty.

The politicization of material goods on the eve of the American Revolution cut across social and gender hierarchies, drawing both high and low, men—and women—into the political maelstrom. From the great planters of Virginia who filled their homes with elegant furniture and Wilton carpets to the small farmers of New York who cherished a looking glass or a teapot, a shared relationship with imported wares, and indebtedness to

British creditors, it has been argued, forged a collective language of resistance that ultimately helped tear Britain's North American empire asunder.[5] Yet the success or failure of these political agendas rested on women's participation in these nonconsumption movements.

Scholars have long recognized that women's roles as consumers and producers of material goods in the service of their households placed them in the public sphere in a unique position to exert political influence, a circumstance not lost on those crafting nonimportation associations.[6] As the first set of nonimportation associations of 1769 took shape in response to the Townshend Duties, a contributor to the *South-Carolina Gazette* was only one among many writers to identify women as "much the properest persons to manage an affair of so much consequence to the American world."[7] And many women responded with alacrity, seizing the opportunity to exercise their influence in the broadened political sphere made possible by the imperial crisis. Not only did women participate in public displays of domestic manufacture, such as the large spinning bee hosted by the Rhode Island Congregational minister Ezra Stiles in May 1770; they also added their names to nonimportation agreements and composed their own. In February 1770, more than three hundred Boston women signed a document pledging to "totally abstain from the use of" tea in their "respective Families," while fifty-one ladies of Edenton, North Carolina, crafted their own association in response to the Coercive Acts of 1774.[8] To focus solely on ladies' patriotic spinning bees and petition signing, however, necessarily privileges the story of those women firmly entrenched within the ideal patriarchal household at the expense of those, like Rathell, who were already independent actors in the marketplace.

Women also formed a substantial, albeit low-level, segment of the business community that similarly needed to be mobilized in support of the nonimportation associations. The same credit systems that ensnared colonists in debt relationships with merchants in Great Britain also created a marketplace in which women were enmeshed in the local economy equally alongside men. The women of eighteenth-century Newport and Charleston acted as confident handlers of finances and enterprising entrepreneurs who strategically employed imported wares in moneymaking ventures, seizing on the opportunities generated by increasing numbers of outsiders passing through port cities in the service of transatlantic trade. Women operated taverns and boardinghouses and set up shop in retailing businesses, serving not only as consumers but also as central players in the distribution of goods.[9] More than four hundred women are known to have kept shop in Boston, New York, and Philadelphia between 1740 and 1775. Of those, the female shopkeepers of the revolutionary era largely opposed the nonimportation agreements in much higher percentages than their male counterparts.[10] Milliners especially, Ellen Hartigan-O'Connor observes with tantalizing lack of detail, became "common business casualties of the nonimportation movement."[11] Such evidence suggests that the story of the impact of the revolutionary politics of the marketplace on women should be evaluated in terms not only of opportunities created but also of independent enterprises stifled.

Extending the story of experiences of female shopkeepers, milliners and mantuamakers in particular, into the Chesapeake raises questions about not only the degree to which the Revolution opened and closed opportunities for women but also the role of indebtedness—not to British merchants, but to one's neighbors—in choosing sides. There, too, the growth of the British Atlantic economy combined with proto-urban developments created space for female entrepreneurs to flourish. Even though the region's urban structure did not provide a base comparable to those found in colonial America's major port cities, creative enterprise and strategic advertising could nonetheless provide a productive and stable support for a single woman. The region also presented distinct challenges that required careful negotiation to ensure success. The ability to navigate the fine line between demanding cash and offering credit could mean the difference between prosperous stability or slavish dependence on one's customers. A paucity of sources makes it difficult to track these tradeswomen past the first rumblings of conflict, but a careful reading of shop advertisements and limited extant correspondence adds complexity to what has been considered a pivotal moment in revolutionary politics for women, establishing Rathell and her fellow milliners and mantuamakers as central actors caught up in both the rise in consumption of British goods and the politicization of those goods on the eve of revolution.

Even as Rathell boldly entered Virginia society, the inclusion of a careful contingency plan at the close of her first advertisement signifies a realistic awareness of the potential difficulties in doing business in an area dominated by the export of a staple crop and accustomed to trading largely on credit. At the end of a long list of fashionable and genteel goods, she asserted that, as she was "but lately come into the country" and "her continuance [there was] very uncertain," she would "sel[l] for ready money only."[12] The advent of the Revolution revealed that those milliners who failed to carefully negotiate this difficulty during the prewar years found their personal choices and livelihoods directly limited by the very economic system on which they relied.

The diversification of Virginia's economy in the 1760s and changes in the marketing of tobacco gave rise to a greater degree of urban development and created both geographic and economic space for Rathell to conduct her business that would have been more difficult in earlier decades. Previously, a combination of geography and the character of marketing Virginia's staple export tobacco had conspired to inhibit town growth for most of the seventeenth and early eighteenth centuries. Throughout the 1750s and 1760s, Virginia's economy witnessed a subtle shift toward grain production in the Northern Neck and backcountry that gave rise to increased trade with the markets of southern Europe, the West Indies, and other mainland colonies; introduced greater cash flow into the region; and fostered the development of towns on the periphery of the tidewater. By the 1770s, the populations of Williamsburg and Annapolis had risen to approximately 2,000 and 3,700, respectively, and Baltimore and Norfolk, as well as smaller towns in the interior, such as Fredericksburg, Richmond, and Petersburg, had begun to take shape. The 1760s also witnessed the arrival of significant numbers of Scottish factors operating directly in the region on behalf of larger Glasgow firms. Dotting the countryside, they established stores that offered wares wholesale to small shopkeepers, as well as directly to small farmers, and helped break the monopoly of the larger planters and consignment merchants in the York River region.[13]

Although she was the first, Rathell was not the only English milliner to envision Virginia as a place of economic opportunity. Although milliners and mantuamakers had been in colonial Virginia as early as the 1730s, they were few in number before Rathell's arrival. The period between the end of the Seven Years' War and the beginning of the Revolution marked the highest concentration of millinery activity in Virginia during the eighteenth century. Rathell was quickly followed by four other single London women of fashion: Jane Hunter, also in 1766; Margaret Hunter, Jane's sister, in 1767; an unidentified London milliner working alongside the Virginia milliner Sarah Pitt, in 1769; and Margaret Brodie, a mantuamaker in 1771.[14] In addition, several Virginia women—Elizabeth Carlos, Mary Dickinson, Mary Davenport, Joanna McKenzie, Sarah Pitt, Elizabeth Russal of Fredericksburg, and sisters Elizabeth, Mary, and Anne Strachan of Richmond— also found ample room to ply their trade.

Having wares on hand and available for immediate inspection gave milliners an edge over consignment merchants based in London. Although many of the prosperous planters tended to give consignment merchants the bulk of their business, the long-distance ordering process was fraught with difficulty, disappointment, and sometimes plain disgruntlement, as a few examples from the Nicholas family correspondence demonstrate. "Several Articles in my last Invoice," Robert Carter Nicholas wrote to the London merchant John Norton on one occasion, "Mrs. Nicholas assures me are charged higher than they could be bought in the Stores of Williamsburg, dear as they are."[15] In another instance, Mrs. Nicholas herself took up her pen to emphatically inform Norton that the "parcel of Fans" she had received "could have [been] bought in a Milliner's shop in Wmsbg for a third of the price wch they cost, besides the difference between Ster. & Curr. Money," and that the "Stays, Bonnets &c" had been "very ill bought & ungenteel."[16] Perhaps one of the greatest difficulties with long-distance shopping by proxy was simply anticipating long-term needs adequately in advance. One can envision a scene in which Robert Carter Nicholas, besieged yet again with belated requests from his wife and children, sat down to write Norton in a tone at once frazzled and apologetic, "I am afraid you will think I shall never be done troubling you with little trifling Commissions, but so many little articles as are wanted in a Family can't well be recollected at once."[17] Rathell and her fellow milliners were only too ready to supply any of those "little articles" found wanting at a moment's notice.

No account books survive for any of the milliners doing business in Williamsburg during this period, but individual entries scattered throughout customers' personal ledger books and other sources indicate that the milliners of Williamsburg did in fact do much of their business by supplying such small, trifling articles in question. A receipt paid by Washington to Jane Hunter Charlton (she ran a shop separate from her sister Margaret following her marriage to the wigmaker Edward Charlton) in 1771 records the purchase of several items of paste jewelry as well as a bit of lace for his stepdaughter, Martha Parke Custis.[18] Similarly, an entry in one of Washington's ledger books dated March 1772 records payment of 5 pence to Jane for "Mounting two fans."[19] Additional entries that do not denote specific items nevertheless remain at or below £2, 15 shillings, and 3 pence in price, suggesting that Miss Custis and Mrs. Washington shopped for a necessary article here and there or simply for recreation. Likewise, John Spotswood purchased two pairs of gloves from Rathell on one occasion and three pairs of shoes on another.[20] The Williamsburg milliners were especially well poised to meet special impromptu needs such as engagements, weddings, and periods of mourning. After a morning's "ramble" through town, Anne Blair, a resident of Williamsburg, wrote to her sister with wry amusement about an encounter with one "deeply Loadn'd" Mr. Price who had been busily "Buying a World of things of Messrs Hunter & Pitt," she "fanc[ied]," while out "geting Wedding geer for his Betsy."[21] In an effort to gain the "Honour of helping to Dress" another young lady on her "day of all Days," Rathell sent a small parcel of goods to the home of the prospective bride so that Mrs. Mercer and her daughter could personally inspect the wares and make a selection.[22] The episode underscores the advantages of doing business with local milliners, particularly on special occasions, for the opportunity to personally select items and solicit the advice of someone who possessed the latest fashion news. Not only did milliners' specialized wares connect customers to the worldwide reaches of British commerce, but their specialized knowledge, skills, and advice provided vital connections with London itself.

A milliner's capacity to establish strong connections with the fashionable world in London validated her expertise and enabled her to better distinguish herself from the competition. When Anne Blair sent word to Fanny Bayler not to worry that Miss Hunter had no caps "reddy made" for she could "make them equal to the English," she paid Margaret Hunter a high compliment.[23] The ability to command financial capital was necessary to the start of any business; the ability to command cultural capital was essential for continued success in the fashion trade. Rathell's choice of the descriptive phrase "Lately arrived from *London*" as a line second in importance only to her name and the repetition of the sentiment "as she was but lately come into the country" at the close of her first advertisement was no accident.[24] When she set up shop temporarily in Maryland after nearly three years' residence in the colonies, she still introduced herself to the citizens of Annapolis as "Catharine Rathell, Milliner From London."[25] Hers was a move consciously calculated to garner prestige and stimulate interest in her wares. Rathell's business partner, the mantuamaker Margaret Brodie, similarly trotted out her credentials on her arrival, citing her training with "the original Makers, at their Warehouse in Pall Mall," the epicenter of London's fashionable world, as well as her continuing connections to "the Queen's" very own "Mantuamaker."[26] Rathell even made one return trip to London to personally select wares. Her advertisement of October 1771 was designed to instill the utmost confidence in her customers that her goods "*Just* Imported *from* London" truly were of the "newest Fashion." They had been purchased as recently as "*July* last" with Rathell's expert knowledge from the most "eminent Shops," and they promised to be a good bargain because they had been bought under Rathell's shrewd eye for "the best Terms."[27] In a society hungry for the latest fashions from the empire's cultural center, Rathell and her fellow milliners held a powerful tool at their disposal in their position to serve as cultural intermediaries, with one foot in the colonies and the other foot, sometimes quite literally, in London.

Milliners could also create ties with the metropole by forming a relationship with someone else whose connections and judgment were known and respected. In addition to two cargoes of wares Rathell was able to boast of having chosen herself, she assiduously cultivated a relationship with John Norton and Sons, one of the oldest and most reputable London merchant houses doing business in Virginia. It was not John Norton, however, with whom Rathell was most interested in dealing; it was his wife, Mrs. Norton.[28] "The very great Character I have had from Many of My Aquaintance of Mrs Norton's great Carefullness in buying & Sending the Neatest and Cheapest goods in, that's sent to Virginia," she wrote eagerly, "Makes One so very desirous of getting goods from your House." "As you must know," Rathell continued with some degree of pride, "I Peigne myself much on having the very best & most fashionable goods in Williamsburg."[29] Presumably, Mrs. Norton could be counted on not only to exercise good taste but also to drive a hard bargain. Since Rathell could not make regular trips to London herself, she took the next best step, carefully surveying the prevailing tastes of the neighborhood and endeavoring to secure the connections necessary to ensure that her goods remained the "very best & most fashionable" in town. Mary Davenport solved the problem of a lack of direct personal connections with London by also dealing with John Norton and, presumably, Mrs. Norton.[30]

Even if a milliner succeeded in establishing cultural capital for herself, acquired the latest in fashionable wares, and framed them with the proper descriptors, the crux remained when and where to effectively market them. Although urban developments in Virginia had improved a great deal since the seventeenth century, Virginia still lagged far behind other colonies in terms of urban sophistication. Despite the economic prosperity of the region, the Chesapeake remained largely rural in character and lacked a substantial urban center comparable even to Newport, the smallest of colonial British America's five major port cities, with a population of eleven thousand. Williamsburg's population of 2,000, approximately half of whom were enslaved, and Annapolis's population of 3,700 seem little more than small, provincial towns.[31] Both of those cities offered mainly seasonal business opportunities contingent on government sessions. The success or failure of Rathell and her fellow milliners depended largely on their ability to assess and respond to the economic circumstances of the Chesapeake.

Milliners were aware that their success, as with all business enterprises in the capital, revolved chiefly around meeting the needs of those who traveled to the city for public times and meetings of the General Assembly. Making the most of those opportunities when the city bustled with activity was crucial to their survival. By the 1760s, the General Court was meeting four times a year. In April and October, the court heard both civil and criminal cases, while June and December sessions were reserved for criminal cases. The civil sessions at the April and October courts appear to have brought the most outsiders to town, and the dates of millinery advertisements reflect that. Advertisements for the month of October constitute one-third of the total millinery advertisements placed from 1766 to 1775. Total advertisements for the months of April and May are equal and together constitute nearly one-third of the remaining advertisements. The rest of the advertisements are concentrated in November and December, with a few scattered throughout the rest of the year, save August. The combined strength of the April and May advertisements suggests an effort to target both the April and June court sessions. The high numbers for November potentially signify goods that arrived too late for the October sessions but were advertised in hopes of selling during the December sessions.

Because business revolved around the courts, Rathell and her fellow milliners were engaged in a constant battle to coordinate supply and demand over long distances amid shifting trends in fashion. A milliner's ability to have the proper goods on hand at the proper moment was critical in generating income and maintaining a loyal customer base. In November 1771, Rathell sent an urgent missive to Norton requesting that he "send & Hurry" one of her direct orders from a London tradesmen. "As Our Assembly meets in March," she continued anxiously, "I must request of all things on Earth, you will by the very first ship that Sails out of London send me those Goods, or I shall at that time totally Loose the Seal of them." She returned to the subject at the close of her letter in a tone almost reaching despair: "These are all the things I at this time want but My greatest distress is for fear I should not have them in March . . . or it will be a very great loss to me."[32] As January 1772 rolled around, Rathell once again found herself nearly out of certain items and sent two letters via separate channels. If Norton could not fill the order, the invoice was to be forwarded to Colonel George Mercer for, she closed, "a disappointment would *totally ruin,* Cath Rathell."[33] Rathell's concern was no mere exercise in female histrionics. Whether or not the goods arrived on time could mean the difference in either selling them immediately or "hav[ing] them on hands for 12 months longer."[34]

Rathell's advertisements spanning April 1769 to March 1770 serve as an insightful illustration of the shelf life of a milliner's wares. In April, Rathell announced to her customers that she "hope[d] to have it in her power to go home after the *June* court, to purchase a cargo against the *October* court" and was therefore "determined to sell."[35] So it might be reasonably presumed that Rathell did not import any further wares after April in anticipation of her travels. Evidently, Rathell did not sell enough of her wares to enable her to return to London as soon as planned. On route to London, Rathell took a detour to Annapolis. Advertisements appear in the *Maryland Gazette* for September 7, 1769, and November 2, 1769, announcing that "Catharine Rathell, Milliner From London, *Has open'd Shop at the House of Mr.* Wm. Whetcroft, *Jeweler, in* West-Street *near the Town Gate.*"[36] One last Annapolis advertisement appears on March 29, 1770, but its language implies that

Rathell had finally returned to London. The location remains the same and the wares listed appear to be Rathell's, but no specific mention of her name is made. The advertisement simply states: "An Invoice of the above Goods to be seen at Mr. *Whetcrofts,* Jeweller in *Annapolis,* who will treat with any one inclinable to purchase."[37]

Although milliners routinely closed their advertisements with the statement that they had "many more Articles too tedious to mention"—making it impossible to ascertain how many wares were simply not named—nearly 60 percent of the goods named in Rathell's April advertisement reappear in both the September and November advertisements, which are nearly equal in length. Only one entry in relation to jewelry gives some indication of the degree to which quantities were diminishing. In her November advertisement, Rathell lists only one paste necklace and earrings, singular, while previous advertisements refer to paste necklaces and earrings, plural. Two orders sent to Norton provide an estimate of the quantity of necklaces with which Rathell might have started. In December 1771, she requested that Norton send "12 Handsome Necklaces of Diferent Sorts & Coulors set in Silver and Some with Parrings," and, in January 1772, she ordered "6 neat newest fashioned folling Necklaces."[38] These orders suggest that Rathell carried only a half-dozen to a dozen of any one kind of necklace at any given time. Thus, it appears that it took her at least eight months to dispose of approximately twelve necklaces. The last advertisement in March is truncated in size, listing only sewing silks, threads, and tapes; fans; various sorts of gloves; and a small range of textiles but estimates the goods to be worth between "Two and Three Hundred Pounds Sterling."[39] Together, these advertisements illustrate that even in the best of scenarios, when goods arrived on time, they could remain on a milliner's shelves for months.

During the slow times between government sessions, Rathell and Mary Dickinson attempted to improve on the time by packing up their wares and traveling to more promising locations. As stated previously, on at least one occasion Rathell endeavored to profit by the lull and gain an edge over her competitors by traveling to London via Annapolis to personally select wares for the upcoming court. The following year, in October 1772, Rathell proposed, "if a House [could] be got, to reside at *Petersburg* from the End of [the October] Court until *April,*" another developing center comparable to Fredericksburg.[40] Similarly, Dickinson attempted to move from one capital to another, trying her fortunes between court sessions twice in Annapolis, in September 1771 and September 1772.[41]

As evidenced by Anne Blair's letter shopping for caps by proxy for Fanny Bayler and the parcel of wedding materials Rathell sent to Mrs. Mercer, cultivating relations with a customer base in the country was another source of income for milliners in Williamsburg during moments between government sessions. At the close of her advertisement for the June 1771 court session, Margaret Hunter finished with a line that anticipated the slow summer season by reminding her customers that "Orders from the Country [would] be faithfully and punctually executed, on the most reasonable Terms."[42] Dickinson's efforts to "particularly" thank "her good friends in the country" and assure them they could continue to "rely on their orders being attended to with the strictest care" in May 1774 indicate that they played an essential role in her business.[43] Although meetings of the General Court and the Virginia Assembly in Williamsburg offered tremendous opportunity for women in the fashion trades, the nature of the seasonal business patterns could potentially leave their small enterprises in a vulnerable spot for much of the year.

The most critical challenge for milliners doing business in the Chesapeake revolved around the perpetual problem of credit. Dominated by the tobacco trade, the Chesapeake economy in which Rathell and her fellow tradeswomen found themselves was largely dependent on a series of short- and long-term credit obligations. To transport tobacco to market, planters, local Scottish factors, and consignment merchants in London first had to have sufficient investment capital to cover the freighting and insurance costs of a transatlantic shipment. Once the tobacco arrived in London, investors had to mobilize enough capital or available credit to cover duties and warehouse costs until the tobacco could be sold and profits realized. Tobacco was sold in London for either cash or short-term credit, which was then used to purchase goods for export back to the colonies. Warehouses and wholesalers in London usually offered long-term credit of twelve months on goods for export merchants but also made extended credit available with interest. Oftentimes these processes overlapped. Price estimates that to open a simple shop in the Chesapeake cost about £200–£300. The estimated value of the goods Rathell left to be sold in Annapolis were worth approximately £200–£300 after twelve months since her last shipment, so it may be assumed that Rathell needed upward of £400 to stock her shelves. A shop that intended to accept tobacco and offer credit in exchange for goods while assuming the risks involved in shipping and selling it needed at least £3,000 to start. Most Glasgow and London merchant firms operated with £10,000–£20,000 worth of investment capital.[44] Operating on much less available capital, Rathell and others had to find ways to compete with consignment merchants and Scottish factors who could afford to extend customers extensive credit. The principal line of defense for the majority of milliners was simply to avoid offering any credit at all. Announcements of goods sold at a "low advance" or "low price" for "cash" or "ready money only" run as a constant refrain through milliners' advertisements.

By demanding cash only, milliners actually increased their chances of gaining access to those with more extended capital. To operate a shop full of imported wares, a milliner needed to secure a reliable source of supply. A milliner could either return to London periodically to purchase goods or, more practically, obtain the services of a London consignment merchant— sometimes one of the very merchants with whom the milliner hoped, in some small measure, to compete. Cash-only business practices made dealing with milliners attractive to consignment merchants for the way such policies ensured that they would be more likely to settle their debts in a timely fashion, unlike the majority of customers, who were all too happy to leave lingering debt on the books. In 1773, for example, John Norton and Sons' list of foreign debtors in Virginia numbered 398 individuals with a combined total of £63,856, 7 shillings, and 5 pence in outstanding debts. Rathell's continual emphasis on cash payments was most likely a conscientious effort to impress creditors.[45] John Norton Jr.'s sole stipulation for doing business with Rathell was that she be "punctual in [her] payments." After speaking in person with John Norton Jr. in Yorktown, she immediately sent a letter to John Norton Sr. in London reassuring him that he could "depend" on her punctuality, adding that she would "always be proud to have Mr. Norton [Jr.] on the spot to receive the cash as it comes in."[46] In January 1773, still only a few months into their business dealings, Rathell again attempted to allay any fears Norton might have about her dependability. "Perhaps, sir, you may scruple sending so much goods to a person who you know so little of," she speculated, "but you may depend on my being very exact in my payments." If Norton entertained any lingering doubts, she directed him to consult with Colonel George Mercer, who, Rathell informed Norton, "is not unacquainted with my Method of Dailing, and . . . Can Inform you I sell for Nothing but ready Cash, So by giving no Credit, I can at all times Either Command Goods or Cash."[47] Likewise, when she asked Roger Atkinson to write a letter of introduction on her behalf in an effort to secure a new supplier, she requested that he inform the merchant house that she dealt "only for ready Money," was "very industrious & frugal," and "propose[d] to pay ye Money to Mr. Hanson . . . as She recovers it."[48] By referring Norton to Mercer and requesting a letter of introduction, Rathell was operating within the usual custom of colonial business dealings, smoothing the way through mutual connections and personal relationships. However, her reference to Mercer almost as an afterthought to verify her main point is suggestive in the way it implies she believed her business dealings should carry nearly equal weight as the recommendation itself. Staying out of extended debt and credit tangles enabled women of limited means to prove that they were a worthwhile credit risk.

Dealing on a cash-only basis also helped milliners offer their goods at competitive prices. One of the chief incentives for planters to do business directly with consignment merchants was the opportunity to obtain goods at reasonable rates. By having a merchant make purchases directly in London, a planter stood to gain by achieving discounts on duties and the exchange rate.[49] As Robert Carter Nicholas remarked to John Norton in 1771, Williamsburg stores had a reputation for being "dear." Setting prices too high could be disastrous, as Mary Dickinson quickly discovered, much to her chagrin, when she found herself having to offer her customers "lower terms than the former" as an "inducement for a continuance of their favours."[50] But the consignment trade was not without its problems. In addition to complaining that Norton had sent her goods that were "ill bought and ungenteel," Mrs. Nicholas objected to both orders on the basis that they were too expensive: they were "charged higher than they could be bought in the Stores of Williamsburg," and the fans were priced so high they "could have [been] bought in a Milliner's shop in Wmsbg for a third of the price," exchange rate aside. The Williamsburg milliners' opportunity for sales lay in their ability to manipulate the credit system to their own and their customers' advantage. By demanding cash only, Rathell was able to price goods to advantage despite the exchange rate because she did not need to allow for the interest that would accrue as she waited for a customer to settle an account on credit. As she explained to her customers, since she "[sold] for ready money only, and at a very low advance; and [was] . . . contented to make a reasonable profit . . . the fall of the exchange" would be "to their benefit."[51]

Most important, Rathell succeeded in keeping prices low through her activities as a shrewd and careful shopper. When milliners advertised their wares as "well bought" and "well chosen," they were not just advertising their expert knowledge of fashion; they were marketing their expert skills as shoppers. One way Rathell secured bargains was by using her specialized knowledge of London to deal directly with the city's wholesalers. In November 1771, Rathell informed Norton that, since she had been "so lately in England," she needed "few goods" and those few "chiefly from Messrs. Wooley & Hemings." However, she had already "sent them . . . directions." All she required of Norton was to "send and hurry them."[52] Similarly, in December 1771, she had "ordered Some Goods from Messrs Flight & Co." directly and begged Norton to "recive and send them."[53] By reducing Norton's role as a middleman, Rathell probably succeeded in minimizing fees. More important, when Rathell used Norton to make purchases, she was very precise about the prices she was willing to pay. Fully cognizant of the prices the market would bear in Williamsburg, Rathell knew exactly what she could pay for an item and still make a profit. If, as in the case of a shipment of toupees, Norton did not follow her instructions precisely, she was not afraid to confront him and send the goods back. When a shipment of toupees arrived that were not of the quality or price she expected, Rathell resolutely packed them up again and sat down to vent her disappointment to Norton: "I sent for woolpacks at 2/6 or 3/ apiece these with Curls, and he sends me 2 Dozn tupees from 6/6 to 12/ a price that would never suffer me to sell them, even at first cost, besides he made a mistake in charging them, he charges one with 7 tupees with 2 curls a 12/ makes 4. 4. o." She closed the letter by giving instructions for their return. Although she did offer an apology that she hoped he would "excuse [her] giving [him] so much trouble," she remained firm with her closing line, stating, "I dar say you approve on being particular as well as I do."[54] Such hard-nosed bargaining would have earned her the praise and custom of her Williamsburg patrons, but it did not endear her to the merchants with whom she did business. Perhaps an exasperated Norton had the last word after all when he wrote to his son, "I am glad you have rec'd Mrs. Rathell's Debt, with several others, her Correspondence is dangerous, & she plagues almost every one she deals with by returning large quantities of Goods yearly which don't suit her to keep."[55]

Not all milliners were as successful as Rathell in working the credit system to their advantage. The wording of Sarah Pitt's advertisements suggests that, while she continually demanded ready money, she was largely unsuccessful in obtaining it. Every single one of Pitt's nine advertisements, starting with her first, placed on November 12, 1767, stipulated that she sold at "a low price" for "ready money only," but her last advertisement, on November 8, 1770, still found Pitt pleading with her customers that as she was "obliged to be punctual in her remittances" she "must sell for ready money only."[56] Although Mary Davenport's sole advertisement does not mention the terms on which she dealt, she appears on both of Norton's list of foreign debtors, in 1770 and 1773, for £153 and £104, 3 shillings, and 3 pence, respectively.[57] In contrast, Rathell, who dealt with Norton on a regular basis, does not appear on either list—suggesting, perhaps, that her cash-only policy was largely successful. It is unclear whether the Hunter sisters ever attempted to demand cash, since their advertisements announce only that the goods were to be sold "on reasonable terms." Although both Margaret Hunter and Rathell ended up in court at least once trying to collect outstanding debts, the debt Margaret was attempting to recover was much larger—"One Hundred five Pounds and nine pence sterling with interest," compared with Rathell's "Twenty four Pounds three shillings and four pence"—indicating that hers may have been part of a long-standing credit arrangement.[58] Even if demanding cash was a prudent path to maintaining solvency, the reality of the business climate in the Chesapeake, where hard specie was scarce and customers could obtain credit easily from local Scottish factors and London consignment merchants, sometimes made offering credit unavoidable.

The Revolution disrupted these carefully constructed enterprises and served as a moment of truth that revealed their vulnerability. The first rumblings of revolutionary interference appear with Sarah Pitt's advertisement in November 1770, in which she excuses herself for selling imported wares after the signing of Virginia's first nonimportation association on the basis that "the above goods were sent for before the association took place, and there has not been time for counter orders."[59] Virginia's first nonimportation resolutions were organized in response to the Townshend Duties in May 1769 by former members of the House of Burgesses after they were dissolved by the royal governor, Norborne Berkeley, Lord Botetourt, for defending the rights of Virginia and other colonies to tax themselves. Although a restored House of Burgesses passed a formal nonimportation association in June 1770, the resolves did little damage to the milliners. British imports into the Chesapeake actually rose 60 percent from 1770 to 1771. In April 1770, John Norton, Rathell's supplier, even noted that he had "shipped considerably more goods this year than I have ever done since my return to England."[60] The gentry, eager to reduce their indebtedness to British merchants, largely embraced the opportunity to economize, not without hopes that participation in the association would similarly allow smallholders and tenants to reduce debt. Many of their tenants were so indebted to British creditors that they lacked hard specie to pay their rents. Smallholders, however, were loath to participate. Still enjoying high prices wrought by a tobacco boom that began following the Seven Years' War, many individuals continued to seize the opportunity to acquire material symbols of status on the credit freely offered by tobacco merchants.[61]

The real trouble for Rathell and her fellow milliners came with the second wave of nonimportation associations following the Coercive Acts in 1774. Initially drafted by former burgesses in May 1774, after the assembly was once more dissolved by the royal governor, John Murray, fourth earl of Dunmore, for passing a resolution for a day of fasting and prayer in conjunction with the closing of the port in Boston, the association was expanded in August 1774 by the First Virginia Convention, meeting in Williamsburg while the governor was away fighting an Indian war in the Ohio Valley. In October 1774, the First Continental Congress adopted Virginia's resolutions, forming a continental association. This time, the nonimportation associations would be effective.[62]

Gripped by a credit crisis resulting from a glut in the tobacco market, small farmers and planters alike seized the opportunity to retrench and stave off creditors under the guise of political protest. Between 1772 and 1773, Virginians watched as the price of tobacco fell almost 40 percent in some regions, nearly too low to make a profit.[63] Debt suits mounted, and credit contracted. Although no extant commentary on the state of affairs from Rathell and her compatriots remains, one Virginia trader, Charles Yates, observed to a contact in London that the thought of receiving a large shipment of goods at such a juncture "throws me into a sweat."[64] In July 1774, Thomas Nelson Jr. of Yorktown conjectured that "the Goods already in the Country, and those expected in the Fall, will be sufficient to supply the Wants of all Virginia for two Years."[65] As a measure of the success of the 1774 associations, the value of goods imported into the Chesapeake from 1774 to 1775 declined from £690,000 sterling to £2,000 sterling.[66]

The milliners in Williamsburg felt the pinch of credit in the midst of the increasing political turmoil deeply. Within fifteen months of the Continental Congress's adoption of Virginia's nonimportation associations, all of the milliners and mantuamakers in Williamsburg who had arrived from London between 1766 and 1771 announced their intention to quit the colony. Yet as they quickly discovered, their plans to leave were directly affected by their success or failure in negotiating the fine line between demanding cash and offering credit over the previous decade.

Jane Hunter Charlton and her husband, Edward Charlton, were the first to advertise their plans to leave Virginia starting in early November 1774, only a couple of weeks after the Continental Congress's adoption of a continental association. Over the next month, the couple ran a pair of advertisements in the *Virginia Gazette*. Although the only explanation Jane offered for leaving was that she "[found] it necessary to go for *England* in the spring," the timing of their departure and Edward's advertisement directly beneath it attempting to sell their house imply that they intended the move to be a semipermanent one, arguably driven by concerns over the political and economic turmoil. Even though they did not plan to leave until the spring, they found it necessary to begin advertising months in advance. Jane's plea to her customers reveals why. "It is hoped those ladies and gentlemen who have favored me with their orders, and have not discharged them," she politely but firmly reminded her customers "will be kind enough to make payment as early as possible, that I may be enabled to put my designs in execution."[67] Jane's ability to finance her return home was directly linked to her ability to collect her outstanding debts. Initially, Jane's sister, Margaret, appears to have been inclined to wait out the situation, but as the political turmoil deepened, she, too, decided it was time to leave. As the Second Virginia Convention was on the brink of its March 1775 meeting at which Patrick Henry famously advocated putting Virginia in an immediate posture of defense, Margaret also placed an advertisement announcing to her customers that she found it "necessary . . . to go to *England* this Spring." Margaret's advertisement makes the problem of uncollected debt even more explicit: "I shall esteem it a particular Favour if those who are indebted to me would be as early as possible in discharging their Accounts, without which it will not be in my power to accomplish my Intention."[68] Because Margaret dealt in credit, her ability to make her own choices was no longer in her power; it was in her customers'. The seriousness of the problem is underscored by Jane and Edward's last appeal to their customers to settle their debts. On April 19, 1775, just days before Lord Dunmore's ill-conceived seizure of the public powder caused tensions within the city to nearly reach the breaking point, Jane and Edward made one more attempt to collect: "The Subscribers intending to leave the Colony as soon as they can settle their Affairs, once more most earnestly entreat the Favour of those who are indebted to them to discharge their Accounts at the ensuing Meeting of the Merchants. The Goods they have on Hand will be sold cheap for Cash; and as their Continuance here is uncertain, it makes such a Notice necessary."[69] Despite their intense desire to remove themselves from the increasingly troubled economic and political climate, they were as indebted to their customers as their customers were to them.

Conversely, when Rathell announced her intention to "g[o] to *England* as soon as I dispose of my Goods . . . until liberty of importation is allowed" the day after Jane and Edward's last advertisement, she was able to set her plans in motion without delay.[70] If she had not perished in a shipwreck in sight of England's coast, she would have been there by October 1775.[71] Although her "request, as a favour, that all who are indebted to me will pay off their accounts this meeting" implies that she had relaxed her policies on cash only, Rathell was still evidently able to "command cash or goods" to the extent that she could finance her passage while leaving the remaining goods with her partner.[72] Gossip around town reported that Margaret Brodie was £2,000 the richer for Rathell's death.[73] Yet even the possession of £2,000 worth of wares did Brodie little good if she could not convert them into cash. Perhaps encouraged by the prospect of running her own shop with the goods inherited from Rathell, Brodie waited out the political situation the longest. But, by November 1775, she also was ready to return to England.

In the intervening months between April and November 1775, the political situation in Virginia had deteriorated drastically. Following the seizure of the gunpowder in April, Lord Dunmore had abandoned the capital in early June, taking up residence aboard the H.M.S. *Fowey* in the York River. During the summer, the Third Virginia Convention sat in Richmond and began to form a provisional government, and October 1775 marked what was to be the last official meeting of the General Court, which typically generated the briskest business a Williamsburg millinery shop would see in a year. Perhaps more disturbing, the fall witnessed the outbreak of skirmishing between Dunmore's small flotilla and Virginia forces in the Hampton Roads area. On November 7, 1775, Dunmore issued his provocative proclamation raising the king's standard and offering freedom to all slaves of rebel masters who would come and join him in taking up arms against the colonists. On November 23, 1775, he occupied Norfolk.[74] The next day, November 24, 1775, Brodie joined the others in making an attempt to leave the colony. "As I intend for *Great Britain* immediately," she alerted the public, "all mrs. *Rathell's* Stock of Goods will be absolutely sold by publick vendue . . . for ready money." All persons "indebted to mrs. *Rathell*" were "requested to discharge their accounts immediately."[75] Whether it was for love or for security in the wake of a failure to turn capital in goods into actual capital in cash, Brodie did not leave Virginia but married a recently emigrated English merchant in 1776.

In the end, out of all five women from London working in the fasion trades, only Rathell succeeded in establishing a business that provided her with enough security to realize her intentions and withstand the pressures of the revolutionary marketplace. Despite their best efforts to return to England, Jane Hunter Charlton, Margaret Hunter, and Margaret Brodie were forced to remain in Williamsburg in the midst of an increasingly volatile political situation. The fate of the unidentified London milliner working alongside Sarah Pitt in 1769 is unknown. On one hand, the riches of the economy generated by tobacco sales following the Seven Years' War and the corresponding demand for imported wares in the Chesapeake combined to create an enormous opportunity for ambitious female entrepreneurs in the fashion trades. On the other, the economy was based on a credit system that could go up in smoke just as easily as the tobacco that supported it. Although the Chesapeake was one of the wealthiest regions of Britain's North American mainland possessions, Maryland and Virginia together were responsible for 58 percent of the total debts outstanding to British merchants following the Revolution, reaching a grand total of £2,876,864.[76]

As Rathell and her fellow milliners learned only too well, the very economic system that afforded them such rich opportunities could, if not carefully navigated, directly circumscribe their personal choices at critical moments. In that light, Rathell's careful contingency plan at the beginning of her first advertisement stipulating that she would do business "for ready money only" was not just a device to impress creditors or achieve lower prices but a deliberate strategy to retain control of her finances and thereby her own independence. The rise of consumer culture in the British Empire enabled Rathell and her fellow milliners to painstakingly establish an economic foothold in the Chesapeake, but the politicization of that very same marketplace also presented them with a very different set of options from those available to the women who participated in sewing bees or proudly affixed their names to nonimportation agreements. When viewed from the opposite side of the shop counter, it becomes apparent that the revolutionary politics of the marketplace did not simply provide women with new opportunities to exercise a political voice. They also held the potential to reduce other women to a greater state of dependence.

Notes

1. *Virginia Gazette* (Purdie and Dixon), April 18, 1766, [3]. Although this advertisement uses the spelling "Rathall," I have found "Rathell" to be more common and have elected to use the latter spelling throughout.

2. John Morton Jordon to Robert Carter, August 25, 1765, Carter Papers, Virginia Historical Society, Richmond (hereafter, VHS), microfilm reel M-82.6, John D. Rockefeller Jr. Library, Colonial Williamsburg Foundation, Williamsburg, VA.

3. [Reverend Thomas Gwatkin], Gwatkin Chorography, [ca. 1774], Tyler Family Papers, mss. 65 T97, Group F, box 8, fol. [8], Special Collections, Earl Greg Swem Library, College of William and Mary, Williamsburg, VA.

4. *Virginia Gazette* (Pinkney), April 20, 1775, [3].

5. T. H. Breen, *The Marketplace of Revolution: How Consumer Politics Shaped American Independence* (New York: Oxford University Press, 2004), see chap. 2, esp. 34, 38–39, 43, 60, chap. 6, esp. 210, 329–30.

6. Ibid., 288; Mary Beth Norton, *Liberty's Daughters: The Revolutionary Experience of American Women, 1750–1800* (Boston: Little, Brown, 1980), chap. 6; Linda K. Kerber, *Women of the Republic: Intellect and Ideology in Revolutionary America* (Chapel Hill: University of North Carolina Press, 1980), chap. 2.

7. *South-Carolina Gazette*, July 13, 1769, quoted in Breen, *The Marketplace of Revolution*, 282.

8. *Boston Gazette*, February 12, 1770, quoted in Breen, *The Marketplace of Revolution*, 287; Kerber, *Women of the Republic*, 38–41.

9. For the female entrepreneurs in eighteenth-century Newport and Charleston, see Ellen Hartigan-O'Connor, *The Ties That Buy: Women and Commerce in Revolutionary America* (Philadelphia: University of Pennsylvania Press, 2009), chap. 1, esp. 23–28, chap. 2, esp. 39, 41–49, 50–51, 68, chap. 3. When viewed as a whole, she contends, "the glass-by-glass and shoe-by-shoe transactions" made by women shaped "the economic landscape of port cities as much as the well-trod paths from wharf to counting-house."

10. For the female entrepreneurs of Philadelphia, New York, and Boston, see Patricia Cleary, "'She-Merchants' of Colonial America: Women and Commerce

on the Eve of the Revolution" (Ph.D. diss., Northwestern University, Evanston, IL, 1989), 2, 163–68.

11. Hartigan-O'Connor, *The Ties That Buy*, 179.

12. *Virginia Gazette* (Purdie and Dixon), April 18, 1766, [3].

13. John J. McCusker and Russell R. Menard, *The Economy of British America, 1607–1789* (Chapel Hill, N.C.: University of North Carolina Press, 1985), 131–33, 139; James O'Mara, *An Historical Geography of Urban System Development: Tidewater Virginia in the 18th Century, Geographical Monographs no. 13* (Downsview, ON: York University, 1983), 87; Jacob Price, *Capital and Credit in British Overseas Trade: The View from the Chesapeake, 1700–1776* (Cambridge, MA: Harvard University Press, 1980), 128–29.

14. *Virginia Gazette* (Purdie and Dixon), October 10, 1766, [3] (Jane Hunter), October 1, 1767, [1] (Margaret and Jane Hunter), December 14, 1769, [3] (unidentified English milliner working alongside Sarah Pitt), October 24, 1771, [2] (Margaret Brodie).

15. Ro[bert] C[arter] Nicholas to John Norton, September 7, 1771, in Frances Norton Mason, ed., *John Norton and Sons: Merchants of London and Virginia* (Richmond: Dietz, 1937), 184–85.

16. Ann Nicholas to John Norton, July 22, 1775, quoted in Patricia Ann Hurdle, "Millinery and Milliners in Colonial Virginia, 1750–1780" (M.A. thesis, College of William and Mary, Williamsburg, VA, 1970), 22–23.

17. Robert Carter Nicholas to John Norton, January 22, 1772, John Norton and Sons Papers, John D. Rockefeller Jr. Library, folder 52.

18. "Col Washington to Edward Charlton for J. Charlton," 1771, Mary Custis Lee Papers, Mss. 1 L5 144 a28–29, Section 2, VHS.

19. George Washington Ledgers A and B, Ledger B, March 26, 1772, United States Library of Congress, Washington, D.C., microfilm reel M-89.2, John D. Rockefeller Jr. Library.

20. John Spotswood in Account with James Hunter, Fredericksburg District Court Papers, microfilm reel M-146, John D. Rockefeller Jr. Library.

21. A[nne] Blair to [Mary Blair] Braxton, September 4, 1769, Blair, Banister, Braxton, Horner, Whiting Papers, Mss. 39.1 B58, folder 1, Item 7, Special Collections, Earl Greg Swem Library.

22. Catherine Rathell to Mrs. Mercer, n.d., Misc. Mss. R., New York Historical Society, transcription on file in York County Records Project, Colonial Williamsburg Foundation's Department of Training and Research, Williamsburg, Virginia.

23. A[nne] Blair to [Mary Blair] Braxton, August 21, 1769, Blair, Banister, Braxton, Horner, Whiting Papers, Mss. 39.1 B58, folder 1, Item 5, Earl Gregg Swem Library.

24. *Virginia Gazette* (Purdie and Dixon), April 18, 1766, [3].

25. *Maryland Gazette*, September 7, 1769, [2].

26. *Virginia Gazette* (Purdie and Dixon), October 24, 1771, [2].

27. *Virginia Gazette* (Purdie and Dixon), October 10, 1771, [3] (quotations). For Rathell's announcement of her intention to return to London to select a cargo of wares, see *Virginia Gazette* (Rind), April 13, 1769, [3].

28. For background on the merchant firm John Norton and Sons, see Jacob M. Price, "Who Was John Norton? A Note on the Historical Character of Some Eighteenth-Century London Virginia Firms," *William and Mary Quarterly*, 3d ser., 19, no. 3 (July 1962): 400–7. For the important role played by female members of

merchant families in the transatlantic trade to Virginia, see Linda L. Sturtz, *Within Her Power: Propertied Women in Colonial Virginia* (New York: Routledge, 2002), chap. 6. For a broader discussion of Mrs. Norton's popularity with John Norton and Sons' Virginia customers, and her appeal with Rathell in particular, see Sturtz, *Within Her Power*, 163–69, esp. 168–69.

29. Catherine Rathell to John Norton, January 31, 1772, John Norton and Sons Papers, John D. Rockefeller Jr. Library, folder 52.

30. Mary Davenport appears on John Norton's list of foreign debtors in 1773: see "A List of Foreign Debtors," July 30, 1773, John Norton and Sons Papers, John D. Rockefeller Jr. Library, folder 88, oversize.

31. McCusker and Menard, *The Economy of British America*, 131.

32. Catherine Rathell to John Norton, November 16, 1771, John Norton and Sons Papers, John D. Rockefeller Jr. Library, folder 50.

33. Rathell to Norton, January 31, 1772, emphasis added.

34. Rathell to Norton, November 16, 1771.

35. *Virginia Gazette* (Rind), April 13, 1769, [3].

36. *Maryland Gazette*, September 7, 1769, [2], November 2, 1769, [4].

37. Ibid., March 29, 1770, 253.

38. Catherine Rathell to John Norton, December 29, 1771, folder 51, John Norton and Sons Papers, John D. Rockefeller Jr. Library; Rathell to Norton, January 31, 1772.

39. *Maryland Gazette*, March 29, 1770, 253.

40. Ibid., October 22, 1772, [2].

41. Ibid., September 26, 1771, 578, September 24, 1772, [2].

42. *Virginia Gazette* (Purdie and Dixon), June 20, 1771, [3].

43. *Virginia Gazette* (Rind), May 12, 1774, [3].

44. For a discussion of the capital necessary to start various businesses, see Price, *Capital and Credit in British Overseas Trade*, 25, 38, chap. 6, esp. 99–103.

45. For John Norton and Son's outstanding foreign debts in 1773, see Mason, *John Norton and Sons*, 293. For Sturtz's discussion of Rathell's cash-only policy, see Sturtz, *Within Her Power*, 173.

46. Rathell to Norton, November 16, 1771.

47. Rathell to Norton, January 31, 1772.

48. Roger Atkinson to Benson Fearon, March 1, 1773, Roger Atkinson Mss. Letter Book, 1769–76, Alderman Library, University of Virginia, Charlottesville, microfilm reel M-51, John D. Rockefeller Jr. Library.

49. Price, *Capital and Credit in British Overseas Trade*, 100–1.

50. *Virginia Gazette* (Purdie and Dixon), November 22, 1770, supp., [2].

51. Ibid., April 18, 1766, [3]. Sturtz has also made this point: see Sturtz, *Within Her Power*, 172.

52. Rathell to Norton, November 16, 1771.

53. Rathell to Norton, December 29, 1771.

54. Catherine Rathell to John Norton, July 22, 1772, John Norton and Sons Papers, John D. Rockefeller Jr. Library, folder 66.

55. John Norton to John Hatley Norton, July 6, 1773, John Norton and Sons Papers, John D. Rockefeller Jr. Library, folder 86.

56. *Virginia Gazette* (Rind), November 8, 1770, [1] ("obliged to be punctual"). For the rest of Pitt's advertisements, see *Virginia Gazette* (Purdie and Dixon), November 12, 1767, [2], October 27, 1768, [3], May 18, 1769, [3], November 2, 1769, [4],

December 14, 1769, [3], April 19, 1770, supp., [2]; *Virginia Gazette* (Rind), October 26, 1769, [2], July 12, 1770, [3].

57. For Dickinson's outstanding debts, see "List of Foreign Debtors," July 31, 1770, John Norton and Sons Papers, John D. Rockefeller Jr. Library, folder 31, oversize; "A List of Foreign Debtors," July 30, 1773.

58. For Hunter's and Rathell's attempts to collect debts in court, see "Margaret Hunter [Plaintiff] against Matthew Marrable [Defendant]," July 19, 1773, York County Records Project, JO-3 (1772–74), 318; "Catherine Rathell [Plaintiff] against Mathew Holt [Defendant]," November 16, 1772, York County Records Project, J O-3 9 (1772–74), 164, transcriptions of both are held at the Department of Historical Training and Research, Colonial Williamsburg Foundation, Williamsburg, VA.

59. *Virginia Gazette* (Rind), November 8, 1770, [1].

60. William J. Van Schreeven and Robert L. Scribner, eds., *Revolutionary Virginia: The Road to Independence, Volume 1: Forming Thunderclouds and the First Convention, 1763–1774, a Documentary Record* (Charlottesville: University Press of Virginia, 1973), 72–77, 78–84; John Norton to Robert Carter Nicholas, April 21, 1770, Wilson Cary Nicholas Papers (no. 5533), Special Collections Department, Alderman Library, quoted in Woody Holton, *Forced Founders: Indians, Debtors, Slaves, and the Making of the American Revolution in Virginia* (Chapel Hill, N.C.: University of North Carolina Press, 1999), 91.

61. Holton, *Forced Founders*, 79–95.

62. Ibid., chap. 3, esp. 91.

63. Ibid., 95.

64. Charles Yates to Samuel Martin, April 2, 1774, Yates Letterbook, Special Collections Department, Alderman Library, quoted in ibid., 99.

65. Schreeven and Scribner, *Revolutionary Virginia*, 102, 116.

66. Holton, *Forced Founders*, 102.

67. *Virginia Gazette* (Pinkney), November 4, 1774, [3], November 10, 1774, [4], November 17, 1774, [4], November 24, 1774, [4].

68. *Virginia Gazette* (Dixon and Hunter), March 4, 1775, [3].

69. *Virginia Gazette* (Dixon and Hunter), April 19, 1775, supp., [4].

70. *Virginia Gazette* (Pinkney), April 20, 1775, [3].

71. A London newspaper carried the announcement of her death in a shipwreck just off the coast of England: see *London Evening-Post*, October 28–31, 1775, [3].

72. *Virginia Gazette* (Pinkney), April 20, 1775, [3].

73. "The Meml: of Margt [Brodie] Mathews Widow of Wm Peter Mathews," in *American Loyalists: Transcript of the Manuscript Books and Papers of the Commission of Enquiry into the Losses and Services of the American Loyalists Held under Acts of Parliament of 23, 25, 26, 28, and 29 of George III. Preserved amongst the Audit Office Records in the Public Record Office of England 1783–1790, Volume 59: Examinations in London, Memorials, Schedules of Losses and Evidences, Virginia Claimants in Two Books (Book ii)*, transcribed for the New York Public Library, 1901, microfilm reel M-73, John D. Rockefeller Jr. Library.

74. For an overview of the collapse of royal government and Virginia's descent into war, see John E. Selby, *The Revolution in Virginia, 1775–1783* (Williamsburg: University Press of Virginia, 1988).

75. *Virginia Gazette* (Purdie), November 24, 1775, [3].

76. Price, *Capital and Credit in British Overseas Trade*, 7, 9.

Marketing Medicine

Apothecary Elizabeth Weed's Economic Independence during the American Revolution

SUSAN HANKET BRANDT

On October 11, 1777, Elizabeth Dickinson Weed announced in the *Pennsylvania Evening Post* that she would carry on the Philadelphia pharmaceutical practice of her deceased husband, the apothecary "Doctor" George Weed. As her newspaper advertisement emphasized, Elizabeth Weed retained her husband's secret medicinal recipes and had, in fact, "been employed these several years past in preparing them herself." Weed's proprietary pharmaceuticals included "the Royal Balsam, the Bitter Tincture, the Essence of Tar . . . sundry patent medicines, ointments, and salves, &c." She advised her patrons that those who experienced the "good effects" of her products might "depend on being supplied with them as usual."[1] Amid the turmoil of the American Revolution and the British occupation of Philadelphia, Weed's customers required reassurance. An adjacent column in the *Evening Post* chronicled the devastating defeat of General George Washington's Continentals at Germantown and alluded to British General Sir William Howe's triumphal entry into the city. Despite the economic dislocations of occupation, Weed had to sustain her apothecary business to support herself and her sickly toddler, George Junior.

Weed's experiences seem mundane compared with the popular tales of patriot women who risked their lives as spies, nurses, and soldiers, or the accounts of enslaved women who fled to the British lines seeking liberty. Nonetheless, Weed's narrative is equally important. She represents free women who faced the political and economic uncertainties of the revolutionary period and preserved their financial self-reliance through creative entrepreneurship. The scarcity of archival sources produced by female entrepreneurs has reinforced free women's misleading invisibility in economic history and has obscured their active participation in an emerging capitalist marketplace. Few artisanal women had the leisure time to write letters or diaries, and most archives preserved only documentation of the American Revolution generated by men.[2] By contrast, this essay recovers free Philadelphia women's engagement in a vibrant consumer marketplace in which health was peddled as a commodity. Far from being sidelined by the rise of medical consumerism, female entrepreneurs marketed themselves as authoritative providers of medicinals and healing advice. Weed and her colleagues developed innovative advertising strategies to convince customers that their panaceas would cure a profusion of ills and restore health. They leveraged rising consumer demand for pharmaceuticals to sustain their businesses in a competitive marketplace during a period of economic and revolutionary ferment.

Indeed, Weed marketed her proprietary Weed's Syrup so effectively that it gained brand-name recognition and was counterfeited by the barber James Craft. In response, Weed used the courts to assert her exclusive intellectual property rights to the authentic Weed's Syrup. She sued Craft, accusing him in the press of "the base act of forgery." As an artisanal woman, Weed defied prescriptive norms of restrained and private elite women's behavior by naming herself in print and promoting her products in public newspaper advertisements. Her use of the courts to battle for her intellectual property rights in her proprietary medicines challenged the stereotypes propounded by Enlightenment philosophers, who argued for women's innate intellectual inferiority compared with men.[3] Weed's assertive actions, her medicinal knowledge, and her marketing savvy were valuable commodities that translated into income for herself and her family. The documentary traces of Weed's apothecary practice underscore free Euro-American women's innovative roles in advertising, marketing, and selling pharmaceuticals as they developed networks of healthcare commerce in the era of the American Revolution.

Women and the Business of Pharmacy

Elizabeth Dickinson Weed had precedents for her apothecary practice. European women's long-standing and legitimate roles as herbalists and domestic healers made pharmaceutical preparation a culturally normative women's practice. Female adepts could redeploy these skills to create healthcare businesses. Historians have described women's work as proprietors of taverns, boardinghouses, millinery stores, print shops, and dry goods emporiums in England and its colonies.[4] Female apothecaries and drug vendors have received less attention. Even in the relatively restrictive environment of late seventeenth-century and early eighteenth-century London, some women assumed their deceased husbands' or fathers' apothecary practices with the approval of the apothecaries' guild, which considered a woman's participation in the family shop equivalent to an apprenticeship.

Other female lay healers, shopkeepers, and tavern keepers sold pharmaceuticals and participated in retail distribution networks for proprietary drugs.[5]

Women also created and sold brand-name proprietary medicines.
Joanna Stephens's discovery of a chemical remedy that dissolved bladder
stones earned her a £5,000 award from the British Parliament in 1740.
Her widely publicized recipe underscored pharmaceuticals' lucrative possibilities. A healer named Mrs. Garway created her own version of a popular
medicinal amulet that she sold at her London coffee shop in the early eighteenth century. Her "Mrs. Garway's Anodyne Necklace" cured babies' teeth-
ing pains, fevers, convulsions, ruptures, and countless maladies. But other
drug vendors argued that their necklaces were the only genuine products,
warning customers against counterfeits in broadsides and newspaper advertisements. Intense debates over Anodyne Necklace purveyors' authenticity
or quackery exemplifies the texture of the consumer market for self-help
pharmaceuticals that emerged in mid-seventeenth-century England and was
transmitted to the British North American colonies. An early discourse of
pharmaceutical trustworthiness and fraud appeared in print and spilled over
into interpersonal healthcare networks, as evidenced in women's manuscript
medical recipe books.[6] In this contentious marketplace, drug vendors sued
one another over exclusive rights to proprietary medicines.

Elizabeth Weed's lawsuit against the alleged pharmaceutical counterfeiter James Craft had English precedents. The women of the Anthony
Daffy family waged public battles in the press and courtrooms over the
rights to Daffy's Elixir. The self-styled "Doctor Daffy, student in Physick,"
a shoemaker in Leicester named Anthony Daffy, created the preparation
in the 1670s. He lambasted a group of London's "upstart counterfeiters,"
including the druggist Jane White, whom he called "Ape-like imitators" and
"sneaking Cub-Quacks, not yet lickt into form, but remaining Moon-blind
brats, (still in swaddling clouts)." Upon Daffy's death, his wife, Elleanor,
marketed the best-selling drug, which was said to cure melancholy, colic,
green-sickness, scurvy, dropsy, consumptions, agues, and numerous other
ills. Elleanor's daughter, Ellen Daffy Trubshaw, also championed her rights
to the elixir in courtroom battles against her estranged husband. In 1765,
the Londoner Mary Swinton successfully sued a competitor for the rights to
her uncle Anthony's Daffy's Elixir, arguing that she was the "sole Proprietor
of the original Receipt." However, a female cousin challenged Swinton's
trademark rights. Swinton's obituary in 1780 was embedded appropriately
in an advertisement for Daffy's Elixir.[7]

Women in another London pharmaceutical dynasty marketed the popular Turlington's Balsam of Life. Its inventor, Robert Turlington, received one
of the first royal pharmaceutical patents in 1744 for the cure-all balsam. The

medication's pear-shaped glass phial was stamped "By the King's Patent" to discourage counterfeiters. Nonetheless, Turlington warned his transatlantic customers about the "Villainy of some Persons, who buying up my empty bottles, have basely and wickedly put therein a vile spurious composition." After Turlington's death, his niece Martha Wray assumed the patent and marketed the drug in the 1750s. Like Elizabeth Weed, these women invoked their panaceas' male creators, but they emphasized their own proprietary rights. In addition to developing skills in sales and marketing, female druggists learned to defend their products in the courts and in print.[8]

This medical consumer culture emerged in the early eighteenth century in the British North American colonies, and female entrepreneurs took advantage of an unregulated environment to start healthcare businesses. Patients facing a profusion of acute and chronic diseases were lured by advertisements promising that health was something that money could buy. Apothecary shops' bow-front windows displayed richly decorated ceramic jars and glassware that enticed customers to purchase distinctive brands of medicine in attractive packaging. Advertisements added the authoritative power of the printed word to practitioners' claims of extraordinary cures and manipulative retail advertising techniques increasingly shaped consumers' desires. Consumer demand for healthcare-related products drove this small but important sector of the developing market in goods. In addition, the minimal regulations regarding the education and licensure of apothecaries and medical practitioners were unenforceable, and codes regarding the safety or efficacy of medicinals were nonexistent. When they purchased panaceas hawked by female and male drug vendors, buyers were torn between fears of harmful counterfeit remedies and the hope of miraculous cures.[9]

In this laissez-faire milieu, Philadelphia-area entrepreneur Sybilla Righton Masters marketed "Tuscarora Rice" in the 1720s, invoking the exotic power of American Indian remedies. Her finely ground corn preparation cured "consumption & other distempers." Masters obtained a royal patent for her unique grain-processing invention. In Boston, healing adept Elizabeth Gooking Greenleaf opened an apothecary shop in 1727 to support her family when her husband was disabled. She was identified as an apothecary in a list of the city's medical professionals. The extent of Greenleaf's pharmaceutical education is unknown, but like many colonial female entrepreneurs she exploited the blurry boundaries among apprentice-trained apothecaries, self-taught medicinal adepts, pharmaceutical merchants, drug retailers, and herb sellers.[10]

Some women who provided free, benevolent healthcare to their communities translated their medical knowledge into paid work. The Philadelphian

Elizabeth Duckworth Whartnaby served as lay healer and itinerant Quaker minister, but she opened an apothecary shop to supplement her ministerial stipends. In March 1721, Whartnaby ran one of the first pharmaceutical advertisements in Pennsylvania newspapers, which appeared in several editions of the *American Weekly Mercury*. She touted her "Spirit of Scurvey-grass" and her "right and genuine Spirit of Venice Treacle, truly and only prepared by her in Philadelphia, who was the original and first promoter of it in this city." Venice Treacle or Venetian Theriac was an expensive universal panacea that consisted of more than fifty ingredients, including opium. It was a common remedy for plague, which was raging in Marseilles, France, in the early 1720s. Whartnaby capitalized on Philadelphians' anxieties that plague might spread to interconnected port cities, and she could price her own shop-compounded Venice Treacle to undercut expensive imported versions.[11]

However, Whartnaby faced competition. On the same page as her ad in the *Mercury*, a woman announced that *her* mother's preparation of Venice Treacle, called Mary Banister's Drops, was the only genuine one. It was available at "reasonable rates" at Francis Knowles's dry goods shop. Female pharmaceutical entrepreneurs sold medicine through retailers such as Knowles or vended them directly at their shops or taverns. Hannah Harkum Hodge, Miles Stricklin, and other Philadelphia shopkeepers advertised and sold Mary Banister's Drops for decades.[12] Hodge, Whartnaby, and Mary Bannister's unnamed daughter represent numerous other female drug vendors of various classes and ethnicities who did not advertise and are less visible in documentary records.

Philadelphia's female entrepreneurs placed fewer formal newspaper advertisements than their male counterparts, which further obscures their practices. However, sometimes family members submitted newspaper notices for female kin. In the early 1730s, the Philadelphia printer Benjamin Franklin announced in his *Pennsylvania Gazette* that his mother-in-law, "The Widow READ," had moved her business into his print shop and continued "to make and sell her well-known ointment for the ITCH [scabies] . . . always effectual for that purpose and never fails to perform the cure speedily." In addition to having a pleasant smell, Sarah Read's salve could be used for infants "without the least Apprehension of Danger." Read and Franklin targeted female clients' interest in safe and effective children's products. Franklin's wife, Deborah, vended her mother's proprietary medicines into the 1740s.[13]

Retailers and printers like the Franklins understood that customers who educated themselves in medical practices were more likely to buy self-prescribed proprietary medicines. The Franklins sold lay medical manuals

such as John Tennent's *Every Man His Own Doctor* that proffered lay pharmaceutical advice. The popular author Eliza Smith advised women readers
that by learning to prepare the medical remedies contained in her bestsell-
ing book, *The Compleat Housewife,* they could procure "a very handsome
Livelihood" selling drugs. By the mid-1750s, when Elizabeth Weed appears
in the documentary record, the commerce in medical print and pharmaceuticals was flourishing as part of an expansion in consumer goods.[14]
Weed joined other female pharmaceutical adepts who earned their livings
by creating innovative pharmaceuticals and developing advertising techniques to shape consumer demand.

Therapeutic Self-Fashioning

Unfortunately, like many female artisanal entrepreneurs of this period,
Elizabeth Weed left few documentary traces. Aspects of her life and her
apothecary practice must be reconstructed from newspapers, wills, city
directories, local histories, and her third husband's commonplace book, as
well as court, church, and hospital records. Prior to her marriage to George
Weed, Elizabeth Delaplaine married her first husband, William Dickinson,
in 1755. A doctor by that name was listed in Philadelphia tax records, and
Elizabeth's first marriage may have been a medical partnership.[15] Her second marriage, to the apothecary George Weed in 1768, was certainly a joint
enterprise. George's background illuminates the experiences that informed
his advertising acumen and the context for Elizabeth's work in the family
apothecary shop. George Weed was born in 1717 in Derby, Connecticut,
and he married his first wife, Esther, in 1740. George was a member of
the "Derby Gang" of counterfeiters led by his eldest brother, Samuel. In
1746, Dr. George Weed was arrested for passing forged 20 shilling bills,
but he escaped from the constable and fled with Esther. Although Samuel
and other family members served jail time, authorities never apprehended
George. In later advertisements, George implied that he was from Haddon-
field, New Jersey.[16]

In 1760, the managers of Philadelphia's Pennsylvania Hospital hired Dr.
George Weed as its steward and apothecary and appointed Esther Weed as
matron (supervising nurse). The Weeds served together in these posts for
seven years. Although George Weed styled himself a doctor, the hospital
managers, who included university-educated physicians, called him a mere
apothecary. George added "Reverend" to his title, augmenting his healthcare expertise with the aura of religious authority. He requested permission
to preach from the elders of the First Baptist Church, but they refused.
To the elders' chagrin, Weed continued his counterfeit preaching at the

hospital, and they struck his name from their roll in 1765. In January 1767, the hospital board noted with regret the death of Matron Esther Weed, "who had been in Service several Years with Credit to herself, & satisfaction to the Managers" and consistently exhibited "Christian Tenderness to the Diseased and Distressed." However, her husband "the Apothecary not being so fully Qualified as we could wish, left the service, by consent, a few Months since." They were now "in want of an Apothecary superior to the last." If we read between the lines, it appears that the managers had retained George because of Matron Esther Weed's administrative and healing acumen, but upon her death, they fired him. George Weed skillfully reconfigured his ouster from the hospital staff as a new beginning in "a more private station" in which he could benevolently "contribute to the relief of the sick, the wounded, infirm and distressed."[17]

George Weed exemplifies the fluidity of healthcare roles in Philadelphia's pre-Revolutionary medical marketplace. A practitioner's title and authority were based on effective self-fashioning and winning patients' hearts and minds. As an experienced counterfeiter, George confidently made extravagant claims regarding his products and credentials. He took advantage of the unregulated boundaries among apothecaries, physicians, surgeons, and drug retailers. The city's small number of university-educated doctors and their nascent medical school could not exert control over the practices of other healthcare providers. Practitioners with more formal-sounding titles competed with other self-styled female and male medical providers, who might include ministers, doctresses, wise-women healers, African American conjure doctors, midwives, bonesetters, American Indian healers, and cancer specialists. Female healing adepts of various classes and ethnicities took advantage of this flexible environment to earn needed income by selling pharmaceuticals and medical advice.[18]

Within a year after Esther's death, George Weed promptly found in Elizabeth Delaplaine Dickinson another skilled woman with whom he could forge a healthcare business partnership. They married in January 1768 at Philadelphia's Anglican Christ Church, which was often the choice for upwardly mobile Philadelphians. After their marriage, George and Elizabeth Weed took advantage of the expansion of the consumer economy during the pre-Revolutionary period. They plied their trade on Front Street, near the bustling Delaware River wharves. Although it is clear from Elizabeth's later newspaper notices that she worked alongside her husband in the apothecary shop, newspaper ads beginning in July 1768 promoted only George's medicines and credentials. Elizabeth's name, like the names of numerous other Philadelphia women who helped to run family businesses, did not appear in print while she was married. However, this invisibility contrasts with women's actual presence in Philadelphia's business community. According to the historian Karin Wulf, women were heads of 20 percent of households in pre-Revolutionary Philadelphia, and Patricia Cleary counted more than 160 female retailers in Philadelphia between 1740 and 1755. Elizabeth likely participated in networks of female and male shopkeepers and drug vendors.[19]

The Weeds compounded drugs to treat a variety of illnesses, including "venereal disease in all its stages," the bloody flux, "colds, coughs, shortness of breath, spitting of blood," consumption, rheumatism, and gout. They also marketed pediatric medicines, including the opiate paregoric for curing children's intestinal complaints and ensuring that an infant is "easy and quiet, more healthy, and requires less tending." Their Syrup of Balsam cured "whooping coughs in children," and the Essence of Tar healed "the greensickness in virgins."[20] Since women traditionally provided the bulk of children's and women's healthcare, advising mothers and dispensing pediatric medications was an obvious practice space for Elizabeth. She may also have discreetly treated female clients for sexually transmitted diseases and women's health issues. Elizabeth's duties required an understanding of botany, chemistry, and apothecaries' weights and measures, as well as methods to produce tinctures, decoctions, distillations, plasters, and ointments. She gained valuable pharmaceutical and marketing experience in her early years in the apothecary shop.

Revolutionary Pharmaceutical Marketing

In the mid-1760s, apothecaries' advertising campaigns were interspersed among newspaper debates over a series of British parliamentary taxation measures that prompted colonial resistance. Consumer goods, including imported pharmaceuticals, became politicized as Pennsylvanians protested Parliament's new taxes on imports and its enforcement of laws against smuggling. Newspaper articles called for colonists to boycott the consumption of imported goods to send a message to Parliament via London merchants. Although the British North American colonies exported some pharmaceuticals, such as ginseng and snakeroot, colonial apothecaries were dependent on products imported from British and European drug manufacturers. The Weeds likely purchased imported medicinals from larger Philadelphia apothecary firms such as Christopher Marshall and Sons or directly from British companies. These imports were potential targets for boycotts. In October 1765, four hundred Philadelphia business owners, including eight female shopkeepers, seven physicians, and fourteen apothecaries, signed a nonimportation petition to protest the Stamp

Act, declaring the direct tax unconstitutional. George Weed did not sign the petition, but as a Pennsylvania Hospital employee he may not have felt it necessary. However, George and Elizabeth Weed were in practice together in July 1768 when the *Pennsylvania Chronicle* published articles admonishing merchants to protest the Townshend Acts by refusing to import British goods. Despite the potential for censure from the business community, they continued to advertise imported pharmaceuticals in the *Chronicle*. Apparently, the Weeds chose not to participate in nonimportation measures that might stifle business.[21]

Despite these political tensions, the Weeds expanded their apothecary practice and deployed marketing techniques developed by retailers on both sides of the Atlantic. To undercut their competition and reach a wider audience, they advertised reasonably priced products so that "the poor may be able to purchase them." The Weeds provided "Printed directions" with their medications "gratis," which empowered and educated patients and served as take-home advertisements to share with family and friends. George deployed his persuasive preaching skills, announcing that "persons in both town and country" testified that the Weeds' remedies had been "under God, the means of saving their lives." There is evidence that the Weeds distributed their pharmaceuticals to other retailers. For example, in December 1773, the New York printer John Holt advertised that he had "just received from Philadelphia, A choice parcel of MEDICINES, Prepared by Doct. George Weed, Late Apothecary to the Pennsylvania Hospital." According to the ad, the Weeds' pharmaceuticals had achieved widespread success in Philadelphia, New Jersey, and "Pennsylvania provinces," suggesting a distribution network.[22]

The Weeds' newspaper advertisements included actual or counterfeit patient testimonials under the guise of benevolent public service announcements. In 1770, the *Pennsylvania Chronicle* printed an affidavit allegedly written by a female patient "with a sincere desire to do good," who had been plagued with sores and facial swellings but was "perfectly cured" by "Dr. George Weed's ROYAL BALSAM." In a newspaper testimonial in 1771, "C. Smith" extolled the Weeds' Tinctura Amara, or Bitter Tincture, that cured a variety of gastrointestinal complaints. Smith declared that he had been "afflicted with a dizziness, swimming of the head," a staggering walk, and a sick stomach that threatened to "turn into fits." He "applied to an able physician" but "received little help." By contrast, Tinctura Amara cured Smith, and he encouraged readers to try it. Both of these endorsements suspiciously repeat particular phrases from the Weeds' previous advertisements, and the apothecaries likely invented them or participated in their production.[23]

The Weeds diversified their practice in the early 1770s by offering smallpox inoculation. George advertised that he had developed a new inoculation method such "as the great Dr. Boerhaave hinted at," which made the ordeal "light and easy for the patient to undergo." By citing the renowned Leiden physician and chemist Herman Boerhaave, Weed appealed to literate patients abreast of innovations in Enlightenment science. New techniques had indeed made smallpox inoculation a safer and more popular procedure. The Weeds' advertisement touted their successful inoculation of eighty patients, noting, "What greater proof can there be of the utility of medicines than the great success that attends them?" Although Elizabeth was not named, her later advertisements clarified that she had actively participated in the business. Elizabeth may well have prepped patients with the pre-inoculation diet and medications and cared for them following the procedure in the rooms above the shop.[24]

As political frictions heightened between Britain and the North American colonies, Germany provided an alternative source for drug imports. Pennsylvania German drug vendors sold alchemically derived medications that were popular among Philadelphia's large German-speaking population. In 1773, a German-language newspaper in Philadelphia advertised "Gold tincture to be sold by the widow of Augustus Schubart."[25] Like Elizabeth Weed, Mrs. Schubart continued the family business and built on her husband's reputation. But newspaper ads reflected only a small percentage of the Philadelphia women in the English- and German-speaking communities who vended medicines in general stores, print shops, and market stalls, as well as door to door. In the early 1770s, Anna Maria Muhlenberg, the wife of the prominent German-born Lutheran minister, Heinrich Melchior Muhlenberg, imported medications from a drug manufactory in Halle, Brandenburg-Prussia. Anna Maria compounded the pharmaceuticals and sold them at the family home in Trappe, and later in Philadelphia. As Heinrich noted in a letter in 1774, "My wife intends to continue the sale of the Halle medications, and although she has not yet used up her entire supply, she would like at all times to have a stock on hand."[26] Anna Maria Muhlenberg marketed her goods by word of mouth within church networks. By contrast, the Weeds continued to purchase advertising space to hawk Daffy's Elixir, Stoughton's Bitters, Anderson's Pills, and their own Weed's Syrup.

When George died in 1777, Elizabeth was experienced in drug compounding, smallpox inoculation, and pharmaceutical marketing. That September, Elizabeth faced the economic crises of the British occupation, as well as the challenge of supporting herself and her son. Like other Philadelphia apothecaries and shopkeepers, Weed had to choose between abandoning her business and remaining in the occupied city. Some apothecaries, such as the avowed patriot Christopher Marshall, fled, along with the members of the

Second Continental Congress, to Lancaster, Pennsylvania. However, apothecary shops were particularly difficult to relocate. Pharmaceuticals were sensitive to heat and moisture, and fragile glassware, ceramics, alembics, and scales had to be transported in wagons that jostled along the roads out of the city. Elizabeth Weed's three-year-old son, George, was ill, which may have influenced her decision to stay in the city rather than flee as a refugee. Some shopkeepers remained in Philadelphia to protect their homes and businesses from looting or confiscation, risking the suspicion of loyalism.[27]

Although Elizabeth Weed reassured her customers that she would carry on her practice "as usual," the war and occupation disrupted businesses, markets, and monetary systems. To aggravate Elizabeth's financial problems, George Weed Senior's will was contested by Elijah Weed, his son from a previous marriage. The will remained unproved until after the Revolution. Philadelphia residents experienced food shortages, and prices for staples increased sixfold. Continental currency deflated, and some shopkeepers exacted payment in scarce specie. British embargoes on colonial ports also interrupted pharmaceutical supply chains.[28] Like munitions, pharmaceuticals were subject to blockades and seizure by opposing military forces. One Philadelphia-area doctor "had all his medicines taken in order to replenish the army medicine chests of His Britannic Majesty." A Continental officer noted that surgeons sought indigenous medicinal herbs, with "American senna and white-walnut bark being substances largely in demand."[29] Female adepts' knowledge of local medicinal flora and their compounding skills were sought-after commodities. Instead of dampening pharmaceutical sales, the occupation provided new opportunities for apothecaries and druggists. As patriot physicians joined the army and loyalist doctors fled the conflict, civilians had less access to physicians' services. Inflated prices combined with decreased availability of doctors increased the value of affordable self-help pharmaceuticals. Weed advertised to a new, transient pool of customers, including British soldiers and speculators.

However, Elizabeth Weed faced stiff competition from other drug retailers. The apothecary William Smith's advertisement in the *Pennsylvania Evening Post* in March 1777 assured customers that despite the British occupation, "they may still be supplied with all kinds of DRUGS AND MEDICINES as usual at his shop . . . on reasonable terms." Smith took advantage of the confusion of occupation and commandeered a shop abandoned by a patriot merchant in a more desirable location. The dry-goods merchant Nicholas Brooks advised clients that he continued to sell "DR. RYAN'S incomparable WORM DESTROYING SUGAR PLUMBS," which "cured a great many children of whooping or chin coughs, and agues." Below this advertisement, the itinerant patent medicine purveyor Dr. Anthony Yeldall, "well known for his travels through most of the United States," offered consultations at his "medicinal warehouse," in patients' homes, or by post. He attracted crowds to his medicine shows with his clown, Merry Andrew. It is possible that Yeldall's use of the term "United States" was provocative to the British occupiers, but his opium prescriptions certainly dulled the pain of the occupation.[30] Elizabeth Weed had to rely on her retailing experiences to differentiate her products in this competitive market.

Weed exemplifies female healthcare entrepreneurs who successfully weathered the economic and political turmoil of the British occupation. In 1779, she married the master carpenter Thomas Nevell, whose reputation, military service, and solid patriot credentials would quell any rumors of loyalism related to Elizabeth's residence in the city. After the British decamped, Thomas, a member of the carpenters' craft guild, supervised the repairs to Carpenter's Hall, where the First Continental Congress had convened. However, he struggled with debt and served time in debtor's prison. Tax records cite Thomas Nevell as a carpenter with only one cow, no property, no servants, and a tax assessment of less than £5. Apparently, Elizabeth did not marry him for his fortune. Despite financial reverses, Thomas remained well connected and would have provided Elizabeth with valuable business contacts.[31]

The Nevells lived in the house and shop that were in Elizabeth's name. Her son George, rather than Thomas, was slated to inherit the property. Elizabeth used the legal system to maintain her own property and to secure a competence for her son. She continued the court battles with Elijah Weed over George Senior's will until it was settled in 1784. Elizabeth received $132 of her $238 inheritance in medicines. In the Nevells' Front Street shop, Thomas contracted work as a carpenter and a coffin maker. Apparently, this grave trade was not off-putting to Elizabeth's sick clients, since her name was juxtaposed with Thomas's in Philadelphia city directories as an apothecary who "prepares medicines against the ague &c." However, Elizabeth continued to face competition from other female healers, such as a Mrs. Kayser, who advertised in the *Pennsylvania Packet* that she "had a safe and peculiar method for the cure of fever and ague . . . and she has great pleasure in the general way of Physic and Surgery." Elizabeth Weed Nevell's practice was not unique.[32]

Mary Watters and Margaret Hill Morris provide additional examples of widowed Philadelphia healing adepts who matched Weed Nevell's business acumen and her desire for financial independence. Mary Watters, an Irish immigrant with a young son, served as a nurse in Continental Army hospitals during the Revolution. After the war, she used her medical contacts with prominent Philadelphia doctors to legitimize her practice and create webs of physician and patient referrals. In addition to the role of nurse, Watters identified herself as an apothecary and doctress in city directories. Through her successful practice, Watters educated her son, James, and advanced his career as a magazine publisher. She advertised and sold pharmaceuticals in James's *Weekly Magazine,* including her proprietary Worm Cakes, which "effectively cleared the body" for only *"one Fourth of a Dollar for a single Cake."* Mother and son sold medicinals and magazines until James's death during the yellow fever epidemic of 1798.[33]

The Quaker healer Margaret Hill Morris opened a medical and apothecary practice in Burlington, New Jersey, in 1779. She diagnosed, prescribed, compounded, and dispensed medicine. She recorded that her practice helped support her family and kept her "a step above absolute dependence." Morris passed down her medical and pharmaceutical skills to a daughter and a son who became a physician. Sadly, he also died in the 1798 epidemic.[34] The economic crises of the revolutionary years posed challenges for Weed, Watters, and Morris. Medicinal knowledge was a commodity that these savvy widows deployed to earn needed income, to secure their children's financial futures, and to attain a measure of financial autonomy. After the war, their healthcare practices helped these women survive the economic volatility of the Early National period.

The Intellectual Property of Women

In early July 1787, while convention delegates in Philadelphia debated the tenets of the U.S. Constitution, Elizabeth Weed Nevell was more concerned about bodily constitutions and the health of her pharmaceutical business. She was shocked to discover that the crafty James Craft, "a barber and a shoemaker" in Burlington, New Jersey, was guilty of counterfeiting her Weed's Syrup. At the Pennsylvania State House, convention delegates recognized that a culture of counterfeiting could discourage innovation, thus dampening the young republic's economic development. Article 1, section 8 of the Constitution assigned the regulation of intellectual property rights to Congress, empowering that body to "promote the Progress of Science and useful Arts, by securing for limited Times to Authors and Inventors the exclusive Right to their respective Writings and Discoveries." Although patent acts in the 1790s further clarified Article 1, section 8 and included language that specifically referred to potential patentees as "she" as well as "he," a formal patent office was not created until the 1830s. In the meantime, pharmaceutical products were prey to counterfeiting.[35]

Like the Daffy and Turlington women, Elizabeth Weed Nevell used the press and the courts to assert her intellectual property rights in Weed's

Syrup. Thomas joined her in filing suit against Craft because, as a married woman, she could not instigate litigation. However, Weed Nevell was the author of her newspaper tirade against the "base counterfeiter." She began with a civic service announcement "TO THE PUBLIC," affirming that "HEALTH" was the "greatest temporal blessing." Weed Nevell advised customers that she possessed the skills to maintain bodily vigor, including "a knowledge of the "virtues [medicinal values]" of "the vegetable and mineral kingdoms" and "the art of restoring health when lost." She reminded readers that she alone possessed "the Doctor's genuine recipe." By peddling his counterfeit cures, Craft "imposed on the public, and may possibly have injured many" with his potentially harmful, fraudulent drugs.[36] Because of her successful marketing, Weed's Syrup gained brand-name recognition, which left it open to forgeries. Perhaps Weed Nevell caught the irony of her situation: the wife of a counterfeiter was now the victim of pharmaceutical fraud.

Although the alleged counterfeiter James Craft worked as a barber/shoemaker, he is listed as a Burlington wholesaler and retailer in a later advertisement for "HOPKINS CELEBRATED RAZOR STROPS," which prevented "HUMAN BLOOD FROM BEING SPILLED" by "blunt razors . . . A Fact Clearly Proved!!!" Craft likely perceived himself as a legitimate healthcare provider, since barbers and barber-surgeons practiced tooth drawing, minor surgery, and therapeutic bloodletting. He confidently countersued Thomas and Elizabeth Nevell for slander, declaring in the press that he was merely reselling Weed's Syrup that he had purchased from Elizabeth. Unfortunately, the Philadelphia County Court of Common Pleas records are not complete for this period, and the outcomes of the lawsuits are unknown. Despite the distraction of litigation, Weed Nevell continued her work and educated George Junior to take over the practice. After twenty-two years in the apothecary business, Elizabeth Weed Nevell died in 1790.[37]

Weed Nevell's successful practice enabled her to secure a legacy for her son. Her legal maneuvers suggest that she was intent on facilitating George's social mobility. The 1790 census lists sixteen-year-old "Doctor" George Weed as head of the household, with the sixty-nine-year-old Thomas Nevell, "house carpenter," listed second. George Weed held the title to the Front Street house. Unlike Watters's and Morris's sons, George Weed Jr. lived to find success, first as an apothecary marketing the only authentic Weed's Syrup, and then as a tavern keeper. In the late 1790s, he purchased and managed Gray's Ferry Inn, a venue with its own pleasure garden, "a veritable fairy scene, with bowers, grottoes, [and] waterfalls." The "eminently successful" George Weed was quartermaster for the Second Troop Philadelphia City Cavalry, whom he entertained in style at his inn. Through her acumen in the apothecary business and shrewd financial planning, Elizabeth Weed Nevell secured for her son a successful livelihood and a place in Philadelphia society.[38]

However, Weed Nevell's medicinal legacy did not remain with her menfolk. In the back of Thomas Nevell's commonplace book is an affidavit written by Rebecca Reed Nicholson dated September 21, 1795, that states, "I certify that the foregoing recipes are in Doctor Weeds own hand writing and that his widow after the Death of her Husband the Doctr. continued to make the preparations agreeable to the foregoing Recipes." Detailed instructions for "Weed's Essence of the Essentials" and "Syrup for the Flux" are crossed out but visible. Nicholson continued, "That for & in consideration of a sum of mony to me in hand paid I now deliver them to Samuel Wetherill & Sons to be prepared & sold by them as they may think proper, & I hereby engage that I will not give or cause to be given the recipes to any other person or persons."[39] Rebecca Nicholson had provided nursing care to the ailing septuagenarian Thomas Nevell. It is possible that Elizabeth gave the secret remedies to Thomas or George, and they bartered the recipes to pay for Thomas's healthcare. Or perhaps Elizabeth Nevell bequeathed them directly to Nicholson. In either case, Nicholson sold them to the prominent Philadelphia druggists Samuel Wetherill and Sons. Another woman, then another business, kept the Weeds' pharmaceutical legacy alive. Weed's Syrup appeared among popular patent medicines in an early nineteenth-century druggist's manual. Its secret ingredients included opium, peppermint, aniseed, and fennel, which were typical for flux (diarrhea) remedies and likely effective. Medicinal knowledge was a valuable and transferrable commodity that networks of women mobilized to generate income and maintain a measure of economic independence.[40]

Elizabeth Weed Nevell and her fellow female drug vendors attest to free Euro-American women's roles as economic actors during the era of the American Revolution. Faced with financial reversals, the loss of male kin, and the dislocations of wartime and occupation, skilled Philadelphia women deployed their specialized knowledge to initiate or maintain entrepreneurial healthcare businesses. They stood on the shoulders of European and mid-Atlantic women who recognized the profitable possibilities of medical consumerism beginning in the late seventeenth century. Partnering with her former counterfeiter husband, Weed Nevell developed creative pharmaceutical marketing strategies to assert their products' amazing cures and to shape customers' expectations that health was an obtainable commodity. After George's death, she invoked his medical legacy while affirming her own formidable expertise.

As the wife of a counterfeiter who later accused another shopkeeper of swindling her, Weed Nevell entered the public debates over commodities' authenticity and fraud that emerged alongside market capitalism. Present-ing herself as a legitimate apothecary in the press and courts, she chal-lenged her counterfeiting competitor and asserted her intellectual property rights. Despite the economic fluctuations of the American revolutionary period, Weed Nevell translated her pharmaceutical skills and marketing experience into a medicinal legacy for herself and financial security for her family. Rather than becoming marginalized by the rise of a consumer med-ical culture, Weed Nevell and savvy female healing adepts like her became successful entrepreneurs who rode the crest of a surge in the popularity of brand-name medicinals.

Notes

Research for this essay was supported by fellowships from the Library Company of Philadelphia; Philadelphia Area Center for the History of Science; American Phil-osophical Society; Quaker and Special Collections Library, Haverford College; and Winterthur Museum and Library.

1. *Pennsylvania Evening Post* (Philadelphia), October 11, 1777. Elizabeth Delaplaine Dickinson Weed Nevell's birthdate is unknown; she died in 1790.

2. Cathy Matson, "Women's Economies in North America before 1820," *Early American Studies* 4, no. 2 (2006): 271–90; Mary Beth Norton, *Liberty's Daughters: The Revolutionary Experience for American Women, 1750 1800* (Ithaca, NY: Cornell University Press, 1996), xi–xx.

3. *Pennsylvania Gazette*, July 11, 1787. For debates on women's innate inferior-ity, see Londa Schiebinger, *The Mind Has No Sex? Women in the Origins of Mod-ern Science* (Cambridge, MA: Harvard University Press, 1989), 220–39; Rosemarie Zagarri, *Revolutionary Backlash: Women and Politics in the Early American Republic* (Philadelphia: University of Pennsylvania Press, 2007), 1–8; Barbara Taylor and Sarah Knott, eds., *Women, Gender, and Enlightenment* (New York: Palgrave Macmil-lan, 2007), 2–18; Patricia Fara, *Pandora's Breeches: Women, Science, and Power in the Enlightenment* (London: Pimlico, 2004), 1–13.

4. Ellen Hartigan-O'Connor, *The Ties That Buy: Women and Commerce in Rev-olutionary America* (Philadelphia: University of Pennsylvania Press, 2009); Karin Wulf, *Not All Wives: Women of Colonial Philadelphia* (Philadelphia: University of Pennsylvania Press, 2000); Patricia Cleary, *Elizabeth Murray: A Woman's Pursuit of Independence in Eighteenth-Century America* (Amherst: University of Massachusetts Press, 2000).

5. Judith S. Woolf, "Women's Business: Seventeenth-Century Female Pharma-cists," *Chemical Heritage Magazine* 27, no. 3 (Fall 2009): 1–4; F. H. Rawlings, "Two Seventeenth-Century Women Apothecaries," *Pharmaceutical Historian* 14, no. 3 (September 1984): 7; Glenn Sonnedecker, *Kremers and Urdang's History of Phar-macy* (Madison, WI: American Institute for the History of Pharmacy, 1986), 68–94, 102–15, 157; Juanita G. L. Burnaby, *A Study of the English Apothecary from 1660–1760* (London: Wellcome Library, 1983).

6. *A Most Excellent Cure for the Stone and Gravel: As Published by Mrs. Joanna Ste-phens* (London: Printed for the Benefit of Mankind in General, ca. 1740), National

Library of Medicine, Washington, DC (hereafter, NLM); M. A. Katritzky, *Women, Medicine, and Theatre, 1500–1750: Literary Mountebanks and Performing Quacks* (Burlington, VT: Ashgate, 2007), 144–49; Francis Cecil Doherty, *A Study in Eighteenth-Century Advertising Methods: The Anodyne Necklace* (Lewiston, NY: Edwin Mellen Press, 1992), 38–58; *Daily Courant* (London), January 6, 1717; Patrick Wallis, "Consumption, Retailing, and Medicine in Early Modern London," *Economic History Review* 61, no.1 (February 2008): 26–53; Lisa Forman Cody, "'No Cure No Money,' or the Invisible Hand of Quackery: The Language of Commerce, Credit, and Cash in Eighteenth-Century British Medical Advertisements," *Studies in Eighteenth-Century Culture* 28 (1999): 103–30; Louise Curth, "The Commercialisation of Medicine in the Popular Press: English Almanacs, 1640–1700," *Seventeenth Century* 17, no. 1 (2002): 61–63; Roy Porter and Dorothy Porter, "The Rise of the English Drug Industry: The Role of Thomas Corbyn," *Medical History* 33 (1989): 277–95. For examples in women's medical manuscripts, see Mary Chantrell, Book of Cookery and Medical Receipts, ca. 1690s, MS 1548, 63, Wellcome Library, London; Elizabeth Coates Paschall, mid-eighteenth-century MS Recipe Book, College of Physicians Philadelphia.

7. Anthony Daffy, *Daffy's Original Elixir Salutis, Vindicated against All Counterfeits* (S.l.: s.n., 1675?), http://name.umdl.umich.edu/A35701.0001.001; "Materials Relating to Daffy's Elixir," William Helfand Collection, Library Company of Philadelphia (hereafter, LCP); *London Evening Post*, July 13–16, 1765; Charles J. S. Thompson, *The Quacks of Old London* (London: Brentanos, 1928), 253–58; David B. Haycock and Patrick Wallis, "Quackery and Commerce in Seventeenth-Century London: The Proprietary Medicine Business of Anthony Daffy," *Medical History Supplement* 25 (2005): 3–12.

8. Robert Turlington, *By Virtue of the King's Patent: Turlington's Balsam of Life* (London: C. Davis, 1754), NLM; "By Virtue of the King's Patent," broadside, ca. 1750s, William Helfand Collection, LCP; David R. Watters, "A Turlington Balsam Phial from Montserrat, West Indies: Genuine or Counterfeit?" *Historical Archaeology* 15, no. 1 (1981): 105–8.

9. Carl Robert Keyes, "Early American Advertising: Marketing and Consumer Culture in Eighteenth-Century Philadelphia" (Ph.D. diss., Johns Hopkins University, Baltimore, 2007), 131–80; J. Worth Estes, "Patterns of Drug Usage in Colonial America," *New York State Journal of Medicine* 87, no. 1 (1987): 37–45; Roy Porter, *Health for Sale: Quackery in England, 1660–1850* (Manchester, UK: Manchester University Press, 1989), 21–29.

10. For Sybilla Righton Masters (ca. 1675–1720), see John Fanning Watson, *Annals of Philadelphia: Being a Collection of Memoirs, Anecdotes, and Incidents of the City* (New York: E.L. Carey and A. Hart, 1830), 616; Frederick B. Tolles, "Sybilla Masters," in *Notable American Women, 1607–1950: A Biographical Dictionary*, 3 vols., ed. Edward T. James, Janet Wilson James, and Paul Boyer (Cambridge, MA: Harvard University Press, 1971), 2, 508. For Elizabeth Gooking Greenleaf (1681–1762), see Norman Gevitz, "'Pray Let the Medicines Be Good': The New England Apothecary in the Seventeenth and Early Eighteenth Centuries," in *Apothecaries and the Drug Trade: Essays in Celebration of the Work of David L. Cowen*, ed. Gregory Highby and Elaine C. Stroud (Madison, WI: American Institute of the History of Pharmacy, 2001), 23–24.

11. For Elizabeth Whartnaby (d. 1734), see *American Weekly Mercury*, March 23–30, 1721; John Richardson, ed., *The Friend: A Religious and Literary Journal*, vol.

29 (Philadelphia: Robb, Pile, and McElroy, 1856), 373–74; Rebecca Larson, *Daughters of Light: Quaker Women Preaching and Prophesying in the Colonies and Abroad, 1700–1775* (Chapel Hill: University of North Carolina Press, 2000); 68, 90–93. For plague, see *American Weekly Mercury*, March 2–16, 1721, August 17–24, 1721.

12. *American Weekly Mercury*, March 23–30, 1721, March 14–21, 1722/3, February 27–March 5, 1726/7, March 28–April 4, 1728, January 28–February 4, 1734/5. See also "Memoirs of Mrs. Hannah Hodge," *General Assembly's Missionary Magazine; or, Evangelical Intelligencer*, vol. 2, no. 2, 1806, 94. For other examples, see Mrs. Joyce's Grand American Balsam, in *Rivington's New-York Gazetteer*, May 6, 1773, and "Mrs. Hughes, Midwife," who sold medicine in the *Virginia Gazette*, December 10, 1773.

13. *Pennsylvania Gazette*, August 19, 1731, October 6, 1739; Keyes, "Early American Advertising," 181–95. For Deborah Read Franklin (ca. 1708–74), see Susan E. Klepp, "Benjamin Franklin and Women," in *A Companion to Benjamin Franklin*, ed. David Waldstreicher (Malden, MA: Wiley-Blackwell, 2011), 237–51; Stanley Finger, *Doctor Franklin's Medicine* (Philadelphia: University of Pennsylvania Press, 2011), 24–26.

14. John Tennent, *Every Man His Own Doctor: or, The Poor Planter's Physician* (Philadelphia: B. Franklin, 1736), LCP; Charles E. Rosenberg, William H. Helfand, and James N. Green, *"Every Man His Own Doctor": Popular Medicine in Early America* (Philadelphia: LCP, 1998); James H. Young, *The Toadstool Millionaires: A Social History of Patent Medicines in America before Federal Regulation* (Princeton, NJ: Princeton University Press, 1974), 3–30; Eliza Smith, *The Compleat Housewife* (London: R. Ware, 1750), preface, LCP; Mary E. Fissell, "The Marketplace of Print," in *Medicine and the Market in England and Its Colonies, c. 1450–c. 1850*, ed. Mark S. R. Jenner and Patrick Wallis (Basingstoke, UK: Palgrave Macmillan, 2007), 108–32; T. H. Breen, *The Marketplace of Revolution: How Consumer Politics Shaped American Independence* (New York: Oxford University Press, 2004), 57–58; Francisco Guerra, *American Medical Bibliography: 1639–1783* (New York: Lathrop C. Harper, Inc., 1962), 9–20.

15. Pard M'Farland Jr., *Marriage Records of Gloria Dei Church, "Old Swedes," Philadelphia* (Philadelphia: M'Farland and Son, 1879), 17; Hannah Benner Roach, *Colonial Philadelphians* (Hanover: Genealogical Society of Pennsylvania, 2007), 113–14.

16. Jeanne Majdalamy, *The Story of the Early Settlers of Stamford, Connecticut, 1641–1700* (Berwyn Heights, MD: Heritage Books, 1992), 67–9, 75, 124; Kenneth Scott, *Counterfeiting in Colonial America* (Philadelphia: University of Pennsylvania Press, 1957), 156–65.

17. Thomas Morton, *The History of the Pennsylvania Hospital, 1751–1895* (Philadelphia: Times, 1897), 527–28; David Spencer, *The Early Baptists of Philadelphia* (Philadelphia: William Syckelmoore, 1877), 83; Pennsylvania Hospital Mangers to Dr. John Fothergill, letter, quoted in Morton, *The History of the Pennsylvania Hospital*, 528; *Votes and Proceedings of the House of Representatives of the Province of Pennsylvania*, 8 vols. (Philadelphia: Henry Miller, 1767), 5:219, 542; *Pennsylvania Gazette*, January 8, 1767, September 3, 1767, July 12, 1770.

18. Mark S. R. Jenner and Patrick Wallis, "The Medical Marketplace," in Jenner and Wallis, *Medicine and the Market in England and Its Colonies*, 2–15; Harold J. Cook, "Good Advice and a Little Medicine: The Professional Authority of Early Modern English Physicians," *Journal of British Studies* 33, no. 1 (1994): 1–31; Susan Hanket Brandt, "'Getting into a Little Business': Margaret Hill Morris and Women's Medical Entrepreneurship during the American Revolution," *Early American Studies* 13, no. 4 (2015): 774–807.

19. John B. Lin and William H. Egle, eds., *Pennsylvania Archives,* 2d ser., 19 vols., Record of Pennsylvania Marriages prior to 1810, vol. 1 (Harrisburg, PA: Clarence M. Busch, 1896),7:80; Wulf, *Not All Wives,* 13; Patricia Cleary, "'She Will Be in the Shop': Women's Sphere of Trade in Eighteenth-Century Philadelphia and New York," *Pennsylvania Magazine of History and Biography* 119, no. 3 (1995): 183.

20. Evan T. Ellis, "The Story of a Very Old Philadelphia Drug Store," *American Journal of Pharmacy* 75 (1903): 50; *Pennsylvania Chronicle,* July 4–11, 1768; *New-York Journal; or, General Advertiser,* December 23, 1773.

21. See, e.g., *Pennsylvania Journal and Weekly Advertiser,* October 31, 1765; *Pennsylvania Gazette,* November 7, 1765. "Non-Importation Agreement Signed by the Merchants of Philadelphia," October 25, 1765, Am 340, Historical Society of Pennsylvania, Philadelphia; *Pennsylvania Chronicle,* July 4–11, 1768; Breen, *The Marketplace of Revolution,* 19–24; Linda K. Kerber, *Women of the Republic Intellect and Ideology in Revolutionary America* (Chapel Hill: University of North Carolina Press, 1980), 37–41; Edmund Morgan and Helen Morgan, *The Stamp Act Crisis* (Chapel Hill: University of North Carolina Press, 1962); Thomas Corbyn, Business Ledger, MS 5442, British Library, London.

22. *Pennsylvania Gazette,* July 12, 1770; Keyes, "Early American Advertising," 22–25; *New-York Journal; or, General Advertiser,* December 23, 1773.

23. *Pennsylvania Gazette,* July 12, 1770; *Pennsylvania Chronicle* (Philadelphia), March 4, 1771, September 3, 1767, June 25–July 2, 1770, July 15–22, 1771.

24. *Pennsylvania Packet* (Philadelphia), March 29, 1773; David van Zwanberg, "The Suttons and the Business of Inoculation," *Medical History* 22 (1978): 71–82; Thomas Dimsdale, *The Present Method of Inoculating for the Small-pox,* 5th ed. (London: W. Owen, 1769).

25. *Der Wochentliche Pennsylvanische Staatsbote* (Philadelphia), January 19, 1773; Sonnedecker, *Kremers and Urdang's History of Pharmacy,* 68, 85–94, 102–15.

26. Heinrich Muhlenberg to Halle Manufactory, 1774, in Renate Wilson, *Pious Traders in Medicine: A German Pharmaceutical Network in Eighteenth-Century America* (University Park: Pennsylvania State University Press, 2000), 145; Lisa Minardi, *Pastors and Patriots: The Muhlenberg Family of Pennsylvania* (Kutztown, PA: The Pennsylvania German Society, 2011), 23.

27. Christopher Marshall, *Extracts from the Diary of Christopher Marshall, 1774–1781,* ed. William Duane (Albany, NY: Joel Munsell, 1877), 118–31.

28. *Pennsylvania Evening Post,* March 11, 1777; George Weed, Will, 1784, no. 66–1777, Philadelphia City Hall; Willard O. Mishoff, "Business in Philadelphia during the British Occupation, 1777–1778," *Pennsylvania Magazine of History and Biography* 61, no. 2 (1937), 166; Anne Bezanson, *Prices and Inflation during the American Revolution: Pennsylvania, 1770–1790* (Philadelphia: University of Pennsylvania Press, 1951), 5–33.

29. J. Smith Futhey and Gilbert Cope, *History of Chester County, Pennsylvania with Genealogical and Biographical Sketches* (Philadelphia: Louis H. Everts, 1881), 101, 106; Erna Risch, *Supplying Washington's Army* (Washington, DC: Center for Military History, 1981), 389–98.

30. *Pennsylvania Evening Post,* March 11, 1777; Rosenberg et al., *"Every Man His Own Doctor,"* 26.

31. Hannah Benner Roach, "Thomas Nevel (1721–1797): Carpenter, Educator, Patriot," *Journal of the Society of Architectural Historians* 24, no. 2 (May 1965):

153–64; Roach, *Colonial Philadelphians*, 113–14. Nevell (also Nevel or Nevill) sold his house for $700 in 1775 to raise needed cash.

32. Weed, Will; Roach, "Thomas Nevel (1721–1797)," 153–64; *Pennsylvania Gazette*, September 17, 1783; Francis White, *Philadelphia Directory* (Philadelphia: Young, Steward, and McCulloch, 1785), 52; *Pennsylvania Packet or the General Advertiser*, September 11, 1779.

33. Benjamin Rush, *The Autobiography of Benjamin Rush His Travels through Life Together with His Commonplace Book for 1789–1813*, ed. George W. Corner (Princeton, NJ: Princeton University Press, 1948), 201; James Hennessey, *A History of the Roman Catholic Community in the United States* (New York: Oxford, 1983), 60; *Transactions of the College of Physicians of Philadelphia* (Philadelphia: T. Dobson, 1793), 191; *Weekly Magazine*, vol. 1, February 3–April 28, 1798, wrapper.

34. Margaret Hill Morris to Samuel Preston Moore, February 1, 1779, G. M. Howland MS Collection 1000, Quaker and Special Collections Library, Haverford College, Haverford, PA, box 1, folder 5; Brandt, "Getting into a Little Business."

35. U.S. Constitution, art. 1, sec. 8; B. Zorina Kahn, *The Democratization of Invention: Patent and Copyrights in American Economic Development, 1790–1920* (New York: Cambridge University Press, 2005), 49–56, 128–33; Stephen Mihm, *A Nation of Counterfeiters: Capitalists, Con Men, and the Making of the United States* (Cambridge, MA: Harvard University Press, 2009), 1–10.

36. *Pennsylvania Gazette*, July 11, 1787.

37. *Philadelphia Gazette and Universal Daily Advertiser*, July 19, 1798; Ian Burn, *The Company of Barbers and Surgeons* (London: Farrand, 2000), 30–38, 196–98; *Pennsylvania Gazette*, August 1, 1787; Roach, "Thomas Nevel (1721–1797)," 155–56; Marylynn Salmon, "The Court Records of Philadelphia, Bucks, and Berks Counties in the Seventeenth and Eighteenth Centuries," *Pennsylvania Magazine of History and Biography* 107, no. 2 (1983): 249–92; Philadelphia County Court of Common Pleas, Appearance Docket, December 1772–March 1789, 20.2, Philadelphia City Archives. An extant appearance docket lists Craft's countersuit initiated in September 1787 (*James Craft v Thos. Neville and Eliza. His Wife*). Neither the appearance docket for the Nevell's initial suit nor the execution dockets are extant.

38. Philadelphia Census, Middle District, 1790, http://us-census.org/pub/us genweb/census/pa/philadelphia/1790/pg0226.txt; *Philadelphia Minerva*, December 3, 1796; W. A. Dorland, "The Second Troop Philadelphia City Cavalry," *Pennsylvania Magazine of History and Biography*, vol. 46 (1922): 36, 74, 265, 350; John Scharf and Thomas Westcott, *History of Philadelphia, 1609–1884*, 3 vols. (Philadelphia: L. H. Everts, 1884), 3:992; *American Daily Advertiser*, July 8, 1794; *The Casket: Flowers of Literature, Wit, and Sentiment* (Philadelphia: Samuel C. Atkinson, 1829), 75.

39. "Thomas Nevell's Day Book," 1762–85, MS Codex 1049, Rare Book and Manuscript Library, University of Pennsylvania, Philadelphia.

40. Joseph W. England, ed., *The First Century of the Philadelphia College of Pharmacy, 1821–1921* (Philadelphia: Philadelphia College of Pharmacy and Science, 1922), 35–37; John W. Jordan, *Colonial and Revolutionary Families of Pennsylvania*, 3 vols. (New York, 1911, repr. Baltimore: Genealogical Publishing, 1978), 1:1022–23; Philadelphia College of Pharmacy, *The Druggist's Manual* (Philadelphia: Solomon W. Conrad, 1826), 32.

PART II

Political Identities

"She Did Not Open Her Mouth Further"

Haudenosaunee Women as Military and Political Targets during and after the American Revolution

MAEVE KANE

Silver shoe buckles, fine silk mantuas, porcelain teacups, peach trees, and cornfields all became targets of political violence during the American Revolution, symbols of Haudenosaunee women's traditional authority within their communities and the threat British-allied Haudenosaunee communities presented to the new American nation.[1] During the war, Haudenosaunee (or Iroquois) women's authority within their own communities came under attack when American combatants destroyed the improved farmland owned by Haudenosaunee women. This land symbolized Haudenosaunee women's traditional claims to authority. Attacks on Haudenosaunee homes and farms for the first time turned violence against Haudenosaunee women for their perceived violation of gendered roles during war. American negotiators' hostility toward Haudenosaunee women's presence at treaty conferences during and immediately after the Revolution grew out of the gendered political violence of the early years of the war. This hostility was fueled by suspicion of women as political actors, even as Haudenosaunee women became more visible at treaty conferences precisely because American negotiators objected to their very presence.

Haudenosaunee women's history is a bit of an "old chestnut": familiar, well-worn, and still something of a problem.[2] The American Revolution often figures as the turning point of colonialism for Haudenosaunee communities, and especially Haudenosaunee women, the point after which women's status and roles in their communities began to decline. These narratives of decline hinge on the punitive destruction of Haudenosaunee settlements and fields wrought by the 1779 Sullivan Campaign, which sent refugee populations of Haudenosaunee families to British forts to shelter through the upcoming winter. The targeted destruction of cornfields and peach orchards was part of a much broader American pushback against Haudenosaunee women's visibility as consumers of symbols of material civility and as political actors.[3] I argue that although American attempts to silence and erase Haudenosaunee women's presence after the American Revolution was a decisive shift away from earlier British practice, Haudenosaunee women's continued presence and influence throughout the revolutionary period prompted these attempts to push them out of spaces Americans perceived as public, political, diplomatic, and masculine.

Attempts to silence and push out Haudenosaunee women stemmed in part from American and British awareness of Haudenosaunee women's central roles in their communities: women's work was at the heart of Haudenosaunee political and military power, which American and British forces alternately courted and feared during the course of the Revolution. The Iroquois Confederacy included five, and later six, loosely affiliated and often independent nations linked by common cultural and political goals, often known as the Six Nations. The Five Nations originally included the Mohawk, nearest to modern Albany; the Oneida; Cayuga; Oneida, Onondaga; and Seneca in the far west, covering the Finger Lakes and stretching to and sometimes past modern Buffalo. After 1722, with the addition of the Tuscarora, the confederation was known as the Six Nations.

Although the nations of the Iroquois Confederacy often differed politically, socially, religiously, and economically, they shared matrilineal accountings of descent and clan organization and maize agriculture in matrifocal towns that expanded and diffused as political and military conditions required. Iroquoia as a territory was relatively unknown to British and American observers until the American Revolution; the political and military strength of Haudenosaunee communities throughout the eighteenth century controlled access and travel through their territories for Europeans and other Native groups well past the American Revolution. With a total population of more than fifteen thousand in the eighteenth century, the Six Nations Haudenosaunee pursued a strategy of neutrality in the early years of the war. But with the increased pressure of the 1777 New York campaigns, as British and American forces increasingly intruded on their territories, the Mohawk, Onondaga, Cayuga, and Seneca joined the British effort, while the Tuscarora and Oneida joined American effort, with Haudenosaunee war parties avoiding direct engagement with other Haudenosaunee war parties for most of the course of the war.[4]

Haudenosaunee women are often not visible in accounts of the American Revolution, due partly to the sparse documentation that affects many areas of women's history; partly to the structure of Haudenosaunee governance; and partly to deliberate efforts by British and American soldiers and diplomats to push Haudenosaunee women out of the sphere of politics over the course of the war, which is the main focus of this essay. Despite the sparse documentation, Haudenosaunee women were active participants in their nations' diplomatic and military decision making. Clan matrons distributed food to war parties from lineage stores, effectively vetoing or supporting military ventures via their control of food stores and agricultural production.

More directly, clan matrons named and deposed the sachems who represented their lineages and who met with British and American diplomats in council. To represent their views, a designated male "speaker for the women" addressed gatherings of men on behalf of the clan matrons. The European-facing men's councils met separately from meetings of clan matrons and are much more visible in the historical record because male outsiders were occasionally allowed to attend, and the men's council addressed issues of warfare and diplomacy at treaty councils. Outside observers were not allowed to attend councils at which clan matrons named and directed their male speaker for the women. In Haudenosaunee gendered governance of the period, consensus was paramount and addressing opposite-gendered councils considered a breach of etiquette.[5] A speaker for the women maintained the appearance of consensus by speaking for the women to the men's council with one voice while respecting gender protocols and conveying the position of the clan matrons to councils of sachems and Euro-American diplomats. Although women themselves rarely spoke in the masculine spaces of treaty councils and diplomatic negotiations that were most visible to outside observers, women's influence permeated such gatherings and these gatherings were often directly shaped by the speeches of the speaker for the women, even if he was not always acknowledged as such by British and American observers.

Over the course of the American Revolution, Haudenosaunee women's importance in their communities made them and their property targets for symbolic political violence as American enemies attempted to push them out of the masculine sphere of politics and diplomacy. First, the consumer symbols of material civility that had brought together Haudenosaunee and settler communities came under attack; then women's land came under attack as the basis of Haudenosaunee political and military strength, as did the women themselves. In the final years of the war and the years that followed, American diplomats attempted to exclude Haudenosaunee women from the political realm entirely, often as they sought to acquire the land that formed the symbolic basis of Haudenosaunee women's authority.

Pewter Dishes and Silk Dresses

In the years leading up to the American Revolution, Haudenosaunee and Euro-American communities grew ever more entangled in their daily lives and in the material goods that at once distinguished each community and tied them together. As David Preston, Gail MacLeitch, and others have shown, Haudenosaunee communities, especially more eastern ones such as the Mohawk and the Oneida, became increasingly entangled with their Dutch, German, and English neighbors over the course of the 1760s. Navigating pressure to sell land, conflicts with Euro-American squatters who encroached on their territories, and changing economic realities, many eastern Iroquois communities engaged in blended economic strategies. Haudenosaunee communities pursued both hunting and market agriculture while purchasing manufactured goods and using them in ways congruent with distinctly Haudenosaunee cultural norms.[6] This economic entanglement provided the basis for gendered attacks on Haudenosaunee property precisely because of the cultural distinctions that it articulated.

The loss claims made by American-allied Oneidas and Tuscaroras after the war provides a snapshot of economically entangled Haudenosaunee communities.[7] About one-third of the eighty-nine claimants were women, submitting claims either on their own behalf or on behalf of deceased fathers or husbands, showing Haudenosaunee women's continued roles as household heads through 1794. While women's claims generally averaged less than $35 per household, the array of household goods claimed illustrates the integration of consumer goods in many Haudenosaunee households. Oneida and Tuscarora veterans filed claims for lost milk cows, horses, and hogs, as well as copper tea kettles, pewter dishes and teapots, looking glasses, porcelain teacups and saucers, silver candlesticks and teaspoons, and Anglican prayer books. They also claimed the loss of items familiar from the fur trade or treaty gifts such as stroud blankets, animal traps, lengths of ribbon, wampum, silver brooches and hair plates, axes, brass kettles, and indigenous clothing. These items were lost or damaged when American-allied Oneida and Tuscarora fled homes of frame, log, and bark construction; some of the bark longhouse-style homes had glass windows and metal door hardware. Families who resided in frame homes reported the loss of strouds and traps alongside prayerbooks and candlesticks, while families who resided in bark homes reported the loss of milk basins, pewter dishes, and tea sets, reflecting communities in which purchased consumer goods denoting civility and sensibility in Euro-American households blended with more typically "Native" items and settings.[8] There was no bright dividing line for Revolutionary-era Haudenosaunee communities between "traditional" and "European" material culture as Haudenosaunee families integrated the world of Atlantic consumer goods in a Haudenosaunee cultural framework.

In the account books of the trader Jelles Fonda dated 1758–63 and 1768–75, Haudenosaunee consumers at the mixed-ethnicity Native, Dutch,

German, and English settlement of Fort Hunter, west of Albany, had access to the same range of Atlantic consumer goods as their white neighbors and made most of their payments with New York currency or work for credit rather than furs, much like their white neighbors, but their purchases display deliberate cultural consistency in clothing choices in line with earlier account books.[9] While Fonda's Mohawk customers purchased many of the same materials and fabrics as their German, Dutch, and English neighbors—osnaburg, linen, fustian, and calico—Fonda's notes suggest that they were used to make indigenous clothing items such as leggings, wrap skirts, and blankets rather than the coats, breeches, and mantuas his white customers purchased linings, buttons, and thread to complete. Mohawk families at Fort Hunter worked alongside, attended church with, and sometimes formed fictive kin ties of godparentage with their white neighbors;[10] yet they maintained a sartorially distinct identity as Mohawk women created distinctly indigenous items from purchased cloth their white neighbors used to create markers of European-style civility. The accounts of Fonda's Mohawk customers suggest simultaneous economic integration and cultural distancing from their white neighbors even as they purchased many of the same materials and items.

The very consumer similarity that linked Iroquois and settler communities to the Atlantic market also made Native property a target during wartime. Mohawk homes at Fort Hunter and nearby Canajoharie were plundered by both Continental soldiers and Committee of Safety members from surrounding white communities in fall 1778. Colonel Peter Ganse voort, the Continental officer who led the expedition, wrote that "this Castle [Canajoharie] is in the Heart of our Settlements, and abounding with every Necessary so that it is remarked that the Indians live much better than most of the Mohawk River farmers their Houses very well furnished with all necessary Household utensils."[11] The local white community, acting on resentment of "the Indians [who] live much better than most" of them, joined in the raids, robbing Mohawk homes and occupying farms and homes after their Mohawk owners fled to safety in Canada. Jelles Fonda, who served during the war as an Indian agent for New York and officer in the Continental Army, was sent to investigate what had caused the previously neutral Mohawk to align with the British.

Fonda took affidavits from white residents who accused the local Committee of Safety of stealing windows, iron hinges from house and barn doors, hogs, cows, and corn from their Mohawk neighbors, as well as consumer goods such as clothing and jewelry. The thefts were so extensive that it was "impossible for me to make an inventory of all the goods taken from the Indians," Fonda wrote, "as I can't find out from any of them [the white deponents] the whole that is missing." Mohawk homes were robbed by "sundry persons in our neighborhood who made it their business to go about plundering" under cover of night with their faces painted black.[12] The raiders also dug up recently buried Mohawk neighbors and stole expensive wool blankets and European-style coats Haudenosaunee men wore at treaty councils to symbolize their intercultural mediation.[13] More than a military attack, the 1778 raids were personal and targeted at material objects that had come to symbolize the entangled yet culturally distinct engagement of Haudenosaunee communities with their white neighbors.

In addition to occupying the homes and farms of their former neighbors, the participants in the 1778 raids also appropriated personal symbols of civility. One of these raids, led by Peter Dygert, head of the local Committee of Safety, targeted the property of Molly Brant. The Brants were exceptional in many ways. Molly was the Mohawk widow of the recently deceased British Superintendent for Indian Affairs Sir William Johnson and a noted diplomat in her own right, and her younger brother Joseph Brant was a vocal proponent and, later, leader of mixed white loyalist and Haudenosaunee attacks against the rebel Americans. Molly Brant was well known before the war both for her political influence as a clan matron and for the fine home she kept at Johnson Hall, and later at Canajoharie, which blended Haudenosaunee and European items and where she wore a striking mix of markers of Anglo femininity, such as mantuas, and Haudenosaunee femininity, such as silver hair plates and brooches.[14]

But despite the influence and prominence of the Brant family, the appropriation of Molly Brant's property by white settlers differed only in degree from that of her Haudenosaunee kin. Fonda wrote to the New York Commissioners of Indian Affairs that, although Molly Brant's losses were most noteworthy, "I believe our Mohawk Indians at Fort Hunter have suffered in the same manner." Dygert took from Brant's home specie, silver shoe buckles, jewelry, and "several silk gowns which has been seen by George Herkimer on the aforesaid Peter S Dygarts [sic] Daughter."[15] Other items taken in the raids were seen on Dygert's wife and other daughters, according to white witnesses. An Oneida ally, Honyary, occupied Molly Brant's home. The attacks were both political and personal, removing the physical markers of consumer civility and severing Native ties to the land by driving the Mohawk residents of Fort Hunter and Canajoharie to Canada. The appropriation of Brant's clothing and jewelry for Dygert's daughter made the personal political. It at once removed the clothing and jewelry from Brant's use in claiming feminine respectability legible in English spaces and asserted a white man's daughter as a more appropriate owner and consumer of those symbols, just as white settlers and—for the moment—their

Oneida allies were the more appropriate owners of the land and homes Mohawk families had abandoned.[16]

A War against Vegetables

As the war progressed, political violence turned not only against Haudenosaunee women's consumer property but also against their real property and persons. In 1779, George Washington dispatched a force to Seneca country that was, to that point, the single largest Continental Army offensive of the Revolutionary War. Washington issued orders that the campaign's

> immediate objects are the total destruction and devastation of [Seneca] settlements . . . parties should be detached to lay waste all the settlements around, with injunctions to do it in the most effectual manner, that the country may not be merely overrun, but destroyed. . . . You will not by any means listen to overtures of Peace before the total ruin of their settlements is effected. . . . Our future security will be in their inability to injure us—the distance to which they are driven, and in the terror with which the severity of the chastisement they receive will insure them— peace without this would be fallacious and temporary.[17]

General Phillip Schuyler further clarified the campaign's aims, writing, "Should we be so fortunate as to take a considerable number of the women and children of the Indians I conceive that we should then have the means of preventing them from acting hostilely against us."[18] The aim was not merely to destroy but to terrify by targeting noncombatants. Although the resulting campaign led by General John Sullivan captured or killed very few Haudenosaunee people, Sullivan's soldiers burned homes, cornfields, and orchards with the aim of destroying Haudenosaunee economic and agricultural support, and they accomplished that aim very well. In the wake of the devastating attacks against Haudenosaunee communities, waves of poorly fed Native refugees crowded British Fort Niagara for the duration of the war, later returning to their homes to find orchards and fields ruined and burned.[19]

The campaign of destruction evoked mixed feelings for Americans even as soldiers cut their way through the country, but Continental soldiers contextualized it with the gendered barbarism they perceived in their Haudenosaunee enemies. As the campaign put thousands of bushels of harvest-ready corn to the torch, one soldier wrote home, "I really feel guilty as I applied the torch to huts that were Homes of Content until we ravagers came spreading desolation everywhere."[20] Continental soldiers perceived themselves as destroying the gendered sphere of home that the British American culture of sensibility associated with women and domesticity, but they rationalized their attacks as just desserts for Native women's unwomanly conduct. Members of the Sullivan Campaign justified the devastation of the attacks as revenge for the actions of "Queen" Esther Montour, a Munsee Delaware of mixed French descent allied with the British and Haudenosaunee.[21] One soldier wrote, "Queen Hester was with Butler last fall at Wyoming & behaved with Barbarity unparalleled in former ages after taking the men prisoners and tying them to trees, the old infernal Savage brute would go with her knife cut their throats with it and scalp them at the same time repeating 'She should never be tired of killing rebels.'"[22] In taking an active role, or being rumored to have taken an active role, in the devastating Battle of Wyoming in 1778, Montour violated gender norms so severely that it justified the vast assault on noncombatants' homes. Reports of Montour's personal role in killing captured American combatants are difficult to verify, but the vast destruction of Seneca country that followed is not.

In August 1779, the Sullivan Campaign began its assault against Seneca country by plundering graves and burning the multiethnic settlement of Chemung, putting bark homes to the torch and cutting down more than a thousand bushels of corn. Throughout the late summer and early fall, the Sullivan Campaign chased Seneca and Cayuga communities from their homes, burning forty towns and destroying more than 160,000 bushels of corn and decades-old orchards.[23] Sullivan's men cut down, burned, or otherwise destroyed corn, cucumbers, beans, squash, melons, and other produce "in such quantities (were it represented in the manner it should be) would be almost incredible to a civilized people. We sat up until between one and two o'clock feasting on these rarities."[24] As Haudenosaunee communities fled before the incursion, they carried what they could with them and left behind bare homes with only the occasional feather bed, abandoned or missed horse, hog or cow, or trunk of household goods buried for safe keeping.[25] In multiple towns, orchards of "appletrees which is a good number & very old was either cut down or killd, likewise the peach trees."[26] By the end of September 1779, General Sullivan wrote, there was "not a single town left in the country of the Five nations."[27]

Members of the Sullivan Campaign further rationalized the destruction of what many lamented was a truly stupendous harvest of corn by reasoning that its planting "was occasioned by the British giving a premium to encourage them in raising it, so as to enable them to come down on our frontiers."[28] The vast cornfields cultivated by women that formed the basis of Haudenosaunee traditional agriculture was, to the American eye, merely a tool of the British to make otherwise nomadic or barbaric Indian allies more effective in their depredations. Never mind the decades-established plum, peach, and apple orchards that were destroyed along with the corn. The Sullivan Campaign has famously been characterized as a "war against vegetables,"[29] a characterization that the literature has largely followed and that the letters and reports of the campaign on their surface support.[30] The Sullivan Campaign was, in actuality, a war against women and women's property, whether the members of the campaign could see that clearly or not. At the end of the Seven Years' War, one Mohawk speaker explained that women were "the Truest Owners, being the persons who labour on the Lands."[31] In destroying fields and orchards, the Sullivan Campaign attacked the basis of Haudenosaunee women's traditional claims to military and political influence, as well as the ability of Haudenosaunee warriors to stage long-distance attacks. For the duration of the war, refugee Haudenosaunee women were to be seen as "useless mouths" by their British allies.[32]

Haudenosaunee women's bodies came under attack for the first time alongside their property and symbolic claims to influence, as well. In late September 1779, Sullivan's men came upon the nude body of a young Haudenosaunee woman who had been shot at one of the destroyed village sites, "supposed to be done by some of the soldiers," committed by "some inhuman villain."[33] Whether murdered because she resisted a sexual assault or left for grisly display, her murder marked a distinct shift in the way the rank and file of the campaign viewed violence against Native women. Although Washington and Schuyler had advised the capture and hostage taking of Iroquois women and children as part of a broader campaign of terror, the single live hostage taken, an elderly Tuscarora woman known as Madam Sacho, was treated with civility by General Sullivan.[34] This disjuncture in the overt display of the murdered young woman's body and the treatment received by Madam Sacho suggests that older women, who held social and political sway in Haudenosaunee decision making, were viewed by Americans as less threatening targets.[35] It also suggests that although Continental soldiers and their commanders may have differed in the level of overt violence they believed appropriate to use against Native women, on some level there was tacit approval for the murder. Despite civil treatment afforded to captured women such as Madam Sacho, there was no suggestion of finding the offending soldiers who murdered the young woman.

In previously neutral Onondaga country, another arm of the Sullivan Campaign led by Colonel Goose Van Schaick was much more successful in the goal of taking hostages. In his report of the expedition, Van Schaick reported thirteen Onondaga killed, including at least one woman, and thirty-three captured, with women and children at work in the fields constituting the majority of those captured.[36] In his instructions, General James Clinton cautioned Van Schaick to be watchful of his men's behavior: "Bad as the savages are, they never violate the chastity of any women, their prisoners. Although I have very little apprehension that any of the soldiers will so far forget their character as to attempt such a crime on the Indian women who may fall into their hands, yet it will be well to take measures to prevent such a stain upon our army."³⁷ After the war, however, an Onondaga sachem accused Van Schaick's men of having "put to death all the Women and Children, excepting some of the Young Women, whom they carried away for the use of their Soldiers & were afterwards put to death in a more shamefull manner."³⁸ Clinton and Van Schaick were aware of the possibility that Continental soldiers might assault Haudenosaunee women, as well as their lands, and the tacit silence in Van Schaick's report of the expedition upheld the polite fiction that American soldiers were at least as civilized as the "savages" whom they sought to subdue. Written reports and letters from the Sullivan Campaign and other American attacks over the course of the war did not record directly the assault or murder of Native women, but Haudenosaunee communities clearly experienced the war as an attack on women's bodies, as well as on their lands. The Sullivan Campaign marked a shift in American views of Haudenosaunee women as targets for political violence, making their very existence and bodies as vulnerable to attack as their property and symbolic claims to authority and civility.

She Did Not Open Her Mouth Further

In the final years of the war and in the years that followed, American negotiators attempted to explicitly erase Haudenosaunee women from diplomatic negotiations and tried to fit Native diplomacy into the American paradigm of gendered political civility. Prerevolutionary British diplomacy had never been overtly welcoming of Native women's presence, but neither had British diplomats been overtly hostile to women's presence.³⁹ In large part this stemmed from acknowledgment that, to keep the Haudenosaunee as allies, the British had to work within the structures of Haudenosaunee diplomacy.⁴⁰ American diplomats were both ignorant of these long-standing protocols and had no such compunctions about compromising with what they saw as a defeated enemy.

By definition in the new republic, women's very presence invalidated political debate.⁴¹ American observers at treaty conferences occasionally noted Haudenosaunee women's role in diplomatic negotiations but found it fundamentally alien, more of a novelty that set "squaws" apart from "ladies" who did not participate. While observing a treaty conference in 1789, the British traveler Anne Powell remarked on the novelty of women's presence in a political arena in the process articulating her understanding of fundamental Haudenosaunee-American differences and women's unsuitability for weighty matters: "Some old squaws [sic] who sat in Council, were present, and also a few young ones to dress the provisions, for their great men, as well as those of our world, like a good dinner after spending their lungs for the good of their country. The old women walked one by one with great solemnity and seated themselves behind the men. . . . These ladies observe a modest silence in the debates. (I fear they are not like the women of other countries), but nothing is determined without their advice and approbation."[42] While Powell approved of the matrons' public silence, mistaking Haudenosaunee gendered etiquette of shared governance for modesty, she viewed Haudenosaunee matrons' very presence as a notable exception and young women's roles in dressing provisions as the norm. Women were, despite observed Haudenosaunee practice, fundamentally unsuited even to being seen in a diplomatic space.

Postwar shifts in American diplomatic overtures coupled blatant disregard for Haudenosaunee political traditions with more subtle disregard for the material and social culture of diplomacy, expressed as lack of interest in Haudenosaunee preferences and hostility to the presence of women in political and diplomatic settings. American diplomats tasked with negotiating peace with the Haudenosaunee at the close of the war had a basic lack of "cultural literacy" in Indian diplomacy.[43] They were often inexperienced in Indian relations and intent on making former enemies "discover some signs of repentance for [their] conduct during the late war."[44] The combination of a basic lack of cultural literacy with a punitive approach to treaty negotiations resulted in a refusal to acknowledge the presence of Haudenosaunee women or their role in Haudenosaunee governance and diplomacy. Where British gifts at treaty conferences had recognized the importance of communal decision making and consensus government by offering presents of needles, women's and children's clothing, and household items intended for wide distribution throughout the community, American gifts in the postwar years were composed mainly of liquor intended for immediate consumption by male council participants and suits of clothing intended for specific male leaders.[45] Even in attempts to conform to Haudenosaunee diplomatic protocols of gift giving, American negotiators materially rejected the possibility of women's participation.

Women's presence was also implicitly rejected in the way American diplomats addressed demands at postwar peace conferences. In February 1789, New York's Governor George Clinton held negotiations for peace and the discussion of reservation boundaries with the previously British-allied Onondaga and acknowledged Onondaga women's participation only insofar as it fell in line with his own gendered expectations for women's participation. Good Peter, the Onondaga speaker for the women, noted that "our Ancestors considered it a great Transgression to reject the Council of their Women, particularly the female Governesses [clan matrons]. Our Ancestors considered them Mistresses of the Soil." The women felt that "their Uncles had of late lost the Power of Thinking, and were about sinking their Territory" and requested that Clinton enforce an equitable peace by protecting their lands from white squatters.[46] In the fictive kinship language of middle-ground diplomacy, "Uncles" referred to American military and political leaders such as Clinton, rhetorically acknowledging their authority in diplomatic negotiations but also invoking familial duties of protection owed to children by their mother's brothers.[47]

In his answer to the women, however, Clinton seems to have missed the significance of this rhetorical move. He expressed regret "that your Uncles by declining to listen to your Voice had so nearly brought Ruin upon your Country and deprived you of your Land," placing the responsibility for land loss on Haudenosaunee men. While Clinton acknowledged Haudenosaunee women's traditional roles as cultivators of the soil, it was their role as mothers, not farmers, that he believed entitled them to respect. Haudenosaunee women could make claims to a place in the councils of their own nations as "mistresses of the soil," but in the diplomatic sphere it was "your Importance to the human Race; without you we could not have Existance; you are the Mothers of menkind, and this of itself entitles you to the greatest Respect" that Clinton viewed as the basis of Haudenosaunee women's right to call for peace in public forums.

In acknowledging the right of Haudenosaunee women to participate in their own nations' governance, away from cross-cultural diplomacy, Clinton articulated a much more limited view of women's right to call for peace as mothers. Haudenosaunee demands that women's rights to land and participation in decisions about land were much more explicitly rejected. At the same meeting, Good Peter later expressed Onondaga clan matrons' request that a certain salt springs be reserved for the use of their own nation. Clinton, who days before had directly addressed his Haudenosaunee "sisters" in response to Good Peter's speech on their behalf, addressed only his "brothers" in discussing land rights. The salt springs, Clinton argued, ought to be held "in common for the Onondagas and our People."[48] While Clinton may have allowed for Haudenosaunee women's limited ability to call for peace and participate out of view in their own communities, he rejected their participation in explicitly political matters of landownership and use.

Women's continued presence at and participation in postwar treaty conferences proved vexing for American negotiators. In an effort to control the cost and terms of treaty negotiations, American commissioners for

Indian affairs such as Timothy Pickering repeatedly requested that the Six Nations limit the number of people attending each treaty, taking specific affront to the presence of women at the negotiations.[49] This was, to Haudenosaunee diplomats, simply unacceptable. Haudenosaunee sovereignty stemmed directly from women's participation, not despite it. Seneca Billy, the Seneca speaker for the women, told Pickering in 1790 that women's political participation was essential to Haudenosaunee diplomacy. The Americans showed their own inexperience and ignorance by demanding that it cease. During tense negotiations regarding the extent of land that would be reserved for Haudenosaunee use, Seneca Billy addressed Pickering on behalf of the women, saying, " 'Tis our mind that you should hear a little from us also. For this reason that the Pres GW may also hear from us: that he may know the women have been at the Council fire to hear what was done: and for this reason also that we are the persons who supported the country. . . . We do this that he may know the women are yet alive, for we suppose he does not know that women attend treaties."[50] Through their designated speakers and their repeated appearance at treaties of the period, Haudenosaunee women assumed the role of political educators, schooling American representatives on the place of women in Haudenosaunee diplomacy. To Haudenosaunee diplomats, American hostility to women's presence was evidence of either profound ignorance or rudeness; the Americans acted as though women were no longer even living by not acknowledging their role in diplomatic negotiations. In negotiations with British diplomats who did not seek to exclude women, Haudenosaunee speakers had rarely felt the need to explicitly tutor their Anglo counterparts in the gendered etiquette of cross-cultural diplomacy. The Americans' lack of cultural literacy and their refusal to acknowledge women's diplomatic and political roles required explicit tutelage and had the contradictory effect of making Haudenosaunee women's presence in diplomatic spaces more visible as Haudenosaunee speakers protested women's exclusion.

American negotiators typically maintained a polite fiction by refusing to directly acknowledge Haudenosaunee women's presence, but an encounter between an American-delegated Mahican diplomat and the formidable Molly Brant exposed tensions over American views of the place of the Iroquois Haudenosaunee in diplomacy. In 1791, the Stockbridge Mahican orator Hendrick Aupaumut stopped at British-controlled Niagara on his way west to negotiate with the multinational Western Confederacy on behalf of the United States and encountered a hostile and suspicious Molly Brant while there. Although Brant had been forced to flee her home in Canajoharie after the 1778 raids that appropriated her property for Peter Dygert's daughter, she maintained an important position in Haudenosaunee-British diplomacy throughout the war and in the years that followed. On behalf of the U.S. government, Aupaumut sought to travel west to ease tensions with the nations of the Ohio Valley and defuse what was to become the Northwest Indian War, but to do so he had to travel through British-controlled territories via the British fort at Niagara, where Brant resided.

In a tense meeting with Brant and Colonel John Butler, the British commander at Niagara, Brant observed the absence of women and accused Aupaumut of spying for the Americans; by pointing out the lack of women in his party, Brant sought to undermine Aupaumut's legitimacy as a Native diplomat uncontrolled by American interests. Traditionally, Brant argued, Native groups traveling for peaceful purposes included women to prepare food, make camp, and maintain kinship ties with other groups. The lack of women indicated that Aupaumut's group either traveled for war or were too ignorant to be counted as legitimate diplomats. In making this accusation, Brant claimed the high ground as a custodian of Native diplomatic mores.[51]

In response, Aupaumut made a jab at Brant's own claims to diplomatic authority: "Then I speak too says I tis true some nations have such custom for certain occasions but I my nation do not follow such custom especially when I travel thro indian country I do not wish that my women should take such tedious journey, especially since there are so many women in every village. Then she did not open her mouth further."[52] In this demeaning implication, Aupaumut articulated a very American understanding of women's roles, and by extension diminished Brant's possible participation at British Niagara to domestic and sexual roles dictated by her gender. Aupaumut pointed out that he needed no women to travel with him, since women were available interchangeably anywhere he might stop while traveling through Indian territory. In Aupaumut's formulation, the only possible roles for women in these places were to provide the reproductive labor of food and shelter, a service that he could have through exchange with any woman, denying the importance of Native women such as Brant as diplomatic actors. The implied sexual availability only furthered Aupaumut's insult in reducing Molly Brant to the private sphere.

Despite American hostility to their presence in diplomatic spaces, their ownership of land, and their claims to symbols of consumer civility, Haudenosaunee women remained a continuous presence in diplomatic negotiations and the governance of their own communities through the nineteenth and twentieth centuries into the present. During the American Revolution, the very significance of Haudenosaunee women in their nations' governance and diplomacy made them and their property targets for political violence. As clan matrons and the traditional owners and cultivators of land, Haudenosaunee women held traditional authority to name and depose male leaders, call for or veto military expeditions, and part with land that was at odds with developing American ideals of women's exclusion from political life.

In the early years of the war, this hostility to Haudenosaunee women's authority came in the form of attacks against communities economically and culturally entangled with their white neighbors, often from those white neighbors. Before the war, Mohawk, Oneida, and other Haudenosaunee communities had increasingly incorporated markers of consumer civility such as European-style clothing; housewares; and hardware such as window glass while maintaining cultural distance from their white neighbors who purchased the same goods by blending clothing and housewares with more typically Indian items of dress in homes that incorporated both Haudenosaunee and Anglo architectural elements. As tensions boiled over and some Haudenosaunee communities joined the British and others attempted to remain neutral, Americans attacked the previously neutral Mohawk communities at Fort Hunter and Canajoharie by appropriating homes, land, and symbols of consumer civility such as jewelry and clothing for the use of their own white families.

As the war progressed, American attacks turned against Haudenosaunee women's lands and bodies. As the basis for Haudenosaunee military and political strength, women's ability to cultivate vast stores of corn came under attack in 1779 by Continental soldiers who marveled at the extent of the fields and orchards that they destroyed. While neither the soldiers who committed the destruction nor the American commanders who ordered and oversaw it viewed the campaign as an attack against women, the goal of terrorizing British-allied Haudenosaunee communities into submission explicitly included taking women and children hostage. American military commanders condemned violence and assault against Native women, but they ignored murder and rape committed by the soldiers under their command, tacitly combining attacks on Haudenosaunee women's lands and bodies. In the years following the war, American negotiators attempted to fit Haudenosaunee diplomacy into their own gendered expectations for political behavior by refusing to acknowledge the presence of women or only acknowledging their very limited participation as dependent mothers. This hostility was expressed materially, in the types of gifts distributed, as well as rhetorically, by asking that women not attend treaty conferences and by addressing answers to women's demands to Haudenosaunee men instead.

Rather than pushing Haudenosaunee women from diplomatic and political spaces, American hostility succeeded only in making Haudenosaunee women and their importance to their own communities more visible as Haudenosaunee diplomats tutored inexperienced Americans in gendered diplomatic expectations. Haudenosaunee women's traditional authority made them targets for symbolic and actual violence during the war, but American attempts to erase women's presence after the war only prompted male Haudenosaunee speakers for the women to articulate their continuing role in Haudenosaunee governance. Rather than forcing Haudenosaunee women to "open their mouths no further," hostility to women's political and diplomatic authority made women more explicitly visible in the diplomatic spaces of the period.

Notes

1. I use "Haudenosaunee" here rather than "Iroquois" to emphasize the indigenous experience and cultural framework for understanding the American Revolution. In doing so, I use "Haudenosaunee" as a political identifier to denote members of the Six Nations rather than the culturally related and sometimes politically aligned Mingo of the Ohio Valley or Laurentian communities of Kahnawake and Akwasasne.

2. Nancy Shoemaker, "The Rise or Fall of Iroquois Women," in *Native Women's History in Eastern North America before 1900: A Guide to Research and Writing*, ed. Rebecca Kugel and Lucy Eldersveld Murphy (Lincoln: University of Nebraska Press, 2007), 303.

3. Judith K. Brown, "Economic Organization and the Position of Women among the Iroquois," *Ethnohistory* 17, nos. 3–4 (1970): 151–67; Elisabeth Tooker, "Women in Iroquois Society," in *Extending the Rafters: Interdisciplinary Approaches to Iroquoian Studies*, ed. Michael K. Foster, Jack Campisi, and Marianne Mithun (Albany: State University of New York Press, 1984); Barbara Graymont, *The Iroquois in the American Revolution* (Syracuse, NY: Syracuse University Press, 1972); Colin G. Calloway, *Crown and Calumet: British-Indian Relations, 1783–1815* (Norman: University of Oklahoma Press, 1987); Robert S. Allen, *His Majesty's Indian Allies: British Indian Policy in the Defence of Canada, 1774–1815* (Toronto: Dundurn, 1992); Colin Calloway, *The American Revolution in Indian Country: Crisis and Diversity in North American Communities* (Cambridge: Cambridge University Press, 1995). For recent Iroquois history, see Joseph T. Glatthaar and James Kirby Martin, *Forgotten Allies: The Oneida Indians and the American Revolution* (New York: Hill and Wang, 2006); Alan Taylor, *The Divided Ground: Upper Canada, New York, and the Iroquois Six Nations, 1783–1815* (New York: Vintage, 2006). For decline narratives in Native history generally, see Richard White, *The Middle Ground: Indians, Empires, and Republics in the Great Lakes Region, 1650–1815* (New York: Cambridge University Press, 2011), 96, 256; Eric Hinderaker, *Elusive Empires: Constructing Colonialism in the Ohio Valley, 1673–1800* (Cambridge: Cambridge University Press, 1997), 226, 267; Timothy J. Shannon, *Iroquois Diplomacy on the Early American Frontier* (New York: Viking, 2008), 192–93. On antideclension narratives, see Kurt Jordan, *The Seneca Restoration 1715–1754: An Iroquois Local Political Economy* (Gainesville: University Press of Florida, 2008), 18, 318; David Preston, *The Texture of Contact: European and Indian Settler Communities on the Frontiers of Iroquoia, 1667–1783* (Lincoln: University of Nebraska Press, 2009), 13; Jon Parmenter, *The Edge of the Woods: Iroquoia 1534–1701* (East Lansing: Michigan State University Press, 2010), xxix, xxxii–xxxiii; Rachel B. Herrmann,

"'No Useless Mouth': Iroquoian Food Diplomacy in the American Revolution," *Diplomatic History* 41, no. 1 (January 1, 2017): 20–49; Shoemaker, "The Rise or Fall of Iroquois Women."

4. For Iroquois population levels, see Richard Aquila, *The Iroquois Restoration: Iroquois Diplomacy on the Colonial Frontier, 1701–1754* (Detroit: Wayne State University Press, 1983), 30; Parmenter, *The Edge of the Woods*, app. 2. For the politics of Iroquois alliances during the Revolution, see Max M. Mintz, *The Seeds of Empire: The American Revolutionary Conquest of the Iroquois* (New York: New York University Press, 2001), 1–4; Glatthaar and Martin, *Forgotten Allies*, 106–23.

5. Barbara Alice Mann, *Iroquoian Women: The Gantowisas* (New York: Peter Lang, 2000), 165–70.

6. Gail D. MacLeitch, *Imperial Entanglements: Iroquois Change and Persistence on the Frontiers of Empire* (Philadelphia: University of Pennsylvania Press, 2011), 175–210; Preston, *The Texture of Contact*, 178–215.

7. Preston, *The Texture of Contact*, 287; Glatthaar and Martin, *Forgotten Allies*, 239–62; Anthony Wonderly, "An Oneida Community in 1780: Study of an Inventory of Iroquois Property Losses during the Revolutionary War," *Man in the Northeast* 56 (Fall 1998): 19–42.

8. "Account of Losses Sustained by the Oneidas and Tuscaroras, in Consequence of Their Attachment to the United States in the Late War," November 27, 1794, Timothy Pickering Papers, Massachusetts Historical Society, Boston; Wonderly, "An Oneida Community in 1780."

9. Jelles Fonda, "Account Book," 1768–75, BV Indian Trader, New-York Historical Society; Jelles Fonda, "Indian Book for Jelles Fonda at Cachsewago," 1758–63, MS651–647, Old Fort Johnson, Fort Johnson, NY.

10. Henry Barclay, Register of Baptisms, Marriages, Communicants and Funerals at Fort Hunter, NY1734. BV Barclay, New-York Historical Society.

11. Peter Gansevoort to John Sullivan, October 8, 1779, Gansevoort Military Papers, New York Public Library. See also Graymont, *The Iroquois in the American Revolution*, 219.

12. Jelles Fonda to the Commissioners of Indian Affairs, Palatine, NY, 21 April 1778, Philip Schuyler Papers, New York Public Library, New York, box 14, 134.

13. Lt. Erkuries Beaty, in Frederick Cook, ed. *Journals of the Military Expedition of Major General John Sullivan against the Six Nations of Indians in 1779* (Auburn, NY: Knapp, Peck and Thomson, 1887), 26. On treaty coats, see Marshall Becker, "Matchcoats: Cultural Conservatism and Change in One Aspect of Native American Clothing," *Ethnohistory* 52, no. 4 (October 2005): 727–87; Laura Johnson, "Goods to Clothe Themselves," *Winterthur Portfolio* 43, no. 1 (2009): 115–40; Maeve Kane, "Covered with Such a Cappe: The Archaeology of Seneca Clothing 1615–1820," *Ethnohistory* 61, no. 1 (Winter 2014): 1–25.

14. George Miles, "A Brief Study of Joseph Brant's Political Career in Relation to Iroquois Political Structure," *American Indian Journal* 2 (December 1976): 12–20; Graymont, *The Iroquois in the American Revolution*, 47, 157–61; Barbara Graymont, "Konwatsi'tsiaenni," in *Dictionary of Canadian Biography*, vol. 4 (Toronto: University of Toronto Press, 1966), accessed September 30, 2018, http://www.biographi.ca/en/bio/konwatsitsiaienni_4E.html; Lois Feister and Bonnie Pulis, "Molly Brant: Her Domestic and Political Roles in Eighteenth-Century New York," in *Northeastern Indian Lives, 1632–1816*, ed. Robert Steven Grumet (Amherst: University of Massachusetts

Press, 1996), 295–320; Jan Noel, "'Fertile with Fine Talk': Ungoverned Tongues among Haudenosaunee Women and Their Neighbors," *Ethnohistory* 57, no. 2 (March 20, 2010): 201–23.

15. Fonda to Commissioners of Indian Affairs, Palatine.

16. On the post-Revolution Oneida experiences, see Glatthaar and Martin, *Forgotten Allies*, 263–314; Laurence M. Hauptman and L. Gordon McLester, eds., *The Oneida Indian Journey: From New York to Wisconsin, 1784–1860* (Madison: University of Wisconsin Press, 1999); George C. Shattuck, *The Oneida Land Claims: A Legal History* (Syracuse, NY: Syracuse University Press, 1991); Karim M. Tiro, *The People of the Standing Stone: The Oneida Nation from the Revolution through the Era of Removal* (Amherst: University of Massachusetts Press, 2011).

17. George Washington to John Sullivan, Middle Brook, NJ, May 31, 1779, HM 1590, Huntington Library, Pasadena, CA.

18. Phillip Schuyler to George Washington, Saratoga, NY, February 4, 1779, quoted in Maryly Barton Penrose, *Indian Affairs Papers, American Revolution* (Franklin Park, NJ: Liberty Bell Associates, 1981), 183.

19. Robert W. Venables, "'Faithful Allies of the King': The Crown's Haudenosaunee Allies in the Revolutionary Struggle for New York," in *The Other Loyalists: Ordinary People, Royalism, and the Revolution in the Middle Colonies, 1763–1787*, ed. Joseph S. Tiedemann, Eugene R. Fingerhut, and Robert W. Venables. (Albany: State University of New York Press, 2009); Graymont, *The Iroquois in the American Revolution*; Herrmann, "No Useless Mouth," 20–49.

20. Quoted in Mintz, *The Seeds of Empire*, 186; Sarah Pearsall, "Recentering Indian Women in the American Revolution," in *Why You Can't Teach United States History without American Indians*, ed. Susan Sleeper-Smith, Juliana Barr, Jean M. O'Brien, Nancy Shoemaker, and Scott Manning Stevens (Chapel Hill: University of North Carolina Press, 2015), 64.

21. Carol Berkin, *Revolutionary Mothers: Women in the Struggle for America's Independence*, repr. ed. (New York: Vintage, 2006).

22. Lt. Samuel Shute, in Cook, *Journals of the Military Expedition of Major General John Sullivan against the Six Nations of Indians in 1779*, 270.

23. Gen. John Sullivan, in Cook, *Journals of the Military Expedition of Major General John Sullivan against the Six Nations of Indians in 1779*, 303.

24. Maj. John Burrowes, in Cook, *Journals of the Military Expedition of Major General John Sullivan against the Six Nations of Indians in 1779*, 44.

25. Lt. Col. Henry Dearborn and Major James Norris, in Cook, *Journals of the Military Expedition of Major General John Sullivan against the Six Nations of Indians in 1779*, 73, 232.

26. Beatty, in Cook, *Journals of the Military Expedition of Major General John Sullivan against the Six Nations of Indians in 1779*, 29.

27. Sullivan, in Cook, *Journals of the Military Expedition of Major General John Sullivan against the Six Nations of Indians in 1779*, 303.

28. Lt. William Barton, in Cook, *Journals of the Military Expedition of Major General John Sullivan against the Six Nations of Indians in 1779*, 9.

29. Graymont, *The Iroquois in the American Revolution*, 213.

30. Graymont, *The Iroquois in the American Revolution*; Calloway, *Crown and Calumet*; Allen, *His Majesty's Indian Allies*; Calloway, *The American Revolution in Indian Country*; Glatthaar and Martin, *Forgotten Allies*; Herrmann, "No Useless Mouth,"

20–49. For a discussion of the Sullivan Campaign that does consider its gendered dimensions, see Pearsall, "Recentering Indian Women in the American Revolution."

31. Canajoharie Mohawk, March 10, 1763, in *The Papers of Sir William Johnson*, ed. James Sullivan, 14 vols (Albany: State University of New York Press, 1921), 4:56, quoted in Taylor, *The Divided Ground*, 18.

32. For analysis of the rhetoric of Iroquois allies as "useless mouths," see Herrmann, "No Useless Mouth," 20–49.

33. Burrowes and Lt. Col. Adam Hubley, in Cook, *Journals of the Military Expedition of Major General John Sullivan against the Six Nations of Indians in 1779*, 49, 164, quoted in Pearsall, "Recentering Indian Women in the American Revolution," 64–65. See also Barbara Alice Mann, *George Washington's War on Native America* (Las Vegas: University of Nevada Press, 2008), 92.

34. Pearsall, "Recentering Indian Women in the American Revolution," 57–70.

35. On the importance of age in how the Sullivan Campaign treated Madam Sacho and the murdered woman, see Pearsall, "Recentering Indian Women in the American Revolution," 63–65.

36. T. W. Egly, *History of the First New York Regiment, 1775–1783* (Hampton, NH: P. E. Randall, 1981), 125.

37. Quoted in William L. Stone, *Life of Joseph Brant* (New York: Alexander Blake, 1838), 1:404. See also Graymont, *The Iroquois in the American Revolution*, 196; Mann, *George Washington's War on Native America*, 32.

38. Quoted in Calloway, *The American Revolution in Indian Country*, 53. See also Taylor, *The Divided Ground*, 98; Graymont, *The Iroquois in the American Revolution*, 192–96.

39. MacLeitch, *Imperial Entanglements*, 113–45.

40. On protocols of European-Haudenosaunee diplomacy, see Nancy L. Hagedorn, "'With the Air and Gesture of an Orator': Council Oratory, Translation and Cultural Mediation during Anglo-Iroquois Treaty Conferences, 1690–1774," in *New Trends in Translation and Cultural Identity*, ed. Micaela Muñoz-Calvo, Carmen Bueso-Gómez, and M. Ángeles Ruiz-Moneva (Newcastle upon Tyne: Cambridge Scholars, 2008), 35; Shannon, *Iroquois Diplomacy on the Early American Frontier*, 78–102; Parmenter, *The Edge of the Woods*, xliii–xlvi. For an overview of the recent historiography of Indian-European diplomacy, see Gregory Evans Dowd, "Wag the Imperial Dog: Indians and Overseas Empires in North America, 1650–1776," in *A Companion to American Indian History*, ed. Philip J. Deloria and Neal Salisbury (Malden, MA: Blackwell, 2002).

41. Mary Beth Norton, *Separated by Their Sex: Women in Public and Private in the Colonial Atlantic World* (Ithaca, NY: Cornell University Press, 2011), 111–15, 125–28, 136–38, 175–82. See also Susan Branson, *These Fiery Frenchified Dames: Women and Political Culture in Early National Philadelphia* (Philadelphia: University of Pennsylvania Press, 2001); Mary Kelley, *Learning to Stand and Speak: Women, Education, and Public Life in America's Republic* (Chapel Hill, NC: Omohundro Institute, 2008); Linda K. Kerber, *Women of the Republic: Intellect and Ideology in Revolutionary America* (Chapel Hill, NC: Omohundro Institute, 1997); Mary Beth Norton, *Liberty's Daughters: The Revolutionary Experience of American Women, 1750–1800* (Ithaca, NY: Cornell University Press, 1996); Rosemarie Zagarri, *Revolutionary Backlash: Women and Politics in the Early American Republic* (Philadelphia: University of Pennsylvania Press, 2008).

42. "Extract from a Letter from Miss Powell Describing a Tour from Montreal to Detroit in 1789," Anne Powell Collection, MS 2958.7900, New-York Historical Society.

43. Alyssa Mountpleasant, "Independence For Whom? Expansion and Conflict in the Northeast and Northwest," in *In The World of the Revolutionary American Republic: Land, Labor, and the Conflict for a Continent,* ed. Andrew Shankman (New York: Routledge, 2014), 121.

44. Speech of Good Peter, "Extracts from the Proceedings of the Commissioners for Making Peace with the Indians in 1784 and 1785," Fort Stanwix, Rome, NY, October 12, 1784, no. 115, Timothy Pickering Papers, Massachusetts Historical Society.

45. On British gift giving, see MacLeitch, *Imperial Entanglements,* 17–19, 66–68, 90–91, 189–90; Commissioners of Indian Affairs, "Accounts of the Commissioners of Indian Affairs," 1784–85, A0802-78, vol. 15, boxes 13–16, New York State Archives, Albany; "Account of Goods Purchased by Order of Tench Coxe Esqr for the Use of the Six Nations of Indians," October 13, 1794, no. 137; "Invoice of Goods Purchased by Tench Francis Agent for the Intended Treaty with the Six Nations of Indians and Delivered by Direction of T Pickering," n.d., no. 128; "Invoice of Sundries Procured by Order of the Honorable Major General Knox Sec at War to be Forwarded to Col T Pickering for the Indian Treaty," May 3, 1791, no. 284; "An Account of the Expences Incurred in Holding a Conference with the Six Nations of Indians at Tioga in the Month of November 1790," November 1790, no. 123, all in Timothy Pickering Papers, Massachusetts Historical Society.

46. "At a Meeting of the Commissioners for Holding Treaties with the Indians within this State," 19 Februrary 1789, in *Proceedings of the Commissioners of Indian Affairs,* ed. Franklin Benjamin Hough, 2 vols. (Albany: Joel Munsell, 1861), 2:279.

47. On the rhetoric of kinship in Haudenosaunee-European diplomacy, see Nancy Shoemaker, "An Alliance between Men: Gender Metaphors in Eighteenth-Century American Indian Diplomacy East of the Mississippi." *Ethnohistory* 46, no. 2 (1999): 239–63; Jane T. Merritt, *At the Crossroads: Indians and Empires on a Mid-Atlantic Frontier* (Chapel Hill: University of North Carolina Press, 2003); Gunlög Fur, *A Nation of Women: Gender and Colonial Encounters among the Delaware Indians* (Philadelphia: University of Pennsylvania Press, 2012); MacLeitch, *Imperial Entanglements,* 191–209.

48. "At a Meeting of the Commissioners for Holding Treaties with the Indians within this State," February 24, 1789, in Hough, *Proceedings of the Commissioners of Indian Affairs,* 2:300–2.

49. Timothy Pickering, 10 July 1791, no. 117; Timothy Pickering, Tioga Point, October 30, 1790, no. 59; Timothy Pickering Journal, November 9, 1790, no. 47, all in Timothy Pickering Papers, Massachusetts Historical Society; Abraham Cuyler to the Commissioners of Indian Affairs, Albany, May 14, 1785, in Hough, *Proceedings of the Commissioners of Indian Affairs,* 1:71.

50. Seneca Billy, November 23, 1790, Family Correspondence, reel 31:97, Timothy Pickering Papers, Massachusetts Historical Society.

51. "Capt Hendrik Aupaumut's Narrative of His Journey in July August, Sept and Oct 1791," Family Correspondence, reel 59:8, Timothy Pickering Papers, Massachusetts Historical Society.

52. Ibid.

"A Lady of New Jersey"

Annis Boudinot Stockton, Patriot and Poet in an Age of Revolution

MARTHA J. KING

The year 1758 marked a crucial turning point in the life of colonial poet, Annis Boudinot Stockton (1736–1801). Not only was it the year she lost a close personal friend, Esther Edwards Burr, to illness and death, but she also had recently gained a spouse in Richard Stockton and, through her marriage, had joined a prominent family in New Jersey's colonial elite. In addition to these personal, relational milestones, Stockton achieved greater, albeit indirect public recognition of her talents as a poet. Although she had written unpublished poems as a young woman, she published her first piece in 1758 in the *New-York Mercury* not as Mrs. Stockton but with the mere attribution of "a young Lady of the Province of New-Jersey."[1] The unnamed letter writer who had submitted the poet's verses in honor of a military leader of the French and Indian War who had stayed briefly in Princeton en route to Trenton touted the "uncommon a Genius" in the *"fair Author"* and suggested that distributing the verse through Hugh Gaine's newspaper would be universally acceptable "but more especially to your female Readers."

While scholars such as Paula Backsheider, Pattie Cowell, and Sharon M. Harris have shown that it was not unusual for eighteenth-century women to be engaged in the production, distribution, and consumption of poetry, others, such as Caroline Wigginton, have argued that we must consider the pervasiveness of manuscript circulation in epistolary neighborhoods, not just the publication of printed verse in newspapers and magazines.[2] Annis Stockton's contributions lie in both worlds—of public print and personal prose. The literary biographer Carla Mulford estimates that Stockton wrote more than one hundred poems that circulated only in manuscript in addition to the twenty-one known published pieces of her extant corpus.[3]

Yet Annis Boudinot Stockton's work and life illumine even more than literary contributions. Constance Greiff and Wanda Gunning, the authors of *Morven: Memory, Myth and Reality,* provided further historical documentation in 2004 and a corrective to the extant literature on the Stockton family and their Princeton home.[4] We no longer question that this "Muse of Morven" should be studied in her own right and not just as a wife and mother-in-law of "signers" of the Declaration of Independence.[5] Some scholars have viewed her as a proto-feminist; others, as a highly political poet.[6] Her husband, Richard, was the only signer who retracted his endorsement of American independence, although he did so most likely under duress. This essay explores several overlapping influences that shaped Stockton's life and helped her navigate many roles during the volatile years of the Revolution and its aftermath. It also examines how her poetry gave her both social and political capital in the destabilizing environment of war-torn New Jersey. Stockton maintained her devotion to her husband at the same time that she forged an identity as a woman loyal to the American cause and as a writer in a world of politicized print and manuscript culture. She used gendered power to negotiate her competing allegiances and responsibilities amid the lived experiences of pressure, scarcity, and uncertainty in a wartime state.

Stockton wrote to president and politician, daughters and doctors, and discussed concerns of hearth and home as well as important issues of the day. She wrote to newspaper printers and editors and politely yet confidently encouraged them to publish her letters and poems. The formative influences in her life helped her cope with separations, anxieties, gender inequalities, and uncertainties about the war's ultimate outcome. The war and widowhood opened new opportunities of expression for her. The perspective of a female member of the white elite both adds to and complicates our understanding of the time. Stockton's life reflects broader issues for women of her generation and locale and reveals unique circumstances for an elite woman of New Jersey who had financial means and family support to encourage her poetic expression. She used poetry and publication in its broadest sense to give voice to larger concerns beyond her domestic circle. This essay seeks to discover what she made out of the authority and agency she found in authorship.[7]

Annis Boudinot was born in Darby, Pennsylvania, near Philadelphia, on July 1, 1736, the eldest daughter of the ten children born to Catherine Williams and Elias Boudinot, a merchant and silversmith of French Huguenot descent. Five of her siblings lived beyond childhood. Annis's education was not unusual for elite women, although it was far from typical for most girls of the time. Reading, some writing, and basic ciphering, as well as the more customary domestic arts and occasional ornamental skills, made up the early training for young girls of her class. While many girls received the rudiments of reading, only a few received a complete education in writing. The learned allusions of her later literary output and correspondence suggest some type of classical education, as well as wide reading and a cultivated writing. Scholars have assumed she was informally educated or perhaps benefited from exposure to teachers at the fledgling Academy and College of Philadelphia, where her brothers Elias and John studied.[8] No girls were enrolled in the academy, although many attended the affiliated Charity School.[9] Clearly, Annis's parents valued education for their children.

Her father's wide-ranging pursuits prompted him to move his family from Pennsylvania to New Jersey in the 1750s when Annis was a teenager. The bilingual Boudinots originally lived in New Brunswick, then moved to Princeton in 1756 and settled on the main street across from Nassau Hall and the new home of Aaron Burr Sr., the president of the College of New Jersey. The college had relocated from Newark to Princeton by the end of that very year and was abuzz with energy and religious enthusiasm. The town, with its fifty to seventy-five families, and the college, with its tutors and students, gave Annis many opportunities for social and intellectual enrichment.[10]

In addition to education, family and friendship would be crucial touchstones and lifelong influences dating from Annis's formative years. Her relationships included close bonds with old and young, men and women, nearby neighbors and faraway friends.[11] While kinship ties are typical for women of this era, Annis maintained a multigenerational family network as well as a broad circle of friends, and each facet is surprisingly well documented across the life cycle. In addition to her poetry, correspondence survives of Annis as sister, mother, wife, friend, in-law, grandmother, and slave owner—a unique and rare documentary treasure for the colonial historian.

One important friend from Annis's early years was Esther Edwards Burr, the wife and daughter of two early presidents of the College of New Jersey. Esther was a twenty-four-year-old matron and the wife of President Aaron Burr Sr. when the single and teenage Annis arrived in town. Esther described this likeable newcomer to the community as "a pretty discreet well behaved girl" in correspondence with a friend in 1756. "She has," Esther wrote, "good sense and can talk very handsomely on almost any subject, I hope a good Girl two—I will send you some peieces of poetry of her own composing that in my opinion shew some genious that way that if proporly cultivated might be able to make no mean figure."[12] A few months later she described Annis as a "pleasant, sociable, Friendly" creature who could write impromptu poetry with finesse and ease.[13] Referring to Annis as "my poetis," Esther acknowledged her literary talents and religious zeal yet wished her friend had "more advantages of improvment." Annis was adept at versifying and her poems had appealed to female companions such as Esther and others of her "knot of friends" who regularly met and circulated writings in manuscript.[14] Their friendship was short-lived, however, as Esther died in April 1758 after succumbing to a fever that had earlier taken the lives of her husband and father.[15]

But Annis long remembered this friend of her young adulthood who had shared spiritual and intellectual interests and no doubt had introduced her to people and ideas from the greater college community, thereby adding to her so-called improvement. Almost twenty years later, Annis sent her late friend's son, Aaron Burr Jr., a poem she had written on the death of his friend General Richard Montgomery. She offered her enclosed lines as "her mite in the treasury to the mighty debt due from America to the memory of that brave man." Annis claimed a share in Burr's friendship "both on her own account and on account of that place she once had the happiness of possessing in the hearts of both your worthy parents; whose remembrance is still dear to her and ever will."[16]

Much has also been written about Annis's friendly devotion to the Philadelphia salonièrre Elizabeth Graeme Fergusson of Graeme Park, outside Philadelphia. Intelligent, well-connected (she had been engaged in 1754 to Benjamin Franklin's loyalist son William), and of suspect political allegiance during the war, Elizabeth was the renowned hostess of Saturday "attic evenings" at Graeme Park, where local intellectually curious men and women gathered to discuss and share readings, culture, and polite conversation. Almost exact contemporaries, Annis and Elizabeth enjoyed their correspondence, used the pen names "Emelia" and "Laura," and relished the occasions when they could be in each other's company. In the interim, they shared commonplace books and exchanged poetry and letters and cultivated an enduring friendship that lasted until their deaths in 1801.[17]

It was in this neighborhood of learning, conversation, and stimulating sociability that Annis came to know the Stockton family. Already acquainted with the Stockton sisters, especially Hannah (who would become her sister-in-law in 1762), Annis befriended and became betrothed to their brother, the lawyer Richard Stockton, who was six years her senior. Annis's marriage in late 1757 or 1758 more fully secured her place in the upper echelon of mid-Atlantic colonial society and immersed her in polite and politic society. The Stockton family had been in America for four generations; Richard was born in Princeton in 1730.[18] He was among the first graduates of the College of New Jersey, situated at Newark, in 1748. The Stockton family was literate, landed, and large. Annis's husband inherited an extensive property from his father, Judge John Stockton, and through her marriage Annis acquired seven siblings-in-law, to boot. Regular visits by and among the kin on both sides of the family became the norm for the couple throughout their marriage.

The couple had six children, including twins, who survived beyond early childhood.[19] Their first child, Julia, was born in 1759, and Stockton's poetic output during the subsequent busy years of childbearing is understandably slimmer than that later in life. The historian Susan Klepp has called attention to the normative condition of procreation and motherhood for Stockton and her mid-Atlantic contemporaries but also suggests that, whereas the imagery of the writing of her earlier years related to "prattling infants," that of her later correspondence and poetry emphasized women's intelligence.[20]

After her marriage, Stockton wrote poems of advice to a niece on upcoming nuptials, impromptus on a daughter's birthday or a son's wedding day, memorials for the deceased, and verses on mundane observations such as icicles on trees.[21] Her poems could be spontaneously written on the fly or brooded over by candlelight late at night when alone in her chamber after the rest of her household had gone to bed.[22]

Richard's law practice, with frequent business in Newark and Philadelphia, often took him from their Princeton home, which Annis named Morven in the late 1760s.[23] When her husband traveled farther afield, to England and Scotland in 1766–67, the young mother was left behind with four small children and little time for leisure. During his fifteen-months abroad, Richard traveled in high society and actively recruited the Scottish Presbyterian John Witherspoon to accept the presidency of the beleaguered College of New Jersey.[24] While Richard visited the first minister, socialized with many members of Parliament, and even had an audience with the king, Annis's experience was circumscribed, local, and mundane. In the kitchen and nursery of her home, she carried out responsibilities of the domestic front while tending to children and looking after family accounts.

Reading, writing, and occasional social calls with friends provided her respite. Annis Stockton's commonplace books and letters suggest that some of her poems were widely circulated, copied, or shared aloud in salon conversations where they might be read over a cup of tea. The authorial process was often collaborative among members of her literary intimates and was largely imbued with a social rather than solitary context. It is not surprising, therefore, that the editorial process that brought these poems into circulation was collaborative.[25]

Stockton's writing also consisted of lively correspondence. In her early writing, she remained deliberately silent on political matters, as she expressed to Elizabeth Graeme in 1769: "I have my system of politicks too—but as you say I Leave the settling of the nation to wiser folks and enjoy my own sentiments."[26] The exchange of letters between the Stockton couple from this period is also mostly devoid of politics, with Richard writing as "Lucius" to Annis, his "Emelia," revealing the strong affection and loving, companionate bonds in their marriage, as well as the deep influences of their shared Christian beliefs and concerns for family.[27]

Upon his return to New Jersey, Richard quickly rose to prominence in colonial affairs. Governor William Franklin (the former fiancé of Elizabeth Graeme) appointed him a royal councilor in 1768 and a judge of common pleas four years later. In 1774, Richard Stockton became a provincial Supreme Court justice. With Richard's star rising, Annis no doubt reaped social benefits from his connections and frequently entertained guests at their home and gardens at Morven. A moderate in the growing rift with Great Britain, Richard was appointed by the New Jersey Provincial Council to the Second Continental Congress on June 22, 1776, arrived in Philadelphia on July 1, and cast his vote for independence the following day. He could hardly be considered one of the long-standing or outspoken advocates for the break with England.

When the Revolution came close to home in 1776, the Stocktons and other families, however, were inextricably caught in a precarious situation as armies from both sides of the conflict marched across New Jersey and quartered in their homes. With allegiances and outcomes uncertain, the world turned upside down for Stockton.[28] Just a few months before, her eldest daughter, Julia, had married Benjamin Rush, and Richard had been a member of Congress in Philadelphia signing the Declaration of Independence. By late November 1776, though, with Washington's forces in retreat and General Cornwallis's troops moving south from New York, the British occupation of Princeton was imminent. The College of New Jersey closed its doors and suspended classes in anticipation of the warfront reaching the campus. Overcoming parental worries for their older son and a servant left behind to look after the property, Annis, Richard, and the younger children feared for their lives and fled their home to seek refuge with friends in Monmouth County. But before they left, Stockton gathered what family papers and treasures she could and buried others. In a daring move described as "isolated, independent action," Stockton also rescued the records and effects of the college's Whig Society, a small literary club whose members knew of her writings and who were mostly of a patriot persuasion.[29] Perhaps she had shared some of her own works with its members and took personally the responsibility of preserving the manuscripts.

Shortly after the Stockton family's arrival at their supposedly safe haven, British troops awakened the household in the middle of the night and captured Richard, subjecting him to a painful march in wintery conditions and ultimate imprisonment in a New York Provost jail, where he was reportedly put in irons and starved. We have no record of how Stockton coped with the dramatic loss of her husband, now a prisoner of war, or how she balanced the increased demands and delicate dance of allegiance. Perhaps at her pleading, Benjamin Rush tried to intervene for his father-in-law.[30] When

George Washington learned of the harsh treatment of the delegate from New Jersey, he ordered Congress to investigate the matter, and by early January 1777, Richard had been released.[31] Annis would never forget this debt of gratitude to the commanding general.

Like any spouse reunited with a loved one, Stockton was overjoyed upon their reunion and thrilled when their family could return to Morven, even though they found property damaged from wartime military occupation. Yet Richard's release was not without sacrifice and cost, for he had to swear to forsake future involvement in the war.[32] Richard returned to his home but never completely to good health, and Annis assumed the more frequent role of his nurse. Surely his return prompted some renegotiation of roles and expectations within their marriage and perhaps some anguished conversations about allegiance and duty. Richard was able to resume some travel and legal practice in the area, and there is no evidence that his family held his retraction against him.[33] Others were warier. John Witherspoon wrote in March 1777, "Judge Stockton is not very well in health & much spoken against for his Conduct. He Signed Howes declaration & also gave his Word of honour that he would not meddle in the least in American affairs during the War."[34]

While many loyalists bore the brunt of political, social, and military persecution, Annis's husband seems to have escaped much public censure. Hardly a political extremist and perhaps only a loyalist on paper, Richard probably acted out of pragmatism. Faced with a potentially long imprisonment, possible execution as a traitor, or confiscation of his property that would have left his family impoverished, he chose an expedient alternative in taking the oath. Although he resigned his congressional seat shortly after capture, he maintained his home at Morven and a sizable estate that he was able to pass on to his widow and children upon his death.[35]

Richard's frequent absences from home—whether from legal business, congressional, or college-related affairs; ill health, or wartime imprisonment—forced Annis to shoulder the weight of parenting and estate management. Like Mary Willing Byrd, she had to act pragmatically but cautiously in a politically charged environment. Troops from the Continental Army took possession of a local church and the College of New Jersey, which were used as barracks and hospital at various times during the New Jersey campaigns of 1777–79.[36] We do not know whether Stockton resented her predicament or feared ridicule, but she did face financial constraints before the war's end and had her patience tested when her sick husband grew increasingly irritable from pain.[37]

While other women of her generation had to assume extra responsibilities in wartime, Stockton benefited from having the financial and emotional support of extended family nearby and sometimes under her roof. Daughter Julia and her offspring often came for extended visits, and Stockton hosted her brother Elisha, who boarded at Morven while the Continental Congress convened at Princeton in 1783. Stockton's upper-class status also gave her the economic means to rely on servants and slaves to run the estate, although the number of slaves the family owned remained small throughout Morven's history and had fallen to as few as two or three in 1779–80.[38] Still, having others laboring on her behalf also provided her with some time to pursue her writing even as she raised a family.

Stockton, like most women who experience the absence of loved ones, confronted loneliness, apprehension, and independent pride, emotions that sometimes found unique creative expression in her pen.[39] For her, poetry and participation in writing circles or salons were not leisure activities but meant to instruct or edify as part of an intellectual exchange. Her motivation in writing poetry was to give expression to her emotions and creative impulses, and it helped her feel connected to a larger world beyond her domestic circle. Her poetry was expansive, not restrictive, and sometimes served a political purpose. Writing and poetry would become both solace and strength and a way to forge an identity. As Rachel Hope Cleves and others have shown, however, "The act of writing poems, even poems about war and politics, did not transgress the appropriate bounds of late-eighteenth-century femininity."[40]

Stockton reevaluated her own prospects in wartime even as her husband's health deteriorated before his death on February 28, 1781. Ever loyal to her husband but not willing to divorce herself from neighbors with whom she needed to remain in good standing, she juggled confusing allegiances and tried to carry on in a colony aligning more heavily with the patriot cause. Certainly she was familiar with "The Sentiments of an American Woman," which first appeared on the front page of the *Pennsylvania Gazette* on June 21, 1780, and which launched the fundraising campaign of Esther De Berdt Reed and Sally Franklin Bache in support of the patriot soldiers in the Continental Army.[41] As Mary Thompson has shown, Martha Washington, the wife of the commanding general, was the figurehead of this national canvassing campaign that organized women in every colony to mobilize for patriot wartime relief.[42] Julia Rush, a member of the Philadelphia Ladies Association, became a collector of funds in the city's sixth ward and likely relayed information about her activities to her mother and encouraged her involvement.[43] Along with dozens of other elite New Jersey women, Stockton signed on to New Jersey's regional Fourth of July fundraising effort in 1780 "for the relief and encouragement of those brave Men in the Continental Army, . . . who have so repeatedly suffered, fought and bled in the cause of virtue and their oppressed country."[44] Inspired by their Philadelphia counterparts, several New Jersey women prepared a statement, "The Sentiments of a Lady in New-Jersey," published in the *New-Jersey Gazette* on July 12, 1780, pledging, "If we have it not in our power to do from the double motive of religion and a love of liberty . . . let us animate one another to contribute from our purses in proportion to our circumstances towards the support and comfort of the brave men who are fighting and suffering for us in the field." By participating in this public display of support for the American cause, Annis (as "Mrs. R. Stockton" of Somerset County) tried to show her own patriotism and perhaps redeem her family's name from any suspicion of treason on the anniversary of independence. Even though Richard had shown support for New Jersey's new revolutionary government after his release from prison, some may have questioned his neutrality. By signing on to this very public Ladies Association effort, Annis was in effect reinscribing the name of Stockton among the supporters of independence. Still, this action was risky business for one devoted to her husband's safety yet wanting to express a commitment in sororal solidarity in the midst of an ongoing war. One also wonders whether such independent actions on her part caused any renegotiation or destabilization in an otherwise companionate marriage.

Throughout the seasons and the vagaries of wartime and family life, the "Muse of Morven" continued to write. She even wrote an especially poignant piece while anxiously watching over her dying husband's bedside and wrote elegies to commemorate him on the annual anniversary of his death. Literary scholars have explored the major themes, classical roots, and traditional style and diction of her poetry, which included odes and elegies, pastorals, and hymns. While the majority of her poetry followed common literary conventions and was intended either for herself or "only for the eye of a friend" (as she often prefaced her commonplace books), it could occasionally be a way to display her learned refinement and her increasingly politicized patriotism.

The American Revolution provided both fuel and fodder for Stockton and other male and female poets in crafting and sharing poetic verse. She wrote tributes on the death of General Joseph Warren at Bunker Hill; on George Washington's leadership after the battles of Trenton, Princeton, and Yorktown; and on the occasions of the surrender of Lord Charles Cornwallis and the British Army and the release of Henry Laurens from imprisonment in the Tower of London. By early March 1781, when the Trenton printer Isaac Collins appended two of her poems to a funeral sermon for Richard Stockton written by Reverend Samuel Stanhope Smith, he noted that Mrs. Stockton's "poetical talents are generally known."[45] Bolstered by her previous success as a known writer in manuscript and print and as a hostess of a local literary salon, Stockton did not shrink from circulating her materials or from writing to printers and publishers in subsequent years, sometimes using strategic anonymity, initials, or simply the pseudonym "Emelia."[46]

Elias Boudinot, a delegate from New Jersey to the Continental Congress who later served as its president in 1782–83, had acted as a sort of literary agent for Stockton's friend and fellow poet Elizabeth Graeme Fergusson, and on more than one occasion, he acted in the same capacity for his sister.[47] Elias and his wife, Hannah, were also on friendly terms with George and Martha Washington.[48] In 1779, after Richard's release from prison but before his death from lip and throat cancer, Annis gave poems to her brother to convey to Washington. Elias enclosed the "few Lines wrote in the fulness of a Ladies gratitude" and revealed a twofold motivation. First, he wanted to "gratify a beloved Sister's Vanity" with the "small effusion of her poetical Genius." Second, he wanted to assure the general that, while some were trying to cast shadows on Washington's public services, the great majority were doing him justice, and "the Ladies, are emulous to be reckoned among this Number." Washington replied that he had been flattered by Annis's poem and recognized it more as a "mark of her genius" than of his merit. Such a favorable response gave reassurance to her not only of her own poetic talent but, perhaps more important, of her family's political standing in the eyes of the general.[49]

For Stockton, Elias provided an entrée to his colleagues in Congress and the larger community and a conduit to a broader distribution of her work in manuscript and print. Francis Hopkinson, Hugh Gaine, Isaac Collins, Peter Edes, John Fenno, and Shepherd Kollock numbered among the printers and publishers who welcomed the inclusion of Stockton's writing in their publications. Her brother also prodded her to make her writing more public and gave her confidence in the face of criticism. At his urging, on May 1, 1789, Stockton sent Elias a version of one of her odes to Washington; she would have otherwise suppressed the poem but was willing to use her talents to laud the general. Happy to comply, Annis told her brother she would "run the risk of being sneered at by *those* who criticise female productions, of all kinds. you can put morven in a blank if you publish it but as you please for they lay a great deal to me that I never did."[50] Not only did she face gender constraints in writing as a woman but she also had to contend with false attributions. Stockton's remarks indicate her awareness of the differences in reception a woman might face within a supportive intellectual community where she had freely circulated her manuscripts with likeminded friends versus the more public distribution of her work in print. Carla Mulford notes that, for Stockton, publication carried burdens of mixed company performance. While print publication was important to her, manuscript circulation was another, and often preferred form, of expression and performance.[51]

Although Stockton likely did not receive payment for her poems, their publication bought her a priceless form of social capital. In seeking to clear her husband's reputation after his death, she further solidified her own reputation even though her name was not explicitly given in her published poems. As Rosemarie Zagarri has demonstrated, print culture gave expanded opportunity for women's political voices to be heard.[52] Stockton and women like her could write anonymously about politics without risk of censure on the basis of their sex. While members of their families and intimate circles might have recognized the women behind the veil of pseudonyms, many in the body politic did not.

For Stockton, the personal became political through the medium of print. Her patriotism became a matter of public record and not merely a private concern circulated solely in manuscript among friends. In her efforts to enter the realm of print under the veil of women's patriotism, she self-consciously constructed an identity. Sharing in a women's literary culture was not an extraordinary heroic act for Stockton, but what she made out of the authority and agency she discovered as an author reveals her strategic use of gendered power. She sent the Federalist editor John Fenno an ode "written and inscribed to General Washington, a short time after the surrender of York-Town," and he promptly printed the unsigned stanzas.[53] While Stockton wrote the piece in 1781, she chose the appropriate moment for its public appearance in 1789. When Fenno established the *Gazette of the United States* that year, he unabashedly announced his intention to promote the new federal Constitution and the new President George Washington. Stockton chose to submit poems to Fenno and not to Philip Freneau, the editor of the opposition press. She was demonstrating in print her support of the federal government and the party in power. In a letter to Elias the following year, she showed her interest in politics and in Fenno's paper: "Deluged in politics, I suppose you never can find a moments time to let such little folks as your sister, have a line from you concerning state affairs or any other—as you know I am a little blasted with the flame of patriotism, I can not but wish to know a little of what is going forward."[54] Acknowledging her circumscribed status in the political sphere because of her gender, she still asserted "the flame of patriotism" and the burning desire to keep up with news of the nation, and with her brother, who held a legitimate role in service to his country. As one scholar has depicted it, a woman could be domestically occupied while politically preoccupied.[55]

Not surprisingly, George Washington was the subject of much news of the day. While he was generally diffident about sentimental expressions of the pen, he also became the reluctant but politely proud subject of numerous poems by Stockton and other poets of the era.[56] His commanding presence on the national stage, as well as his local appearances from Philadelphia to New York, attracted many authors, including Phillis Wheatley, to render literary praise. It gave Stockton an opportunity to showcase her talent and reassert her family's loyalty to the American cause and the first federal government of which Washington was the head.[57] Her poetry and accompanying correspondence became a bold statement of her own assent to the new government and, by association, a posthumous reclamation of her husband's suspect loyalties during wartime.

On the day Stockton heard news of Cornwallis's surrender, she wrote a heartfelt letter to Elias expressing her "joy on the happy Success of our arms in this great Event," which "must cause the heart of Every Lover of their Country, to beat high." Continuing in this state of near-rapture, she added, "You will smile at my being so interested but tho a female I was born a patriot and I cant help it If I would." She acknowledged that her "most fervent Daily prayers" had been answered in the outcome of the battle at Yorktown and never forgot Washington's visit to Morven en route to the campaign. "If we womin cannot fight for our beloved country," she wrote, "we can pray for it, and you know the widows mite was accepted."[58] Stockton asserted her patriotism and her desire to support the patriot cause, if not through martial participation, then by spiritual succor. Whereas her husband once had waited on George III in a royal audience in England, Stockton reminded George Washington of waiting on him as their guest at the Stockton home and hoped for another audience with the general. Family allegiances had certainly evolved.

In her letter to her brother, Stockton wrote a few lines of verse that were later expanded and printed in the *New-Jersey Gazette* by "Emelia" on November 28, 1781. But she did not send the poem to Washington until the following summer, and he immediately replied that the occasion she commemorated was among "the happiest events" of his life.[59]

The Washingtons resided in nearby Rocky Hill, New Jersey, in the summer of 1783 when Congress convened in Princeton. On September 1, 1783, within a few days of Washington's attendance at a session held at the college's Nassau Hall in late August, Stockton sent him another poem of welcome with an apology for her "Effusions of Gratitude and Esteem." Among the stanzas she wrote, "Say; can a female voice an audience gain / And Stop a moment thy triumphal Car / And will thou listen to a peaceful Strain: / Unskill'd to paint the horrid Scenes of war." She ended the poem, signed "Emelia": "And oh if happly in your native shade / One thought of Jersey Enters in your mind / Forget not *her* on morvens humble glade / Who feels for you a friendship most refin'd."[60] Washington wasted no time, responding the next day from Rocky Hill to accept her pardon and invite her to dinner. Without hesitation, he commended "the Muse not to be restrained by its grounded timidity, but to go on and prosper."[61] Having Washington's encouragement of her creative endeavors gave Stockton both validation and motivation.

Stockton wrote to Washington again in the summer 1788 when she learned of the likely ratification of the new Constitution, although her letter is lost. Washington acknowledged the recent letter from the "Muse of Morven," as he called her, for "the pleasing compositions of our female friends" and gratefully accepted her felicitations. "Nor would I rob," he added, "the fairer Sex of their share in the glory of a revolution so honorable to human nature, for, indeed, I think you Ladies are in the number of the best patriots America can boast. And now that I am speaking of your Sex, I will ask whether they are not capable of doing something towards introducing foederal fashions and national manners? A good general government, without good morals and good habits, will not make us a happy People."[62] Washington wrote to Stockton not just as a personal female friend but as a representative of American womanhood.

In early spring 1789, when Washington was elected the first president of the young nation, Stockton once again felt compelled to write. On March 13, she sent her congratulations from Morven along with an expression of understanding of the sacrifice for the public good that had induced him to leave his domestic comforts: "Ah! my beloved friend, you have an arduous task to perform, a severe Science to encounter but you are equal to it. I bless my self—I bless posterity— but I feel for you." She knew all too well the pain of leaving behind one's home—whether to flee to safety during wartime or, in his case, to accept a high office. She realized the pressures of public business might keep him from replying to her correspondence but stated the pleasure she felt on receiving a letter from him and looked forward to future occasions for visiting with the general and his wife. She added the respectful thanks of her "young folks" who were always pleased to see themselves mentioned in his letters.[63]

Washington sent a brief and hurried reply before he left home to be inaugurated as president at the new seat of government in New York. Along the way, his northern journey resembled a triumphal procession. On April 21, 1789, the ladies of Trenton gathered to greet Washington as he passed through town by erecting a triumphal arch on the bridge across Assunpink Creek. Girls dressed in white robes and carrying baskets of flowers lined the general's path with petals and greeted him in song. Washington expressed his appreciation for the elegant style of the festive occasion before he left the city that day.[64] Stockton remained speechless on the spot by the fanfare, but in May 1789 she sent another sample of her poetic veneration for the president and drew on imagery from the event:

> The muse of morvens peaceful shade
> Gave way to all the gay parade.
> For transport of her own.
> She felt the tear of pleasure flow
> And gratitudes delightful glow
> Was to her bosom known.
> Triumphal arches, gratulating song
> And shouts of welcome from the mused throng.[65]

In a letter to her daughter Polly, begun on September 15, 1790, Stockton had much news to report, including how she had seen the Washingtons as they passed through Princeton and provided them a hospitable welcome as they visited the college in attendance with Annis, her son, and Samuel Stanhope Smith and his wife. She recounted how Martha Washington sat with them until one o'clock and "partook of a collation of fruit and cake and wine and sweet meats, which I had in readiness for I had heard the ettiquete of the Journey was settled that they were not to lodge or dine at a private house, the whole Journey the president gave audience to all the gentlemen of the neighbourhood at the tavern, and when the dinner was ready the gentlemen in waiting attended Mrs Washington back—the two Doctors Witherspoon and Smith with your Brother were the only gentlemen asked to dine with them."[66]

But Stockton did not always accept sex-segregated relegation from conversations of politics or affairs of state. On March 12, 1793, after reading about several resolutions passed in Congress against the banking schemes of the Secretary of the Treasury, she deliberately dipped her quill and wrote an impromptu rustic verse to shine "new lustre on *our* HAMILTON." She then addressed a letter to John Fenno, whose readers, she hoped, would appreciate her enclosed poem. "I am no politician," she deferentially conceded, "but I *feel* that I am a patriot, and glory in that sensation." She decried the accusations against Hamilton that did not seem based in fact, questioned the motivations of his accusers, and concluded by noting that all of her neighbors shared her sentiments.[67] Aware of the gendered bias against women's partisan political activity, Stockton portrayed herself not as a politician but as a patriot. Yet the very subjects of her writing and the act of submitting them to a partisan press were political moves. Her declaration that she was "no politician" may have represented her strategic and self-conscious effort to enter the realm of print under the veil of patriotism without worrying about being "sneered at" for her poetry.[68]

As the previous examples illustrate, Stockton continued to be actively engaged in society—entertaining and being entertained, keeping up with current events and government news, and writing with increased confidence in her authorial voice. She was also not without suitors: the new widowers Samuel Stanhope Smith and John Witherspoon both took interest in the matron of Morven.[69] But after Richard Stockton's death in 1781, Annis remained a widow for almost twenty years and never remarried. She also stood to lose real property and assets if she remarried. Like many widows of her day, she faced financial disarray, unpaid debts, and frightening prospects in the initial aftermath of loss, but this did not seem to result in permanently reduced means.[70] In March 1781, less than a month after her husband's death, the forty-four-year-old, cash-strapped widow advertised for rent a farm with barn and extensive land.[71] In a partially undated letter to Hannah Stockton Boudinot shortly after Richard's death, Annis mourned her husband's passing and lamented that geographic distance kept her from being able to find solace in the company of her sister-in-law. She resigned herself, observing that "to lose the partner of your life in your declining years, and be separated from the only intimate friend of your youth on whose bosom you could pour all your sorrows, is to me daily sources of trouble, but the cross we must bear."[72] If patriotism was her national duty, stoicism in the face of grief was her Christian duty.

Stockton was certainly provided for in her husband's will—as long as she remained unmarried. Richard left her his real and personal estate "during the time She Shall continue to be my Widow, that thereby she may be amply provided with Means to Support herself, and finish the Education of my Younger Children as well as Support and provide for the Children who are already grown up, in such Manner as their Obedience and Affection to her, and the nature of their Situation may require." The language was typical of testamentary practices. Each of the Stockton children received specific bequests of land totaling more than 1,300 acres in New Jersey, with his sons receiving vast additional land interests in Nova Scotia. In the bequest, Annis also received 350 acres of land in Northampton, Pennsylvania, as well as Richard's permission to "free what slaves she wishes."[73]

This last provision sheds light on Annis's role as a slave owner and how the work of unfree labor allowed her the free time to pursue interests such as writing and reading. Although slavery was in slow decline in New Jersey by the late eighteenth century, Annis and Richard Stockton had relied on slave and servant labor to run their family, farm, and estate.[74] By 1790, there were still approximately 11,500 slaves in New Jersey.

Stockton regarded at least some of the enslaved people of her estate almost as family. She maintained an especially close personal bond with one of her slaves, Marcus Marsh, who was born at Morven in 1765, supported the family throughout the Revolution, and obtained his freedom sometime after Richard's death in 1781. He settled in Philadelphia, where he worked as a manservant in the household of Julia and Benjamin Rush.[75] Inquiries about Marcus's well-being, especially when he was sick with influenza and when he was helping Dr. Rush during the yellow fever epidemic of 1793, were a regular part of Stockton's correspondence with the Rush family.[76] Rush updated his wife with reports of Marcus succumbing to the disease and of being twice bled and well purged. When Marcus continued to mend, his value increased, as he could "turn his two hands to a hundred different things" by mixing powders, spreading blisters, and giving clysters (enemas) "equal to any apothecary in town." He served as a courier and caretaker to the ailing doctor and fed him beef soup to restore his health. When Rush recovered, he commended Marcus to his wife, who no doubt related to her mother the feelings expressed in her husband's letter of October 18, 1793: "I cannot tell you how much I owe to the fidelity and affection of our humble black friend. He has been a treasure to us in all our difficulties."[77]

One rainy Sunday morning in early November 1793, when the rest of the family had gone off to church, Stockton, who was homebound with an indisposition, wrote a revealing letter to her son-in-law, who had stayed in Philadelphia to tend to yellow fever patients. In a postscript she wrote, "I can not close this letter without saying a word about my poor Marcus—I cannot express to you what I felt when I read what you have said of the poor fellow in several of your letters when I think of the poor fellow having numberless times sucked at my breast, and of my having brought him up almost as my own son, that he should have been made an instrument of Comfort to my dear Doctor Rush, and of good to any of his fellow creatures, I can not help being truly thankful." She resolved to "write to him by the first private opportunity."[78] Evidently she stayed in touch with the slave whom she had granted freedom. In accordance with her husband's will of May 1780, she could and did use her discretion to manumit any of the family's slaves who behaved with "obedience & fidelity" toward her.[79] She deemed Marcus's service to her and her extended family worth rewarding, for she had freed him after Richard's death and vouched for his liberty in a signed seaman's certificate for the young former slave-turned-mariner in 1798.[80] While we do not know Stockton's attitudes and opinions per se as a slave owner, or whether she had any affiliation with the New Jersey Abolition Society or its members, we do have this glimpse of her intimate affection for an individual household slave whom she later manumitted. At least in this particular slave-mistress relationship, she saw and expressed more of a common humanity than a generalized assumption of power and subordination based on difference.

In her later years, Stockton enjoyed a growing family as sons-in-law and daughters-in-law joined the clan and introduced new children into the group. She delighted in her grandchildren and their learning and welcomed their extended visits.[81] She benefited from ongoing education through her literary salon and polite conversations, from an expanding circle of friends, and from the opportunity to pursue the creative impulses for which she rarely had time as a young wife and mother in the 1760s.

While many women of the Revolution acted on behalf or in place of their husbands, Stockton's use of the pen to redeem the family name and reputation in the eyes of her contemporaries is exceptional. If her husband's loyalties were suspect, it never seemed to harm her seriously as she played the patriot in independent actions and in showing repeated support of Washington and the new federal government.

Stockton was typical of women of her time in her fear of the uncertain outcome of the war and her strategic navigation of conflicted loyalties. Her devotion to immediate and extended family, her lifelong pursuit of spiritual and intellectual improvement, her literacy, and her status as a well-connected member of the wealthy upper class set her apart. These formative influences defined her life and remain evident in the expressions of her pen.

While white women of the eighteenth century often acted as arbiters of credit and reputation, Stockton in wartime and in widowhood expertly navigated this terrain. Her life story seems to parallel New Jersey's own political awakening for women. An expanded franchise for a certain class of propertied white women gave them a chance to exercise their political power, although not all did. We have no ballot proof of whether Stockton joined them, but her story reflects the limits of revolutionary ideology for women. She certainly was privy to the local and national conversation about women's place in civil society.[82] The sites for women's political participation of the era did not lie in the franchise and office holding. Her poems and letters reveal women's increased political consciousness, which was yet to break free fully from patriarchal constraints and the presumed natural order of feminine domesticity.[83]

An active contributor to the republic of letters, Annis Boudinot Stockton, as a woman, could not yet fully participate in the republic of governance. The burden of the family's reputation rested on her shoulders—or, rather, on her pen—as she voiced allegiance to the patriotic cause, visited with George Washington, and helped raise money for his troops with other women of New Jersey. By caring for her family, manumitting her slave Marcus Marsh, and writing and publishing her verses, Stockton participated in a public dialogue that helped forge national identity. Her actions had consequences and reverberations. She used her gendered power armed with emotional effusion and deferential discourse, as well as the agency of authorship, to negotiate her sometimes competing allegiances amid the lived experience of war. By participating as a writer and reader, she contributed to the diffusion of revolutionary sentiment, even though her poetry was revolutionary neither in form nor content.[84] Like Phillis Wheatley, Annis Stockton should be seen as an actor in, and not just a reactor to, the Revolution.[85] Her poetry challenged contemporaries to see women's participation in culture and politics, whether or not women had a full and equal share as that of men.

Notes

1. Her first published poem, "To the Honourable Col. Peter Schuyler," appeared in the *New-York Mercury* on January 9, 1758. The poem's prominent, well-ornamented public debut on the first page of the newspaper appeared with an introductory headnote addressed to the printer Hugh Gaine. See also L. H. Butterfield, "Morven: A Colonial Outpost of Sensibility, with Some Hitherto Unpublished Poems by Annis Boudinot Stockton," *Princeton University Library Chronicle* 6 (November 1944): 8.

2. Paula R. Backsheider, *Eighteenth-Century Women Poets and Their Poetry: Inventing Agency, Inventing Genre* (Baltimore: Johns Hopkins University Press, 2005); Pattie Cowell, *Women Poets in Pre-Revolutionary America, 1650–1775* (Troy, NY: Whitston, 1981); Sharon M. Harris, "Whose Renaissance? Women Writers in the Era of the American Renaissance," *ESQ* 49, nos. 1–3 (2003): 59–80; Caroline Wigginton, *In the Neighborhood: Women's Publication in Early America* (Amherst: University of Massachusetts Press, 2016); Carla Mulford, "Writing Women in Early American Studies: On Canons, Feminist Critique, and the Work of Writing Women into History," *Tulsa Studies in Women's Literature* 26 (Spring 2007): 107–18. For the concept of an epistolary neighborhood, I draw on Caroline Wigginton, "A Late Night Vindication: Annis Boudinot Stockton's Reading of Mary Wollstonecraft's *A Vindication of the Rights of Woman*," *Legacy* 25 (2008): 226–28. She suggests that a woman such as Stockton writing in an epistolary neighborhood engages directly with political and domestic concerns, gaining an audience that allows her to blur lines between public and private. Wigginton also defines a publication as any communication that "*makes public* an expression of its author, invites a reading, submits itself to circulation": Wigginton, *In the Neighborhood*, 5.

3. Carla Mulford, *Only for the Eye of a Friend: The Poems of Annis Boudinot Stockton* (Charlottesville: University Press of Virginia, 1995).

4. Constance M. Greiff and Wanda S. Gunning, *Morven: Memory, Myth and Reality* (Princeton, NJ: Historic Morven, 2004). The introduction is an invaluable assessment of the veracity of the secondary sources and shows how "history can be colored by omission as well as invention" (p. 10).

5. Annette Gordon-Reed, "Writing Early American Lives as Biography," *William and Mary Quarterly*, 3d ser., 71 (October 2014): 491–516. Contrast this with the outdated approach of Elizabeth F. Ellet in *The Women of the American Revolution*, 3 vols. (New York: Scribner, 1856), 3:13.

6. See Wigginton, "A Late Night Vindication," 225–38; Wendy Weston McLallen, "Affectionately Yours: Women's Correspondence Networks in Eighteenth-Century British America" (Ph.D. diss., Florida State University, Tallahassee, 2007), 40–44.

7. For shared manuscript culture and scribal publication and the prevalent existence of literary culture for women, see Angela Vietto, "Daughters of the Tenth Muse: New Histories of Women and Writing in Early America," *Early American Literature* 41 (2006): 555–67, esp. 566.

8. Mulford contends that Stockton was taught reading, writing, and ciphering by a private master alongside her brother Elias: see Carla J. Mulford, "Political Poetics: Annis Boudinot Stockton and Middle Atlantic Women's Culture," *New Jersey History* 111 (Spring–Summer 1993): 72. Greiff and Gunning emphasize Stockton's poor-quality schooling compared with that of the pious and well-educated Esther Edwards Burr: Greiff and Gunning, *Morven*, 27–28. Martha Slotten concludes Annis Boudinot Stockton and Elizabeth Graeme "had received an excellent education": Martha C. Slotten, "Elizabeth Graeme Ferguson: A Poet in 'The Athens of North America,'" *Pennsylvania Magazine of History and Biography* 108 (1984): 276; Annis Boudinot Stockton to Mary Stockton, September 15, 1790, photostat in Stockton Family Additional Papers, C0491, Department of Rare Books and Special Collections, Princeton University Library (hereafter, NjP), box 1, folder 10.

9. "Book of Accounting Belonging to the Academy in Philadelphia," tuition book, January 7, 1751–January 26, 1757, UPA 3, item 1558, Archives General Collection of the University of Pennsylvania, 1740–1820, 1. For girls' education, see *Minutes of the Trustees of the College, Academy and Charitable Schools, Volume 1: 1749–1768*, UPA 1.1, University of Pennsylvania Archives and Records, 37. In her chapter "The Education of a Woman of Quality," Sarah Fatherly stresses the importance of the British educational model for gentry women and the role played in their instruction by advice literature such as *The Female Spectator*: Sarah Fatherly, *Gentlewomen and Learned Ladies: Women and Elite Formation in Eighteenth-Century Philadelphia* (Bethlehem, PA: Rowman and Littlefield, 2008), 68–91. See also Carla Mulford, "Benjamin Franklin, Traditions of Liberalism, and Women's Learning in Eighteenth-Century Philadelphia," in *"The Good Education of Youth": Worlds of Learning in the Age of Franklin*, ed. John H. Pollack (New Castle, DE: Oak Knoll, 2009), 100–21.

10. Alfred Hoyt Bill, *A House Called Morven: Its Role in American History*, rev. ed. (1954; reprint, Princeton, NJ: Princeton University Press, 1978), 19.

11. For heterosocial friendships in the early republic, see Cassandra A. Good, "Friendly Relations: Situating Friendships between Men and Women in the Early American Republic, 1780–1830," *Gender and History* 24 (April 2012): 18–34. See also Jacob Read to Annis Boudinot Stockton, February 1, 1784, in *Letters of Delegates to Congress, 1774–1789*, ed. Paul H. Smith, 26 vols. (Washington, DC: Library of Congress, 1976–2000): 21:320–22.

12. Esther Burr to Sarah Prince, December 10, 1756, in Carol F. Karlsen and Laurie Crumpacker, eds., *The Journal of Esther Edwards Burr, 1754–1757* (New Haven, CT: Yale University Press, 1984), 236.

13. Esther Burr to Sarah Prince, April 11, 1757, in Karlsen and Crumpacker, eds., *The Journal of Esther Edwards Burr*, 256.

14. For "knot of friends" metaphor, see Annis Boudinot Stockton to Elizabeth Graeme, January 28, 1769, Stockton Family Additional Papers, CO491, NjP, box 1, folder 9.

15. Aaron Burr's death from malaria in 1757 left Esther a young widow with small children and in dire need of close friends: Karlsen and Crumpacker, eds., *The Journal of Esther Edwards Burr*, 13–18.

16. Annis Boudinot Stockton to Aaron Burr, [1776], notice in Henkels dealer's catalogue, December 6, 1892, item 328, in Mary-Jo Kline, ed., *The Papers of Aaron Burr, 1756–1836*, microfilm ed., 27 reels (Glen Rock, NJ: Microfilming Corporation of America, 1978): 1:185.

17. Among those who frequented these literary salons were Benjamin and Julia Rush, Francis Hopkinson, John Morgan, Thomas Godfrey Jr., Nathaniel Evans, Jacob Duché, and Anna Young Smith. For Elizabeth Graeme Fergusson, see Anne M. Ousterhout, *The Most Learned Woman in America: A Life of Elizabeth Graeme Fergusson* (University Park: Pennsylvania State University Press, 2004). Annis Boudinot Stockton's son-in-law Benjamin Rush introduced Elizabeth to her future husband, Hugh Henry Fergusson, in late 1771, and the couple secretly married five months later. Elizabeth endured the reputed infidelities of her husband, as well as his frequent absences and ultimate alignment with the British Army after he spent much time abroad. There was also a shadow over Elizabeth's allegiance to the patriot cause when she became involved as a courier for some assumed traitorous correspondence. Her Graeme Park home was seized in 1778, and colonial authorities did not restore its title to her until 1781. Stockton probably had to juggle compassionate loyalty to a beloved friend who had been a deserted wife of a loyalist husband during the war with the need to balance her own family's reputation: Rodney Mader, "Elizabeth Graeme Fergusson's 'The Deserted Wife,'" *Pennsylvania Magazine of History and Biography* 135 (April 2011): 151–90.

18. Greiff and Gunning, *Morven*, 16, 24, 27.

19. The Stockton children who lived beyond infancy were Julia (b. 1759), the twins Mary and Susan (b. 1761), Richard (b. April 1764), Lucius Horatio (b. 1768), and Abigail (b. 1773).

20. Susan E. Klepp, "Revolutionary Bodies: Women and the Fertility Transition in the Mid-Atlantic Region, 1760–1820," *Journal of American History* 85 (December 1998): 920–21, 927, 930. Klepp focuses selectively on a poetic stanza circa 1793: "They despise us poor females, and say that our sphere/Must move in the kitchen or heaven knows where/The nursery, the pantry, the dairy is made/The theatre on which our worth is display'd."

21. The fullest anthology of Stockton's dated and undated poems on these and other themes and occasions is Mulford, *Only for the Eye of a Friend*.

22. Rachel Hope Cleves shows that spontaneous poems or extempore rhymes demonstrated one's cultural capital in the Anglo-American world: Rachel Hope Cleves, "'Heedless Youth': The Revolutionary War Poetry of Ruth Bryant (1760–83)," *William and Mary Quarterly*, 3d ser., 67 (July 2010): 533.

23. Greiff and Gunning, *Morven*, 7.

24. "Richard Stockton," in John A. Garraty and Mark C. Carnes, eds., *American National Biography*, 24 vols. (New York, 1999): 20:813–14. L. H. Butterfield, *John*

Witherspoon Comes to America: A Documentary Account Based Largely on New Materials (Princeton, NJ: Princeton University Library, 1953). It was during his trip to Edinburgh that Richard Stockton got to know the young Philadelphia doctor Benjamin Rush, fellow signer of the Declaration of Independence and frequent visitor at the Stockton home.

25. Robb K. Haberman, "Periodical Publics: Magazines and Literary Networks in Post-Revolutionary America" (Ph.D. diss., University of Connecticut, Storrs, 2009), chap. 2, esp. 54–59.

26. Stockton to Graeme, January 28, 1769.

27. Religion and spirituality were important supports for Stockton throughout her life. Although she was baptized in the Anglican Christ Church in Philadelphia, she attended the Presbyterian church in Princeton with her husband: Greiff and Gunning, *Morven*, 10. Ellet gives extensive treatment of Richard's letters to his wife from his time abroad: Ellet, *Women of the American Revolution*, 3:14–34. For an especially poignant letter that captures the mutual love, religious foundations, and health anxieties of the couple, written while Richard was in Philadelphia recovering from surgery for his cancerous lip, see Richard Stockton to Annis Boudinot Stockton, December 9, 1778, Etting Papers, Signers, Historical Society of Pennsylvania, Philadelphia (hereafter, PHi), box 18, vol. 5:90.

28. For the Revolution in New Jersey, see Larry R. Gerlach, *Prologue to Independence: New Jersey in the Coming of the American Revolution* (New Brunswick, NJ: Rutgers University Press, 1976); James J. Gigantino II, *The Ragged Road to Abolition: Slavery and Freedom in New Jersey, 1775–1865* (Philadelphia: University of Pennsylvania Press, 2015), 34–39; Bill, *A House Called Morven*, 38–42. For insights on the Revolution as civil war and the difficult choices members of the same family faced in wartime alignments, see Sheila L. Skemp, *Benjamin and William Franklin, Father and Son, Patriot and Loyalist* (Boston: St. Martin's, 1994); Judith Van Buskirk, "They Didn't Join the Band: Disaffected Women in Revolutionary Philadelphia," *Pennsylvania History* 62 (Summer 1995): 306–29.

29. Mulford, *Only for the Eye of a Friend*, 24, 52 n. 89; J. Jefferson Looney, *Nurseries of Letters and Republicanism: A Brief History of the American Whig-Cliosophic Society and Its Predecessors, 1765–1941* (Princeton, NJ: Trustees of the American Whig-Cliosophic Society, 1996), 9. In addition to the society's papers, Stockton took into safekeeping its brass andirons, a pair of candlesticks, a mirror, and a copy of Samuel Johnson's *Dictionary*. For her actions, she was given retroactive recognition and, in 1869, awarded honorary membership in this all-male society.

30. Benjamin Rush to Richard Henry Lee, December 30, 1776, in Smith, *Letters of Delegates to Congress*, 5:706.

31. Worthington C. Ford, ed., *Journals of the Continental Congress*, 34 vols. (Washington, DC: U.S. Government Printing Office, 1904–37): 7:12–13.

32. In late November, Lord William Howe offered full pardon with assurance of liberty and enjoyment of their property to all who within sixty days would "remain in a peaceful Obedience to His Majesty and not take up arms, nor encourage others to take up arms, in Opposition to His Authority": quoted in Bill, *A House Called Morven*, 41).

33. Ibid., 35.

34. John Witherspoon to David Witherspoon, March 17, 1777, in Smith, *Letters of Delegates to Congress*, 6:455–56.

35. Bill, *A House Called Morven*, 40–41. Will of Richard Stockton, May 20, 1780, Stockton Family Additional Papers, CO491, NjP, box 1, folder 64.

36. Robert Stockton's report on damage to college and church at Princeton by the Continental Army, 1777–78, Stockton Family Additional Papers, CO491, NjP, box 2.

37. See, e.g., Annis Boudinot Stockton to Elisha Boudinot, June 15, 1784, Boudinot Family Collection, CO725, NjP, box 1, folder 8; Annis Boudinot Stockton to Elizabeth Graeme Fergusson, November 24, 1780, Simon Gratz Collection, PHi, box 7/9, folder 42.

38. Greiff and Gunning, *Morven*, 44–45.

39. See Dena Goodman, "Enlightenment Salons: The Convergence of Female and Philosophic Ambitions," *Eighteenth-Century Studies*, 22 (1989): 329–50; Susan Stabile, "Salons and Power in the Era of Revolution," in Larry E. Tise, ed., *Benjamin Franklin and Women* (Philadelphia: Pennsylvania State University Press, 2000), 129–48.

40. Cleves, "Heedless Youth," 524.

41. On the Philadelphia Ladies Association, see Vivian Bruce Conger, "Reading Early American Women's Political Lives: The Revolutionary Performances of Deborah Read Franklin and Sally Franklin Bache," *Early American Studies* 16 (Spring 2018): esp. 341–49.

42. See Mary V. Thompson, " 'As if I Had Been a Very Great Somebody': Martha Washington's Revolution," in this volume.

43. Mary Beth Norton, *Liberty's Daughters: The Revolutionary Experience of American Women, 1750–1800* (Ithaca, NY: Cornell University Press, 1980), 178–81.

44. *New-Jersey Gazette* (Trenton), July 5, 1780.

45. Samuel Stanhope Smith, *A Funeral Sermon, on the Death of the Hon. Richard Stockton, Esq. Princeton, March 2, 1781* (Trenton, NJ: Isaac Collins, 1781), Early American Imprints, Series 1: Evans no. 17371, 45.

46. For an insightful argument on strategic anonymity, see Gay Gibson Cima, "Black and Unmarked: Phillis Wheatley, Mercy Otis Warren, and the Limits of Strategic Anonymity," *Theatre Journal* 52 (December 2000): 465–95.

47. Elias Boudinot to Elizabeth Graeme Fergusson, May 11, 1796, Stimson Collection of Elias Boudinot, CO228, NjP, box 1, folder 19; Elias Boudinot to George Washington, January 4, 1779, Revolutionary War Series, June 16, 1775–December 31, 1783, in *The Papers of George Washington Digital Edition*, ed. Theodore J. Crackel (Charlottesville: University of Virginia Press, 2007–), http://rotunda.upress.virginia.edu/founders/GEWN-03-18-02-0634.

48. See, e.g., Elias Boudinot to George Washington, January 11, 1784, Confederation Series, and Elias Boudinot to George Washington, April 6, 1789, Presidential Series, September 24, 1788–March 3, 1796, both in Crackel, *The Papers of George Washington Digital Edition*, http://rotunda.upress.virginia.edu/founders/GEWN-04-01-02-0022, http://rotunda.upress.virginia.edu/founders/GEWN-05-02-02-0023.

49. Elias Boudinot to George Washington, January 4, 1779. For Washington's reply, on February 27, 1779, see Revolutionary War Series, June 16, 1775–December 31, 1783, in Crackel, *The Papers of George Washington Digital Edition*, http://rotunda.upress.virginia.edu/founders/GEWN-03-19-02-0306

50. Annis Boudinot Stockton to Elias Boudinot, May 1, 1789, quoted in L. H. Butterfield, "Annis and the General: Mrs. Stockton's Poetic Eulogies of George Washington," *Princeton University Library Chronicle* 7 (November 1945): 39.

51. Mulford, "Writing Women in Early American Studies," 112–13.

52. Rosemarie Zagarri, *Revolutionary Backlash: Women and Politics in the Early American Republic* (Philadelphia: University of Pennsylvania Press, 2007), 58–61.

53. *Gazette of the United States* (New York), May 13–16, 1789.

54. Annis Boudinot Stockton to Elias Boudinot, February 23, 1790, Boudinot Collection, CO725, NjP, folder 19. For a helpful analysis of John Fenno, see Jeffrey L. Pasley, *"The Tyranny of Printers": Newspaper Politics in the Early American Republic* (Charlottesville: University Press of Virginia, 2001), 51–60.

55. Cleves, "Heedless Youth," 526.

56. Ibid., 536–37. Elegies were considered an acceptable form of poetry for women authors. See also Wigginton, *In the Neighborhood*, 96–97.

57. Butterfield, "Annis and the General," 1–39.

58. Annis Boudinot Stockton to Elias Boudinot, October 23, [1781], quoted in ibid., 25.

59. George Washington to Annis Boudinot Stockton, July 22, 1782, PHi, quoted in Butterfield, "Annis and the General," 26.

60. Annis Boudinot Stockton to George Washington, September 1, 1783, in *George Washington Papers, Series 4, General Correspondence,* Library of Congress, https://www.loc.gov/item/mgw434510. The poem is dated August 28, 1783.

61. George Washington to Annis Boudinot Stockton, September 2, 1783, quoted in Butterfield, "Annis and the General," 28–29.

62. George Washington to Annis Boudinot Stockton, August 31, 1788, Confederation Series, January 1, 1784–September 23, 1788, in Crackel, *The Papers of George Washington Digital Edition,* http://rotunda.upress.virginia.edu/founders/GEWN -04-06-02-0442.

63. Annis Boudinot Stockton to George Washington, March 13, 1789, Presidential Series, September 24, 1788–March 3, 1796, in Crackel, *The Papers of George Washington Digital Edition,* http://rotunda.upress.virginia.edu/founders/GEWN-05 -01-02-0298.

64. George Washington to the Ladies of Trenton, April 21, 1789, Presidential Series, September 24, 1788–March 3, 1796, in Crackel, *The Papers of George Washington Digital Edition,* http://rotunda.upress.virginia.edu/founders/GEWN-05-02-02 -0095. The Trenton printer Isaac Collins produced a broadside of the sonata to mark Washington's inaugural journey: Early American Imprints, Series 1: Evans no. 22094.

65. Annis Boudinot Stockton to George Washington, May 1, 1789, and enclosure, Presidential Series, September 24, 1788–March 3, 1796, in Crackel, *The Papers of George Washington Digital Edition,* http://rotunda.upress.virginia.edu/founders /GEWN-05-02-02-0136.

66. Annis Boudinot Stockton to Mary Stockton, September 15 and 24, 1790, Stockton Family Additional Papers, photostat in CO491, NjP, box 1, folder 10.

67. *Gazette of the United States* (Philadelphia), March 13, 1793. For the resolutions against the official conduct of Treasury Secretary Alexander Hamilton that were debated in the House of Representatives on March 1, see *Gazette of the United States* Philadelphia, March 6, 1793. Carla Mulford was the first to attribute this poem to Stockton: Mulford, *Only for the Eye of a Friend*, 174–75.

68. Stockton used the common poetic convention of deference and appearing weak and in so doing acknowledged a system that subjugated women while mocking the very men who would do so: ibid., 9.

69. For Smith's effusive letters, see Samuel Stanhope Smith, 1786–91, General Manuscripts Bound, CO199, NjP. For Witherspoon's interest, see Bill, *A House Called Morven*, 67.

70. Annis Boudinot Stockton's financial concerns in early widowhood, in which she was "so dependant on other people" and "so cruely used in money matters" that she contemplated exercising her right to sue debtors or seize and sell their property, are evident in Annis Boudinot Stockton to Elisha Boudinot, June 15, 1784.

71. Isaac Collins ran the ad, dated March 26, 1781, in his *New-Jersey Gazette* on April 4, 1781. Four years later, he ran another, this time for the sale of "a valuable farm" of 280 acres near Princeton and covered mostly with "excellent timber" with a dwelling house and barn in need of repair. The sale was offered with easy terms of payment and enquiries to be directed to Benjamin Rush of Philadelphia or Richard Stockton Jr. of Princeton: *New-Jersey Gazette*, September 26, 1785.

72. Annis Boudinot Stockton to Mrs. Elias Boudinot, March 24, [1781?], Boudinot Family Collection, CO725, NjP, folder 19.

73. Will of Richard Stockton; Elmer T. Hutchinson, ed., *New Jersey State Archives, Calendar of New Jersey Wills, Administrations, Etc.*, 1st ser., vol. 6 (Trenton, NJ: MacCrellish and Quigley, 1939), 375.

74. For recent scholarship on the role of slavery in New Jersey, see Gigantino, *The Ragged Road to Abolition*, chaps. 1–4, esp. chap. 2.

75. On December 5, 1793, Marcus Marsh married Martha Wright at Old St. Paul's Church in Philadelphia. Philadelphia directories for 1796 and 1797 list his occupation as "mariner" and his residence as Spruce Street: Historic Pennsylvania Church and Town Records, reel 240, PHi; *Stephen's Philadelphia Directory for 1796* (Philadelphia: William W. Woodward, 1796), 117; Cornelius William Stafford, *Philadelphia Directory for 1797* (Philadelphia: William W. Woodward, 1797), 123.

76. Jacquelyn C. Miller, "The Wages of Blackness: African American Workers and the Meanings of Race during Philadelphia's 1793 Yellow Fever Epidemic," *Pennsylvania Magazine of History and Biography* 129 (April 2005): 163–94, esp. 176, 188; Alexander Biddle, *Old Family Letters Relating to the Yellow Fever*, ser. B (Philadelphia: J. B. Lippincott, 1892), 4, 36–38, 40, 46–47, 71, 75, 79–89, 101. See also Emily Rush to Benjamin Rush, October 18, 1793, Benjamin Rush Papers, ser. 1, Yellow Fever, PHi, vol. 36:90.

77. Benjamin Rush to Julia Stockton Rush, October 17, 1793, in *Letters of Benjamin Rush*, ed. L. H. Butterfield, 2 vols. (Princeton, NJ: Princeton University Press, 1951), 2:717.

78. Annis Boudinot Stockton to Benjamin Rush, November 3, 1793, Benjamin Rush Papers, ser. 1, Yellow Fever, PHi, vol. 36:120. Annis was likely still nursing her own son Richard, born April 1764, at the time Marcus Marsh was born in 1765. For the practice of mixed-race wet nursing, see Diane Mutti Burke, *On Slavery's Borders: Missouri's Small Slaveholding Households, 1815–1865* (Athens: University of Georgia Press, 2010), 157–60; Nora Doyle, "'The Highest Pleasure of Which Woman's Nature Is Capable': Breast-Feeding and the Sentimental Maternal Ideal in America, 1750–1860," *Journal of American History* 97 (March 2011): 958–73; Janet Golden, *A Social History of Wet Nursing in America: From Breast to Bottle* (New York: Cambridge University Press, 1996).

79. Will of Richard Stockton; Greiff and Gunning, *Morven*, 45.

80. Seaman's Protection Certificate for Marcus Marsh, March 2, 1798, in *Proofs of Citizenship Used to Apply for Seamen's Certificates for the Port of Philadelphia, 1792–1861*, RG 36, National Archives and Records Administration, Washington, DC.

81. For her "dear little flock" of grandchildren, see Annis Boudinot Stockton to Mary Stockton, September 15–24, 1790.

82. See, e.g., her commentary on women's equality to men and on women's intellectual development after reading Mary Wollstonecraft in Annis Boudinot Stockton to Julia Rush, March 22, 1793: Wigginton, "A Late Night Vindication," 225–38; Mulford, *Only for the Eye of a Friend*, 304–7.

83. For New Jersey's temporary suffrage for women, see Zagarri, *Revolutionary Backlash*, esp. 30–37. For Annis Boudinot Stockton's ultimate acceptance of patriarchal structures by the end of her life, see Mulford, "Political Poetics," 78–79. On feminine domesticity, see Brian Steele, "Thomas Jefferson's Gender Frontier," *Journal of American History* 95 (June 2008): 17–42.

84. Cleves, "Heedless Youth," 523, 526.

85. See David Waldstreicher, "The Wheatleyan Moment," *Early American Studies* 9 (Fall 2011): 522–51, esp. 527, and David Waldstreicher, "Women's Politics, Antislavery Politics, and Phillis Wheatley's American Revolution," in this volume.

"As if I Had Been a Very Great Somebody"

Martha Washington's Revolution

MARY V. THOMPSON

For years, Mount Vernon has told visitors during their tours of the mansion that Martha Washington spent every winter of the Revolution with her husband at his military headquarters. Often, the trunk her eldest granddaughter identified as the one Martha used in the war has been pointed out to them, along with Eliza Custis Law's note detailing her sadness when, as a small child, she watched her grandmother packing each fall, but also her joy the following spring, when her beloved "Grandmama" would unpack this same trunk, filled with toys for the youngest members of her family.[1] Visitors would seem interested, but I am not sure that they, or even we, really understood the impact of the statement "Martha Washington spent every winter of the Revolution with her husband at his military headquarters." That changed in 2002, when we began the commemoration of the two-hundredth anniversary of Martha Washington's death and suddenly realized that very little scholarly research had been done on her. That year I looked into many aspects of her life but spent most of my time concentrating on her experiences during the war.

What does not really strike home with the words "Martha Washington spent every winter of the Revolution with her husband at his military headquarters" is the impact of this travel and these events on her life. Now, when a person can, in theory, drive from Mount Vernon to Boston in eight hours or less—or even fly there in an hour—there is no appreciation of the physical punishment of several weeks to a month of travel, one way, to go the same distance. "Military headquarters" suggests parties and interactions with other officers and their wives but seems relatively comfortable, without any hint of threat to personal safety. "Spending the winter" sounds as though she was in camp for maybe three months at most each year. Actually, while she was with her husband for only two to three months in the second year of the war, in some years the Washingtons were together more than they were apart—for example, for eight to nine months in the first year of the war; four months in the third; six months in the fourth and sixth years; seven months in the fifth year; eight months in the seventh year; and eleven months in the last year of the war. In total, Martha Washington spent 52–54 of the roughly 103 months of the war (April 1775–December 1783)—or almost half of the time—either with her husband in camp or nearby in the hope that they could spend more time together.

Our knowledge about this period in Martha Washington's life has been hampered by several factors, the most important being a dearth of direct information. Except for a brief time during the Yorktown campaign, George Washington did not keep a diary during the war years; his wife never kept one. In addition, two important sets of papers were destroyed, probably to protect the privacy of the people involved. In the first instance, many letters from George Washington to his cousin Lund, who managed Mount Vernon during the war, were burned by Lund's widow sometime after his death in 1796. Then, in the two-and-a half years between George Washington's death and her own, Martha likewise burned forty years of correspondence between herself and her husband.[2] Additional obstacles to understanding Martha Washington's life during the war have been thrown up by earlier biographers of both her and her husband. Nineteenth-century treatments of Martha Washington typically depict a saintly woman, constantly knitting stockings for soldiers and caring for the sick, generally without citing the sources of that information, which in several cases are surely fabricated.[3] In the twentieth century, historians focused on George Washington have shown a tendency to dismiss any impact Martha may have had on his life, save for a financial one, which enabled his rapid ascent into the upper strata of the Virginia gentry.[4] As a result, comparatively little is known about Martha Washington's life as a whole, and especially about the period of the Revolution. Privately, she and George shared experiences during the war—victory, adulation, defeat, hardship, separation, the loss of loved ones—that brought them immeasurable sadness and great joy, the kinds of things that either break or strengthen the bond between couples. During those eight long years, she came to know many of the most important figures of the day; traveled to other parts of the country, where life was very different from Virginia; and served as a bridge between her very busy husband and officials, foreign and domestic, who came to meet him. In the process, Martha Washington was quietly transformed into the new nation's First Lady, something she would not even realize until many years later.

On the plus side, this project was undertaken eight years after the publication of Martha Washington's surviving correspondence, in a volume edited by Joseph E. Fields fittingly titled, *"Worthy Partner": The Papers of Martha Washington*. A second thing for which to be thankful was that a new edition of George Washington's papers was in the process of being pub-lished by the University of Virginia Press. Including both his incoming and outgoing correspondence, and enhanced with excellent footnotes identify-ing people, places, and incidents mentioned in the text of the letters, this edition of the Washington papers has about another decade to go before it is finished. In addition, surviving financial records from both Mount Ver-non and Washington's headquarters during the war provide insights not found in the correspondence.

The loss of so many family papers from the period of the war made it necessary to turn to sources left by the Washingtons' contemporaries. The papers of Thomas Jefferson, Alexander Hamilton, the Marquis de Lafa-yette, and Nathanael Greene have been especially helpful. Further down the social ladder, the diaries and reminiscences of American and French soldiers often mention Martha Washington, as do period newspapers.

A number of historians have turned their attention to the roles women played during the Revolution. Throughout the war, both out of love for their spouses and because many could not support themselves in the absence of their husbands, the wives of common soldiers often followed their husbands during their campaigns, many with small children in tow. In camp they took on the important and necessary, but still largely unofficial, roles of cooks, laundresses, and nurses for the army. The exact number of American women who lived this rugged life is unknown; however, at least one historian has noted that there were fewer women with the Continen-tal Army than among their enemies. British forces during the Revolution, for example, averaged about one woman for every one-and-a-half soldiers, while the Hessians had one woman for every fifteen men, the same ratio allowed the Continental Army by Congress. Although they slowed down an army on the march, these women provided services that were invaluable.[5]

Unlike those married to soldiers, the wives of American generals and other officers rarely traveled with the army during campaigns, but they did spend time with their spouses when the army went into winter quarters. There they typically had no responsibilities beyond teas, dinners, dances, and keeping up the morale of the army—and one another. In short, their "value to the army was symbolic rather than practical. . . . [Their] presence, even under privileged conditions, was a declaration that everyone, even wealthy wives and mothers, was willing to make sacrifices for the Revolution."[6]

The buildup to war began slowly, over a period of about a dozen years, from the end of the Seven Years' War in 1763 to the spring of 1775, when fighting broke out in the towns of Lexington and Concord, near Boston. Martha Washington, while preoccupied with raising children during much of this time, would have been aware of the growing discontent with British colonial policy through her husband's position in the House of Burgesses, as well as from reading newspapers and conversing with family, friends, and neighbors throughout Virginia.[7] In September 1774, George Washington and two other Virginia delegates left from Mount Vernon to attend the First Continental Congress in Philadelphia, where representatives from each of the colonies could discuss the deteriorating political situation and determine the best way to respond to it. As he, Patrick Henry, and Edmund Pendleton prepared to set off, Martha Washington made clear her loyalty to the American cause, inspiring this verbal portrait of her by Pendleton as her world began to change: "I was much pleased with Mrs. Washington and her spirit. She seemed ready to make any sacrifice and was cheerful though I knew she felt anxious. She talked like a Spartan mother to her son on going to battle. 'I hope you will stand firm—I know George will,' she said." As the gentlemen left, "She stood in the door and cheered us with the good words, 'God be with you gentlemen.'"[8]

Martha Washington would remain loyal to the Revolution, but a large part of her faithfulness to the American cause grew out of her attachment to her husband. This comes through most strongly when the illnesses and deaths of family members pulled her in several directions. Shortly before Christmas in 1777, for example, she learned that her favorite sister had died. She wrote from Mount Vernon to assure her newly widowed brother-in-law, "[N]othing in this world do I wish for more sincerly than to be with [you], but alass I am so situated at this time that I cannot leve home. . . . [T]he General has wrote to me that he cannot come home this winter but as soon as the army under his command goes into winter quarter[s] he will send for me, if he does I must go."[9] A letter written the following year shows just how contrary to her own wishes all this travel actually was. Upon learning of the severe illness of her mother, she remarked wistfully to one of her brothers, "I wish I was near enough to come to see you and her. I am very uneasy at this time—I have some reason to expect that I shall take another trip . . . northward. The pore General is not likely to come to see us from what I can hear—I expect to hear seertainly by the next post . . . if I am so happy [as] to stay at home."[10]

Throughout the Revolution, clues to the Washingtons' relationship pop up in many different places. George Washington's worries about his wife come across strongly in a series of letters he sent to relatives shortly after his appointment as commander of the Continental Army in the summer of 1775. Seventeen years earlier, according to an Englishman who knew the Washingtons before the Revolution, Washington had exchanged his military career for life on a plantation and a seat in the Virginia House of Burgesses because of the "entreaties" of his wife-to-be, the twenty-six-year-old widow Martha Dandridge Custis.[11] Now, as he was telling his stepson Jack about his new responsibilities, Washington confided, "My great concern upon this occasion is, the thought of leaving your mother under the uneasiness which I fear this affair will throw her into; I therefore hope, expect, and indeed have no doubt, of your using every means in your power to keep up her spirits, by doing everything in your power to promote her quiet." He told Jack that he and his bride, Nelly, were always welcome to stay at Mount Vernon, especially at this juncture, "when I think it absolutely necessary for the peace and satisfaction of your mother."[12] It was not just the immediate family who were asked to help Martha Washington get over the shock and loneliness of her husband's absence; relatives and even friends from quite some distance away were also recruited for the task.[13]

Several people who saw the Washingtons during the war recorded the couple's delight at being reunited at camp. The year 1777 was the one in which they were able to spend the least amount of time together. Following Washington's victories at the end of 1776 and the beginning of 1777, his army made its way to winter quarters at Morristown, New Jersey, for the remainder of the season. Martha Washington left Mount Vernon in March, spending a few days in Philadelphia before traveling on to headquarters.[14] One officer, Nathanael Greene, commented to his wife that "Mrs Washington and Mrs Bland [another officer's wife] from Virginia are at Camp, happy in their better halves. Mrs Washington is excessive fond of the General and he of her. They are very happy in each other."[15] Mrs. Bland sent her sister-in-law a long description of how the Washingtons spent their days in camp that year, noting that George Washington's "Worthy Lady seems to be in perfect felicity while she is by the side of her *Old Man* as she calls him, we often make partys on Horse back." Washington's cheerfulness at the presence of his wife was noted, as well, for Mrs. Bland wrote that during these riding parties "General Washington throws of[f] the Hero—and takes on the chatty agreable companion—he can be down right impudent sometimes—such impudence, Fanny, as you and I like."[16]

These descriptions were echoed the following year, as the Continental Army struggled to survive at Valley Forge. The Marquis de Lafayette wrote to his young wife in France about the presence of other officers' wives that year: "Several general officers have brought their wives to camp, and I am very envious . . . of the pleasure they have in being able to see them. General Washington has also just decided to send for his wife, a modest and respectable person, who loves her husband madly."[17]

In traveling to meet her husband for each of the eight years of the war, Martha Washington had to overcome a number of obstacles, including threats to her safety. Early in the war, much of the surviving correspondence between George Washington and his cousin Lund Washington dealt with concerns that the wife of the commanding general of the Continental Army might be targeted by the British. The general wrote in late August 1775 that he could "hardly think that Lord Dunmore [the royal governor of Virginia] can act so low, so unmanly a part, as to think of seizing Mrs. Washington by way of revenge upon me." He was comforted that for the next couple of months she would be away from home, visiting friends and relatives, and so would "be out of [Dunmore's] reach for 2 or 3 months to come," after which, he hoped, events would play out in such a way "as to render her removal either absolutely necessary, or quite useless." He thanked some unnamed "Gentlemen of Alexandria for their friendly attention on this point" and asked that, should Lund believe there was any hint that Martha was in danger, he "provide a . . . place of safety elsewhere for her and my Papers."[18] In preparation, Martha insisted on packing her husband's papers in a trunk by herself, making them ready for a speedy evacuation if necessary.[19]

Concerns that Martha Washington might be a target of the British continued throughout the war. In the late spring of 1780, military action began after the winter hiatus with a British push into New Jersey. George Washington and his staff had been gone from his Morristown headquarters for several days in early June when a young officer assigned to guard Martha left an interesting description of the commander's wife: "I am at present enjoying myself incomparably well in the family of Mrs. Washington, whose guard I have had the honor to command since the absence of the General. . . . I am happy in the importance of my charge, as well as the presence of the most amiable woman upon Earth, whose character should I attempt to describe I could not do justice to. . . . [T]he first and second nights after I came it was expected that a body of the Enemy's horse would pay us a visit, but I was well prepared to receive them."[20]

There was also a threat of physical harm from enemy bombardment. During the first winter of the conflict, Martha Washington wrote to a friend about her concern for the citizens of Boston and Charlestown and how shaken she was at hearing British artillery:

[S]ome days we have a number of cannon and shells from Boston and Bunkers Hill, but it does not seem to surprise any one but me; I confess I shudder every time I hear the sound of a gun . . . I just took a look at pore Boston & Charlstown—from prospect Hill Charlestown has only a few chimneys standing in it, thare seems to be a number of very fine Buildings in Boston but god knows how long they will stand; they are pulling up all the warfs for firewood—to me that never see any thing of war, the preparations, are very terable indeed, but I endever to keep my fears to myself as well as I can.[21]

Not just capture and wayward artillery but also illness threatened Martha Washington's safety during the war. The military camps brought together men from different parts of the country, from relatively isolated farms and small communities, into crowded conditions, where they came into contact with disease-causing agents from other areas to which they had no immunity. With their resistance stressed to the breaking point from various factors—being away from home, inadequate food, lack of proper hygiene, introduction to military discipline, and understandable fears about being in battle—disease was rampant. Especially in the early years of the Revolution, one of the biggest challenges to the survival of the American army was smallpox, which remained a threat until George Washington instituted a regular program of quarantine and inoculation to deal with the problem.[22] Martha Washington would have been introduced to these conditions, especially to the danger of smallpox, during that first winter in Cambridge, and it was sometime during that initial stay that she made the decision to be inoculated herself, a choice that would have an impact on her future ability to come to headquarters. Washington wrote from New York at the end of April 1776 that his wife was considering inoculation, although he doubted "her resolution."[23]

In expressing concern that Martha might not go through with the procedure, George was undoubtedly thinking back several years to when his stepson was a teenager. Jack Custis's schoolmaster had insisted that the boy be inoculated before making a Grand Tour to Europe, a trip that never materialized. Inoculation involved inserting a bit of infectious material from the sores of a smallpox patient into the arm of a person who had never had the disease, leading to a very mild—and less dangerous—case and consequent lifelong immunity from this dreaded scourge. Martha Washington had been so anxious about the possibility that young Custis might die as a result of the procedure that she was not told until after he had completely recovered.[24] The fact that, five years later, she was willing to risk inoculation herself probably says as much about her attachment to her husband as does her willingness to travel such great distances during the war to be with him.

In May 1776, Martha Washington underwent inoculation in Philadelphia.[25] The result was a very mild case of smallpox—George Washington noted that after thirteen days she had only a "very few Pustules" and eventually reported that she had "got through the Fever and not more than about a dozen Pustules appearing."[26] When he learned how successful the procedure had been, her son Jack Custis responded with a very telling statement about his parents' relationship: "[It] gave Me the sincerest pleasure: to hear; that my dearest Mother had gone through the Smalpox so favourably . . . as

She can now attend you to any Part of the Continent with pleasure, unsullied by the Apprehensions of that Disorder." Noting that her "Presence will alleviate the Care and Anxiety which public Transactions may occasion" for his stepfather, he closed with the observation, "[your] Happiness when together will be much greater than when you are apart."[27]

It was during the same month-long period that Martha was recovering from the inoculation that the first hints came of the couple's growing popularity: John Hancock ordered portraits of them both. On May 19, the artist Charles Willson Peale, who had first painted the couple in 1772, recorded in his diary that "Mr. Hancock bespoke the Portrait of Genl Washington & Lady." Six days later, Martha sat for a half-length portrait, as she did again on May 30. George Washington went to Peale's to have his started on May 29.[28] Peale kept the paintings on view in his studio for the remainder of the year so other potential customers could see them and order copies.[29] Later in the war, on March 26, 1782, a pair of companion portraits of the Washingtons was published in Boston by John Coles. Among the earliest engraved portraits of these subjects, they were the work of John Norman, an English-born engraver who was probably the first in America to do a printed portrait of George Washington in about 1779. The Norman engravings were based on drawings done by Benjamin Blyth, an engraver and portrait draughtsman, who worked in pastels.[30] In almost full-face views of the couple, George was depicted in his Continental Army uniform surrounded by cannons, drums, and flags, while Martha, wearing a ribbon around her neck, a beribboned cap, and a low-cut gown, was set among floral garlands.[31] Less expensive than the paintings done earlier for John Hancock, the engravings were intended for a wider audience, where they would not only provide income for their creators but would also meet a need for those Americans, with fewer financial resources than Hancock, who also wanted to have something tangible in their homes to express their political affiliations and their affection for the Washingtons.

While Martha Washington sometimes acted as a secretary in the busy headquarters, making copies of letters for the record, her most important function, as for the other generals' wives, was social.[32] George Washington found himself with a diplomatic role during the war. Prominent Americans and Europeans came to camp to meet him, closely observing both him and his soldiers, to determine the viability of the American cause. Washington's ability to come across as a well-mannered and educated gentleman lent credibility to the American government in the eyes of both fellow citizens and foreigners.[33] Having an experienced hostess at his side who naturally drew people to her helped that impression as much as the fact that fashionable ceramics and silver were used on the table at headquarters. Martha

Washington's warmth and friendliness could also make up for George's reserved temperament and preoccupation with affairs of war.

Through her husband's role, Martha Washington met influential members of society in Boston, New York, and Philadelphia, expanding her social circle dramatically. She also found herself entertaining diplomats from other nations and cultures. In January 1776, John Adams recorded that he had had dinner at a home in Cambridge "with G. Washington, and [General Horatio] Gates and their Ladies." It proved to be an interesting occasion, primarily because of the other guests that day: six Native American leaders and warriors, with their wives and children, who had come to offer their services to the Americans. Adams found the little group quite interesting, though lacking in table manners: "There is a Mixture of White Blood French or English in most of them. Louis, their Principal, speaks English and French as well as Indian. It was a Savage feast, carnivorous Animals devouring their Pray. Yet they were wondrous polite. The General introduced me to them as one of the Grand Council Fire at Philadelphia, upon which they made me many Bows, and a cordial Reception."[34]

Martha Washington's reaction to this dinner was not recorded. While George Washington had spent considerable time among Native Americans on the frontier, it is not known whether this was the first situation in which his wife found herself in company with Indian people. It would certainly, however, not be the last. An oral tradition among the Oneida suggests that Martha Washington presented a shawl, still treasured by the tribe, to Polly Cooper, an Oneida woman who accompanied a group of their men to Valley Forge, where she helped to feed the starving American soldiers.[35]

Later in the war, the Washingtons met the ministers of Spain and France—Don Juan de Miralles and Monsieur Gerard, respectively—during the Christmas season of 1778 in Philadelphia. They welcomed these gentlemen to the winter encampment at Middlebrook on May 1, 1779, where they were greeted with a salute from thirteen cannons. This was followed, the next day, with an another cannon salute, a mounted parade and review of the army, and additional military exercises.[36] About a year later, in April 1780, Miralles paid a visit to the Morristown headquarters with the new French minister, the Chevalier de la Luzerne. The planned entertainments for the two men were carried out, although Miralles became gravely ill; he died on April 28 and was buried at a nearby church following a resplendent procession more than a mile long and graveside funeral rites by a Spanish priest.[37]

Even when she was home at Mount Vernon, Martha Washington found herself acting in a public role, entertaining visiting officers and foreign dignitaries. In November 1780, for example, a group composed of officers of at least three nationalities stopped to visit her on their way to Richmond and were invited to stay to dinner with Mrs. Washington and "a young lady, a relative, whose name, I think, was Miss Custis" (she was actually Martha Washington's daughter-in-law, Eleanor Calvert Custis). One of the men recorded, "I had the honour of sitting in the parlor tete-a-tete with Mrs. Washington [after dinner]. I shall never forget the affability, and, at the same time, the dignity of her demeanour. Our conversation was on general subjects. I can only remember the impression it left upon my mind; she reminded me of the Roman matrons of whom I had read so much, and I thought that she well deserved to be the companion and friend of the greatest man of the age."[38]

There were times when Martha Washington was obliged to stand in for her husband. In the summer of 1777, she paid a long visit to relatives in Virginia. On August 5, while at Eltham, the home of her sister and brother-in-law Anna Maria and Burwell Bassett, she made a side trip to Williamsburg to visit Bassett's mother, Elizabeth Churchill Bassett Dawson. She was met upon her arrival in the city with a salute of "cannon and small arms" before being escorted to Dawson's home. Several days before, the Virginia General Assembly had decided to let Martha know "of the high sense this hall entertains of General Washington's distinguished merit, as the illustrious defender and deliverer of his country," and to present her with a specially designed gold medal. Through her, George Washington was given "the freedom of this city."[39]

Martha Washington also found herself playing hostess to prominent civilians, who made their way to headquarters to request assistance. It was early spring in 1778 when Elizabeth Drinker and three other Quaker women from Philadelphia arrived at the Valley Forge headquarters one afternoon, carrying a petition signed by eighteen of their fellow believers—wives, parents, and friends of a group of Quaker men who had been exiled to Virginia because of their refusal to take an oath of loyalty to the Americans. The little delegation, having failed to win permission from Congress to let the men go home, was trying its luck with George Washington. Mrs. Drinker and her party sat and chatted with Martha Washington until the general was free to join the conversation. Washington invited these guests to stay for dinner, which they later described as "eligant." Apart from the guests, Martha Washington was the only woman present at the table with eighteen officers. She later took the guests up to her room so they could visit a little longer while her husband and his staff got back to work.[40]

The mission of the Quaker women was a partial success: George Washington gave them a pass through the American lines so they could take their petition to the Supreme Executive Council of Pennsylvania, the political body that by then controlled the fate of their men. They were released at the end of the month. The historian Linda Kerber has suggested that George Washington "carefully used" the "custom of separating the ladies from the gentlemen" after dinner "to limit his dealings with the importunate Quaker women." She makes nothing, however, of Martha Washington's presence, her role in dealing with these women, or any influence she, having spent considerably more time with the women than he, may have had on her husband's decision-making process. When George Washington gave the women permission to pass through the American lines, he wrote that "humanity pleads strongly in their behalf," a statement that led Kerber to suggest, "It may be that the case was given more human resonance through the women's presence." It is entirely possible that his wife's support for the Quaker women's cause also gave the issue "more human resonance" in Washington's eyes.[41]

It was Martha Washington's concern for the plight of the common soldiers that probably led to one of the most interesting incidents of the war. The winter of 1779–80 was not a happy one, as the countryside around George Washington's headquarters at Morristown labored under four feet of snow, with drifts reaching as high as twelve feet, making this—meteorologically, at least—the worst winter of the war. Supplies were short, and both men and animals suffered terribly. The army was angry about the lack of support from Congress and the states, and at one point the entire Connecticut line threatened to leave en masse. Washington wrote that if the Connecticut soldiers had not been persuaded to stay, the rest of the army might well have gone with them. The anger of the men was mirrored by their officers, and the constant tension sometimes erupted in quarrels and violence during social gatherings in the officers' quarters that winter.[42] Months later, in writing about the situation at Morristown, Martha Washington noted that "there was not much pleasure thar the distress of the army and other difficultys th'o I did not know the cause, the pore General was so unhappy that it distressed me exceedingly."[43]

In June 1780, following that terrible winter, as she stopped once again in Philadelphia on her way home, Martha Washington had the opportunity to do something about the problems facing the army. In Virginia she had a reputation as someone who cared for the poor, something that would have been expected of a devout Anglican woman of her social class. Officers from Virginia told others in camp of her reputation at home as "a lady of distinguished goodness," who was "full of benignity, benevolence and charity, seeking for objects of affliction and poverty, that she may extend to the sufferers the hand of kindness and relief."[44]

Now Martha Washington, along with several other prominent ladies, including Benjamin Franklin's daughter, became involved in a campaign to get American women to provide aid to the Continental Army. The project was spearheaded by Esther DeBerdt Reed, the young wife of Joseph Reed, a former military secretary to George Washington who was then serving as president of the Supreme Executive Council of Pennsylvania (equivalent to governor). The Reeds invited Martha to stay with them on her way home from Morristown that year, but she had already accepted an earlier invitation from someone else. The happiness Martha expressed when she learned that Esther was able "to receive company" after giving birth suggests the possibility of an upcoming visit. Through her own husband's position, Esther Reed undoubtedly knew something about the problems that had plagued the army at Morristown. Around this time, she published her ideas for a women's fundraising campaign in the newspaper. It is very likely, however, that conversations with Martha Washington provided enough firsthand examples of suffering and need in camp to encourage Esther and the other women.[45]

The Ladies Association, as it came to be known, has been described by other historians, as has Martha Washington's role as the figurehead of their efforts.[46] Briefly, the basic idea was that the women of each county would choose one of their number to act as a local treasurer, gather in funds, and keep a record of each donation. Once the money was collected, each county treasurer would send both the contributions and the registers to the first lady of her state, who in turn would send it along to Martha Washington. Because she might not be at camp when the contributions were sent in, the ladies asked that General Washington receive them on behalf of his wife. At that point, Washington was to use the money "in the manner that he shall judge most advantageous to the Soldiery." The women cautioned that the money was not intended "to procure to the army the obje[c]ts of subsistence, arms or cloathing which are due to them by the continent," meaning the government. They stressed that this was "an extraordinary bounty, intended to render the condition of the soldier more pleasant, and not to hold the place of the things which they ought to receive from the Congress, or the States."[47]

Farther south, Martha Washington turned to Martha Jefferson, the wife of Virginia Governor Thomas Jefferson, as the logical head of the campaign in their state. Martha Jefferson followed up with an announcement of the plan in the *Virginia Gazette* on August 9, 1780, and with at least one personal letter on the subject: "Mrs. Washington has done me the honor of communicating the inclosed proposition of our sisters in Pennsylvania and of informing me that the same grateful sentiments are displaying themselves in Maryland. Justified by the sanction of her letter in handing forward the scheme I undertake with chearfulness the duty of furnishing to my country women an opportunity of proving that they also participate of those virtuous feelings which gave birth to it. I cannot do more for its promotion than by inclosing to you some of the papers to be disposed of as you think proper."[48]

According to the Virginia newspapers, the collections were to be taken up in the churches "at which sermons suited to the occasion will doubtless be preached by the several Ministers of the Gospel."[49] Records from Virginia are incomplete but indicate that Alexandria contributed $75,800 "under the lead of 'Lady Washington'"; Fredericksburg, the home of George Washington's mother and sister, sent £1,600; $7,506 came from the women of Prince William County; and £1,560 came from Albemarle County.[50] Evidence from one of the Mount Vernon account books indicates that Martha Washington herself donated $20,000, the equivalent of £6,000, to the campaign in October 1780. Listed as "Mrs. Washington's Bounty to the Soldiers," the money was turned over to a Mrs. Ramsay, who was probably the woman in charge of the collection in Alexandria.[51] Ultimately, *the offering of the Ladies* was primarily used, as George Washington suggested, to supply his soldiers with clothing, including shirts and stockings.[52]

In many ways, the Martha Washington of 1783 was a very different woman from the sheltered and rather fearful person who gave George Washington so much concern as he went off to the Revolution eight years before. She had faced her fears: traveling to unfamiliar parts of the country; undergoing smallpox inoculation; living in a camp full of men; trying to seem unconcerned as enemy artillery shelled her quarters; taking on very public roles, both on behalf of her husband and in a campaign to help the common soldiers of the Continental Army. In the process, she won the heart of a nation.

She was honored by great and small. After her arrival in Cambridge that first year, she wrote in some mystification about her reception along the way in Philadelphia, noting that when she resumed her journey, she left the city "in as great pomp as if I had been a very great somebody."[53] Children were named for her, even very early in the war. In 1789, for example, the Washingtons were sent a portrait of a set of twins who had been born in 1775 and had "the Honor of bearing the Names of your Exc[ellenc]y & Lady."[54] When Nathanael Greene's wife wrote in the spring of 1777 to let him know that she had given birth to a little girl, he replied, "I am happy to hear you have such a fine daughter. . . . Mrs Washingtons [sic] Christian name is Martha. I shall have no objection to that or any other name you think proper to give her."[55] Not just children but at least three ships were named for the American commander's wife, as well. A schooner called *Lady Washington* was commissioned as a privateer by the Massachusetts Council in the spring of 1776.[56] Operating in New York waters that year was a galley of the same name, while a brig in Virginia that summer and fall was known as the *Lady Washington*.[57] At least two pieces of music were written in Martha Washington's honor during the Revolution: the first, known variously as "Lady Washington's Reel" and "Lady Washington's Quick Step," in 1777; the second, "Saw You My Hero, George," or "Lady Washington," two years later.[58] All of these instances, together with gifts presented to her during the war and the fact that artists were providing clients with companion portraits of her and her husband, suggest the love and respect that Marth Washington inspired in her countrymen, from very early in the war.

Something else may have been going on, as well. Starting during the war and continuing for the rest of his life, the American people began celebrating George Washington's birthday. The earliest instances of this took place in military settings—the first at Valley Forge in 1778, when money was paid to a military band to play on February 22; and the second, three years later at Yorktown.[59] By 1788, the city of Alexandria, Virginia, was holding an annual ball to celebrate the birth of its favorite son; other cities would follow Alexandria's lead in the years to come.[60] All of these hark back to the way Americans had celebrated the birthdays of the British king before the Revolution and suggest that George Washington was taking the place of the king in the hearts of Americans, who gave him a new title: "Father of his Country."[61] At the same time, his wife was becoming its mother.

Notes

1. Eliza Parke Custis, July 4, 1830, typescript, Fred W. Smith National Library for the Study of George Washington, Mount Vernon, VA (hereafter, FWSNL). See also accession and catalogue records for the trunk, W-368, in Mount Vernon Ladies' Association of the Union, Mount Vernon, VA.

2. Revolutionary War Series, June 16, 1775–December 31, 1783, *The Papers of George Washington Digital Edition*, ed. Theodore J. Crackel (Charlottesville: University of Virginia Press, 2007–), 2:65n. Joseph E. Fields, ed., *"Worthy Partner": The Papers of Martha Washington* (Westport, CT: Greenwood, 1994), 464–65.

3. Nancy K. Loane, *Following the Drum: Women at the Valley Forge Encampment* (Lincoln: University of Nebraska Press, 2009), 149–64.

4. Flora Fraser, *The Washingtons: George and Martha, "Join'd by Friendship, Crown'd by Love"* (New York: Alfred A. Knopf, 2015), xii–xiv; Patricia Brady, *Martha Washington: An American Life* (New York: Viking, 2005), 1–2, 232–36.

5. Linda Grant De Pauw, *Founding Mothers: Women of America in the Revolutionary Era* (Boston: Houghton Mifflin, 1975), 179–81, 184–86. For more on the lives of camp followers, see Mary Beth Norton, *Liberty's Daughters: The Revolutionary Experience of American Women, 1750–1800* (Boston: Little, Brown, 1980), 212–13; Linda K. Kerber, *Women of the Republic: Intellect and Ideology in Revolutionary America* (New York: W. W. Norton, 1980, 1986), 55–58; Holly A. Mayer, *Belonging to the Army:*

Camp Followers and Community during the American Revolution (Columbia: University of South Carolina Press, 1996).

6. Mayer, *Belonging to the Army*, 15, 145, 149–50; quote taken from Carol Berkin, *Revolutionary Mothers: Women in the Struggle for American Independence*, repr. ed. (New York: Vintage, 2006), 68.

7. For the buildup to war in Virginia, see Philip Vickers Fithian, January 24, 1774, in *Journal and Letters of Philip Vickers Fithian, 1773–1774: A Plantation Tutor of the Old Dominion*, ed. Hunter Dickinson Farish (Williamsburg, VA: Colonial Williamsburg, 1957), 59; John Harrower, *The Journal of John Harrower: An Indentured Servant in the Colony of Virginia, 1773–1776*, ed. Edward Miles Riley (Williamsburg, VA: Colonial Williamsburg, 1963), 44. For an example of Washington's feelings on these issues, see George Washington to Bryan Fairfax, July 20, 1774, in John C. Fitzpatrick, ed., *The Writings of George Washington from the Original Manuscript Sources, 1745–1799; Prepared under the Direction of the United States George Washington Bicentennial Commission and Published by Authority of Congress*, 39 vols. (Washington, DC: U.S. Government Printing Office (1931–44), 3:231–32, 233–34.

8. Edmund Pendleton to [?], [September 1774?], *The Letters and Papers of Edmund Pendleton, 1734–1803*, ed. David John Mays, 2 vols. (Charlottesville: University Press of Virginia, 1967), 1:98.

9. Martha Washington to Burwell Bassett, December 22, 1777, in Fields, *"Worthy Partner,"* 175.

10. Martha Washington to Bartholomew Dandridge, November 2, 1778, in Fields, *"Worthy Partner,"* 180.

11. Entry dated July 13, 1777, in Nicholas Cresswell, *Journal, 1774–1777* (New York: Dial, 1924), 253.

12. George Washington to John Parke Custis, June 19, 1775, in Fitzpatrick, *The Writings of George Washington from the Original Manuscript Sources*, 3:295–96.

13. See George Washington to Burwell Bassett, June 19, 1775, and George Washington to John Augustine Washington, June 20, 1775, in Fitzpatrick, *The Writings of George Washington from the Original Manuscript Sources*, 3:298, 300.

14. For the military situation in late 1776 and early 1777, see James Thomas Flexner, *Washington: The Indispensable Man* (New York: Signet, 1984), 77–98. For Martha Washington's departure from Mount Vernon in March 1777, see George Washington, "An Acct of Mrs. Washington's Expenses from Virginia to my Winter Quarters & back again to Virginia according to the Memms. and accts. which I have received from her & those who accompd. her," July 1, 1783, photostat, A-581, FWSNL. For other details of her trip north, see George Washington to Samuel Washington, April 5, 1777 and George Washington to Captain Caleb Gibbs, May 3, 1777, Fitzpatrick, *The Writings of George Washington from the Original Manuscript Sources*, 7:361, 8:11.

15. Nathanael Greene to Mrs. Catherine Greene, April 8, 1777, in *The Papers of General Nathanael Greene*, ed. Richard K. Showman and Dennis M. Conrad, 9 vols. (Chapel Hill: University of North Carolina Press, 1980), 2:54.

16. Martha Dangerfield Bland to Frances Bland Randolph, May 12, 1777, *Proceedings of the New Jersey Historical Society* 51, no. 3 (July 1933): 152.

17. The Marquis de Lafayette to Adrienne de Noailles de Lafayette, January 6, [1778], in *Lafayette in the Age of the American Revolution: Selected Letters and Papers, 1776–1790*, ed. Stanley J. Idzerda and Robert Rhodes Crout, 5 vols. (Ithaca, NY: Cornell University Press, 1977–83), 1:225.

18. George Washington to Lund Washington, August 20, 1775, in Fitzpatrick, *The Writings of George Washington from the Original Manuscript Sources*, 3:432–33. For similar correspondence, see Lund Washington to George Washington, October 5, 1775, October 15, 1775, Revolutionary War Series, June 16, 1775–December 31, 1783, in Crackel, *The Papers of George Washington Digital Edition*, 2:116, 174–75; George Washington to John Augustine Washington, October 13, 1775, in Fitzpatrick, *The Writings of George Washington from the Original Manuscript Sources*, 4:28.

19. Lund Washington to George Washington, October 29, 1775, in Crackel, *The Papers of George Washington Digital Edition*, 2:257.

20. John Steele to William Steele Jr., June 14, 1780, in *A Salute to Courage: The American Revolution as Seen through Wartime Writings of Officers of the Continental Army and Navy*, ed. Dennis P. Ryan (New York: Columbia University Press, 1979), 186–87.

21. Martha Washington to Elizabeth Ramsey, December 30, 1775, in Fields, *"Worthy Partner,"* 164.

22. For smallpox during the Revolution, see Mary V. Thompson, "'More to Dread ... than from the Sword of the Enemy': Smallpox, the Unseen Killer," *Annual Report 2000*, Mount Vernon Ladies' Association of the Union, Mount Vernon, VA, 2001, 22–27.

23. George Washington to John Augustine Washington, April 29, 1776, Revolutionary War Series, June 16, 1775–December 31, 1783, in Crackel, *The Papers of George Washington Digital Edition*, 4:173.

24. For John Parke Custis's inoculation, see Jonathan Boucher to George Washington, May 9, 1770, October 1, 1770, April 11, 1771, April 19, 1771, May 9, 1771; George Washington to Jonathan Boucher, May 13, 1770, April 4, 1771, April 20, 1771, Colonial Series, July 7, 1748–June 15, 1775, in Crackel, *The Papers of George Washington*, 8:333, 335, 387, 442–43, 443–44, 446–47, 448–49, 464–65.

25. John Hancock to George Washington, May 16, 1776, May 21, 1776, Revolutionary War Series, June 16, 1775–December 31, 1783, in Crackel, *The Papers of George Washington Digital Edition*, 4:313, 352, 353n.

26. George Washington to John Augustine Washington, May 31[–June 4,] 1776, George Washington to Burwell Bassett, June 4, 1776, Revolutionary War Series, June 16, 1775–December 31, 1783, in Crackel, *The Papers of George Washington Digital Edition*, 4:413, 435.

27. John Parke Custis to George Washington, June 10, 1776, June 16, 1775–December 31, 1783, in Crackel, *The Papers of George Washington Digital Edition*, 4:484–85.

28. Charles Willson Peale, 19, 25, 29, and May 30, 1776, in *The Selected Papers of Charles Willson Peale and His Family*, vol. 1, ed. Lillian B. Miller (New Haven, CT: Yale University Press, 1983), 182–83.

29. Lauren Suber, "The Many Faces of Martha," *Colonial Williamsburg* 17, no. 3 (Spring 1995): 62–63; Robert G. Stewart, "Portraits of George and Martha Washington," *Antiques* 135, no. 2 (February 1989): 474–75; Charles Willson Peale, June 4, 1776, July 26, 1776, 4, 10, 16, 19, 20, 23, August 25, 1776, in Miller, *The Selected Papers of Charles Willson Peale and His Family*, 184, 191–94.

30. For information on Blyth and Norman, see Mantle Fielding, *Dictionary of American Painters, Sculptors and Engravers*, ed. Glenn B. Opitz (Poughkeepsie, NY: Apollo, 1986), 81, 672.

31. *Annual Report 1968*, Mount Vernon Ladies' Association of the Union, Mount Vernon, VA, 1969, 7, 28–29, 37.

32. For an example of a letter copied by Martha Washington, see George Washington to the Duc de Lauzun, May 1, 1783, in Fitzpatrick, *The Writings of George Washington from the Original Manuscript Sources*, 26:370–71, 371n. She also copied letters from George Washington to Alexander Hamilton, dated March 31 and April 11, 1783: see Fields, *"Worthy Partner,"* 190n.

33. For examples of Washington's diplomatic role in the American Revolution, see Benjamin Huggins, "General George Washington: Diplomat," *Journal of the American Revolution*, April 26, 2017, accessed June 5, 2017, https://allthingsliberty .com/2017/04/general-george-washington-diplomat.

34. Entry dated January 24, 1776, in John Adams, *Diary and Autobiography of John Adams*, ed. L. H. Butterfield, 4 vols. (Cambridge, MA: Harvard University Press, 1961), 2:226–27, 227n.

35. Joseph T. Glatthaar and James Kirby Martin, *Forgotten Allies: The Oneida Indians and the American Revolution* (New York: Hill and Wang, 2006), 208.

36. James Thacher, *Military Journal of the American Revolution, from the Commencement to the Disbanding of the American Army; Comprising a Detailed Account of the Principal Events and Battles of the Revolution, with Their Exact Dates, and a Biographical Sketch of the Most Prominent Generals* (Hartford, CT: Hurlbut, Williams, 1862), 162–63.

37. Ibid., 191–93; Mabel Lorenz Ives, *Washington's Headquarters* (Upper Montclair, NJ: Lucy Fortune, [1932]), 216–17.

38. Pierre Etienne Du Ponceau to his daughter, Anna L. Garasche, September 9, 1837, in James L. Whitehead, "Notes and Documents: The Autobiography of Peter Stephen Du Ponceau," *Pennsylvania Magazine of History and Biography* (July 1939): 312–13.

39. For the presentation of this gift and its accompanying sentiments, see Revolutionary War Series, June 16, 1775–December 31, 1783, in Crackel, *The Papers of George Washington Digital Edition*, 10:554n–555n.

40. Elaine Forman Crane, editor, *The Diary of Elizabeth Drinker*, vol. 1 (Boston: Northeastern University Press, date unknown), 297.

41. Kerber, *Women of the Republic*, 93–98, 98n.

42. For conditions in camp, see Flexner, *Washington*, 133–36; Ives, *Washington's Headquarters*, 207–8.

43. Martha Washington to Burwell Bassett, July 18, 1780, in Fields, *"Worthy Partner,"* 183.

44. Thacher, *Military Journal of the American Revolution*, 160–61. See also Lund Washington to George Washington, January 17, 1776, Revolutionary War Series, June 16, 1775–December 31, 1783, in Crackel, *The Papers of George Washington Digital Edition*, 3:129.

45. For the campaign being headed by Mrs. Reed, see *The Papers of Thomas Jefferson*, ed. Julian Boyd et al., (hereafter, *PTJ*), 43 vols. (Princeton, NJ: Princeton University Press, 1951), 3:532n–33n. For the Reeds' invitation to Mrs. Washington and the identification of Joseph Reed, see Martha Washington to Joseph Reed, [June 1780], in Fields, *"Worthy Partner,"* 173, 173n–74n. For the participation of Mrs. Bache, see John Frederick Schroeder, *Life and Times of Washington: Containing a Particular*

Account of National Principles and Events, and of the Illustrious Men of the Revolution (New York: Johnson, Fry, 1857), 107n.

46. See, e.g., Berkin, *Revolutionary Mothers*, 44–49.

47. "The SENTIMENTS of an AMERICAN WOMAN," *Pennsylvania Gazette*, June 21, 1780, Accessible Archives CD-ROM edition of the *Pennsylvania Gazette*, with additions from the *Pennsylvania Packet*, folio 3: American Revolution, 1766–83.

48. Martha Wayles Skelton Jefferson to Eleanor Conway Madison, August 8, 1780, *PTJ*, 3:532.

49. *PTJ*, 3:533n.

50. For the collection in Alexandria and Fredericksburg, see Elizabeth R. Varon, *We Mean to be Counted: White Women and Politics in Antebellum Virginia* (Chapel Hill: University of North Carolina Press, 1998), 128. For the collections in Prince William and Albemarle Counties, see Norton, *Liberty's Daughters*, 184.

51. "Lund Washington . . . Contra," October 1780, in Ledger B, bound photostat, FWSNL, 160b. See also Helen Bryan, *Martha Washington: First Lady of Liberty* (New York: John Wiley and Sons, 2002), 242.

52. Kerber, *Women of the Republic*, 99–103. For the fact that each shirt bore the name of the woman who made it, see Norton, *Liberty's Daughters*, 183, 185–87. For the phrase *"the offering of the Ladies,"* see ibid., 185.

53. Martha Washington to Elizabeth Ramsay, December 30, 1775, in Fields, *"Worthy Partner,"* 164, 165n.

54. Mr. and Mrs. Anderson to George Washington, May 11, 1789, Presidential Series, September 24, 1788–March 3, 1796, in Crackel, *The Papers of George Washington Digital Edition*, 2:264.

55. Nathanael Greene to Catharine Greene, May 3, 1777, in Showman and Conrad, *The Papers of General Nathanael Greene*, 2:67.

56. Maj.-Gen. Artemas Ward to George Washington, May 20, 1776, May 27, 1776, Revolutionary War Series, June 16, 1775–December 31, 1783, in Crackel, *The Papers of George Washington Digital Edition*, 4:347, 348n, 397, 398n.

57. For the galley in New York, see Lt.-Col. Benjamin Tupper to George Washington, August 3, [1776], in ibid., 5:553–54; George Washington to John Hancock, August 17, 1776, Maj.-Gen. William Heath to George Washington, August 17, 1776, August 31, 1776, in ibid., 6:49, 49n–50n, 51, 51n–52n, 181n; Major General William Heath to George Washington, November 26, 1776, December 11, 1776, in ibid., 7:214, 216n, 299, 300n. For the Virginia brig, see George Washington to Lund Washington, August 26, 1776, in ibid., 6:136, 137n. For Lund Washington's sale of pork and beef to the brig *Lady Washington*, see "Cash Recieved [sic] on Act. of General Washington," November 4, 1776, Lund Washington Account Book, 1774–86, typescript, FWSNL, 54.

58. Kate Van Winkle Keller and Charles Cyril Hendrickson, *George Washington: A Biography in Social Dance* (Sandy Hook, CT: Hendrickson Group, 1998), 41, 58.

59. For Valley Forge, see Caleb Gibbs [steward] and Mary Smith [housekeeper at headquarters], "Revolutionary War Journal of Household Expenses, July 1776–November 1780," *George Washington Papers, Series 5, Financial Papers*, Library of Congress, item 28. I thank Dona McDermott, the archivist at Valley Forge, and Bruce Kirby of the Manuscripts Division at the Library of Congress for sharing this information with Mount Vernon. For Yorktown, see Comte de Rochambeau

to George Washington, February 12, 1781, and George Washington to Comte de Rochambeau, February 24, 1781, in Fitzpatrick, *The Writings of George Washington from the Original Manuscript Sources,* 21:217n29, 286.

60. Lt. John Enys, February 11, 1788, in *The American Journals of Lt. John Enys,* ed. Elizabeth Cometti (Syracuse, NY: Syracuse University Press, 1976), 244–45, 350n23; Donald Jackson and Dorothy Twohig, eds., *The Diaries of George Washington,* 6 vols. (Charlottesville: University Press of Virginia, 1976–79), 60:30n.

61. For examples of George Washington attending celebrations in Williamsburg for the birthdays of British royals, see entries dated May 19, 1769, June 4, 1770, in Jackson and Twohig, *The Diaries of George Washington,* 2:153, 153n, 246, 246n. For George Washington as Father of His Country, see W. S. Baker, *Itinerary of General Washington from June 15, 1775, to December 23, 1783* (Philadelphia: J. B. Lippincott, 1892), 211.

Women's Politics, Antislavery Politics, and Phillis Wheatley's American Revolution

DAVID WALDSTREICHER

By 1773, when Phillis Wheatley was about nineteen years old, her poetry made her a famous one-woman antislavery argument. Yet the politics of slavery and race was not the only political context for her work. Antislavery politics took particular shape because of the imperial controversy. Aware that her own enslavement was being used against the patriots even as she wrote sympathetically of the American—or, at least, New England—cause, Wheatley carefully kept her options open. Consequently, her public actions garnered studied responses from leading statesmen such as Lord Dartmouth, Benjamin Franklin, George Washington, and Thomas Jefferson. She became, in other words, a significant player in the intertwined politics of slavery and Revolution. It is time we asked why it was a woman, not a man, who played such a singular role.

Wheatley's death in 1784, at what some have called the high point of revolutionary-era radicalism in several realms, makes it hard to test whether she suffered, or would have suffered, a "backlash."[1] Perhaps for this reason in part, Wheatley has not had much of a place in the recent reevaluation of women's politics in the late eighteenth century. Political historians generally keep their distance, ceding such territory to literary scholars, who rightly see Wheatley as a pioneer and have made increasingly bold claims for her political savvy in recent years. Historians of slavery, meanwhile, wonder whether she is typical enough to warrant sustained attention. And historians of women have to face her unusual mix of slave status and unprecedented, publicized interactions with elites.[2] Popular historical treatments of women in the revolutionary era sometimes give her a celebratory chapter but not much in the way of analysis. The result is some confusion about her role and her intentions. For example, Gary Nash depicts Wheatley as lobbing her fascinating critique from the pious, feminine margins, to little effect. By contrast, Henry Wiencek has Wheatley helping to convince

Washington to reverse his initially negative policy on free black soldiers in tacit exchange for the laurels Wheatley could supply.[3]

But what if we considered Wheatley in relation to recent descriptions of elite and ordinary women's political activities and the recent scholarship on slaves' politics? Categories such as "mortuary politics," and expanded definitions of public diplomacy, may indeed apply to Wheatley. Certainly, a heightened appreciation of the role of the press in the politics of the Revolution helps explain the threat she posed to revolutionaries such as Franklin and Jefferson, who needed to spin the slavery question the Americans' way.[4] Careful attention to her actions suggests that Wheatley accomplished something that only a woman—and, perhaps, only a slave woman who could balance religious, classical, and secular political idioms—could have done: she helped force the issue of the relationship of slavery to the Revolution and American identity.

During the mid-eighteenth century, slavery became implicated in the seemingly separate issues of economy and sovereignty. These implications shaped both the Revolution itself and the ensuing creation of the federal republic. Anglo-Americans faced the fact that the colonies were different from England not only because they had more liberty or more land or less aristocracy but also because they had slavery; that they had slavery because they were colonies; and that the same justifications for that or any distinctly colonial state of affairs might also justify limits on colonists' power, their liberties, or their equality as British citizens. When the patriot side of the pamphlet debate is read for "the ideological origins of the American Revolution" and the British side—along with its tendency to bring up slavery—is rendered backward, irrelevant, and ultimately foreign to American history, we miss a crucial, shaping dimension of our past.[5] Moreover, the era's striking mix of antislavery and backlash—or radicalism and retrenchment— have their parallels in the experience of women. Wheatley operated at the nexus of the politics of slavery, the imperial controversy, and the ambiguous, shifting opportunities and risks that both presented for women.

Closer attention to Phillis Wheatley suggests a Wheatleyan moment circa 1772–73 that becomes a landmark in the struggle against slavery and a moment of crisis for the revolutionaries. For an alternative "primal scene" to the apocryphal (and politically isolated) "Wheatley Trial" before Boston's worthies first imagined by the young adult biographer Shirley Graham DuBois and more recently reimagined as "lost to history" (and thus to research) by Henry Louis Gates Jr., we might look to the events of October 10, 1772, when Wheatley took advantage of a visit from Thomas Woolridge, a traveler looking for exotic colonial goods, to get the attention of Lord Dartmouth, the colonial secretary. The poem Wheatley produced suggested that the newly appointed Dartmouth might simultaneously recognize the justice of the colonists' claims *and* why an African might "pray/Others may never feel tyrranic sway?" In fairly short order, Wheatley traveled to England to get her book published, got shown around the Tower of London by none other than the abolitionist Granville Sharp, and became an antislavery celebrity—and personally emancipated, thanks to the sarcastic comments in the London press about how Americans could hold such a prodigy in chains. For many contemporaries, the issue of the colonial controversy and the matter of slavery had been, effectively, linked, with consequences that shaped both the Revolution and the nascent antislavery movement.[6]

Wheatley's career is as clear a demonstration of this potentially emancipatory process of politicization as we are likely to find. Wheatley brought out the double meaning, and risks, of the classical (and republican) revival in the context of slavery. She did this in part by re-creating herself through the Greek and Roman classics—as a neoclassical poet—and by making the relationship of the patriots' dilemma to the ancient and modern politics of slavery a key theme of her very public project. The key question is not whether she was so exceptional as to perhaps mean nothing outside of, perhaps, intellectual or literary traditions; it is what she accomplished politically—and maybe even as a woman in particular.

We need to return to the notion of a "moment" to emphasize these were not just ideologies or words on a page but *events*. Imaginative leaps *and* a new kind of political and cultural practice occurred. In the *Somerset v. Steuart* case of 1772, Granville Sharp's reading of the ancient constitution meshed with James Somerset's inspired fugitivity and with King's Bench Chief Justice Lord Mansfield's desire to enforce parliamentary supremacy to produce a juridical dimension of this happening—a decision. They suggested limits to, and perhaps a coming end of, African slavery. During that same year, a pious Boston slave girl with an astoundingly sensitive ear, an awareness of exactly what it meant to be called "an uncultivated Barbarian from Africa," and a hard-won talent for putting herself in others' shoes provided the other happening, at the other end of the Atlantic, in another sector of the public sphere.[7] Wheatley's realization that she could address her African and enslaved experience as well as her captors' prejudices and practices through an engagement with the Mediterranean heritage—a heritage seen by her captors as at once distant (ancient) and universal—was pivotal, especially when integrated with her evangelical piety and ability to engage with both patriot and metropolitan skeptics. Her profundity and political effectiveness derived not just from her classicism but from its studied inflection of her Africanism—and her womanhood.

Wheatley's African Worlds

What can we know of Wheatley's African experience and what it meant to her in the absence of other, or more direct, testimony? We know that Wheatley came over on the *Phillis* in 1761, at about age seven or eight. That is a lot to know about an individual enslaved person during the revolutionary era. It has been tempting in recent years to presume she came directly from Senegambia, since she later mentions Gambia as an origin, and the shipowner Timothy Fitch directed the captain to that region. But she could have been taken or retaken at any number of West African ports. Like many slaving ships in this era, the *Phillis* was directed by its owner to make as many stops as necessary to fill the cargo. Senegambian voyages did not stay long in port at mid-century, if only because of a high ratio of shipboard revolts there.[8]

So we do not know where Wheatley was from. Yet if we apply what we do know about West Africa and slavery in the late 1750s and think of those facts as things Wheatley knew (better than us), a meaningful picture emerges that allows us to make sense of what she brought to the writing table. It was not unusual for young female children to be caught up in the slave trade. They were more easily captured and pawned; their sale was in some ways where the more traditional forms of enslavement and the newer more market-oriented forms overlapped, resulting in an intensified kidnapping of women and children. Historians of Senegambia and West Africa agree that the 1750s saw a ramping up of wars within Africa, violent European competition for trading posts, and pressure from African coastal merchants on their warlord suppliers to liquidate human assets. In general, "Most people who found themselves in slave ships did so in the aftermath of war." She may have traveled significantly before arriving in a West African port—indeed, a sizable chunk of the seven-year-old's life might have been spent within the slave trade before her Middle Passage. A precociously bright and observant child would have learned quite a bit about trade in women, about travel, about the commonality of slavery and its spread, and about war and change in the African inland and Atlantic.[9]

The recent literature on the slave trade and oral culture in West Africa stress the role of women as poets who represented, and often glorified, (male) authority figures. Roger Abrahams has described "verbal play directed at powerful figures" as a West African tradition that made it to the Americas. Other scholars of this period underline the importance of death rituals both in African cultures and in the changing Africa emerging from the slave trade. The one detail that exists in Wheatley family lore about Phillis's

African memories involved her mother pouring out water to the sun in the morning as part of what the recorders understood as a religious ritual.[10]

Much of this background would have played directly into the role of the poet in eighteenth-century Anglo-America—the poets of empire described by David Shields, the elegiac tradition interpreted by Max Cavitch, and the lamentations and narrations of African women in Atlantic slavery analyzed by Vincent Brown and others.[11] In both Africa and America during the eighteenth century, a woman could become a more valued member of an intimate and political community by talking eloquently about war and death. It might even be a way to reestablish kin ties in a real, substantive sense. Many of Wheatley's poems, especially the early ones, were in effect gift offerings for the bereaved—offered in a Christian idiom, to be sure, but universalizing in effect. We know that her poems circulated first in manuscript, among acquaintances, and that she was asked to read or recite in parlors long before male authorities wondered who could have taught her or whether she actually wrote the poems.[12] The female networks she found were most likely her first indication that some aspects of her African knowledge of how to be in the world, how to relate to others, and how to survive and even thrive amid strangers might, indeed, translate.

Recent studies of Atlantic cultures stress syncretism despite—and sometimes because of—uneven power relationships: even exploitative relations are, after all, relationships. People did not simply choose assimilation or cultural autochthony any more than our grandparents did or do today. What would the various middle grounds have looked like to a slave in Boston? It surely varied depending on who was listening. Jeffrey Bruce, who was captured in the Niger Valley, spent a few months in Barbados, and arrived in Boston the summer before Wheatley, remembered that Africans there "asked me many questions about my native country." At the same time, as Anne Bailey suggests, the slave trade had an effect on individuals of the sort we associate with modern wars: veterans often do not like to talk about war directly, and certainly not to people who not only do not share the experience but, more important, do not admit their responsibility for the horror of it all.[13]

It is entirely possible to interpret Wheatley, then, as not experiencing complete culture shock even as she converted and acculturated enough to write contemporary English verse. It seems likely that she chose poetic roles and forms for their very continuities with her West African memories. The issue here is not whether Wheatley had African or slave trade memories, kept them alive, or knew how and when to share them; it is how they related to the idioms she did choose in her writing, which made her a public figure at an astonishingly young age.

Wheatley's Ancient Worlds

Most scholars have neglected, or continued to condescend to, what to most of us is most foreign and inaccessible about Wheatley (besides her African-ism)—that is, her classicism.[14] We have been so shaped by our generation's lack of a classical education, and perhaps by the idea that, as Bernard Bailyn argued, the American founders were not real classical scholars and that their appropriations of classics had no substantive meaning, that we tend to view classicism in this period as mere window dressing or the playful and pragmatic use of pseudonyms—a kind of heady yet superficial identity politics, the equivalent of a toga at a frat party.[15]

But what does the naïve reader of Homer, Terence and Virgil, who were so central to mid-eighteenth-century education both in the original and in translation, discover? Tricksters and gods who intervene in human lives. Gods that behave like humans; humans who are godlike. Direct speech with the dead. An overwhelming importance given to eloquent acts of speech and to "professional rhapsodists" who represent "the dead and defeated" while singing of gods, of battles, and of heroes who might even be present at the feast. Libations poured out for the gods, ritually, regularly. A world of war (*The Iliad*). A world of consequential, tragic, and yet sometimes redemptive travels (*The Odyssey*). Women as prizes—booty of war—and as slaves: most of the slaves in *The Odyssey* are women. Individual women who are on the bottom but seem to have the power to determine the doings of men, and not merely as catalysts. A "dread of enslavement" as a central trope, as slaves are made free and men and women are made slaves.[16]

The reader also discovers slaves who are smarter than their masters, who manipulate situations to their own ends, as in Terence's comedies, or who may be the loyal keys to the reclaiming of the kingdom, like Eumaeus in *The Odyssey*. Eumaeus is a boy prince who was sold away, captured: he indicates a world in which anyone might be enslaved but still might come to love his captors and be in some sense a member of the family. In their careful words and whispered intimacies with the storm-tossed and for-merly captive Ulysses, Eumaeus and the maid Eurycleia, a parallel female figure, emerge as central to the plot and denouement of the epic poem. They appear at first to be bit players, happy slaves, but they make history happen—and gain at least the prospect of freedom as a result.

Indeed, in Homer's ancient world there is a discernible relation among travel, encounter, war, and enslavement that would have meant all the more because of the several mentions of Egypt and Ethiopia in the text. In the later Greek and Roman literature, the importance of slaves in everyday life, as "vibrant violators and exploiters of the intimacies of family life" only intensifies. So does the ubiquity of war as a cruel leveler. Africa appears with even greater clarity and frequency as a place on the map. The very first of Virgil's *Eclogues,* often used as a teaching text for children, is a dialogue in which one interlocutor speaks of his escape from slavery while the other forecasts exile to, among other places, Africa in the wake of the forcible transfer of land to soldiers. And Horace, so clearly a favorite of Wheatley, as of her other favorite, Alexander Pope, repeatedly makes a theme of how patronage *and* his talents made it possible for him to live a better life despite his father's low status as a former slave.[17]

Students of slavery have made much of the travesty committed by masters who gave names such as Caesar and Pompey to their household bondsmen. Wheatley carried the name of the slave ship she was bought from, the *Phillis.* But was it refreshing to learn that the name referred to a beautiful woman in Virgil's third *Eclogue?* A tragic, eloquent figure in Ovid's *Heroides?* Or that, in one of Horace's odes, Phillis is a slave so virtuous that "she must Have come down from kings!"[18] If the late colonial master class fulfilled its imperial fantasies by imagining its slaving as akin to Greek and Roman varieties, that required—or, at least, allowed—them to do more than merely condescend to their slaves as primitive and pagan. Like the Christian and republican traditions, classical idioms had universalizing, as well as inegalitarian, potential.

In short, by the time Wheatley opened her *Poems on Various Subjects, Religious and Moral* (1773) by citing the Roman slave poet Terence, "African by birth," as a precedent in a poem titled "To Maecenas," the patron of Horace, she had connected a certain set of dots. The classical world, her Africa, and her America exist in the same universe. Poets are actors in this world. They make sense of war, cross-cultural encounters, enslavement, the supernatural. Women can be central to a cultural and political drama: the traffic in women is a kind of original sin that makes and unmakes the world—the real origins of slavery, in fact—and it is the job of the poet to knit the world back together, and maybe free herself in the process. Classical example and models do not consist of unattainable brilliance (the best that has been thought and said) or primitive exoticism to be appreciated, if at all, for its very difference from a modern Christian world; rather, the classics are classic because they apply to her worlds. They are pagan, but they are witty, playful, worldly. Squaring what is good and what is not so good, what is the same and what is different, what is sacred and what is profane about the ancient and the modern is like any other act of comparing times, places, and mores.[19]

And most of all, if a women and a slave seeks to hitch her desires to those of men and nations, it is wisest to work by indirect comparison. The classical revival provided Wheatley with a way of talking about her experience without talking about it directly. In that light, I would like to propose another, earlier primal scene of the Wheatleyan moment—perhaps the moment when she first made real in practice the possibilities of a dialogue among the African, the classical, and the contemporary. Wheatley's first published poem, "On Messrs. Hussey and Coffin," which appeared in a Newport newspaper in 1767, is about a near-shipwreck of two Nantucket Quaker merchants. Written by a Bostonian, it nicely exemplifies a kind of archipelagic New England experience analogous to the ancient Greek world and resolves a distinctly Homeric set of queries about the causes of a shipwreck into a Christian salvation:

> Did Fear and Danger so perplex your Mind,
> As made you fearful of the Whistling Wind?
> Was it not Boreas knit his angry Brow
> Against you? Or did Consideration bow?
> To lend you Aid, did not his Winds combine?
> To stop your passage with a churlish Line,
> Did haughty Eolus with Contempt look down
> With Aspect windy, and a study's Frown?
> Regard them not;—the Great Supreme, the Wise,
> Intends for something hidden from our Eyes.[20]

It is not hard to imagine why the survivor of a slave ship would identify with another storm-tossed voyage.

But these lines are also literally evocative of *The Odyssey* and Virgil's *Aeneid*. In Pope's translation of *The Odyssey*, the ghost of Agamemnon asks the ghost of Amphideon, one of the suitors slain by Odysseus, "What cause compell'd so many, and so gay,/To tread the downward, melancholy way? . . . did the rage of stormy Neptune sweep/Your lives at once, and whelm beneath the deep?" There are many such storm-tossed voyages in Homer, accompanied by questions about the gods' intentions. An even more direct thematic link lies in Dryden's *Aeneid*, which begins with Juno asking Eolus, who rules the winds and the waves, to bring down the ship of the Trojans, whom she calls "a race of wandering slaves." He does so with the help of Boreas, the north wind. Ultimately, Neptune calms the waves. Aeneas and his Trojans land in Libya—later described as part of "Africk," one of numerous references in the poem to northern and eastern African peoples.[21]

The poem to Hussey and Coffin is also typical of Wheatley's later work in calling attention to the inspired poet's role as a mediator between God and the subject, simultaneously humbling herself and exalting her role.

The poet, in Pope/Homer's version of such a scene, channels the dead; in Dryden/Virgil, he channels the gods, the ultimate religious act and act of translation. In Wheatley's version, the poet and the audience come together in response to trauma and a Christian supersession that is beyond the ancients. Yet the entire project presumes a careful building on the classics—classics that, for Wheatley, depict a world and a set of experiences that are not only analogous to her voyage but also refer directly to Africa, to slaves, and to women as central actors.[22]

When we pay careful attention to the contextual information we have, we see the thirteen-year-old Wheatley writing the role of her lifetime. The preface to the poem published in the newspaper describes her hearing the story of Hussey and Coffin's voyage while waiting table—precisely the kind of banquet scene, with slaves and poets in attendance, that recurs throughout *The Odyssey*. Moreover, Nathaniel Coffin, one of the merchants she addresses, was a member of what would become a staunchly antislavery family. In 1767, this Nathaniel Coffin or one of his kin of the same name held a pair of slaves named Sapho (!) and Tombo. They had formed a close friendship, in Boston, with a man named James Somerset, the slave of Coffin's fellow customs officer Charles Steuart.[23]

Wheatley chose this occasion because she knew that her (Quaker) subjects were more than usually sympathetic to her situation, perhaps more open to the possibility of a special status for her. What is most striking here is the boldness of the identification: we are all on the same Christian and classical team. Poetry linked these worlds in a universal culture. Wheatley does insist on progress from the pagan worldview to the Christian, and in that sense she is certainly a "modern," but she manages to do so in a way that levels the playing field.

If the ancient Mediterranean is standing in for Africa—for her and for her audience insofar as she is speaking the language of neoclassicism—her performance opens up another, more historicized way to view her seeming self-distancing from Africa. Wheatley's relationship to Africa in her poems has been the subject of much angst and speculation. It is usually construed in a negative fashion, most famously in "On Being Brought from AFRICA to AMERICA," a poem Henry Louis Gates Jr. reports as "the most reviled . . . in African-American literature" because of its seeming thankfulness for enslavement, refigured as conversion:

> TWAS mercy brought me from my pagan land
> Taught my benighted soul to understand
> That there's a God, that there's a *Saviour* too:
> Once I redemption neither sought nor knew.

Wheatley moves on immediately, however, to question her readers' racism: "Some view our sable race with scornful eye,/'Their colour is a diabolic dye." Recent readings argue there is a more challenging antiracist statement in the final couplet—"Remember, *Christians, Negros,* black as *Cain,*/ May be refin'd, and join th' angelic train"—if one pays attention to the italics and imagines the voice as ironic rather than pleading. But even a more literal reading of the middle of the poem must admit that at its center is a critique of those who focus on race.[24] The would-be Christians are the only ones in the poem not moving forward. The poem is an attempt to seize control of the meaning of Africa and America in time and to say that race is a static, ahistorical way to think about slavery, Christianity, and civilization. The ambivalence about Africa parallels her contemporaries' ambivalence about the ancient world.

Even from 1767, Wheatley's invocations of Africa are decidedly double-edged. They use presumptions of African pagan backwardness to challenge easy notions of progress. "Must Ethiopians be imploy'd for you/Greatly rejoice if any good I do," she asks in "Deism," an early unpublished poem that went through a number of extant variants and might also be seen as following a self-hating script—if it did not end in a prose encomium that sounds precisely like an adaptation of her African mother's morning sun rite, but Christianized: "May I O eternal salute aurora to begin thy Praise, shall mortal dust do that which immortals can scarcely comprehend."[25] In a similar poem from 1767 that was later revised, an appeal to wayward Harvard students, she refers to "the Sable land of error's darkest night/ There, sacred Nine! For you no place was found,/Parent of mercy, 'twas thy Powerfull hand/Brought me in safety from that dark abode." Christianity saves—but it also allows Wheatley access to the "sacred" classical muses. If this is a refusal of Africa on behalf of Christianity, it is also a valorization of her authority to mediate between *that* ancient world and this modern one.

And that is the real game changer. When Wheatley successfully entered into the colonial controversy and won her transatlantic audience, she found herself enabled to say rather different things about Africa. In her poem for Lord Dartmouth of 1772, she can mock Anglo presumptions that Africans remember their home country as a "fancy'd happy seat," given that it is a place where fathers lose their daughters to the slave trade. This is not the first reference to paternity in the poem: in the first eight lines celebrating Dartmouth's ascent to the secretaryship and its possibilities for the preservation of colonial liberties, the new secretary is the "sire" as well as the "friend, [and] messenger" of peace and liberty. Wheatley improves on patriots' hopes for Dartmouth, the "psalm-singer" Lord, by celebrating

New England liberties revived and then intuiting that the good Lord is wondering how and why she would care. Her African experience, she insists, is precisely what allows her to understand liberty deprived and the generational discourse through which patriots sought to influence imperial politics. The praise song, in other words, permits her to criticize slavery, participate in the Anglo-American conversation about liberties, and seem very, very discerning as well as polite.[26]

Even given the enhanced appreciation of young women as a demographic and cultural force and as potential symbols of and participants in rebellion in the late eighteenth century, this is a remarkable bid to link antislavery to the patriot appeal.[27] It seems time to ask whether it would have been possible if Wheatley had not been a woman. To be blunt: could a man have done it and in the process become a touchstone of the debate about slavery and American protest? I do not think so. Wheatley's ability to coyly shame Anglo-Americans while praising the colonial secretary depends on her feminine perspective, as well as her African and slave identity. The presentation of the poem, as recounted by Thomas Woolridge in the letter sent enclosing the poem to Lord Dartmouth, supports such a gendered reading of Wheatley's actions. When Woolridge showed up in the Wheatleys' parlor and asked to see the goods, Phillis told him "she was then busy and engaged for the Day," but he could "propose a subject" and return in the morning. This is a slave woman turning the tables, acting like a lady, at once acknowledging her servitude and seducing the genteel visitor because she has something that he wants.

Wheatley did not always play the daughter, the child prodigy, or the feminine mourning specialist. She could also play it as a romance. In a verse dialogue with British officers in 1775, she accepts their feminizing pastoral reading of Africa, which makes her the bard of the continent. Like Virgil, Horace, and Alexander Pope, she retails pastoral nostalgia in part to be able to comment on the effects of war, including enslavement. Who, indeed, is a barbarian in a world at war? Wondering, in early 1776, about "the proceedings of nations that are fav'd with the divine revelation of the gospel," sharing her "anxious suspense concerning the fortune of this unnatural civil contest," she lays the stakes on the line: maybe the British "thirst of Dominion" was "design'd as the punishment of the national views of others," the Americans, "tho' it bears the appearance of greater Barbarity than that of the unciviliz'd part of mankind."[28] We ought to wonder, more than we have, what she did during the rest of the Revolutionary War in her lost second book manuscript, and what she might have done had she survived past 1784.

Sometimes by Simile

Ultimately, Wheatley followed through on an analogy that proved useful in confronting the American Revolution: as she put it in her last published poem in 1784, "new born Rome shall give Britannia law."[29] The missing term, the simile implicit, I think, for many readers, as well as for Wheatley, was Africa. As in the poem to Lord Dartmouth, in which she does explicitly compare her enslavement to the oppression of the colonists by way of explaining why she can understand the latter, Wheatley's great theme is one of triangulation by analogies—or, in her preferred term, in the most resonant description she gave of her own craft, "Sometimes by Simile, a victory's won."[30]

These similes depend on something very important that modern scholarship on slavery has reasserted, but that American slaveholders came to deny in the wake of antislavery: the exceptional, not at all progressive or even timeless, quality of American racial slavery. The first, crucial step was the realization that, as Joseph Miller writes, "For the ancient Mediterranean . . . more relevant analogies come from Africa than from the modern Americas."[31] The relationship of Africa to Atlantic America might still be analogous (not reducible) to the relationship between classical world and modern, but it was neither a simple equivalence—empire's historical return—nor, given the spread of racial slavery as a sine qua non of new world empire, necessarily an improvement or supersession.

The implications are stunning. If you say that the modern is superior, you can be shamed when you do "ancient" practices, including slavery. If you think the ancients are a worthy model—or, at least, not inferior in certain regards—then comparisons between them and the present are warranted, and Africa might be part of the conversation. Wheatley engaged in precisely these sorts of comparisons in a letter to Samson Occom published in eleven New England newspapers in 1774:

> I have this Day received your obliging kind Epistle, and am greatly satisfied with your Reasons respecting the Negroes, and think highly reasonable what you offer in Vindication of their natural Rights: Those that invade them cannot be insensible that the divine Light is chasing away the thick Darkness which broods over the Land of Africa; and the Chaos which has reign'd so long, is converting into beautiful Order, and [r]eveals more and more clearly, the glorious Dispensation of civil and religious Liberty, which are so inseparably Limited, that there is little or no Enjoyment of one Without the other: Otherwise, perhaps, the Israelites had been less solicitous for their Freedom from Egyptian slavery;

I do not say they would have been contented without it, by no means, for in every human Breast, God has implanted a Principle, which we call Love of Freedom; it is impatient of Oppression, and pants for Deliverance; and by the Leave of our modern Egyptians I will assert, that the same Principle lives in us.[32]

Referring to modern Egyptians, and calling them "ours," raises the question of American slavery *and* its modernity. Wheatley insists that slavery is implicated in the very meaning, and thus the future, of America.[33]

These were practical as well ideological questions. In Boston, Wheatley was caught between slavery's possible or incipient amelioration and its extension—that is, between slavery's seemingly ancient persistence (indeed, its cycles in imperial histories) and its modern American apotheosis in race. One of the things that has led historians away from Wheatley is that her experience does not look like typical plantation slavery. Wheatley's slavery looks like some aspects of ancient slavery. She was taught, like a member of the family; she was emancipated because of her skill. Our imaginations are so shaped by the later use of classical precedents by antebellum southerners, and perhaps by similar polemical battles over the character of African slavery and the role of Africans in the slave trade, that we forget the basic differences between varieties of ancient and traditional slavery and the North American variant. In Africa and in the classical world, slavery was brutal and ubiquitous, but slavery was not racial, and slaves, especially in the Roman world, could become—or, more often, became—free.[34] Homer, indeed, seems to dwell on precisely this process of people becoming enslaved and becoming free.

But it is precisely this that made Wheatley a potential threat to the American revolutionaries, such that the patriot newspapers and printers began to decline to publish her around, interestingly enough, 1772. It is not just that she proved Africans can write poetry, that they are capable, so race as a justification for slavery was a lie. It is that she showed that modern, American slavery was worse than the ancient kind precisely insofar as it did not celebrate or even free individuals such as her. She raised the distinct possibility that history was going backward, not forward, in America and signaled the implications in numerous ways, even as she kept lines of communication open with both sides of the imperial controversy. A London reviewer of her *Poems* registered the possibilities here by spending his first paragraph mocking her use of solar imagery as all too African and not really classical ("Homer and Hesiod breathed the cool and temperate air of the Meles, and the poets and heroes of Greece and Rome had no very intimate commerce with the sun"), only to conclude by stating how poorly it reflected on "the people of Boston" and their "principles of liberty" to keep even a "merely imitative" African poet in bondage. Similarly, some months later, Thomas Day, in the preface to the second edition of his popular antislavery poem "The Dying Negro" (1774), chided American "inconsistency" and called Americans worse than Spartans.[35]

This is why Thomas Jefferson built the "Manners" chapter of *Notes on the State of Virginia* around his famous cocktail party-like slam, "Religion, indeed could produce a Phillis Whately; but it could not produce a poet. The compositions published under her name are below the dignity of criticism. The heroes of the Dunciad are to her as Hercules to the author of that poem." Jefferson had a copy of Wheatley's *Poems* in his library, and marginalia in the Library of Congress copy that appear to be his handwriting suggests that he tracked her appearances in newspapers in 1773.[36] The misspelling of her name may be in the manner of a Freudian slip, but I think he knew exactly what he was doing. Jefferson accepts the classical context for Wheatley and its implications for the future of slavery (and America) but inverts it. Her poetry is merely religious, not classical; mock-epic, not epic.[37] The short-guy joke on Pope and his *Dunciad* evokes Jefferson's lengthy attack, in earlier chapters, on Comte de Buffon's notion that the new world had led to a natural degeneration of mammalian life—a degeneration that Buffon and others had seen in the practices of the colonizers, including the shocking revival of slavery. The discussion of Wheatley and other black writers parlays directly into Jefferson's insistence that American slavery is kinder and gentler than the Roman kind. Jefferson disparaged Wheatley, in other words, because Wheatley herself had become a protagonist as well as a subject in the controversy about empire, slavery, and the meaning of America.[38]

Jefferson's response to Wheatley is complex, but its most telling aspect may be his handling of the precedent of the Afro-Roman slave poet Terence. He does not tell us that Wheatley claimed Terence (why would a merely religious writer do that?), but he asserts that Terence does not prove anything about black slavery, since he was "of the race of whites." He also ignores the other dimensions of Wheatley's identification with Terence as "African by birth": Terence, too, was suspected of getting help in writing, and he earned his freedom by his pen.[39] Wheatley put herself in the tradition of classical—male—writers with something to say about political men and about the relationships between slaves and masters. Jefferson denies the qualifications of a few male slaves to participate in the republic of letters and thus to suggest the possibility of emancipation on the grounds of African equality.

Why must Wheatley—or "the poems published under her hand"— be dismissed out of hand? Why must her religion be stressed and her engagement with Pope and the very poets Pope translated—Homer, Horace—be winked away? Ultimately, Jefferson resolves the classical, or temporal and spatial, question of slavery and American modernity in one of race—the hallmark of American slavery. In short, in the aftermath of Phillis Wheatley, Jefferson has to reply on race (and, for the international audience of his *Notes*, a promise of eventual emancipation and an admission of slavery's wrongs) to establish a virtuous Virginian American identity. Wheatley's nonracial, Christian universalist, neoclassical, feminine antislavery testimony is inadmissible because of Jefferson's need to claim aspects of universalism, classical revival, and antislavery for the Americans. In Jefferson's emerging world, nothing but race can trump the suspicion of colonial and early national inferiority in the face of the classical—nothing, that is, but the stunning achievement that is Wheatley's poems or the establishment of the American nation, which, as Jefferson writes, is not yet certain. If Wheatley is a poet, arguments for America as an improvement over European corruption, as a selective "countercultural" classical revival, do not stand up—at least, not yet; not with slavery. If people are listening to Wheatley, the founders have not "dr[iven] the ancients from their pedestals and occupied their places," unless it is the other ancients—the barbarians and Spartans—we are talking about.[40] And the best way to make Wheatley something other than what she was is to get the audience to not read her or think about the world that had made her. Instead, they are to read her race and sex, supported by an exaggeration of her piety as a kind of feminine foible. When Jefferson makes Pope and Terence his instead of hers, he denies the very grounds of both Wheatley's art and her politics while reducing them to a feminized religion that, he has already argued in another chapter, ought to be separated from truly political questions. He shows just how much was at stake in seemingly literary matters and that the segregated and gendered boundaries of American independence could not be taken for granted. They had to be rewritten, in part because Phillis Wheatley had rewritten them.

The patriot movement and its call for liberties created a crisis that gave an extra charge to the reasonable question about whether the American colonists, in the wake of world wars and a heightened slave trade, were, in fact, (still) barbaric—that is, ancient in all the wrong ways. Is it too much to claim that the very public entry of an African woman into the conversation about ancients, moderns, Africans, and Americans in as informed a manner as Wheatley helped precipitate a cultural and political crisis every bit as much as the *Somerset* case discussed earlier? If not, it is little wonder that Jefferson began, around 1774, to deny the relevance of classical precedents for public matters, insisting that the uses of the classics were wholly private—not unlike the way his fellow southerners would begin to describe slavery itself.[41]

Wheatley will not be fully understood or appreciated as an actor in history until we realize the striking multiplicity of reasons that she was Jefferson's kryptonite. It was not just that she was an African and a slave writing, or writing poetry, or writing Christian poetry: it is that she was writing neoclassical poetry and, in so doing, bringing by stealth (or by simile) her African and feminine experience to bear on various aspects of secular as well as religious life, including the politics of the Revolution. Wheatley's emergence, like those other moments when blacks became participants in the imperial struggle, was a moment in which mutually serving Anglo-American myths, and with them the colonial structures they sustained, began to break down—when the factors that created liberties were perceived to threaten them. That a woman played a significant role in this process also has implications for our understanding of the American Revolution.

The problem of the empire, whether looked at from Boston, Norfolk, or London, proved inseparable from the politics of slavery. Empire, republicanism, and slavery implicated one another. *Somerset v. Steuart* is one index of this; Wheatley's emergence shortly thereafter is another, as is the likely personal link between Somerset and Wheatley in Boston. Jefferson, being Jefferson, understood Wheatley as a political as well as an intellectual problem, and it seems to have required the patriot victory, and perhaps her death in 1784, for him to resolve it on paper to his own satisfaction. Wheatley lived long enough to propose a postcolonial identity for America that was rather different from Jefferson's, and even if the story of the American Revolution must be a story of Jefferson's real and imagined victories, it cannot be an accurate story until it shows how Phillis Wheatley and James Somerset actually chose some key battlegrounds, in verse as in the courtroom, well before their fellow slaves chose Dunmore's and Washington's armies.

Notes

1. Rosemarie Zagarri, *Revolutionary Backlash: Women and Politics in the Early American Republic* (Philadelphia: University of Pennsylvania Press, 2007).

2. For examples, see Karen Weyler, *Empowering Words: Outsiders and Authorship in Early America* (Athens: University of Georgia Press, 2013); Catherine Adams and Elizabeth Pleck, *Love of Freedom: Black Women in Colonial and Revolutionary New England* (New York: Oxford University Press, 2010).

3. Gary B. Nash, *The Unknown American Revolution: The Unruly Birth of Democracy and the Struggle to Create America* (New York: Penguin, 2005), 137–39; Henry Wiencek, *An Imperfect God: George Washington, His Slaves, and the Creation of America* (New York: Farrar, Straus and Giroux, 2003), 205–14.

4. Vincent Brown, *The Reaper's Garden: Death and Power in the World of Atlantic Slavery* (Cambridge, MA: Harvard University Press, 2008); Vincent Brown, "Social Death and Political Life in the Study of Slavery," *American Historical Review* 114 (2009): 1231–49; Catherine Allgor, *Parlor Politics: In Which the Ladies of Washington Help Build a City and a Government* (Charlottesville: University of Virginia Press, 2000).

5. David Waldstreicher, *Runaway America: Benjamin Franklin, Slavery, and the American Revolution* (New York: Hill and Wang, 2004), chap. 7; David Waldstreicher, *Slavery's Constitution: From Revolution to Ratification* (New York: Farrar, Straus and Giroux, 2009), chap. 2; Staughton Lynd and David Waldstreicher, "Free Trade, Sovereignty, and Slavery: Toward an Economic Interpretation of American Independence," *William and Mary Quarterly* 68 (October 2011): 597–630.

6. "To the Right Honorable WILLIAM, Earl of DARTMOUTH, His Majesty's Principal Secretary of State for North-America," in Phillis Wheatley: *Complete Writings*, ed. Vincent Carretta (New York: Penguin, 1999), 38; David Waldstreicher, "The Wheatleyan Moment," *Early American Studies* 9, no. 3 (Fall 2011): 522–51; David Waldstreicher, "Phillis Wheatley, the Poet Who Challenged the American Revolutionaries," in *Revolutionary Founders: Rebels, Radicals, and Reformers in the Making of the Nation*, ed. Alfred F. Young, Gary B. Nash and Ray Raphael (New York: Vintage, 2011), 97–113; Christopher L. Brown, *Moral Capital: Foundations of British Abolitionism* (Chapel Hill: University of North Carolina Press, 2006); David Brion Davis, *The Problem of Slavery in the Age of Revolution, 1770–1823* (Ithaca, NY: Cornell University Press, 1975). For further reflections on the historiography, see my "Ancients, Moderns and Africans: Phillis Wheatley and the Politics of Empire and Slavery in the American Revolution," the version of this essay published in *Journal of the Early Republic* 37 (Winter 2017): 701–33.

7. Thomas Hutchinson et al., "To the Publick," in Phillis Wheatley, *Poems on Various Subjects, Religious and Moral* (London: A. Bell, 1773), vii

8. Tim Fitch to Capt. Ellery, January 14, 1759; Timothy Fitch to Peter Gwinn, January 12, 1760, November 8, 1760, September 4, 1761, November 1, 1761, October 1762, Medford Historical Society, Medford, MA; Alexander X. Byrd, *Captives and Voyagers: British Migrants across the Eighteenth Century Atlantic World* (Baton Rouge: Louisiana State University Press, 2008), 21–22; G. Ugo Nwokeji, *The Slave Trade and Culture in the Bight of Biafra: An African Society in the Atlantic World* (Cambridge: Cambridge University Press, 2010), 38–39, 137; Claude Meillassoux, *The Anthropology of Slavery: The Womb of Iron and Gold*, trans. Alide Dasnois (Chicago: University of Chicago Press, 1991), 67; Vincent Carretta, *Phillis Wheatley: Biography of a Genius in Bondage* (Athens: University of Georgia Press, 2011), 7–9.

9. Joseph C. Miller, "Introduction," in *Women and Slavery*, vol. 1, ed. Gwyn Campbell, Suzanne Miers and Joseph C. Miller (Athens: Ohio University Press, 2006), 17; Philip D. Curtin, *Economic Change in Precolonial Africa: Senegambia in the Era of the Slave Trade* (Madison: University of Wisconsin Press, 1975), 110; David Eltis, "The Volume and Structure of the Transatlantic Slave Trade," *William and Mary Quarterly* 58, no. 1 (2001): 44; John K. Thornton, *Warfare in Atlantic Africa, 1500–1800* (London: Routledge, 1999), 146–47; Joseph C. Miller, "The Dynamics of History in Africa and the Atlantic Age of Revolutions," in *The Age of Revolutions in Global Context, 1750–1840*, ed. David Armitage and Sanjay Subrahmanyan (New York: Palgrave Macmillan, 2010), 118; James F. Searing, *West African Slavery and Atlantic*

Commerce: The Senegal River Valley, 1700–1860 (New York: Cambridge University Press, 1993); Rebecca Shumway, *The Fante and the Transatlantic Slave Trade* (Rochester, NY: University of Rochester Press, 2011); Audra A. Diptee, "African Children in the British Slave Trade During the Late Eighteenth Century," *Slavery and Abolition* 27 (2006): 183–96; Paul Lovejoy, "The Children of Slavery—The Transatlantic Phase," *Slavery and Abolition* 27 (2006): 197–219; Marcus Rediker, *The Slave Ship: A Human History* (New York: Penguin, 2006), 98, 201.

10. Ruth Flanagan, *The Oral and Beyond: Doing Things with Words in Africa* (Chicago: University of Chicago Press, 2007); Roger D. Abrahams, *The Man-of-Words in the West Indies: Performance and the Emergence of Creole Culture* (Baltimore: Johns Hopkins University Press, 1983); Roger D. Abrahams, *Singing the Master: The Emergence of African American Culture in the Plantation South* (New York: Penguin, 1992), 111; George E. Brooks, *Eurafricans in Western Africa: Commerce, Social Status, Gender, and Religious Observance from the Sixteenth to the Eighteenth Century* (Columbus: Ohio University Press, 2003), 31; Robert M. Baum, *Shrines of the Slave Trade: Diola Religion and Society in Precolonial Senegambia* (New York: Oxford University Press, 1999); Margaretta Odell, "Memoir," in Phillis Wheatley, *Memoir and Poems of Phillis Wheatley, a Native African and a Slave* (Boston: George W. Light, 1834), 11.

11. David S. Shields, *Oracles of Empire: Poetry, Politics, and Commerce in British America, 1690–1750* (Chicago: University of Chicago Press, 1990); Max Cavitch, *American Elegy: The Poetry of Mourning from the Puritans to Whitman* (Minneapolis: University of Minnesota Press, 2006); Brown, *The Reaper's Garden;* Brown, "Social Death and Political Life in the Study of Slavery"; Stephanie Smallwood, *Saltwater Slavery: A Middle Passage from Africa to American Diaspora* (Cambridge, MA: Harvard University Press, 2007), 196–98; John C. Shields, *Phillis Wheatley's Poetics of Liberation: Backgrounds and Contexts* (Knoxville: University of Tennessee Press, 2009), 103–4, 117, 122.

12. In this respect, Gates's imagined "trial" is also a particularly gendered telling of her story: Henry Louis Gates Jr., *The Trials of Phillis Wheatley: America's First Black Poet and Her Encounters with the Founding Fathers* (New York: Basic Civitas, 2003). It is necessary only if one cannot imagine or recover women's practices of circulating manuscripts and poetry. For Wheatley's support network of women, see esp. David Grimsted, "Anglo-American Racism and Phillis Wheatley's 'Sable Veil,' 'Lengthn'd Chain,' and 'Knitted Heart,'" in *Women in the Age of the American Revolution*, ed. Ronald Hoffman and Peter J. Albert (Charlottesville: University Press of Virginia, 1989), esp. 370–94; Caroline Wigginton, *In the Neighborhood: Women's Publication in Early America* (Amherst: University of Massachusetts Press, 2016), chap. 3.

13. Jeffrey Brace, *The Blind African Slave: Memoirs of Boyrereau Brinch, Nicknamed Jeffrey Brace*, ed. Kari J. Winter (Madison: University of Wisconsin Press, 2005), 152; Anne C. Bailey, *African Voices of the Atlantic Slave Trade: Beyond the Silence and the Shame* (Boston: Beacon, 2005), 161–62.

14. With exceptions, including John C. Shields, *The American Aeneas: Classical Origins of the American Self* (Knoxville: University of Tennessee Press, 2001), chap. 6; Shields, *Phillis Wheatley's Poetics of Liberation;* John C. Shields and Eric D. Lamore, eds., *New Essays on Phillis Wheatley* (Knoxville: University of Tennessee Press, 2011), pt. 1; Martha Watson, "A Classic Case: Phillis Wheatley and her Poetry," *Early American Literature* 31 (1996): 103–30.

15. Bernard Bailyn, *The Ideological Origins of the American Revolution* (Cambridge, MA: Harvard University Press, 1967), 26; contrast Richard Gummere,

The American Colonial Mind and the Classical Tradition (Cambridge, MA: Harvard University Press, 1963); Eran Shalev, *Rome Reborn on Western Shores: Historical Imagination and the Creation of the American Republic* (Charlottesville: University of Virginia Press, 2009); Caroline Winterer, "From Royal to Republican: The Classical Image in Early America," *Journal of American History* 91 (2005): 1264–90; Caroline Winterer, "Model Empire, Lost City: Ancient Carthage and the Science of Politics in Revolutionary America," *William and Mary Quarterly* 67 (2010): 3–30. Other scholars emphasize the multivalent and sometimes subversive potential of various ancients in early modern contexts: see Sabine MacCormack, *On the Wings of Time: Rome, the Incas, Spain and Peru* (Princeton, NJ: Princeton University Press, 2007); Eric Nelson, *The Greek Tradition in Republican Thought* (Cambridge: Cambridge University Press, 2004); Eric Nelson, *The Hebrew Republic: Jewish Sources and the Transformation of European Political Thought* (Cambridge, MA: Harvard University Press, 2010).

16. Homer, *The Illiad*, trans. Robert Fagles (New York: Penguin, 1990); Homer, *The Odyssey*, trans. Robert Fagles (New York: Penguin, 1996); Page DuBois, *Slaves and Other Objects* (Chicago: University of Chicago Press, 2008), 102, 128, 134–35; Orlando Patterson, "Slavery, Gender, and Work in the Pre-modern World and Early Greece: A Cross-Cultural Analysis," in *Slave Systems: Ancient and Modern*, ed. Enrico Dal Lago and Constantina Katsari (Cambridge: Cambridge University Press, 2008), 62–63; Moses I. Finley, *The World of Odysseus*, 2d ed. (New York: Viking, 1965), 39, 46, 53–54, 59, 145; Page DuBois, *Trojan Horses: Saving the Classics From Conservatives* (New York: New York University Press, 2001), 66, 114; Edith Hall, *The Return of Ulysses: A Cultural History of Homer's Odyssey* (Baltimore: Johns Hopkins University Press, 2008), 36, 101, 116, 120, 132, 203; Alberto Manguel, *Homer's The Iliad and The Odyssey: A Biography* (Vancouver: Douglas McIntyre, 2007), citing Peter Levi at fifty-four ("dead and defeated"); William Fitzgerald, *Slavery and the Roman Literary Imagination* (Cambridge: Cambridge University Press, 2000), 87, 90; David Graeber, *Debt: The First 5000 Years* (Brooklyn, NY: Melville House, 2011), 189, 208.

17. Homer, *The Odyssey*; Terence, *The Comedies*, trans. Peter Brown (New York: Oxford University Press, 2006); Joseph C. Miller, *The Problem of Slavery as History* (New Haven, CT: Yale University Press, 2011), 67; Peter Hunt, "Slaves in Greek Literary Culture," in *The Cambridge World History of Slavery, Volume 1: The Ancient Mediterranean*, ed. Keith Bradley and Paul Cartledge (New York: Cambridge University Press, 2011), 22–47; Virgil, *The Eclogues*, trans. Guy Lee (New York: Penguin, 1984), 22, 33; Horace, *The Complete Odes and Epodes*, trans. David West (Oxford: Oxford University Press, 1997), v, 4–5, 12; Niall Rudd, ed., *The Satires of Horace and Persius* (New York: Oxford University Press, 1987), 16, 18, 66–70, 118–20.

18. Virgil, *The Eclogues*, 51, 53; Eric Ashley Hairston, "The Trojan Horse: Classics, Memory, Transformation, and Afric Ambition in *Poems on Various Subjects, Religious and Moral*," in Shields and Lamore, *New Essays on Phillis Wheatley*, 66–67; Ovid, *Heroides*, trans. Harold Isbell, Rev. ed (New York: Penguin, 2004), 10–16.

19. She shares, in short, her model Alexander Pope's ambivalence about the classics, an ambivalence that led him to translate Homer and to use classical forms as models for Christian and Enlightenment arguments. For Pope and the ancients and moderns, see, e.g., Steven Shankman, "Pope's Homer and his Poetic Career," and Howard D. Weinbrot, "Pope and the Classics" in *The Cambridge Companion to Alexander Pope*, ed. Pat Rogers (New York: Cambridge University Press, 2007),

63–75, 76–88; Howard D. Weinbrot, *Britannia's Issue: The Rise of British Literature from Dryden to Ossian* (Cambridge: Cambridge University Press, 1995), chaps. 6–7.

20. "On Messrs. Hussey and Coffin," in Carretta, *Phillis Wheatley: Complete Writings*, 73–74.

21. Homer, *The Odyssey of Homer in the English Verse Translation by Alexander Pope* (New York: Heritage, 1942), 345; John Dryden, trans., *Virgil's Aeneid*, ed. Frederick M. Keener (New York: Penguin, 1997), 6–8, 91, 101, 235, 305.

22. For trauma, see Phillip M. Richards, "Phillis Wheatley: The Consensual Blackness of Early African American Writing," in Shields and Lamore, *New Essays on Phillis Wheatley*, 262. Wheatley could be talking about herself, imagining herself into the world of the poem—as storm-tossed hero, as voice of the dead, as vessel of the Gods. More important, however, is how she is in control of the ancient references, the presence of the ancient that she comes to inhabit as much as she inhabits her Africanness for the reader.

23. Jeanine Falino, *Lives Shaped by the Revolution: Portraits of a Boston Family: Speakman, Rowe, Coffin, and Amory* (Cambridge, MA: Harvard University Art Museums, 2005), 36–37. For Coffin, Steuart, Somerset, Sapho, and Tambo, see Mark S. Weiner, *Black Trials: Citizenship from the Beginnings of Slavery to the End of Caste* (New York: Random House, 2004), 77; Kirsten Sword, "Remembering Dinah Nevil: Strategic Deceptions in Eighteenth Century Antislavery," *Journal of American History* 97 (September 2010): 9; Coffin to Steuart, August 7, 1769, October 12, 1770, Charles Steuart Papers, reel 2, John D. Rockefeller Jr. Library, Colonial Williamsburg Foundation, Williamsburg, VA.

24. Carretta, *Phillis Wheatley: Complete Writings*, 13; Gates, *The Trials of Phillis Wheatley*, 71; William W. Cook and James Tatum, *African American Writers and the Classical Tradition* (Chicago: University of Chicago Press, 2010), 11; Tara Bynum, "Phillis Wheatley's Pleasures," *Common-Place* 11, no. 1 (October 2010), http://www.common-place.org/vol-11/no-01/bynum. Dwight McBride makes a useful distinction in noting that, in her writings, Wheatley "does not hate Africa; she hates 'pagan' or 'Egyptian' Africa": Dwight McBride, *Impossible Witnesses: Truth, Abolitionism, and Slave Testimony* (New York: New York University Press, 2001), 113.

25. Carretta, *Phillis Wheatley: Complete Writings*, 70–71, 105. Carretta places "Deism," dated 1767, before "On Messrs. Hussey and Coffin," probably because the latter appeared in a newspaper on December 15 of that year.

26. Carretta, *Phillis Wheatley: Complete Writings*, 130–31; *New York Journal*, June 3, 1773, and Thomas Woolridge to Lord Dartmouth, November 24, 1772, in William H. Robinson, ed., *Phillis Wheatley and Her Writings* (New York: Garland, 1984), 388–89, 454; Joseph Rezek, "The Print Atlantic: Phillis Wheatley, Ignatius Sancho, and the Cultural Significance of the Book," in *Early African American Print Culture*, ed. Lara Langer Cohen and Jordan Alexander Stein (Philadelphia: University of Pennsylvania Press, 2011), 35.

27. I am thinking here in particular of Cathy N. Davidson, *Revolution and the Word: The Rise of the Novel in America* (New York: Oxford University Press, 1986); Julia Stern, *The Plight of Feeling* (Chicago: University of Chicago Press, 1997); Susan E. Klepp, *Revolutionary Conceptions: Women, Fertility, and Family Limitation in America, 1760–1820* (Chapel Hill: University of North Carolina Press, 2009).

28. Carretta, *Phillis Wheatley: Complete Writings*, 40, 83–87; Phillis Wheatley to Obour Tanner, February 14, 1776, in "The Hand of America's First Black Female

Poet," National Public Radio, November 21, 2005, http://www.npr.org/templates/story/story.php?storyId=5021077.

29. "Liberty and Peace," in Carretta, *Phillis Wheatley: Complete Writings*, 101.

30. "America," in ibid., 75. It seems important in this context that in this unfinished mini-epic poem, the next line—the simile—is explicitly gendered: "A certain lady had an only son" (referring to Britain and America and, allusively, to Mary and Jesus).

31. Joseph C. Miller, "Slavery as a Historical Process: Examples from the Ancient Mediterranean and the Modern Atlantic," in Dal Lago and Katsari, *Slave Systems*, 98.

32. Carretta, *Phillis Wheatley: Complete Writings*, 152.

33. In *Poems on Various Subjects, Religious and Moral*, Wheatley had revised her 1767 reference to her homeland as a "sable Land of error"—too racial?—to "land of errors, and Egyptian gloom": Kimberley Clay Bassard, *Spiritual Interrogations: Culture, Gender and Community in Early African American Women's Writings* (Princeton, NJ: Princeton University Press, 1999), 43–44. For the debate over "slavery and the meaning of America" in the early modern period, the essential starting point is David Brion Davis, *The Problem of Slavery in Western Culture* (Ithaca, NY: Cornell University Press, 1966), chap. 1.

34. Sandra Joshel, *Slavery in the Roman World* (Cambridge: Cambridge University Press, 2010), 41; Page DuBois, *Slavery: Antiquity and Its Legacy* (New York: Oxford University Press, 2009), 101; Jean Andreau and Raymond Descat, *The Slave in Greece and Rome*, trans. Marion Leopold (Madison: University of Wisconsin Press, 2011), 10, 25; Robert Knapp, *Invisible Romans* (Cambridge, MA: Harvard University Press, 2011), 172–94.

35. *Monthly Review*, vol. 49, December 1773, 457–59, reprinted in Mukhtar Ali Isani, ed., "The British Reception of Wheatley's *Poems on Various Subjects*," *Journal of Negro History* 66 (1981): 147–48; Eric Slauter, *The State as a Work of Art: Cultural Origins of the Constitution* (Chicago: University of Chicago Press, 2009), 192; Brycchan Carey, "A Stronger Muse: Classical Influences in Eighteenth-Century Abolitionist Poetry," in *Ancient Slavery and Abolition: From Hobbes to Hollywood*, ed. Edith Hall, Richard Alston, and Justine McConnell (New York: Oxford University Press, 2011), 131–32.

36. James Gilreath and Douglas L. Wilson, eds., *Thomas Jefferson's Library: A Catalog with the Entries in His Own Order* (Washington, DC: Library of Congress, 1989), 117; Wheatley, *Poems on Various Subjects, Religious and Moral* (London, 1773), v, Library of Congress.

37. Emily Greenwood deftly observes, in a mode reflective of the new interest in classical receptions, of the larger tradition of dismissing Wheatley, "You know you have been well and truly marginalized when even your neoclassicism is held to be derivative," but in this regard Jefferson's refusal to even admit of her neoclassical dimension seems most telling: Emily Greenwood, "The Politics of Classicism in the Poetry of Phillis Wheatley," in Hall et al., *Ancient Slavery and Abolition*, 165.

38. Thomas Jefferson, *Notes on the State of Virginia with Related Documents*, ed. David Waldstreicher (Boston: Bedford, 2002), 178–79; Caroline Winterer, *The Mirror of Antiquity: American Women and the Classical Tradition, 1750–1900* (Ithaca, NY: Cornell University Press, 2007), 31–35.

39. "To Maecenas," on in Carretta, *Phillis Wheatley: Complete Writings*, 10; Terence, *The Comedies*, 101, 316n; Betsy Erkkila, *Mixed Bloods and Other Crosses:*

Rethinking American Literature from the Revolution to the Culture Wars (Philadelphia: University of Pennsylvania Press, 2005), 87.

40. Gordon S. Wood, "Prologue: The Legacy of Rome in the American Revolution," in *Thomas Jefferson, the Classical World, and Early America,* ed. Peter S. Onuf and Nicholas P. Cole (Charlottesville: University of Virginia Press, 2011), 15; Carl J. Richard, *Greeks and Romans Bearing Gifts: How the Ancients Inspired the Founding Fathers* (Lanham, MD: Rowman and Littlefield, 2008), ix.

41. Eran Shalev, "Thomas Jefferson's Classical Silence, 1774–1776: Historical Consciousness and Roman History in the Revolutionary South," in Onuf and Cole, *Thomas Jefferson, the Classical World, and Early America,* 219–47.

PART III

Marriage and the Family

"What Am I but an American?"

Mary Willing Byrd and Westover Plantation during the American Revolution

AMI PFLUGRAD-JACKISCH

In the years surrounding the American Revolution, the Virginia plantation mistress Mary Willing Byrd faced a series of sizable challenges. In 1777, her husband, William Byrd III, died, leaving her to act as the sole executrix of his considerable but heavily indebted estate. She also had the responsibility of caring for and supporting their eight surviving children by herself. The complex nature of her husband's estate and the inimical legal and economic realities of the day for women drew Byrd into series of stressful auctions, court proceedings, and speculations about how she would continue to run Westover plantation in her husband's absence and protect the inheritance of his children.

In 1781, the British Army's repeated invasion and occupation of her plantation on the James River compounded this already demanding personal and economic situation. Troops seized and destroyed her crops, tools, livestock, food, furniture, cooking implements, and farming equipment. In addition, half of Byrd's slaves saw their opportunity for freedom and ran behind British lines as the army descended upon her plantation. To make matters worse, local American military leaders suspected Byrd of being disloyal to the patriot cause during these invasions, and she was tried in the General Court of Virginia for actions "injurious" to her country.

During this tumultuous time in her life, Byrd was catapulted into an unfamiliar world of legal problems, financial upheaval, and wartime dangers. She was forced to interact with the state, the military, the market, and the legal system in ways she likely never imagined. It was in the midst of the twin challenges of war and widowhood that Byrd formulated, articulated, and defined her political identity.

Although William Byrd's will directed that Mary Byrd have a life estate only in Westover, under the law she was a *feme sole* as a widow. Consequently, the government considered her a head of household and required her to pay taxes on her land and the numerous slaves she possessed. Like other white property holders awash in the republican political ideology of the day, Byrd believed that the state was obligated to protect her land and slaves, represent her political interests, and secure her legal authority as a slave owner. In short, as a taxpaying head of household Byrd, expected to be granted the same legal protections as a white man. Under Virginia law, however, only property-owning men had the privilege of *also* being "freeholders." This inherently male classification entitled free white men who owned at least twenty-five acres of land to vote and hold office over and above their right to the legal protection of their property.[1]

By the legal standards of the day, Byrd occupied an ambiguous place in this new nation, in which domestic relationships served as the root of all social, political, and legal order. She paid taxes, acted as a slave owner, and cared for her dependents in all of the same ways that an ideal republican patriarch should. Yet as a woman she could not vote, sell Westover, or make a fee simple claim to the plantation she managed for half her life.

In the end, Byrd drew on this dual status. This essay explores the identity that Mary Willing Byrd fashioned for herself as a citizen, plantation manager, mother, and slaveholding mistress, an identity that allowed her to negotiate the rapidly shifting economic and political sands of postrevolutionary Virginia. It argues that Byrd's experiences as a slave-owning widow during the American Revolution prompted her to devise and implement her own conception of women's citizenship rights that rested on her dual roles as mother and head of household.

Plantation Mistress

Mary Willing Byrd was not entirely unfamiliar with slavery before she moved from Pennsylvania to Virginia with her new husband. She was born into two powerful and well-connected Philadelphia merchant families: the Willings and the Shippens. As a young girl, she grew up in a household with at least three slaves, and trading in slaves was one part of her father and brother's successful business firm, Willing & Son.[2] Her experiences growing up in an urban merchant household in Philadelphia, however, could not have prepared her for her new role as plantation mistress on William Byrd's sprawling estate.

In 1760, twenty-year-old, Mary Willing met the thirty-three-year-old widower William Byrd III. Colonel Byrd was in Philadelphia as a result of his service in the French and Indian War. They married in January 1761, and she was pregnant with their first child by the end of March. In 1762, the family moved to Byrd's grand plantation in Virginia, Westover.[3] Unfortunately, we do not have an account of how Mary Byrd reacted to moving from a society with slaves to a slave society after her marriage, but we know she was impressed by her husband's beautiful and substantial properties, writing to her sister back in Philadelphia, "This is the most beautiful delightful place in the world!"[4] In her new role as the wife of William Byrd of Westover, Mary Byrd was known for her charm, hospitality, and her seemingly effortless performance of her duties as a plantation mistress.[5]

Between 1762 and 1777, Byrd was almost continuously pregnant or raising an infant. She gave birth to ten children, eight of whom lived to adulthood. Her pregnancies had caused several dangerous illnesses, and by November 1767, at twenty-seven, she had four children younger than six. She also faced personal hardships. One year earlier she had suffered the tragic loss of her eighteen-month-old son Charles. She watched him die right in front of her after a nurse dropped him on the brick piazza at Westover, crushing his skull.[6] In 1768, when Byrd's sister Eliza learned that she was pregnant for a sixth time, she commented, "Why don't you exercise female Taste and love of Veriety [sic] and fall on the Platonic System[?] [Y]ou have realy [sic] Children Enough."[7] Sadly, that child, a little girl named Dorothy, lived for only ten days.

During this time, Byrd was celebrated for creating an inviting home and hosting impressive dinners. Certainly, none of this would have been possible without slaves to help care for the children, wash and press the linens, clean her home, prepare and serve the food, and attend to the needs of guests and residents.[8] The many slaves who lived and worked at Westover allowed Byrd to maintain her reputation as a refined hostess, and they made possible the lavish lifestyle to which she and her children became accustomed.

As a plantation mistress, Byrd held power and authority within her home. Although she arrived at Westover with relatively little experience managing a plantation household, she surely would have learned much from her mother-in-law, Maria Taylor Byrd. Maria Byrd had been in charge of the domestic affairs of Westover since her marriage to William Byrd II in 1724. After her husband's death in 1744, Maria continued to manage the household until William Byrd III moved back to the plantation with Mary (although she seems to have limited or no experience in the nondomestic aspects of plantation life). Maria Byrd remained at Westover until her death in 1771.

Maria would have taught Mary how to oversee the slaves in her household. As a plantation mistress, Mary Byrd was responsible for acquiring clothing for slaves; purchasing and preparing food; providing medical care for and disciplining slaves; and making decisions about the buying and selling of slaves. During these formative years as the household manager of Westover, Byrd shaped and developed her persona as a plantation mistress, one that she would build on after her husband's death.[9]

Unfortunately for Byrd, not long after she moved to Virginia, her husband's dismal financial situation began to unravel. William Byrd had accrued enormous debts that he was not able to pay. Despite the sale of several properties, slaves, and a lottery to raise funds, William Byrd was insolvent by 1769.[10] He drew up a trust for his wife in 1772, undoubtedly both to protect and provide for her and to shield his estate from creditors. As part of this jointure agreement, Mary Byrd gave up rights to her dower. The arrangement granted her the estate of Westover and adjacent property Buckland, and it allocated ninety-nine slaves by name to work on the plantations.[11]

William Byrd's financial insolvency augmented and further exposed the ugly realities of slavery. As his finances unraveled during the 1760s, he was forced to hold several large and well-publicized slave auctions that broke up numerous slave families. He also mortgaged more than one hundred slaves to the Bristol tobacco merchants Farrell and Jones, including those at Westover with whom Mary interacted on a daily basis. Likewise, her husband attempted to recapture runaway slaves and sent disobedient slaves to his lead mines, and he had at least one slave jailed and hanged.[12]

The extent to which Mary Byrd participated in these events is unknown. As recent research has demonstrated, historians have often obscured white women's stake in slavery by emphasizing white men's authority in the household, especially among married women.[13] Yet whether a slaveholder was male or female, ultimately the system of slavery was predicated on violence and threat of sale. We do not know whether Mary Byrd personally disciplined her slaves or had an overseer do it or whether she had outbursts in which she slapped, hit, or verbally assaulted slaves. Regardless, her position of authority in the household, even in a domestic capacity, relied on a system of violence *and* the legal authority the state granted her as a plantation mistress to exercise that violence. Everyone knew this, especially the slaves. Thus, in the fifteen years that Byrd spent as the household manager of Westover and as the wife of William Byrd, she gained an intricate understanding of what it meant to live in a slave society. And while she was perhaps subordinate to her husband, she held authority in her household that helped to shape her later identity as a plantation manager after her husband's death.

Executrix

As the Revolution drew near, William Byrd's debts mounted while his reputation declined. Initially sympathetic to the Crown, he offered his substantial military experience and service to the British in July 1775 but quickly changed his mind after Lord Dunmore's Proclamation in November 1775. In December, he offered his services to the Americans, but it was too late, and the Virginia convention turned down his offer.[14] Drowning in debt and humiliated, William Byrd committed suicide in January 1777, at forty-eight.[15] Mary Byrd was pregnant for the tenth time when her husband died.

William Byrd's will bequeathed to "his dearest and best of wives for her life" the plantations of Westover and Buckland "with all the remaining negroes & stocks of all sorts," as much of his "plate" and household furniture as she chose to keep, and his carriage and coach horses. William directed that at the death of Mary Byrd, the remainder of his estate be sold and the proceeds be distributed equally among his surviving children.[16] In addition, he gave Mary the option of being his sole executrix, a task that she accepted. This was an increasingly rare occurrence in colonial Virginia and speaks to William's confidence in the abilities of his wife. By the last third of the eighteenth century, husbands were giving less and less power to their wives, and few deemed their wives capable of serving as their executrix.[17] Mary's sister, Eliza Powel, explained to her friend Martha Washington why Mary chose to take on this monumental task: she accepted the job with "A Hope of being able to serve the Heirs of Col. Byrd, where interests of her own Children were involved, & a Desire to comply with his Will."[18]

As directed by the terms of the will, Byrd auctioned off slaves, silver, dishware, and other valuable personal property that she could spare; her father-in-law's valuable library; and the remainder of William Byrd's real property.[19] An ad for the auction in the Virginia Gazette boasted, "To be sold . . . 100 Virginia born SLAVES," and listed a variety of tradesmen, a washerwoman, a dairy maid, and a cook, many of whom Byrd would have known well and who were important members of the plantation community. These auctions surely ripped apart slave families and disrupted daily life on the plantation. The first auction was held at Westover in April, where Byrd had just given birth to her last child only weeks earlier, and a second auction was held in November.[20]

Byrd then did her best to pay off her husband's creditors, but there was not enough money left after the remainder of the estate was sold, and she continued to struggle financially. Yet she moved forward with running Westover, raising and selling crops of wheat, corn, and tobacco.[21] Byrd adjusted slowly to her new life as a plantation manager in the years immediately following her husband's death. But it was the British invasion of Virginia in 1781 that would force Byrd to fully embrace her new identity as executrix, head of household, single parent, and slaveholder.

Invasion

Early in the morning on January 4, 1781, the newly commissioned British officer Brigadier-General Benedict Arnold moved up the James River and disembarked approximately 750 soldiers at Westover.[22] The troops stayed there for about a week and used the plantation as a base from which to launch an attack on Richmond. The financial damage to Byrd was enormous. She lost grain, household goods, livestock, and a large number of slaves.[23] Shortly after Arnold's departure, Byrd secured a flag of truce from the Continental Army officer Major-General Friedrich Wilhelm von Steuben, which allowed her to communicate with the British about the recovery of her slaves and other property.[24] On hearing that Byrd had received a flag, however, her slaves "hid themselves" and "could not be found," despite a thorough seven-day search by the British.[25]

Despite the unsuccessful search for her slaves, Arnold sent Lieutenant Charles Hare to Westover in his vessel the H.M.S. *Swift* with one of her daughter's riding horses and a number of other goods to convince Byrd that he would keep his promise to return her slaves eventually.[26] This transaction did not go as planned, and the Americans intercepted Hare and detained him and the *Swift* at Sandy Point. After a series of unpleasant exchanges between Hare and the Americans, the commanding officer at Sandy Point ordered Major George Lee Turberville to search Hare's vessel.

On the *Swift*, Turberville found a letter from Mary Byrd and a collection of goods including brandy, wine, linen, china, and broadcloth. Hare insisted these were sea stores, but Turberville was suspicious. He moved quickly (and without authorization) to gather a party of armed soldiers and rode to Westover to forcibly search Byrd's belongings for evidence of illegal trading. The men arrived before sunrise and charged into Byrd's bedroom while she and her daughters were still sleeping. Turberville made prisoners of Byrd, her family, and her guests (neighbors David and Sarah Meade) and placed men with drawn swords at the bottom of her staircase to prevent them from leaving the second floor. Among Byrd's papers Turberville found invoices and bills of cost that, he believed, suggested she had been trading with the British.[27]

Byrd was livid that American soldiers would invade and search her home in such a way. She immediately sent a letter to Steuben describing Turberville's conduct: "This surely can not be stiled [*sic*] liberty. It was Liberty that Savages would have blushed at[.] These Gentlemen used many civil expressions, but I think indecent actions. . . . They beged [*sic*] me not to be uneasy, I assured them my uneasiness was for them."[28] In addition, she condemned the soldiers for not respecting her rights as a property holder and an American citizen: "Good God what a situation am I in. I have paid taxes, during a tedious War; and now am not protected by my Country-men."[29] Her letter reflects not only her awareness and command of revolutionary political rhetoric, but also her convictions regarding the republican state's obligation to her as a citizen.

Throughout the end of February and early March, Byrd continued to correspond with Steuben and with Governor Thomas Jefferson to explain the documents Turberville found on Hare's ship and persuade them that "no action of my life has been inconsistent with the character of a virtuous American." In these letters, she expressed her devotion to America, claiming to have "a perfect love for her country."[30] Moreover, she articulated a notion of patriotism that was coupled to both her personal relationships and her status as a property owner. Speaking the language of republicanism, she wrote, "What am I but an American? All my friends and connexions [sic] are in America; my whole property is here—could I wish ill to everything I have an interest in?"[31] Surely, this would have resonated with Jefferson in particular, who believed that landownership endowed individuals with a vested social attachment and civic interest in their community.[32]

Despite Steuben's and Jefferson's kind responses to Byrd, neither was happy that she appeared to have arranged to receive goods from the British in compensation for her loss of her slaves. Jefferson explained that these concerns about the misuse of a flag were military, not civil, matters, and he had referred them to Steuben. Nevertheless, Jefferson also communicated to Byrd that it was up to the state's attorney-general to proceed as the treason laws required.[33] The letters Byrd wrote to Hare (found on the *Swift*) had caught the attention of several military officials, including Colonel John Nicholas, who wrote to Jefferson, "Since I wrote last I have discovered many other Letters from Mrs. Byrd which exasperates me in such a manner that I have determined to keep the one I mentioned to you secure with the rest for my own justification. . . . I have made discoveries on our part which tend to the injury of America."[34] Unfortunately, the letter has been lost, so we may never know what it contained. Whatever it was, it prompted the Executive Council to advise Jefferson to direct the judges of the General Court to set up a trial for Byrd: "Whereas it hath been represented, and there appears cause to suspect, that Mrs. Mary Byrd hath, during the present invasion, committed an offence."[35] The trial was originally scheduled for March 15, 1781, but was postponed until March 23.[36]

About the now lost letter, Byrd wrote to Jefferson, "I do not recollect the contents of this letter, but am easy about it, for my heart never dictated aught that was dishonorable, so my pen could never have expressed anything that I could not justify. If policy had not forbid it, I owe too much to my honor to betray my Country."[37] She adamantly denied that she had broken any laws or done anything that might have harmed her country. Still, in the same letter she inquired about Virginia's treason law, writing that "if any unavoidable things have happened that the law forbids," she would surely prove her innocence.[38]

Some of Byrd's neighbors also questioned her political loyalties. After Arnold's raid at Westover, leading men such as Arthur Lee referred to Mary Byrd as one of Arnold's "tory friends."[39] These accusations were linked to her treatment of several British soldiers who had occupied her plantation. After a skirmish at Charles City Court House between some of Arnold's men and the Virginia militia, wounded British soldiers were brought back to their encampment at Westover. Byrd reportedly nursed these men and showed them kindness (one eventually died and was buried at Westover).[40] Byrd claimed that because of this, local patriots had even made private attempts to "ruin" her and burn down her home. In fact, patriots did burn homes and destroy crops of suspected loyalists in areas where there was fighting to keep the British from accessing supplies that might benefit them.[41]

Byrd was devastated by the loss of her reputation. She repeatedly claimed that she preferred death to betraying her country.[42] She wrote to Jefferson regarding the hospitality she offered the British soldiers, "When the officers landed, I received them according to my idea, with propriety. I consulted my heart and my head, and acted to the best of my judgment, agreeable to all laws, human and divine. If I have acted erroneously, it was an error in judgment and not of the Heart."[43]

That her neighbors believed Byrd could be a traitor to her country and that the state's Executive Council thought she should be called to trial for her actions implied that Mary Byrd possessed her own, individual political agency. Byrd had exercised independent judgment during Arnold's raids, and consequently—as both Jefferson and Steuben made clear—Byrd would be judged according to Virginia's treason laws.[44] These laws specified that women, married or single, could be guilty of treason or injuring their country. The state's 1776 treason law used the gender-neutral "all persons."[45] In May 1780, the Virginia General Assembly further refined the law to include acts of "crimes injurious to the Independence of America, but less than treason." This law included women as independent actors capable of choosing their individual political allegiance.[46] The crimes carried a substantial fine or up to five years of imprisonment as punishment, and convictions were to be printed in the *Virginia Gazette*.[47]

According to Jefferson, the Executive Council sought in Byrd's case to investigate the part of the law that dealt with political allegiance in the case of invasion. He explained that Byrd could face civil charges if the court found that she had injured the state. The question at hand was whether or not she might "have been able to steer with Precision between the will of those in whose Power [she was—that is, Arnold and the British], and the Laws of [her] Country."[48] At the heart of these laws was the republican idea of volitional allegiance. Under the new republican government, citizenship and allegiance to the state were voluntary acts of individuals. Virginia's citizens had exercised their free political will and pledged their loyalty to Virginia and America.[49] Byrd herself believed that she had the power to choose her political allegiance. She wrote to Steuben, "I may perhaps have the power of serving [my country], it was what I always had in view, but I can not injure it."[50]

In the end, the details of precisely what happened at her trial are unclear. According to family accounts, Byrd did appear before the court. However, one account claims that the witnesses against her never showed up (one of whom was Turberville), and another asserts that she defended herself so effectively that the charges were dismissed. Arthur Lee speculated that Byrd was never prosecuted because "means" were "taken to keep the witnesses out of the way."[51] Each of these accounts could be true, but, unfortunately, we may never know what really happened. In any event, Byrd was never charged with a crime.

Despite the lack of clarity about the trial's details, one thing was evident: no one dismissed the possibility that Byrd could have injured the state simply because she was a woman. Moreover, these suspicions about her political loyalty prompted her to formulate a defense that articulated her relationship to the republican state and fostered the development of her political identity. Whether Byrd's statements during these episodes are expressions of authentic patriotism or strategic self-interest, her letters clearly demonstrate that she not only possessed a clear understanding of republican citizenship, but also that she thought she was entitled to certain citizenship rights as a white property holder, regardless of her gender.

Despite these dramatic events, the war was still not over for Mary Byrd. In late April 1781, three hundred British soldiers under the command of Major-General William Phillips hovered off the coast of Westover, then rejoined soldiers under Arnold. In May, these troops combined with Lord Charles Cornwallis's troops that were moving north after unsuccessfully trying to capture Nathanael Greene in the Carolinas. On May 24, approximately four thousand British soldiers under Cornwallis once again besieged Mary Byrd at Westover.[52]

According to Byrd's granddaughter, Byrd watched from a second floor window as Cornwallis's troops slaughtered her dairy cows and destroyed her crops, and as "her servants were enticed to go and [join] the British in great numbers."[53] Her total losses from both British invasions included grain, hay, and "pasturage"; cattle and horses; clothes; household linens; blacksmith, carpenter, and shoemaker's tools; garden "utensils"; all of her kitchen furniture; saddles, chariots, and harnesses; and a ferry boat, totaling £1,460.[54] The most severe loss, however, was that of her forty-nine slaves. They constituted approximately half of the slaves William Byrd had bequeathed to her in his will, and they were crucial to the financial success of her plantation.

One of Byrd's slaves who had left with the British during the first invasion was Walter (Wat) Harris. He had worked as a "waiting man" at Westover when Arnold arrived, and he volunteered to serve as Arnold's local guide and spy. He continued to work with Arnold until Cornwallis arrived in Virginia, after which time he worked as a guide for Cornwallis.[55] Byrd attributed the loss of her slaves to the "infidelity of those unhappy people."[56] Certainly, the hope of freedom would have motivated her slaves to take advantage of the opportunity the war had presented. Many slaves who had heard about the Dunmore and Philipsburg proclamations hoped to secure their freedom by running behind British lines. Byrd, of course, was not the only slave owner to lose slaves to the British. As the British moved through Virginia, more than 4,500 slaves saw their opportunity for freedom and flocked to join them.[57]

To make matters worse, beginning in early July and through the end of September 1781, the Continental Army moved up and down the roads near Westover that connected Williamsburg and Richmond. The Charles City county commissioners, under orders from the new governor, Thomas Nelson, made demands of the local residents to help supply the troops. Byrd provided the commissioners with large amounts of beef, bushels of wheat, horses, and other supplies. In addition, many troops foraged the countryside. In July, five hundred soldiers under General Anthony Wayne arrived in Virginia starved and half-naked after a grueling march from Pennsylvania. They then joined with the Marquis de Lafayette's 2,200 soldiers and engaged with Cornwallis just down the road from Westover in Green Spring.

Two weeks later, Cornwallis noted the presence of two hundred Continental and militia troops encamped at Westover. He sent Wat Harris with six men to the house to try to bring Byrd's slave Jack "off undiscover'd," but a party of American soldiers spotted Harris's group, and they were forced to retreat after killing one of the American soldiers.[58] According to Byrd's American public service claims, she helped supply Wayne's troops; provided Lafayette with two horses; and supplied corn, beef, fodder for the horses, wagons, carts, and wheat to numerous other local military units acting on behalf of the Continental Army. In 1782, she put forth no fewer than twenty-two public claims and certificates, totaling approximately £1,565 in specie.[59]

Clearly, Mary Byrd suffered extreme financial losses and the destruction of her property during the war, which compounded her preexisting struggles as a widow and executrix. Likewise, she had endured the stresses of having her plantation invaded by both British and American soldiers, of a trial for disloyalty, and of living in the center of a war zone for nine months. These ordeals spurred Byrd to assert her rights as a property holder and to define and communicate her ideas about both her relationship to the state and the state's obligation to her as a property owner. As a result, Byrd came away from the war believing that she was a rights-bearing individual and that the rhetoric of the Revolution applied to her, too, regardless of her gender. She had met the obligations of citizenship by paying taxes and acting as a virtuous citizen, and she expected the state to fulfill its duties to her in return.

Recovery

Once the immediate physical crises of the war ended, Byrd turned her attention to her role as provider for her children. Despite her financial difficulties, she was injected with a new consciousness of her political rights as a property owner. This new political awareness shaped Byrd's vehement campaign to recover the slaves who had emancipated themselves during the British occupations of Westover. In doing so, she intertwined her perceived citizenship rights as a property holder with her authority as a mother and as the head of her household.

As slaveholding widows such as Byrd knew well, their status and economic security rested on slave ownership. She linked explicitly the survival of her family to the return of her escaped slaves. "If I do not recover my people, my family are ruined," she wrote to Governor Nelson in August 1781.[60] In the letters she sent out in the final years of the war, she connected her family's "want of necessities" and the "expectations of [her] children" to the loss of her enslaved labor. Byrd claimed that the loss of her slaves prevented her from being able to provide a proper education for her three boys.[61] She noted that she had suffered not just the loss of the price for which the slaves would have sold but the loss in profits for the crops they would have cultivated.[62]

In addition, slaveholding widows routinely pursued their own financial interest above the comfort of their slaves to maintain the lifestyle of their families, feed and clothe their households, pay their taxes, and settle their debts.

As the historian Kirsten Wood notes, the loss of a husband made women into misers; as a result, slaves owned by widows were at greater risk of being sold and separated from their families.[63] Byrd was no different from other women in this regard. As the war drew to a close, Byrd, in desperate financial straits, sold off thirteen slaves for £900 "for the benefit of the estate."[64]

Clearly, Byrd and her family were not able to live in the high style they had known before the war, but whether or not they were truly impoverished is questionable. After his stop at Westover in 1782, the Marquis de Chastellux noted that the plantation was "still the most celebrated and the most agreeable in the neighbourhood," and Thomas Lee Shippen, who visited Westover in 1783, described the home's gilded portraits, beautiful china, rich silk damask furniture, and finely worked muslin.[65] At the very least, however, Byrd perceived herself as impoverished. She wrote to a female friend that she and her family were "pinched by cold and hunger, for want of servants to provide us with necessaries," and that "no body existed on earth less able to bear the calamities of poverty than myself."[66]

This sense of impoverishment and its perceived effect on her children fueled her determination to recover or be compensated for her escaped slaves and do so as a household head. In the two years following the British occupation of Westover, Byrd repeatedly and doggedly inquired of American and British officials about the recovery of her lost slaves. Channeling privileges typically reserved for white husbands and fathers, she stressed the importance of the return of "my people."[67] Historians have noted that male slave owners used "my people" as a euphemism to avoid using the word slave. Yet the license of using this phrase conveyed a masculine authority that came with being the head of a household and signaled that her "people" were dependents in her household.

Linked to this idea was Byrd's belief that her status as a citizen and a taxpayer entitled her to government protection of her slave property. In trying to obtain another flag of truce from Governor Nelson in August 1781, she forcefully asserted her right to recovery or compensation for her slave property. To do so, she used the language of republicanism and connected her status as property owner with her responsibilities as a female head of household and provider: "This claim I surely have a right to make as a female, as the parent of eight children, as a virtuous citizen, as a friend to my Country. . . . I have lost 49 of my people, 3 fine Horses and two fine Ferry Boats. . . . I have paid my taxes and have not been Personally, or Virtually represented. My property is taken from me and I have no redress."[68] This was a different kind of republican motherhood in which Byrd linked her mastery over her dependents and household authority to her status as a property owner and responsibilities for sustaining the needs of her family. Although she may have believed that raising up the next generation of virtuous citizens was an important part of her duties as a female citizen, it was not the only part. Byrd did not parse out public and private roles for herself but, instead, seamlessly merged one identity as citizen-taxpayer, mother, and slave owner.

By the late summer in 1781, rumors swirled among Virginia's slaveholders about the fate of slaves who had escaped with the British. Byrd wrote to Governor Nelson, "I hear repeatedly of the death of my people, some who wished much to return; others are gone to New York."[69] Disease reportedly raged among the slaves who had followed Arnold and "swept off great numbers of them."[70] A few months later, smallpox killed an untold number of the slaves who were with Cornwallis and his troops in the summer of 1781. Finally, in October Cornwallis drove the slaves out of British camps, where, trapped between the American and British lines, they suffered terribly from disease and starvation. For those who survived, a crueler fate awaited them as the British simply left them behind to be returned to their former masters. Some, however, were able to evacuate with the British and were transported to New York City.[71]

One of the slaves lucky enough to survive Yorktown and leave for New York with the British was Wat Harris, Byrd's waiting man. Immediately after the Articles of Capitulation had been signed, the Americans permitted the H.M.S. *Bonetta* to sail for New York carrying whomever Cornwallis selected, without approval or inspection. Cornwallis had given Harris permission to board the ship with a number of other slaves. Although Governor Nelson correctly suspected that escaped slaves were hiding on the *Bonetta,* there was nothing he could do. Harris arrived in New York with a handsome certificate from Cornwallis that testified to his fervent devotion to the British cause.[72]

After the British surrender at Yorktown, Byrd continued to appeal for compensation for the items she lost during Arnold's and Cornwallis's invasions and for and the return of her slaves. She petitioned the British Claims Commission without success. She then wrote again to Cornwallis and to Henry Clinton. Her writing reveals a sense of urgency to reclaim her slaves before the British left North America, which was coupled with a firm insistence that she had a right to secure her human property. She wrote to the British Claims Commission in August 1782, "I had received the most positive assurances from all the Generals who were up James River that I should not Lose a single Negro . . . , that not a sail should go out of the river without being searched and that if I lost any of my people they should be found and returned [to] me."[73]

Sir Guy Carleton, commander-in-chief of British forces in America, arrived in New York in May 1782. Throughout the summer and fall, he evacuated the rest of the British troops and slaves from the South. The Treaty of Paris was signed that November and included Article VII, which prohibited the British from carrying away any slaves that belonged to the Americans. Carleton, however, was determined to keep British promises to slaves who had assisted them during the war, and he chose to interpret Article VII selectively. He asserted that slaves who had joined the British before November 1782 had become free earlier in the war and could not be considered American property.[74]

After the terms of the treaty became publicly known in early 1783, Byrd joined other wealthy Virginians in trying to track down their slaves in New York City. She believed that seven or more slaves from her estate were there, and at least two of her slaves are listed in the *Book of Negroes*.[75] Byrd knew for certain that Wat Harris was in New York. In April 1783, she wrote to the loyalist Neil Jamieson in New York asking him to speak to Harris and convince him to return to Westover. She also hoped that Harris would assist her in locating other Westover slaves. She offered to pay Harris for his assistance and assured his safety in returning to Westover, noting that his wife, Jenny, and child were very anxious to see him.[76]

Byrd knew that, if located, her slaves would not cheerfully relinquish their newfound freedom. She directed Jamieson, "There is one woman in particular her name is Betty, who will not return I expect having a free Husband if she can avoid it[,] nor do I expect any of them will return willingly what ever they may pretend to."[77] Thus, as a way "to make them more happy," she tried to convince them that she would not punish them for running away: "These poor people may show an unwillingness to return, dreading punishment but I can with truth declare that . . . mine may rely on the best useage [*sic*] from me, if they will merit it."[78] In essence, if they returned to Virginia without giving her any trouble, they could expect not to be punished. An implicit threat existed, though, for her statements implied that punishment would await slaves whose behavior was not in line with what she wanted.

Here we get a glimpse into Byrd's personality as a slave owner. She considered her slaves untrustworthy and believed that they owed her loyalty. She hoped to avoid disciplining them but was willing to punish them if necessary. Most of all, she was entirely unsympathetic to their desire to be free. This is consistent with the findings of Kirsten Wood and others regarding female slaveholders. Like male slaveholders, women almost always put the comfort of their own families above the needs and wants of their slaves.[79] Thus, the fact that her slave Betty had a husband in New York was entirely irrelevant to Byrd's decision to bring her slaves back to Westover.

Instead of helping Byrd, Harris fled to England, leaving behind his friends and family. He claimed that he feared for his safety because he had helped the British. Harris later expressed a desire to return to Virginia, and in 1785 he applied to the British government for funding to return to America. He was given £25 and at some point did return to New York.[80] There is no evidence that he ever returned to Westover, but he somehow kept in touch with his family there. From Westover in 1795, Mary Byrd's son Richard reported to his brother Charles in Ohio that Wat Harris had died in New York, and his wife and family at Westover "were much grieved."[81]

Not getting the results she wanted from Jamieson or Harris, Byrd finally wrote directly to Guy Carleton himself in June 1783. Again, she rested the authority for her claim on her joint roles as mother and property owner/provider: "I am Sir the Mother of eight children. . . . [T]hey are now deprived of the support [their father] left them; fallen from a state of affluence to know the want of many of the necessaries of life. . . . [Lord Cornwallis and others] assured me that not one single Vessel should be allowed to depart this river until they had undergone a search for my people, and every soul of them returned me."[82] By late summer of 1783, it had become clear to most Virginia slaveholders that Carleton was not going to facilitate the return of their slaves. Carleton told Byrd that "as there was not proper vouchers he could do nothing. . . . [H]e pitied her but that was all."[83]

She again wrote to Cornwallis, who was now commander-in-chief of British forces in India, and he responded that, because he was no longer in England, it was not in his power to help her. He did, however, write a letter on her behalf vouching for the worthiness of her claim.[84] The British never compensated Byrd for her losses, and none of the slaves who had escaped during the war ever returned to Westover.

Conclusion

As Byrd attempted to establish a new normal on her plantation after the war, she was increasingly besieged by her husband's creditors and was forced to turn her focus toward the growing number of lawsuits against William Byrd's estate. Yet by the late 1780s, Byrd had grown more comfortable with her role as head of household, and she shrewdly managed the affairs of her plantation. After hiring out her slave Ned to William Cocke of Bremo in 1788, perhaps in exchange for the purchase of another slave, she did not mince words about ensuring that Cocke return her property to her on time: "Sir, I perceive you have forgot the agreement we made. . . . I have fully paid for Old Ben, Ned's time being expired—I have our agreement written by Mr. Page taken from your mouth and mine. . . . If you wish to have Ned, he shall be at your service at my [price] if not—I beg this favor of you to send him down tomorrow. I had expected to see him this evening."[85] Throughout the remaining years of her life, Mary Byrd continued to manage Westover. She produced successful wheat and barley crops, bought and sold slaves, posted ads for runaways, and managed her overseers.[86]

Byrd's unique conception of women's citizenship rights was born of trial during a distinctive set of circumstances. Her experiences as a slave-owning widow during the American Revolution led her to fashion her own political identity that explicitly linked her status as a property owner to her identity as a mother. In the new republican culture that idealized sovereignty of property, Byrd claimed as many of the rights of the Revolution for herself as she could—including the ownership of slaves.

Slowly over the course of the early republic, however, changing ideas about women's capacity for political participation diminished, along with the possibility of property-owning widows such as Mary Byrd asserting themselves as rights-bearing citizens. As Americans moved further and further away from the disruption and dislocations of war, they began to conceive of more explicit ways to reconcile and maintain old gender hierarchies with their new republican government.

Increasingly by the 1820s the sexes had separate and distinct rights. Unlike the promises of liberty and choice granted to white men in exchange for their service to the state, early American authors and political commentators placed growing emphasis on women's duty and obligation to the state and on their commitment to social order. In doing so, they effectively circumvented the universal application of natural rights ideology, ensuring that women would lay claim to their rights only within their own, appropriate sphere.[87]

This watered-down form of political identity made it easier to believe growing claims that women were not capable of exercising their own political will and that the founders had never intended full citizenship rights to apply to women. Thus, although Mary Byrd's granddaughters would fulfill their obligation to the state by raising virtuous, well-educated citizens and benefit from being white in a slaveholding republic, their claims to household mastery and civic participation could never be based on anything but their status as mothers.[88]

Notes

1. Christopher Michael Curtis, *Jefferson's Freeholders and the Politics of Ownership in the Old Dominion* (Cambridge: Cambridge University Press, 2012), 53–54.

2. Will of Charles Willing, Philadelphia County, Pennsylvania, Will Books nos. I-K 1748–57, Historical Society of Pennsylvania, Philadelphia; Robert E. Wright,

"Thomas Willing (1731–1821): Philadelphia Financier and Forgotten Founding Father," *Pennsylvania History* 63 (Autumn 1996): 527–29.

3. Marion Tinling, ed., *The Correspondence of the Three William Byrds of Westover, 1684–1776*, vol. 2 (Charlottesville: University Press of Virginia, 1977): 610, 757n1.

4. Regarding the concept of a society with slaves, see Ira Berlin, *Many Thousands Gone: The First Two Centuries of Slavery in North America* (Cambridge, MA: Harvard University Press, 1998), 1–14; Mary Willing Byrd, quoted in Sophia Cadwalader, ed., *Recollections of Joshua Francis Fisher Written in 1864* (Philadelphia: Privately Printed, 1929), 95.

5. Charles Royster, *The Fabulous History of the Great Dismal Swamp Company* (New York: Vintage, 1999), 223.

6. Biography of Mary Willing Byrd written circa 1850 by an unidentified granddaughter, unpublished ms., Robert A. Brock Collection, Huntington Library, miscellaneous microfilm reel 5074, Library of Virginia, Richmond (hereafter, unpublished ms.) My sincerest thanks to Brent Tarter of the Library of Virginia for his assistance with this document.

7. Elizabeth Willing Powel to Mary Willing Byrd, August 15, 1768, Powel Family Papers, 1681–1938, Collection 1582, ser. 3b, Historical Society of Pennsylvania, box 4, folder 3.

8. For a broader of discussion of this idea among the wives and other female relations of the founders in Virginia, see Lorri Glover, *Founders as Fathers: The Private Lives and Politics of the American Revolutionaries* (New Haven, CT: Yale University Press, 2014), 185–87.

9. See Stephanie Jones-Rogers, "'Nobody Couldn't Sell 'em but Her': Slave-owning Women, Mastery, and the Gendered Politics of the Antebellum Slave Market" (Ph.D. diss., Rutgers University, New Brunswick, NJ, 2012), 15–72. For a description of the daily tasks and interactions with slaves that were involved in managing a large plantation household such as the one at Westover, see Elizabeth Fox-Genovese, *Within the Plantation Household: Black and White Women of the Old South* (Chapel Hill: University of North Carolina Press, 1988); Cara Anzilotti, *In the Affairs of the World: Women, Patriarchy, and Power in Colonial South Carolina* (Westport, CT: Greenwood, 2002).

10. Timothy H. Breen, *Tobacco Culture: The Mentality of the Great Tidewater Planters on the Eve of Revolution* (Princeton, NJ: Princeton University Press, 1985), 169–71; For a succinct overview of Byrd's enormous debts, see Emory Evans, "William Byrd," in *The Dictionary of Virginia Biography*, vol. 2, ed. Sara B. Bearss (Richmond: Library of Virginia, 2001), 471–72.

11. Benjamin B. Weiseiger, ed., *Charles City County, Virginia Records, 1737–1774* (Richmond: B. B. Weiseiger, 1984), 52. Buckland was a property adjacent to Westover.

12. Royster, *The Fabulous History of the Great Dismal Swamp Company*, 191–92; Breen, *Tobacco Culture*, 208–9; See *Virginia Gazette* (Purdie and Dixon) runaway and sale ads for December 8, 1768, June 1, 1769, January 31, 1770, May 24, 1770, November 19, 1772, September 23, 1775; "Bill of Complaint: Robinson's Admr's vs. Byrd, et. als." (1786), in Peyton Rhodes Carrington, ed., *Extracts from Various Virginia Records*, compiled 1904, VHS, 222; "Estate of William Byrd in Account with Mary Byrd His Executrix," Charles City County Will Book 2, 1808–24, Library of Virginia, Richmond, 363.

13. For an excellent overview of this scholarship, see Thavolia Glymph, *Out of the House of Bondage: The Transformation of the Plantation Household* (Cambridge: Cambridge University Press, 2008), 18–31. For more on the role of white female slaveholders, see Jones-Rogers, "Nobody Couldn't Sell 'em but Her"; Kirsten E. Wood, *Masterful Women: Slaveholding Widows from the American Revolution through the Civil War* (Chapel Hill: University of North Carolina Press, 2004).

14. Evans, "William Byrd," 472; James Gordon Buelow, "The Last Patriarch of Westover: The Life, Legend, and Legacy of Colonel William Byrd III (1728–1777)," M.A. thesis, College of William and Mary, Williamsburg, VA, 1999, 83–95.

15. Royster, *The Fabulous History of the Great Dismal Swamp Company*, 235–36. Currently, most scholars accept that Byrd committed suicide, although his death notice in the *Virginia Gazette* states that he died of a quick illness. James Gordon Buelow presents an interesting counterargument, claiming that it was historians who labeled Byrd's death a suicide in the twentieth-century: see Buelow, "The Last Patriarch of Westover," 101–3, 125–30. Buelow argues persuasively that there is no definitive proof that Byrd committed suicide.

16. "The Will of Colonel William Byrd, 3d," *Virginia Magazine of History and Biography* 9, no. 1 (July 1901): 86.

17. Joan Hoff, *Law, Gender, and Injustice: A Legal History of U.S. Women* (New York: New York University Press, 1991), 81–85.

18. Elizabeth Willing Powel to Martha Washington, November 31, 1787, in Joseph E. Fields, ed., *"Worthy Partner": The Papers of Martha Washington* (Westport, CT: Greenwood, 1994), 199–200.

19. Royster, *The Fabulous History of the Great Dismal Swamp Company*, 236–37. On William Byrd II's library, see Edwin Wolf, "The Dispersal of the Library of William Byrd of Westover Wolf," *Proceedings of the American Antiquarian Society* (April 1958), 19–109.

20. *Virginia Gazette* (Purdie and Dixon), March 21, 1777.

21. Humphreys Richard to Mary Willing Byrd, March 24, 1780, in William Byrd Papers, 1624–1800, sec. 7, VHS.

22. Benjamin Harrison to Thomas Jefferson, January 4, 1781, in *The Papers of Thomas Jefferson*, ed. Julian Boyd et al., 43 vols. (Princeton, NJ: Princeton University Press, 1951), 4:304 (hereafter, *PTJ*).

23. American Loyalist Claims, Series I, Minutes, 1783, Public Records Office, Audit Office (hereafter, PRO, AO) 12/117/32–37. The originals are housed at the National Archives of the United Kingdom, Kew, Surrey, England. Although Mary Byrd repeatedly mentions the numerous slaves she lost during Arnold's invasion, she does not provide a number until after Cornwallis's raid in May 1781. Overall, she claims to have lost forty-nine slaves, but it is unclear how many she lost in each raid.

24. "The Affair of Westover," *PTJ* 5:675–76.

25. Mary Willing Byrd to Baron von Steuben, February 15, 1781, *PTJ* 5:688.

26. Ibid.; Baron von Steuben to Thomas Jefferson, February 21, 1781, in *PTJ* 4:679–80. There are two relationships that should be noted here. Mary Willing Byrd's sister Margaret was married to Robert Hare, a recent English immigrant to Philadelphia. Robert and Margaret had fled Philadelphia during its occupation by the British in 1778 and stayed with Byrd in exile at Westover. Lt. Charles Hare was Robert Hare's brother, although it is unclear how well Byrd knew him, if at all. Byrd made no attempt to defend Hare's poor judgment and conduct in this whole affair

and, in fact, seemed to distance herself from him. In addition, Margaret Shippen Arnold (the wife of Benedict Arnold) was Mary Willing Byrd's first cousin once removed. It is unclear whether they even knew each other, as Margaret was an infant when Byrd left Philadelphia for Virginia, and there is no evidence that she had any contact with her before or after the war.

27. Mary Willing Byrd to Baron von Steuben, February 23, 1781, *PTJ* 5:689–90; James Innes to Baron von Steuben, February 27, 1781, *PTJ* 5:695.

28. Byrd to von Steuben, *PTJ* 5:689–90.

29. Ibid.

30. Mary Willing Byrd to Thomas Jefferson, February 23, 1781, *PTJ* 4:691. This letter was recently redated to February 28, 1781, by the editors of *PTJ*. In my citations, I have maintained the original date in the printed collection edited by Julian Boyd, since that is how the letter is printed in Boyd's edition and that is the source I used.

31. Byrd to Jefferson, *PTJ* 5:691–92.

32. Curtis, *Jefferson's Freeholders and the Politics of Ownership in the Old Dominion*, 54–55.

33. Thomas Jefferson to Mary Willing Byrd, March 1, 1781, *PTJ* 5:31–32; H. R. McIlwaine, ed., *Journals of the Council of State of Virginia*, vol. 2 (Richmond: Virginia State Library, 1932), 298.

34. Innes to von Steuben, *PTJ* 5:695–96; John Nicholas to Jefferson, [February 20, 1781], *PTJ* 4:680.

35. McIlwaine, *Journals of Council of State of Virginia*, 302–3.

36. Thomas Jefferson to the Marquis de Lafayette, March 19, 1781, *PTJ* 5:180.

37. Byrd to Jefferson, *PTJ* 5:691–92.

38. Ibid.

39. Arthur Lee to Theodorick Bland, March 21, 1781, Arthur Lee Papers, VHS.

40. Cadwalader, *Recollections of Joshua Francis Fisher Written in 1864*, 99; John Graves Simcoe, *A Journal of the Operations of the Queen's Rangers from the End of the Year 1777 to the Conclusion of the Late American War by Lieutenant-Colonel Simcoe Commander of that Corps* (Exeter: Printed for the author, 1789), 110–15.

41. Byrd to von Steuben, *PTJ* 5:689; Wood, *Masterful Women*, 20

42. Unpublished ms., 8; Byrd to von Steuben, *PTJ* 5:689; Byrd to Jefferson, *PTJ* 4:691.

43. Byrd to Jefferson, *PTJ* 4:692.

44. Baron von Steuben to Mary Willing Byrd, February 23, 1781, *PTJ* 5:692; Jefferson to Byrd, *PTJ* 4:31.

45. William Waller Hening, ed., *The Statutes at Large: Being a Collection of All the Laws of Virginia from the First Session of the Legislature, in the Year 1619*, 10 vols. (Richmond: George Cochrane, 1822), 9:170; Linda K. Kerber, *Women of the Republic: Intellect and Ideology in Revolutionary America* (Chapel Hill: University of North Carolina Press, 1980), 121.

46. Hening, *The Statutes at Large*, 10:268.

47. Hening, *The Statutes at Large*, 10:268–70, 386–89.

48. Jefferson to Byrd, *PTJ* 5:31.

49. James H. Kettner, *The Development of American Citizenship, 1608–1870* (Chapel Hill, University of North Carolina Press, 1978), 207, 269–74; Kerber, *Women of the Republic*, 121; Joan R. Gundersen, "Independence, Citizenship, and the American Revolution," *Signs* 13, no. 1 (Autumn 1987): 60–68; Hoff, *Law, Gender,*

and Injustice, 80; Brian F. Carso, *"Whom Can We Trust Now?": The Meaning of Treason in the United States, from the Revolution through the Civil War* (Lanham, MD: Lexington, 2006), 74.

50. Byrd to von Steuben, *PTJ* 5:690.

51. Jefferson to Lafayette, *PTJ* 5:180; unpublished ms., 6–7; Cadwalader, *Recollections of Joshua Francis Fisher Written in 1864*, 99–100; Lee to Bland.

52. John E. Selby, *The Revolution in Virginia, 1775–1783* (Williamsburg, VA: Colonial Williamsburg Foundation, 1988), 272–75; Royster, *The Fabulous History of the Great Dismal Swamp Company*, 269.

53. Unpublished ms., 4–5. As the historian Alan Taylor notes, the idea that the British lured slaves away from patriot masters instead of stating that they ran away with the hope of gaining their freedom was a common interpretation of revolutionary events among antebellum Virginians: see Alan Taylor, *The Internal Enemy: Slavery and War in Virginia, 1772–1832* (New York: W.W. Norton, 2013), 25.

54. American Loyalist Claims, PRO, AO/12/117/32–37.

55. Ibid., PRO, AO 12/99/33; ibid., PRO, AO 13/31/97.

56. Ibid., PRO, AO 12/117/34.

57. Sylvia Frey, "Between Slavery and Freedom: Virginia Blacks in the American Revolution," *Journal of Southern History* 49, no. 3 (1983): 381–83; Taylor, *The Internal Enemy*, 26–27; Michael A. McDonnell, *The Politics of War: Race, Class and Conflict in Revolutionary Virginia* (Chapel Hill: University of North Carolina Press, 2007), 437–40.

58. "Note of Operations from 18th to 22nd July 1781," in Ian Saberton, ed., *The Cornwallis Papers: The Campaigns of 1780 and 1781 in the Southern Theatre of the American Revolutionary War*, vol. 5 (Uckfield, UK: Naval and Military Press, 2010), 221.

59. Selby, *The Revolution in Virginia*, 289–92, 296–98; public service claims, reel no. 1, Charles City County Court Booklet, claims 213–34, Library of Virginia.

60. Mary Willing Byrd to [Thomas Nelson], August 10, 1781, in *PTJ*, 5:703–4.

61. Rebecca Aitchison to James Parker, March 10, 1789, in Parker Family Papers, 1760–95, Liverpool Public Library, Liverpool, UK. In fact, Byrd's son Charles was sent to live with her brother-in-law Samuel Powel in Philadelphia because she could not afford to provide for him. Later in life, Charles lamented in a letter to his sister Ann, "Poverty dragged me at the distance of 600 miles from my brothers and sisters": see Charles Willing Byrd to Ann Willing Byrd, June 26, 1796, Charles Willing Byrd Papers, Lilly Library, Indiana University, Bloomington (hereafter, CWB), folder 1.

62. American Loyalist Claims, PRO, AO 12/117/32–37.

63. Glover, *Founders as Fathers*, 174, 180–83; Wood, *Masterful Women*, 37.

64. "Estate of William Byrd in Account with Mary Byrd His Executrix," 363–68.

65. Basil Hall, ed., *Chastellux's Travels in North America in the Years 1780-81-82* (Carlisle, MA: Applewood, 2007), 280; L. H. Butterfield, ed., *Westover Described in 1783: A Letter and Drawing Sent by Thomas Lee Shippen, Student of Law in Williamsburg, to his Parents in Philadelphia* (Richmond, VA: William Byrd, 1952), n.p.

66. Unpublished ms., 8.

67. She uses "my people" repeatedly: see Byrd to von Steuben, *PTJ* 5:688; Byrd to [Nelson], *PTJ* 5:703–4; Mary Willing Byrd to Guy Carleton, June 5, 1783, in *PTJ* 5:704–5.

68. Byrd to [Nelson], *PTJ* 5:704.

69. Ibid., 5:703–4.

70. David Jameson, March 10, 1781, quoted in Frey, "Between Slavery and Freedom," 392.

71. Frey, "Between Slavery and Freedom," 392–94; Cassandra Pybus, *Epic Journeys of Freedom: Runaway Slaves of the American Revolution and their Global Quest for Liberty* (Boston: Beacon, 2006), 47–55.

72. Pybus, *Epic Journeys of Freedom*, 55.

73. American Loyalist Claims, PRO, AO 12/117/32–37; Aitchison to Parker.

74. Pybus, *Epic Journeys of Freedom*, 57–68.

75. Pybus, *Epic Journeys of Freedom*, 63, 65–66; American Loyalist Claims, PRO, AO 12/117/32–37. One of the slaves listed in the *Book of Negroes* was Fanny Harris, who was likely a relative of Wat Harris. His wife, Jenny Harris, and son Wat remained at Westover, along with several other Harrises: see Graham Russell Hodges, ed., *The Black Loyalist Directory: African Americans in Exile after the American Revolution* (New York: Garland, 196), 171. Among those who also lost slaves were Thomas Jefferson, Benjamin Harrison, St. George Tucker, George Washington, and James Madison: see Taylor, *The Internal Enemy*, 25, 28; Eva Sheppard Wolf, *Race and Liberty in the New Nation: Emancipation in Virginia from the Revolution to Nat Turner's Rebellion* (Baton Rouge: Louisiana State University Press, 2009), p.15

76. Mary Willing Byrd to Neil Jamieson, April 1783, Neil Jamieson Papers, 1757–89, Correspondence, Library of Congress, Washington DC, box 5.

77. Ibid.

78. Ibid.

79. Wood, *Masterful Women*, 36–37, 48; Glover, *Founders as Fathers*, 174, 182–84; Cynthia A. Kierner, *Martha Jefferson Randolph, Daughter of Monticello: Her Life and Times* (Chapel Hill: University of North Carolina Press, 2012), 252–54.

80. American Loyalist Claims, PRO, AO 13/31/ 98; ibid., PRO, AO 12/101/290.

81. Richard Willing Byrd to Charles Willing Byrd, June 20, 1795, CWB.

82. Byrd to Carleton, *PTJ* 5:704–5.

83. Aitchison to Parker.

84. Pybus, *Epic Journeys of Freedom*, 67–69; Aitchison to Parker; Charles Cornwallis to Alexander Ross, April 9, 1784, in Charles Ross, ed. *The Correspondence of Charles, First Marquis Cornwallis*, 2d ed., vol. 1 (London: John Murray, 1859), 173.

85. Mary Willing Byrd to William Cocke, April 10, 1788, Armistead-Cocke Papers, series 4, Swem Special Collections Research Library, College of William and Mary, Williamsburg, VA, box 2, folder 16.

86. "Estate of William Byrd in Account with Mary Byrd His Executrix," 363–88; William Powel Byrd to Charles Wiling Byrd, June 20, 1795, CWB; *Virginia Gazette and Public Advertiser*, September 17, 1794; Mary Willing Byrd to Charles Willing Byrd, July 11, 1812, CWB; Evelyn Taylor Byrd Harrison to [her daughter], June 29, 1813, Byrd Family Papers, 1791–1867, sec. 10, VHS.

87. Rosemarie Zagarri, "The Rights of Man and Woman in Post-Revolutionary America," *William and Mary Quarterly* 55, no. 2 (April 1998): 203–30.

88. See Wood, *Masterful Women*, 9, 52–60, 193–94; Stephanie McCurry, *Masters of Small Worlds: Yeoman Households, Gender Relations, and Political Culture of the Antebellum South Carolina Low Country* (Oxford: Oxford University Press, 1995).

Intimate Ties and the Boston Massacre

SERENA R. ZABIN

Familiar even to American schoolchildren, the Boston Massacre is one of the American Revolution's dramatic events. To most historians it is likewise simple and self-explanatory. Rising confrontations between apprentices and other male teenagers, on the one hand, and young and underpaid British soldiers, on the other, led to an armed confrontation on the Boston streets in March 1770. Five Boston men were killed; eight soldiers and one officer were triumphantly acquitted (or just about) when John Adams took their case. Bored adolescent boys roving the streets and bored men with guns: scholars are not surprised that blood was shed. Over the past forty years, historians who have looked at this incident—like the politicians who lived through it—have simply debated who was to blame. It hardly seems like a topic ripe for women's history.[1]

Yet the story of the first occupation of Boston has women at its heart. In the four years from 1768 to 1772, not only did British soldiers move into civilian Boston; civilian Bostonians blended their families with the British Army. Through courtship, marriage, and childbirth Boston women redefined the imperial relationship in the handful of years before the Declaration of Independence. As the records of some forty marriages of military men and more than a hundred baptisms of their children make clear, women constituted a fundamental component of the army's experience in Boston.

In this essay, drawn from my larger study of the intimate occupation of Boston, I examine the personal, social, and political meanings of these new families. In an eighteenth-century world where the "social" was both private and public, flirtations between young women and soldiers were not simply personal matters; heterosexual relationships between soldiers and civilians were an issue of significant political concern for Boston's Sons of Liberty and other Whigs. The public nature of courtship raised the political stakes for military-civilian relationships. Even women whose families had not yet declared a political position found that their decision to marry into the army had momentous implications. When they married these men, Bostonians did not reject their families or their town. They did, however, extend their familial bonds out of Boston and into the larger empire. If she married a soldier, a woman shifted her legal and personal commitments from a father settled in a community to a man whose world was both peripatetic and unforeseeable. Although neither sex with nor marriage to a soldier declared a woman's political loyalty, such acts did reshape the connections that she and her family had to the British Empire. The connection was not always positive, and not every parent embraced a soldier son-in-law. One way or another, for many Bostonians these troops came to be part of their most personal society. As a result, the military and the familial came to be intertwined in Bostonians' experience of occupation and of the British Empire. Commentary from the eighteenth century onward has spoken of the Revolution as a family drama between the mother country and its ungrateful child. The presence of these women in Boston helps us see that this family conflict was not simply metaphorical. Bostonians and soldiers alike understood at a deeply personal, even physical level that the sundering of the bonds of empire was a hard and painful choice.

The Courtship of William Clark

William Clark had attitude. While his comrades in the Twenty-Ninth Regiment were camping on the Common or meeting their new Boston neighbors, Private Clark was spending time with literature: his own. Two months after his arrival in Boston, Clark announced that his play, *The Miser, or the Soldier's Humour: A Comedy of Three Acts,* was available for purchase by subscription. With a flourish that revealed his devil-may-care attitude, the broadside announcing the subscription included a brief and nearly correct Latin tag, *Non possunt placeto omnibus* (I can't please everyone). Presumably, Clark got enough subscriptions to print his play, since the following February Ezekiel Russell advertised in all of the Boston papers that he had just published *The Miser* and would sell it, with a blue paper cover, for 8 pence. Sadly, no copies of the play are extant. It is possible, of course, that in the winter of 1769 not many Bostonians were particularly eager to read about "the soldier's humour." Given his disclaimer that the author was not trying to please everyone, one can only wonder what comedy an audience would have found in those three acts.[2]

Undaunted, however, Clark continued to write. In August 1770 he took out another advertisement, this one for his new memoir, *A True and Faithful Narrative of the Love Intrigues of the Author, William Clark, Soldier in his*

Majesty's 29th Regiment of Foot. As it happens, Clark's "love intrigues" reveal a great deal about life in occupied Boston.[3]

Clark did indeed have a story to tell. Soon after a small contretemps in May with the Boston watchmen, in which he threatened to burn down the workhouse and the town of Boston with it, he managed an even more dramatic scene with Boston locals. Coming in to his married daughter's house one June day in 1769, seventy-five-year-old Joseph Lasenby was shocked to find Clark in bed with his twenty-year-old granddaughter, Mary Nowell. He ordered Clark out of the house, but the insouciant soldier declined to leave. He had every right to have sex with her, Clark asserted: Mary was his wife, Clark told the astonished old man, and he was going nowhere without her.[4]

Clark might have stretched the truth a bit. The story Mary told was that they had been married one evening "by a person who was drest as a priest." In fact, they were not married until four months after being caught *in flagrante*. But married they were, much to the distress of Mary's parents. So devastated were they, the newspaper claimed, that the news of the affair "much impaired their health." Two weeks later, Mary's father had an altercation with his son-in-law in which Clark shoved a loaded pistol into his chest. Joseph pressed charges, and after many adjournments, William found himself in jail in April 1770 until he could pay a 40 shilling fine.[5]

There Clark languished for three months. He had company: eight soldiers from his regiment were already in the Boston jail after the shooting in King Street in March. Meanwhile, in May 1770 the rest of his regiment would be moved to New Jersey. As the summer heat crept in, it must have become obvious to Clark that his in-laws did not intend to pay his bail. In July, he wrote a letter to the lieutenant governor, pleading with him to remit the fine. In the end, Captain Thomas Preston, imprisoned with Clark for his role in the March shooting, agreed to pay it.[6]

Clark was released immediately and went to join his regiment in New Jersey. By the end of August he was ready to sell subscriptions to his memoir. He clearly meant his sixty-page narrative to be a tell-all; polite conventions of the time usually replaced at least some of the letters of personal names with dashes, but Clark was not polite. The long title of his memoir reads, *In Which Is Given a Faithful Account of his Courtship, Marriage and Bedding with Mary Nowel, Daughter of Joseph Nowel, Boat-Builder at North End Boston; with a Description How Much He Suffered on Said Account.*

The memoir, if it was ever completed, has not survived. Nonetheless, even this bare outline of Clark's picaresque tale offers a rare glimpse of a courtship between an enlisted man and a civilian woman, revealing both the young people's desire to take matters into their own hands and the frustration of their parents. It even offers a cameo appearance by Captain

Preston, a man who at that moment was the most notorious soldier in British America. Clark was undoubtedly a man with a sense of humor, which may have been what attracted Mary Nowell to him in the first place.

The story of Joseph Lasenby finding Clark in his granddaughter's bed was printed as part of the *Journal of the Times,* a series of articles written by radical Whigs that retailed spicy stories of sex, violence, and political scandal. The Clark story is typical of the *Journal* in its combination of editorial writing and slanted, if essentially accurate, reporting. More polite than Clark's account, the *Journal* usually replaced many of the personal names in its stories with dashes. Of course, Bostonians obviously knew something of the story before it was printed. When the Boston shopkeeper Harbottle Dorr read the account in the *Boston Evening Post,* he carefully annotated the article, recording that the young woman in question was Mary Nowell, and her grandfather was "Mr. Lasenby."[7]

Yet despite the attention-grabbing salaciousness of the affair, the *Journal* reserved more than half its article for an editorial comment on the political implications of this illicit marriage, urging its readers to reflect on the inevitable impact of troops on Boston's families: "that the most *dear & tender* connections must be *broken & violated.*" The ultimate blame for this seduction, the article concluded, must fall on those imperial officials "who have been the authors of those scenes of *public* and *private* distress." The old man stumbling in on his favorite granddaughter was only an introduction to the primary protest: the "quartering of a standing army in times of peace." As the *Journal* saw clearly, in the context of a military occupation bonds of affection were both personal and political. In the world of occupied Boston, "*public* and *private*" affairs of the heart were one and the same.[8]

When the four regiments of troops that Governor Bernard had requested in 1768 arrived in Boston, it was not immediately obvious where they would live. The governor wanted them quartered in the center of Boston, while his council and the selectmen insisted that the only space the military could legally claim was the barracks on Castle Island in Boston Harbor. After a standoff of several months, they reached an agreement that the army would pay to rent empty warehouses, rooms, and buildings from Bostonians around the town. The result of this political compromise was the creation of an entirely new social world.

As they found homes scattered around the city, soldiers and their families worked themselves into the daily fabric of Bostonians' lives and the city itself. But such a relationship was a two-way street. In ways quite different from the stresses of living with neighbors that brought the army into the town, Bostonians also entered into the lives of the army. Town and army integration was neither complete nor absolute, but it was significant. As men and women created families through courtship, marriage, and baptism, the bonds that held civilians and military together became ever more personal and intimate.

Courtship

As the affair of Clark and Nowell shows, courtship could never be hidden for long. Relatives, neighbors, and friends all kept their eye on the progression of a romantic relationship. Unlike in earlier moments in Massachusetts history, however, by the time the regiments came to Boston, parents had lost much of their authority over their children's marriage choices. Increasingly, teenagers and adult children were deciding for themselves whom they would marry, leaving parents with little power over their pick of a daughter- or son-in-law. At the same time, courtship between soldiers and civilians was undoubtedly a political concern for Boston's Sons of Liberty and other Whigs. The public nature of courtship raised the political stakes for military-civilian relationships.[9]

Fathers who were deeply opposed to the presence of soldiers did their best to keep their daughters away, although with limited success. Justice of the Peace Richard Dana used every possible occasion to show his rage at the presence of troops in Boston. In a proceeding that made a deep impression on several of the officers, Dana used his courtroom to inveigh against the regiments' practice of challenging passersby and to question their right to be in the town at all.[10] Dana spent most of the occupation binding miscreant soldiers over for trial. In letters to his son Edmund, living in England, Dana found it hard to restrain his reflections on liberty and "arbitrary tyrannical principles," finally concluding, "Must here break off my political remarks, lest I be insensibly carried too far for the company of a letter. But could easily write a large pamphlet on the subject."

When it came to his fourteen-year-old daughter Lydia, however, Dana saw no point in policing himself. He reassured Edmund in August 1769 that he planned to take every precaution that Lydia would have no opportunity to mingle with military men:

> You need not have reminded me of your Sister. Have had too much experience . . . to be off my guard, or taken in by any of 'em. Have the fore taken due care & precaution. Have no familiarity with any of 'em nor shall any in my family. Nor do any of 'em come under my roof, but when bro't by a civil officer to answer for some offence. They know me too well to expect any freedom with me or mine. I seldom suffer your sister to be out in an event—save at a next door neighbor—& this but rarely. This is a standing ordinance of my house.

Dana drew the lines sharply between his public (and distasteful) interactions with the military and his family's social world. This Son of Liberty clearly thought it better to put his own daughter under house arrest than allow her to socialize with soldiers.[11]

Marriage

When Mary Nowell married William Clark in the fall of 1769, she may simply have enjoyed annoying her parents. She may have felt that at twenty, with fewer men than women in Boston, her chances of marriage were decreasing.[12] Perhaps a romantic appreciation of Clark's uniform swayed her, or it may have been that she wished to escape from a household in which her grandfather still ruled the roost. It does not appear that she was pregnant. Two-and-a-half centuries later, her personal motives for marriage have been lost. The broader meanings of marriage in occupied Boston, however, may still be discernable. The *Journal of Occurrences* that reported her affair saw this marriage in explicitly political terms, but it is far less clear that either Mary or William shared this perspective. After all, marriage in eighteenth-century Boston was not, overall, a concern of imperial politics. It may have excited the concern of families and neighbors, and it certainly had implications for property and standing, but it rarely seemed to have political ramifications.[13]

The army condoned marriage for privates because it believed such relationships would ultimately have benefits for the army itself. Army regulations were supposed to monitor privates' marriages carefully, as privates were, one pundit wrote, "too likely to fix their affections" on women who were sexually promiscuous and unaccustomed to work. Handbooks on army discipline suggested that officers should not allow privates to marry without their permission. Acceptable women had to prove themselves to be "honest [and] laborious." If, upon inquiry, a commanding or noncommissioned officer found that a private was involved with a woman known to be "infamous," he should do his best to discourage the marriage.[14] However, the same handbooks cautiously admitted that "honest, industrious women are rather good for the company." Women attached to the regiments could do laundry and nurse the sick. Conversely, Boston families assumed that women would marry for affection, for family harmony, for financial stability, or for procreation. Christian Barnes's arch and gossipy letter to Elizabeth Murray in 1770 reveals all of these concerns:

Coll. Murray is married to Miss Debby Brindley, as this is the most interesting piece of news to you I thought proper to begin with it. Don't let it afflict you too much as we have more Colls [colonels] at your service. Miss Polly Neven is married to Mr. Smith. The Gentleman is a stranger in the country but every body speaks highly in his favor. Miss Sally Hatch is a going to be married to Mr. Isaac Winslow of Roxbury . . . and if Parson Pemberton's wife dies it is supposed he will marry the widow Gardener. . . . [Mrs. Amiel's] son Jack is married to a very genteel Lady at New York but no fortune.[15]

Marriage was equally pragmatic an act among civilians as among the military, but politics would seem to have played no part in the making of a family.

Among Bostonians, some made closer connections with the troops than others. Not every eligible woman married a soldier. A careful and conservative combing of church and civil records from the nearly four years of the occupation, 1768–72, reveals forty probable marriages between soldiers and civilians. This total far outnumbers the military marriages during the previous four years, when the Twenty-ninth and Fourteenth regiments were stationed in Nova Scotia; records in Halifax reveal only a single marriage between a private and civilian woman. Nonetheless, these forty are only a handful relative to the roughly 1,200 marriages in Boston during 1768–72.[16]

Yet the absolute number of military marriages is less important than their meaning. The marriages themselves, regardless of the number of young men and women who chose to wed, were important filaments of this intimate occupation, for what the marriages reveal is that attempts to make sense of the relationship between the empire and the colonies were not simply "political" in the ways that one might assume. The struggles against the army made by the radicals and articulated by the *Journal of the Times*—or, for that matter, the connections made by loyalists and officials of the Crown—were not limited to politically aware men. Working out this relationship involved women as well as men, just as it involved many people who did not identify themselves as clearly Whig or Tory.

For some of these women, marriage with a soldier changed their lives radically. Marriage is not, of course, simply the culmination of courtship. As an event, it implied permanence and decision. As a relationship sanctioned by the state, it was a public act. Marital status mattered to communities, as well as to individuals. Most of all, marriage made an enormous difference in a woman's legal standing. Not only were married white women generally subsumed under their husbands' legal personalities; these women also lost their legal claim to poor relief from the communities in which they had been born. Instead, married women could claim their husbands' birth communities as their own. In theory, by marrying into a community, a woman both lost her old connections and made new ones. In practice, of course, these transitions could look quite different.

In the abstract, marriage to soldiers could seem like a public declaration of a political alliance. In part, this was due to the place that marriage as an act held in the imaginations of Bostonians. Like other parts of the political movements of the 1760s and 1770s, in which personal acts such as consumption, shopping, and fashion took on new political implications, even marriage could be part of a protest movement. Both radicals and conservatives used the idea of marriage, especially with soldiers, to make their points. In January 1770, for example, the government supporter John Mein published a satirical piece in the *Boston Chronicle* mocking the nonimportation agreements (which he had refused to sign). The article proposed that Bostonians should boycott marriage, as well as consumption, until the Revenue Acts were repealed. Like the taxed goods listed in the Revenue Acts, the author suggested, women should be locked up in warehouses. "Were the Women thus confined for the sake of Liberty," he wrote sarcastically, "there can be but little doubt, that the troops, at least, would soon leave us."[17] The idea that women are marketable items is a very old trope, but in parodies such as this one, marriage becomes not just an economic exchange but a political tool.[18]

Not surprisingly, the idea of Boston women marrying into the British Army seemed especially distasteful to radicals. In 1771, for example, the *Massachusetts Spy* republished a poem from 1745 by the British poet Robert Dodsley entitled "An Epistle from a Society of Young Ladies" that mocked the single life of a bachelor and urged young men to marry. One reader at least seemed to take the poem as a personal attack. "A Bachelor" responded the next week with a bit of rhyming invective that excoriated local women for their interest in soldiers. The only choice now left for young men, the poet claimed, was to decide "is it worse/To marry red coats leavings, or a [whore]!!!?/Read this, and trouble bachelors no more."[19] Women who had so much as flirted with soldiers, who had become redcoats' "leavings," were nothing more than prostitutes, unworthy of marriage with the male readers of the *Massachusetts Spy*.

There are few hints to help us discern who might have decided to marry a soldier. Was it primarily a woman who had few connections to her community of birth and was eager to create a new life who would commit to such a marriage? Given the hostile reaction to the presence of troops in Boston, was it only women who were already at the political or social margins who would make such a choice? Did women who married soldiers forfeit their social or familial as well as political ties to Boston?

Surprisingly, looking at the women and their families does not reveal any clear pattern. Susannah Sloper, for example, had borne a daughter in the almshouse in 1767. Throughout the late 1760s and early 1770s, both of Susannah's sisters had also spent some time in the almshouse. Her sister Lydia, who had served as a godparent to Susannah's illegitimate child, had several illegitimate children of her own. In 1769, when she was twenty-one, Susannah married Private John Brand of the Fourteenth Regiment.[20] Susannah would seem to be exactly the sort of unstable, unsteady woman that officers feared their men would pick up. But for every Susannah Sloper, there were two or three like Katherine Skillings, who married George Simpson of the Fourteenth eleven months before their first child was born, or Mary Welch, who married her soldier in January 1770 and had no child until the following autumn.[21]

Nor does any pattern appear to distinguish privates from commissioned officers. Notwithstanding the disdain Lieutenant Stanton showed for the daughters of local elites, in April 1769 Captain Ponsonby Molesworth of the Twenty-Ninth Regiment eloped with one of those defended in the newspaper poem: Susanna Sheaffe, the fifteen-year-old daughter of a customs official. Although they married out of state, they returned to Boston to baptize their first child ten months later. Captain-Lieutenant Samuel Kathrens, from the same regiment, married Mary Haynes "some months before she was delivered of John Kathrens." While the Hayneses and the Sheaffes were too elite to consider an alliance with any mere private soldier, both families had long and significant ties to Massachusetts.[22] Certainly, Susanna Sheaffe's father was deeply unpopular among Boston radicals, but it seems unlikely that Susannah, at fifteen, married a soldier because she feared she was unlikely to find a husband any other way.

Most surprising of all, perhaps, is that even after they married soldiers, some of these women continued to be part of Boston's social world. Eight months after Margaret Sullivan married Corporal Alexander McGregory of the Fourteenth Regiment, she was publicly welcomed into the congregational community of New North Church after testifying to her religious convictions.[23] Even more strikingly, some women who married soldiers between 1768 and 1772 remarried once their soldier husbands had been redeployed elsewhere. Far from becoming outcasts, women such as Hannah Osborn Dundass and Elizabeth Hillman Lindley remarried local Bostonians. It seems possible that soldiers found appealing the opportunities to be a part of a local community that these women offered.[24]

On occasion, the legal implications of these marriages seem to have been somewhat uncertain in Bostonians' minds. In November 1769, John Slayman of the Fourteenth Regiment married Sarah Smith in the King's

Chapel, having previously published their intentions to wed. There was nothing underhanded or hidden about this wedding. Both the church clerk and the town clerk clearly recorded Slayman as a soldier of the Fourteenth Regiment. Yet Smith was hardly a model citizen. A year and a half after her marriage, Smith was prosecuted under her previous name for keeping a disorderly house and found guilty. Both Justice Richard Dana, who originally bound her over the Court of General Sessions, and the court itself recognized that she had changed her name, referring to her as "Sarah Smith alias Sleming [Slayman] of Boston . . . Spinster." Clearly, the courts did not treat her as a fully married woman who had undergone all the legal permutations of a new status. Apparently, Boston officials were not convinced that this marriage was genuine. Perhaps Justice Dana and others did not wish to believe it. However, when a year later, in 1772, the poorhouse accepted "Mary Slemmond," the overseer clearly identified Mary as "a Child of Sarah Slemmond." Over the course of time, Sarah's new family identity had become public.[25]

In other marriages, the status of the men might be in doubt. A wide range of women married soldiers in the years that they occupied Boston (and a few even married them afterward). Less than four months after the soldiers first came ashore, Annis Parcill married Private Walter Jack of the Fourteenth Regiment. The town clerk's record of their intention to marry did not record that Jack was a soldier. Yet at other times, the clerks of both the town and the churches did note the regiment of bridegrooms. Both Trinity Church and the civil authorities noted that Katherine Skillings married "George Simpson a soldier in the 14th Regt" in April 1769, just a few months after the wedding of Parcill and Jack.[26] Although the recording of the regiment in such cases was no doubt haphazard and somewhat random, the very casualness of the recordkeeping hints at the ambiguity of the men's place in Boston. Should they be thought of as invading soldiers or as sons-in-law?

A still clearer sign of the confusion surrounding these marriages is preserved in the few records that identify men as "of Boston," sometimes while also recording their regiments. The term "of Boston" indicated a precise legal status. In 1761, John Adams pondered the specific meaning of the term in his diary. He began with a straightforward definition of what it meant to be legally identified as "of Boston." He reminded himself, "Now it has been adjudged, that, when a Man is called of such a Town, the meaning is that he is an Inhabitant of that Town, a legal Inhabitant of that Town, entitled to all the Priviledges, and compellible to bear all the Burdens of that Town." But simply to live in a place is not to be of it. Adams clarified that there was a significant difference between the status "of Boston" and "resident in Boston," and he took as his example British Regular officers who spent winters during the Seven Years' War in Boston: "They are never styled of Boston, but only resident in Boston." As a rule, military men passing through without living continuously in the town were not inhabitants but merely visitors who could not "gain a settlement in any Town."[27] In short, to be "of Boston" and to be "of X Regiment" were mutually exclusive categories. A man could be an inhabitant or a temporary resident but not both. So what were these soldiers in legal or social terms? How incorporated into the town of Boston were they? And most important, if a Boston woman married a soldier, had she married a new local or a stranger? The answers had real implications for Boston women.

Despite the clear hostility between some soldiers and some townspeople, these men were far from foreigners. As noted earlier, by marrying a soldier, a woman shifted her legal and personal commitments; the clearest indication of this shift is apparent in the town's system of "warning out." By the middle of the eighteenth century, Massachusetts law assumed that one's legal residence—and the community obligated to give poor relief—was the one into which one was born. Women could acquire a new legal settlement by marrying into a new community, in which case they would take on the legal residence of their husbands. If married women required public support, they would have to turn to their new communities to find it. A woman who married a legal inhabitant of Boston would be eligible for Boston's poor relief, but if she married a man who was only a "resident of" Boston, she could be warned that the town had no responsibility to care for her.[28]

Mary Welch married Lawrence Northam of the Fourteenth Regiment in January 1770, and they had a baby boy ten months later. In December of that year, however, after Lawrence was moved to Castle Island from his barracks in Boston, a representative from the town's selectmen sought out Mary and warned her that she had lost the right to claim poor relief in Boston.[29] After growing up in Boston, Mary perhaps had come to find this surveillance of possible drains on the public funds unsurprising. It was, nonetheless, a stark reminder of the choice she had made by marrying a soldier. She might have opportunities to see the world, but the costs could be high, and they might be more than simply the loss of financial support. And while church clerks might have come to think of soldiers as members of the community, the selectmen clearly did not agree.

For some soldiers' wives, the emotional price of shifting one's community from family to army was overwhelming. Across the centuries, some of the pain of these losses still resonates. Isabella Graham was a Scottish woman who married a surgeon of the Sixtieth Regiment, which was deployed to North America at the same time as the Twenty-ninth and Four-teenth regiments. When she left Scotland in the spring of 1767 with her husband of two years, Graham left behind their first child, still an infant, as well as her husband's two sons by his first marriage. As she settled into their first posting in Quebec, she confessed her homesickness in a letter to her mother: "Had I my dear parents near me, our dear boys, and a few other friends, I might be reconciled to this country; but no place or com-pany, however agreeable, can compensate for their absence."[30]

Graham's regiment was eventually reassigned to Fort Niagara, and four years into their tour of duty she was no longer homesick, but she contin-ued to long for her mother's presence. Describing her daily round to her mother, she concluded cheerfully: "In short, my ever dear parents, my life is easy and pleasant. The Lord my God make it pious and useful. Could I place myself and family in the same circumstances, and every thing go on in the same manner, within a few miles of you, I should be happy for life; and were it not for this hope, which my heart is set upon, I could not be so, with all I have told you."[31]

Isabella eventually did forge close friendships with other officers' wives, especially those in her regiment. Yet these connections did not compen-sate for the loss of her family in Scotland. First, Graham's infant died soon after she had arrived in Quebec. Although Graham drew comfort from a Presbyterian belief that the death of an infant "is no real cause of grief," she nonetheless admitted to shedding "many tears" at his death. The apprehension of her mother's death, however, hung over all of her letters. Even the letter from her mother informing her of the child's death was a welcome sign of her mother's health. She poured out her relief in her acknowledgment of the child's death, confessing that she had never suspected bad news concerning her child, "for my fears were entirely for you."[32] The distance between Graham and her mother exacerbated her fears. In 1773 she wrote desperately, "My ever dear Mother, I have not received one line from you for eight months; judge if my mind can be easy."[33] As it happened, her mother had indeed died, news that devastated Graham. As she tried to comfort her father, she could not contain her own grief at being so far from her family, scribbling through her tears, "I am distressed that I can scarcely write. . . . My dearest father, I cannot tell you how much I feel for you; my tears will not allow me, they flow so fast that I cannot write; what would I give to be with you."[34]

When Graham's husband died in 1773, she returned to Scotland and her father as quickly as she could. Her husband's fellow officers paid for her return, and she remained close to some of them and especially their wives for the rest of her life. But her connections with the regiment never rivaled those with her original community.

As the educated wife of an officer, Graham was able to sustain her relationship with her family to the extent that letters between the backwoods of New York and central Scotland could carry news. Nonetheless, her decision to marry a military man meant that she never saw her mother or son again. Only the death of her military husband facilitated her return home.

The familial and personal nature of marriage did not obviate its political implications; marriage to a soldier might indeed matter to future politics. Even so, marriages with soldiers did not automatically either proclaim or create a family's partisan loyalties. Mary Nowell Clark's grandfather Lasenby was a Son of Liberty, and it is possible that Susannah Sloper's brother helped toss tea into Boston Harbor in 1773.[35] The divisions into patriots and loyalists did not yet exist.

In fact, even after the shooting on March 5, 1770, Boston women continued to marry soldiers stationed in the city. Nearly half of the marriages with soldiers happened after the shooting. Andrew Eliot, the same minister who bewailed the coming of the troops, married Alexander McGregory and Margaret Sullivan in his Congregational church just six weeks after the fracas in King Street. Jane Crothers married Joseph Whitehouse three weeks later. Another dozen or so continued to marry over the next two years. When it came to deciding whether or not to marry a soldier, the Boston Massacre, despite its transformation into brilliant political propaganda, did not seem to play much of a role.[36]

Instead, the relationship between civilians and soldiers was transformed through a different process. Marriage and other social bonds helped convert soldiers into men by shifting their identities from a generalized "standing army" to individuals, with names and bodies. At the same time, marriage drew Boston women into a military community.[37]

Even for these individuals who became—at least to their wives—more than simply the members of a standing army, their marriages had political implications quite different from those that came with marrying a local man. Indeed, for them the meaning of marriage shifted altogether. Not only did it create new ties to an individual, a family, and a military community; it also formed new and more robust links to the empire that sustained the army. Sometimes, in some relationships, the bond was closer than in others. Some of these women chose to remarry, and not all marriages lasted long. But marriages were one step in making an imperial family that the birth of children, and particularly the bonds of godparents, often reinforced.

Baptism

One of the most surprising results of the military's integration into Boston was the participation of its members in the town's churches, particularly the Anglican ones. Although some of the military marriages appear to have been performed by regimental chaplains, the majority are recorded in both civil and religious lists.[38] Even more frequently, however, soldiers' families asked local churches to solemnize their children's birth through baptism. There are records of more than one hundred such church baptisms from 1768 to 1772.[39] These records preserve the connections radiating outward from the nuclear family that parents made for their children, as well as the friendships among women and the links that townspeople made to military families. Possibly even more than sex or marriage, acting as a godparent allowed women and men to make public their ties to a community.

In the eighteenth-century Anglican Church, where most of these military children were baptized, parents chose three or four other adults to serve as godparents. The godparents served as links in networks of honor, obligation, and commitment. Sometimes they were aspirational connections: a private might ask his sergeant or his sergeant's wife to be a godparent as a sign of respect. Other godparents were clearly friends or others with whom the parents had forged, or hoped to forge, connections.[40]

A marriage to a soldier did not necessarily sever a woman's ties to her old community. Hannah Dundass, who married as a pregnant bride and then remarried a few years after her husband's regiment left, used her child's baptism to strengthen her ties to her natal community. When her child was born in February 1770, only one godparent, a fellow corporal from another company, was from the army. The other two godparents were Bostonians, possibly members of the same congregational church, Old South, in which Hannah Osborn had grown up. Those two godparents had not rejected their longtime family friend when she married a soldier. Instead, they joined with a noncommissioned officer to sponsor the child of a soldier.[41]

But even parents who had both come into Boston with the army might choose as their children's godparents people with strong ties to the civilian communities. When Joseph Brocklesby was baptized, for example, his godparents included his father's sergeant from the Fourteenth Regiment, a man who had married a local woman the previous year. His second godparent was a local woman, Frances Sheldon, who three months later would marry a man from the same company. Baby Joseph's godparents were deeply connected to Boston. At the same time, some of those godparents were people like Frances Sheldon, who, even before she formally married into the army, used the social world of baptism to make yet another tie to the British military.[42]

In conclusion, young men and women in the second half of the eighteenth century chose mates not only to annoy their parents or create stable households. The companionate marriages they sought were marriages for love. Bonds between soldiers and civilians, soldier's wives and their friends, even infants and their godparents rested on an ideal of affection. Yet affection did not refer solely to personal feelings. It was a political emotion, as well, one that referred as much to one's disposition toward Great Britain or George III as toward one's spouse.[43]

It is these two meanings that shaped the families made by soldiers and Bostonians. The visible expression of these bonds of affection—marriage and children—shows the ways in which the very personal and the clearly political were entwined in the family. When women chose to marry soldiers, or when fathers tried to keep soldiers from becoming their sons-in-law, the imperial power that the British Army represented became very personal indeed. These struggles with the British Empire were not the domain of men alone. Instead, Bostonians came to understand that the fight against Great Britain was truly, literally, a family argument.

We often think of Boston as the birthplace of revolution precisely because of the conflicts that culminated in the Boston Massacre, as though there were a straight line from the selectmen's dismay at finding troops quartered in Boston to the massacre and on to the battles of Lexington and Concord and the Declaration of Independence. But it was not so. Politicians and political elites *were* dismayed at the news that troops were coming to Boston, and others may have been, as well. But a closer look actually shows us that the army's time in the city was not characterized by unmitigated hostility. Far from it: soldiers and townspeople invited each other into their social, sexual, and familial worlds.

Then they grew closer apart. Intimacies at the personal and domestic levels of life began to run counter to and reinforce widening political divisions. The more connected townspeople and the army became, the fiercer and brighter would glow the line that separated them. The violence that ultimately led to the Boston Massacre was the result of people who had come to know one another all too well.

Notes

1. The authoritative, but strongly partisan, account is Hiller Zobel, *The Boston Massacre* (New York: W. W. Norton, 1970). More recently, Richard Archer, *As If an Enemy's Country: The British Occupation of Boston and the Origins of Revolution*

(Oxford: Oxford University Press, 2010), has followed a similar line. Accounts more favorable to Revere's interpretation in his engraving of the "The Bloody Massacre" include Gary B. Nash, *The Urban Crucible: Social Change, Political Consciousness, and the Origins of the American Revolution* (Cambridge, MA: Harvard University Press, 1979); Dirk Hoerder, *Crowd Action in Revolutionary Massachusetts, 1765–1780* (New York: Academic, 1977).

2. Elisha Brown, "Proposals for Printing by Subscription, The Miser: Or The Soldier's Humour. A Comedy of Three Acts, as It Is Acted by His Majesty's Servants." (Boston: Elisha Brown, 1768), Early American Imprints, Series 1: Evans no. 41700; *Boston Gazette*, March 6, 1769. For William Clark's enlistment record, see War Office (hereafter, WO) 12/4493/17, WO 12/4493/27, WO 12/4493/33, National Archives of the United Kingdom, Kew, Surrey, England (hereafter, TNA).

3. *New-York Journal*, August 18, 1770.

4. On the threats, see Superior Court of Judicature docket book, 1769, Massachusetts Judicial Archives, Boston (hereafter, MJA), 252. On the affair with Mary Nowell, see *Boston Evening-Post*, July 31, 1769.

5. On the pistol, see Superior Court of Judicature record book, 1770, MJA, 29.

6. On Clark's petition, see Court of General Sessions of the Peace Record Book, July 10, 1770, MJA. On the Preston memorial, see Massachusetts Archives Collection, vol. 44, Massachusetts State Archives, 704.

7. For the *Journal of the Times*, see O. M. Dickerson, *Boston under Military Rule, 1768–1769: As Revealed in a Journal of the Times* (Westport, CT: Greenwood, 1971). See also *The Annotated Newspapers of Harbottle Dorr, Jr.*, online ed., Massachusetts Historical Society, Boston, http://masshist.org/dorr.

8. There is a rich and robust debate over the relationship between "expression and emotion": see Nicole Eustace et al., "AHR Conversation: The Historical Study of Emotions," *American Historical Review* 117, no. 5 (December 1, 2012): 1487–1531. William Reddy's argument for "emotives" is useful for understanding that the language of affection and distress is not either rote or empty but emotionally meaningful. This is not to suggest that Eustace's insights into "emotional expression" as a means of exerting power are not relevant here also. In these family formations, individual emotion and imperial politics come together in the acts of sex, marriage, and baptism: William M. Reddy, *The Navigation of Feeling: A Framework for the History of Emotions* (Cambridge: Cambridge University Press, 2001); Nicole Eustace, *Passion Is the Gale : Emotion, Power, and the Coming of the American Revolution* (Chapel Hill: University of North Carolina Press, 2008).

9. Richard Godbeer, *Sexual Revolution in Early America* (Baltimore: Johns Hopkins University Press, 2002), 227–98l; Lisa Wilson, *Ye Heart of a Man: The Domestic Life of Men in Colonial New England* (New Haven, CT: Yale University Press, 1999), chap. 2.

10. "There is no occasion to trouble you with the particulars [of an assault case against a private], my only reason for mentioning it, is to acquaint you with the behavior of one of the justices on the Bench, his name Dana, a man as I am well informed of notorious character, as I think many expressions in his speech to the jury, of a very inflammatory nature": John Pomeroy to William Gage, Boston, February 2, 1769, in Gage Correspondence, American Series, William L. Clements Library, University of Michigan, Ann Arbor.

11. Richard Dana to Edmund Dana, August 9, 1769, Dana Family Papers, Massachusetts Historical Society, Boston, (hereafter, MHS), box 1.

12. In Boston in 1765, there were 122 adult women for every 100 men. The influx of military men three years later would have gone far in redressing the imbalance—a point that no demographic historian has yet investigated: see Elaine Forman Crane, *Ebb Tide in New England: Women, Seaports, and Social Change* (Boston: Northeastern University Press, 1998), 13.

13. Mary Beth Norton, *Liberty's Daughters: The Revolutionary Experience of American Women, 1750–1800* (New York: Little, Brown, 1980), chap. 2.

14. Bennett Cuthbertson, *A System for the Compleat Interior Management and Oeconomy of a Battalion of Infantry, by Bennett Cuthbertson, Esq., Captain in His Majesty's Fifth Regiment of Foot, and Late Adjutant to the Same* (Dublin, 1768), 193.

15. Christian Barnes to Elizabeth Murray, February 9, 1770, Christian Barnes Papers, Library of Congress, Washington, DC.

16. Boston Church Records, New England Historic Genealogical Society, AmericanAncestors.org.

17. *Boston Chronicle*, January 18, 1770.

18. On the political meanings of marriage in the later United States, see Nancy F. Cott, *Public Vows: A History of Marriage and the Nation* (Cambridge, MA: Harvard University Press, 2000); Jan Lewis, "The Republican Wife: Virtue and Seduction in the Early Republic," *William and Mary Quarterly* 44, no. 4 (October 1, 1987): 689–721.

19. *Massachusetts Spy*, January 7 and 14, 1771.

20. For Sloper's career in the almshouse, see Eric Guest Nellis Anne Decker Cecere, and the Colonial Society of Massachusetts, *The Eighteenth-Century Records of the Boston Overseers of the Poor* (Charlottesville: University of Virginia Press, 2007), 55, 64. For Lydia Sloper, see ibid., 98, 125. For Mary Sloper, see ibid., 21. For Susannah's first child, "Henrietta of John Jones & Susanna Sloper," see "Records of the King's Chapel in Boston," January 21, 1767, AmericanAncestors.org. For the marriage record, see "Christ Church Records" June 22, 1769, AmericanAncestors.org.

21. Although there is an extensive Skillings family in Boston, I have not yet been able to identify Catherine's baptism. For the marriage of Katherine Skillings and George Simpson on April 9, 1769, see Andrew Oliver and James Bishop Peabody, eds., *The Records of Trinity Church, Boston, 1728–1830* (Boston: Colonial Society of Massachusetts, 1980–82), 730. The marriage intention listed her as Skillingsby: see Boston Registry Department, *A Volume of Records Relating to the Early History of Boston, Containing Boston Marriages from 1752–1809* (Boston: Printing Office, 1903), 400. For the baptism of George Simpson on March 14, 1770, see King's Chapel Records, Register of Baptisms, MHS. For the marriage of Mary Welch to Lawrence Northam on January 24, 1770, see Oliver and Peabody *The Records of Trinity Church*; Boston Registry Department, *A Volume of Records Relating to the Early History of Boston*, 400. For James Northam's baptism on October 28, 1770, see "King's Chapel Records," AmericanAncestors.org.

22. The Molesworth-Sheaffe marriage was reported in the newspaper and elsewhere: see *Boston Evening-Post*, May 1, 1769. See also J. L. Bell, "Carried Miss Suky Sheaffe to Hampton," November 3, 2009, accessed November 1, 2013, http://boston1775.blogspot.com/2009/11/carried-miss-suky-sheaffe-to-hampton.html. For Mary Haynes and James Kathrens, see Ruth Long, *The Genealogy of Captain Samuel Kathrens of the 29th Regiment of Foot of the British Army, and his Wife Mary (Haynes) Kathrens of New England Planter Family Origin, 1736–1997* (Needham, MA: R. A. Long, 1997), esp. 3.

23. "Records of the New North Church," December 9, 1770, Boston Church Records, AmericanAncestors.org.

24. "John Love & Hanah Dundas," August 13, 1774, in Boston Registry Department, *A Volume of Records Relating to the Early History of Boston*, 435; "William Moarn & Elisabeth Lindley," November 16, 1773, in ibid., 338.

25. For the marriage on November 9, 1769, see "Records of the King's Chapel"; Boston Registry Department, *A Volume of Records Relating to the Early History of Boston*, 363; Richard Dana, "Justice of the Peace Records," July 24, 1771, MHS; "Court of General Sessions Record Book," July 30, 1771, MJA. On the almshouse, see Nellis, *Boston Overseers*, 231.

26. For the marriage of Annis Parcill and Walter Jack on January 14, 1769, see Boston Registry Department, *A Volume of Records Relating to the Early History of Boston*, 428. For Skillingsby and Simpson, see n. 21 in this essay.

27. Entry dated January 2, 1761, in *Diary of John Adams*, vol. 1, ed. C. James Taylor (Boston: Massachusetts Historical Society, 2007).

28. For the legal issues of settlement, see Cornelia H. Dayton and Sharon V. Salinger, "Was the Warning of Strangers Unique to Colonial New England?" in *Making Legal History: Essays on the Interpretation of Legal History in Honor of William E. Nelson*, ed. Daniel J. Hulsebosch and R. B. Bernstein (New York: New York University Press, 2013).

29. On the Northam warning, see Suffolk Files no. 90077, MJA; "Warning [Out] Book from January 4, 1745 to 1770," December 22, 1770, Boston (Mass.) Overseers of the Poor, reel 1, vol. 1 (Extra-Tall), in "Boston Overseers of the Poor Records, 1733–1925," P-368, MHS.

30. Isabella Graham and Joanna (Graham) Bethune, *The Unpublished Letters and Correspondence of Mrs. Isabella Graham, from the Year 1767 to 1814; Exhibiting Her Religious Character in the Different Relations of Life* (New York, J. S. Taylor, 1838), 23.

31. Ibid., 50.

32. Ibid., 2.

33. Ibid., 89.

34. Isabella Graham, Joanna Bethune, and Divie Bethune, *The Power of Faith: Exemplified in the Life and Writings of the Late Mrs. Isabella Graham* (New York: American Tract Society, 1843), 23.

35. Benjamin L. Carp, *Defiance of the Patriots: The Boston Tea Party and the Making of America* (New Haven, CT: Yale University Press, 2010), 238.

36. On the marriage of Alexander McGregory and Margaret Sullivan marriage on April 17, 1770, see "List of Marriages, 1742–1778," Andrew Eliot Papers, MHS. Baptism: "Records of the New North Church," December 16, 1770. For the marriage of Joseph Whitehouse to Jane Crothers on March 27, 1770, see Old North Church (Christ Church in the City of Boston) Records, Baptismal Registers, MHS, box 18.

37. For a thoughtful discussion of families and military communities, see Holly A. Mayer, *Belonging to the Army: Camp Followers and Community during the American Revolution* (Columbia: University of South Carolina Press, 1996).

38. For a marriage by regimental chaplains, see the legal document reproduced in Long, *The Genealogy of Captain Samuel Kathrens of the 29th Regiment of Foot of the British Army*, 3 ("Mary Kathrns . . . sath that she was Lawfully Married to the aforesaid Samuel Katrins by the Chaplin of the twenty ninth Regiment of futte").

39. Again, this is a small fraction of the baptisms in Boston over the same period, which number 1,478: Boston Church Records, AmericanAncestors.org.

40. David Cressy, *Birth, Marriage, and Death: Ritual, Religion, and the Life-Cycle in Tudor and Stuart England* (Oxford: Oxford University Press, 1997), 156–61.

41. For William Dundass Jr.'s baptism on February 4, 1770, see "King's Chapel Records," AmericanAncestors.org. His godparents were Corporal Alexander Friendly (WO 12/3117/119, TNA), James Preston, and Martha Powell. Powell was baptized on February 17, 1750 in the New South Church.

42. For Joseph Brocklesby's baptism on February 24, 1771, see "King's Chapel Records," AmericanAncestors.org. His godparents were Sgt. John Wright, Fanny Sheldon, and Ann Woolhouse. On Wright, see WO 12/3117/121, TNA; on his marriage to Anne Belshaw on January 15, 1769, see King's Chapel Records, MHS. Sheldon would marry Sgt. Robert Barton (see WO 12/3117/121, TNA) on May 28, 1771 in the Brattle Street (Congregational) Church: see "Records of the Church in Brattle Square"; Boston Registry Department, *A Volume of Records Relating to the Early History of Boston*, 330. Ann Woolhouse was the wife of Cpl. John Woolhouse (see WO 12/3117/158, TNA).

43. For this point, see Brendan McConville, *The King's Three Faces: The Rise and Fall of Royal America, 1688–1776* (Chapel Hill: University of North Carolina Press, 2006), esp. 105–12.

Left Behind

Loyalist Women in Philadelphia during the American Revolution

KIMBERLY NATH

On September 16, 1777, the Philadelphia Quaker Sarah Logan Fisher wrote, "My mind so deeply affected with the absence of my beloved husband, and my heart so much sunk with the gloomy prospect before and the little probability there is of our meeting with each other soon again." Sarah greatly missed her husband, Thomas, who had been exiled from Philadelphia in September 1777 for his refusal to sign an oath of allegiance on the patriots' behalf. Thomas, a member of the Quaker community, found himself targeted for his refusal to take up arms against the British. He had left Sarah behind in Philadelphia, where she also refused to support the patriot cause and instead remained ambivalent about siding with patriots, defying the patriots who sought to take advantage of her husband's absence. She recorded in her diary on September 22, 1777, that patriot captains and soldiers demanded blankets or old carpets for the war. Sarah, trying to care for her children in her husband's absence, wrote, "I told them I had never given them any, but that they had robbed me of what was far dearer than any property I had in the world, that they had taken from me my husband." Local authorities decided to seize and exile Philadelphia's prominent Quaker leaders in September 1777, and as Thomas Fisher was forced from Philadelphia, Sarah felt a profound loss and hardship in his absence.[1]

Sarah Logan Fisher's experience during the war was not unique, particularly in war-torn Philadelphia. The city was occupied by the British in 1777–78, and this occupation tore apart families as loyalties were called into question. As a result of the occupation and the increasing British presence in the region, some Philadelphia loyalists joined the British campaign, while others were exiled, fleeing the city before, during, and after the occupation to save their lives. While loyalist men and men who refused to choose a side during the Revolution fled in the name of self-preservation, their wives and children were frequently left behind in Philadelphia to support themselves and protect their property from confiscation.[2] In Philadelphia, many loyalist women found their lives upended, but they rose to the challenge by protecting their estates, providing for their families, remaining in contact with their separated families, and even embracing new business ventures in the wake of their husbands' departures. Not all women, however, identified with their husbands' political perspectives. Some women refused outright to identify as loyalists and instead created a new life independent of their husbands' politics and based on pragmatic adjustments to the local crises of daily life.[3] The varied reactions of these wives demonstrate the jarring impact of the Revolution on loyalties, families, and daily life. Women were left behind to negotiate the everyday realities of war, and the responses were as varied as the experiences of the Revolution.

This essay argues that by looking at women who stayed behind, and particularly loyalist women, their contributions to the war are fully realized because of their perseverance in the face of revolution. War disrupted nearly every aspect of everyday life, and the realities of war were felt most strongly by these women; many did not initially flee, they often did not take up arms, and they did not cower to the patriots. Instead, women left behind did their best to provide stability in a time of chaos.

The study of loyalists, the American Revolution, and women is a complex and vast field. However, many historians have neglected to focus on the significance of those women who stayed behind and how they created a space for themselves in the midst of Revolution. Even fewer scholars have focused on the role of loyalist women and what it meant for the wife of a British subject to stay behind, among the patriots. A great debt is owed to the historians Mary Beth Norton and Linda Kerber for their significant contributions in the study of women, the Revolution, and the political spaces women occupied. Norton's *Liberty's Daughters: The Revolutionary Experience of American Women, 1750–1800,* states that women were essential and active participants in the revolutionary cause. Women eagerly participated in the revolution by forming political associations, such as the Daughters of Liberty. Kerber's *Women of the Republic: Intellect and Ideology in Revolutionary America* also gave women a much needed space and voice in the historiography of the American Revolution.[4] More recent scholarship focuses on the activities of women out of doors, noting the ways in which women made spaces in politics and commerce. Rosemarie Zagarri's *Revolutionary Backlash: Women and Politics in the Early American Republic* extends the historiography beyond the Revolution, arguing that women built on their informal political status gained during the war. Others have emphasized the ways in which women operated in the economic sphere in the absence of men. For example, Ellen Hartigan-O'Connor's *The Ties That Buy: Women and Commerce in Revolutionary America* looks at how women used networks, credit, and money to shape consumer culture.[5] Historians have shown that women were active participants in all facets of life in the years leading up to and during the Revolution.

Another approach to the study of women in the Revolution is evident in scholarship that emphasizes the nuances of the war in day-to-day events, with many scholars looking at occupied cities as sites of study. Both Judith Van Buskirk's *Generous Enemies: Patriots and Loyalists in Revolutionary New York* and Ruma Chopra's *Unnatural Rebellion: Loyalists in New York City during the Revolution* look at the actions of loyalists on the ground. Van Buskirk argues that civilians frequently ignored political divides in daily affairs, and Chopra finds that loyalists in New York worked collectively, also crossing political lines when necessary.[6] Both of these texts begin to unravel the impacts of war on daily life and add to a growing body of scholarship that complicates and even blurs the line between patriot and loyalist.

Additional scholarship has focused on the global effects of the Revolution, emphasizing the movement of people across different spaces. These studies emphasize the obviously disruptive nature of the American Revolution and the choices to relocate because of the war. Maya Jasanoff, for example, focuses on the flight of loyalists, exploring the ways in which the American Revolution created a loyalist diaspora in the Atlantic. Her sweeping argument looks at the global impact of loyalist movements throughout the British Empire.[7] Jim Piecuch has also studied loyalist movement, but his book *Three Peoples, One King: Loyalists, Indians, and Slaves in the Revolutionary South, 1775–1782*, examines movement and new patterns of settlement with the conclusion of the war. He provides a narrower focus on the years during the war.[8] Shifts in geographical focus have provided new way to interpret the revolution and the spaces of the revolution. For example, Kathleen DuVal's *Independence Lost: Lives on the Edge of the American Revolution* moves farther south, studying the Gulf Coast during the Revolution with the clash of empires, interest, and interdependence. She argues that by studying the Gulf Coast, a new global perspective is used and brings to light differing motives in the war for independence.[9]

This essay contributes to studies of women and the American Revolution by arguing that loyalist women who remained behind created their own space during the war and used this moment, although perhaps not always willingly, to exert independence. Although there was a spectrum of how women exerted their independence, those left behind used every means necessary to overcome the challenges of the American Revolution. Arguably, the responses of loyalist wives varied based on financial challenges, childcare responsibilities, and fear for personal safety. For some, the war presented seemingly insurmountable challenges because of responsibilities at home and the heartache of a departed husband. Yet for others, it represented opportunity and a moment to exert independence beyond anything previously experienced. This essay argues that those left behind showed remarkable tenacity as their families, lives, and security were stripped during the war.

Disaffected and loyalist women took extraordinary measures to provide for their families during the American Revolution and showed remarkable resilience in a time of chaos. They ran businesses, circumvented the law, and sought to protect their families, as evidenced by Susanna Marshall. Susanna Marshall resided in Baltimore at the beginning of the Revolution and supported the British troops on their way to the Philadelphia campaign. Her husband, William Marshall, originally from Ireland, refused to sign an oath of allegiance and was "obliged to quit the country and leave his wife and children" behind. In her husband's absence, Susanna feared that she, too, would be targeted for loyalism and packed up her children to search for Lord Dunmore in June 1776. However, not finding Dunmore, she journeyed instead to Head of Elk, a small town on the way to Philadelphia in Cecil County, Maryland, hoping to intercept the British troops on their rumored journey to Philadelphia. Once at Head of Elk, Susanna realized her food supplies were running low, and she lacked the ability to provide for her children. So she stayed on and decided to run Elk Tavern, which provided shelter and a livelihood for her and her children. But it was a difficult adjustment, and all the while Susanna longed to be reunited with her husband. In March 1777, she heard of a proclamation by Congress that would allow loyalists to "quit" the colonies without taking any of their goods. This appealed to Susanna as a supporter of the British Crown; however, she found the idea of leaving behind her possessions appalling. In defiance of the law, Susanna held a public vendue, or auction, to raise funds for travel so she and her children could reunite with her husband.[10]

Susanna's dreams of finding Lord Dunmore and heading to Philadelphia changed course suddenly when she realized she was no longer safe in the American colonies. Following the sale of her goods, Susanna charted a schooner to sail to the West Indies, where she learned her husband had fled. Susanna and her children traveled on the schooner with everything they owned that had not been sold at auction, which included a small amount of venison, hams, bacon, and a hogshead of flour. While en route to the West Indies, she allowed aboard the schooner three men also "quitting America." But together the small party was taken by an armed patriot boat to St. Augustine, where American soldiers stole some goods from her ship but allowed Susanna and her children to leave soon thereafter. She and her children left St. Augustine aboard the *Hawk Transport*, seeking refuge in England after she discovered that her husband had died in Saint-Domingue. While Susanna never made it back to Philadelphia and the protection of the British lines, she provided for her family by any means necessary in England. Many years later, in June 1785, she petitioned the Loyalist Claims Commission in London for support and repayment for losses of her property to the American soldiers while in St. Augustine.[11]

While Susanna's journey to England was remarkable, her desire to care for children was not unique. Women were forced to make these decisions on their own and often faced jarring realities in the midst of war. As families were torn apart, women were often left to care for families on their own. Sarah Logan Fisher, like Susanna Marshall, was separated from her husband as the war was beginning to take shape. Her husband, referred to as "My Tommy" in her diaries, was imprisoned and exiled because of his Quaker sensibilities and his refusal to take the Test Act oath, which proclaimed allegiance to the patriot cause.[12] On September 4, 1777, just two days after her husband was taken to a Philadelphia prison, Sarah heard that her husband would be sent to Augusta County, Virginia, nearly three hundred miles away. She found this "cruel and wicked," a particularly deep hardship, as was pregnant. She noted, "My husband, in whom is centered too much of my earthly comfort, is likely to be torn from me by the hands of violence and cruelty, and I left within a few weeks of lying-in, unprotected and alone." Thomas was taken to Virginia on September 13, and Sarah wrote about her distress and anxiety over their separation. Sarah felt a great separation from her husband, describing herself as "solitary and alone."[13]

Like Marshall, Fisher feared her inability to provide for her children's basic needs during her husband's absence, but she did not have a choice. At the end of her pregnancy, Sarah noted that she had scarcely any milk, butter, or eggs for her children. She feared her children would have "nothing to eat but salt meat and biscuit" in November 1777. Fortunately, friends brought her butter and eggs. However, Sarah constantly worried because, in Tommy's absence, she alone was responsible for supporting her children. Sarah wrote less than a month before she gave birth to a girl, "I have to think and provide everything for my family, at a time when it is so difficult to provide anything at any price."[14]

In April 1778, Sarah and her husband were reunited after a seven-month separation. She wrote of his return "thankfully," saying that her husband and other Philadelphia Quakers "were restored to their families and honorably discharged." The return of her husband and reunification of her family brought her "peace of mind, which unspeakable favor I earnestly wish I may keep in grateful remembrance." Although Philadelphia was volatile at the time of her husband's return and the British were beginning to lose control, Sarah's family was reunited.[15] Her separation from her husband was brief, but Sarah had to step up as the sole provider for her family as the Revolution began.

Other women faced prolonged separations from husbands with pronounced loyalist sympathies during the British occupation of Philadelphia, which began in late summer 1777. Once in Philadelphia, General Howe and his soldiers, aided by loyalist regiments from across Pennsylvania, New Jersey, and Maryland, took control of the city. Joseph Galloway, a loyalist from Philadelphia, advised Howe and served as the "virtual" governor of Pennsylvania. Moreover, an estimated two thousand deserters came in from the Continental Army and joined the loyalist cause during the occupation.

Fugitives from Virginia, Maryland, and New Jersey also entered the city for protection. British sanctuary in Philadelphia was brief. In the spring of 1778, the patriots began to encroach, and Howe knew the loyalist occupation was nearing its end.[16] In May 1778, General Howe relinquished his command of the army to Sir Henry Clinton and set sail for England. In the following month, loyalists and troops evacuated Philadelphia for New York and New Jersey, and some removed to the countryside as prisoners of the Patriots. By June 18, the British had formally given up their occupation of the city, but not before destroying large sections of the city.[17]

One consequence of the evacuation was property confiscation, the same property loyalist women had defended desperately for months. As loyalist men fled, women stayed behind to preserve family and property, often without direction or a plan. During the occupation in 1777–78, the Pennsylvania legislature passed additional legislative acts that targeted questions of loyalty and citizenship rights.[18] The Commonwealth of Pennsylvania declared on October 21, 1777, that "all personal estates and effects belonging to those who supported the King of Great Britain and gone within the British lines" were to be seized.[19] The legislature appointed commissioners to confiscate, keep a record, and oversee the sale and auction of loyalist property. Patriots assigned commissioners to most counties in Pennsylvania, but Philadelphia had its own commissioners to handle its significant loyalist population.[20] In 1778, the Provincial Assembly passed additional acts to hasten the seizure of loyalist estates in Philadelphia.[21]

This legislation forced numerous loyalist women, now acting as proxy heads of households, to flee from the city in the hope of protecting their property, including their land, homes, and goods, from confiscation. These women knew their behavior defied the law, yet they seized this moment to challenge the existing legal system. Grace Growden Galloway, wife of the notorious loyalist and Pennsylvania statesman Joseph Galloway, stayed behind following the occupation of Philadelphia to do just this. Joseph and Grace Galloway had married in 1753 and lived in Philadelphia with their daughter, Elizabeth.[22] At the beginning of the American Revolution, Joseph, an active politician, became attainted as a loyalist and found his life in chaos. In the following months, Grace stayed behind in the Philadelphia area with the goal of retaining property included in her dowry and the goods and possessions in her home. Joseph and Elizabeth returned to Philadelphia during the period of occupation but fled at the conclusion of occupation and ultimately left again for England in October 1778.[23]

Given Joseph Galloway's prominent political position, Grace Growden Galloway faced certain scrutiny. Beginning in 1778, Grace was warned by Charles Wilson Peale, one of the agents in charge of confiscating British estates in Philadelphia, that he would be taking possession of her house and estate. The threat of property confiscation was dire for Grace because she and Joseph possessed a number of estates and homes, and had extensive possessions.[24] In July, a friend advised her to seek the counsel of lawyers to prevent the confiscation, especially that of property left to her by her father. The reality of confiscation, however, was growing and very possible. On July 21, another friend told her that the Committee of Confiscation had begun its work. Neighboring loyalists, the Shoemaker family, had watched as their property was inventoried and confiscated the day before, and hearing that Samuel Shoemaker was charged with treason, Grace surmised this would also be her fate. At 2 P.M., the agents in charge of confiscating estates came to her home and took an inventory of her goods. Grace wrote, "They took an inventory of everything even to broken China and empty bottles."[25]

The loss of her estate, now very real, presented a great challenge for Grace. She knew she was openly challenging the confiscation laws, but she maintained her position. In addition to seeing her possessions seized and sold, she faced the loss of her home. Grace feared she would be "brought to beggary" when agents of confiscation told her she could no longer stay in her own home. She lamented, "What shall I do there is No dependence on the arm of flesh; nor have I one hope in this world nor any thing to rely on and am afraid my child and husband came out of New York all hope is over." Grace wrote that she had "no hope of saving anything," although she did try to seek legal counsel in the hope of recovering her estate. Grace also discovered she would not recover her dowry with the confiscation, but she was advised to petition the chief justice for the recovery of her land estates. Grace wrote, "I find I am a beggar indeed I expect every hour to be turn'd out of doors and where to go I know not."[26] The loss of her property, coupled with the absence of her husband, threatened Grace's ability to survive.

Grace was adamant about retaining her property as long as possible, even telling confiscation agents she would not give up her house. She wrote, "[I] will not go out of My house till I know the opinion of ye council."

On August 20, 1778, she remained true to her word: she refused to open the door to Commissioner Charles Peale, and he forced his way into her home through the kitchen. Grace refused to leave, and, as she wrote later, she pleaded with Peale to leave: "I was at home and in my house and nothing but force shou'd drive me out of it." Peale then took Grace by the arm and led her from her home. She reported that her fellow loyalist Rebecca Shoemaker "had agreed to go quietly out of her house," but Grace could not go quietly.[27] In the midst of losing her property and being separated from her family, Galloway's health began to decline. Throughout the remainder of 1778, she noted her failing heath, anxiety due to separation, and overall failing quality of life due to her losses because of the Revolution. In December 1778, she wrote, "I was taken very bad in the morning. . . . I am now quite overcome at being kept out of my estate."[28] Although Grace showed great tenacity and strength in the absence of her husband and daughter, she lost nearly everything.

Women in Philadelphia sought to maintain ownership of loyalist property but faced significant challenges while acting independently in the absence of their husbands. In many cases, attempts were made to manipulate ownership, claiming that property rightly belonged to the women, who were not loyalists. Sarah Shepherd, wife of the Philadelphia loyalist William Shepherd, attempted this strategy to save the family property. William Shepherd was "zealously attached to the British government" and had fled Philadelphia in 1777. After witnessing the execution of a fellow loyalist associate, he went to Brunswick, New Jersey, leaving behind Sarah and their three children, who were "maltreated" in his absence and saw all of their property destroyed. Sarah had attempted to protect the property she inherited from her uncle and held in her own name, but she lost it, as well, due to her husband's loyalism. Eventually, Sarah and the children rejoined William, and together they fled North America and arrived in England in January 1783, forgoing any claims of property.[29]

Like Sarah Shepherd, the Philadelphian Margaret Locke eventually rejoined her husband after prolonged separation. Margaret and her husband, Joshua, were separated for nearly four years. He joined the British troops and left Margaret to care for their home and their three-month-old infant. During the occupation of Philadelphia, General Howe approached Margaret about nursing wounded soldiers. She came to the aid of wounded Hessian soldiers and offered them a place to recuperate during the war. However, nursing the wounded Hessian troops was costly, and Margaret struggled to provide bedding and clothing for them. She claimed that during her separation from her husband she received no financial support from Howe's coffers for either herself or their child; yet, she managed to care for herself, her child, and the wounded Hessians, as General Howe requested, though we can only surmise that she used her own resources.[30]

Prolonged separation anguished the sisters Anna and Peggy Rawle, too, young women who stayed behind in Philadelphia while their loyalist mother, Rebecca Shoemaker, and her husband, their stepfather Samuel Shoemaker, fled the city. Samuel fled during the evacuation of Philadelphia because of his British sympathies. He and Rebecca were both highly regarded in the Philadelphia merchant world and the Quaker community in the years preceding the Revolution. Samuel had served his community in a variety of capacities, holding public offices from 1755 to 1776. He had served as a member of the Philadelphia Common Council and as an alderman, city treasurer, associate justice of the court, mayor of the city, and justice of the peace. He was also a notable member of the community, belonging to the American Philosophical Society and a founder of the Pennsylvania Hospital.[31] He married the widowed Rebecca Rawle in 1763 and took in her three children from her previous marriage: Anne, William, and Margaret (Peggy) Rawle.[32]

Anna and Peggy were daughters of Francis Rawle, a well-established merchant who passed away in 1761. The sisters remained in Philadelphia during the occupation of the city and after the British left. They were separated from their mother in June 1780, when she left Philadelphia for loyalist-occupied New York, and they did not see one another for three years. Anna wrote to her mother on June 7, 1780, begging her to return: "I have every day for this fortnight been expecting to hear from my dear mother, and yet three have elapsed since she left us and I have not yet had that pleasure." Anna described the separation from her mother as a "disagreeable and painful circumstance," although it was "not an hundred miles asunder." Anna seldom heard from her mother, and the silence between letters was painful for her.[33]

Nine months after her mother had left Philadelphia, Anna Rawle heard a rumor that her mother might leave New York for England. The thought of an Atlantic separation caused Anna great discomfort. She wrote, "Tho' I should be distressed at your staying in New York a moment longer than it was safe to do so, yet the thought of being a greater distance, and for how long a time we know not, is most afflicting." Rebecca replied quickly to her daughter's concern, assuring Anna that she had sent earlier word, but the letter must have gotten lost. She tried to alleviate Anna's worries, writing, "I hope that movement [to England] will never be necessary . . . but we must submit if it should be required, at present there is not the least appearance." Despite her mother's reassurances that she would not cross the Atlantic, Anna continued to worry about their separation in New York and continued to write about her worries. In April 1781, a month after hearing rumors that her mother was leaving for England, Anna reported she heard "by a resolve of Congress they talk of absolutely preventing all correspondence between here and New York. . . . [S]urely no honest person would wish to impose laws on another [that interfere] with that first of all human consideration, duty to one's parents, and abstaining from writing would be a great failure of what is owing to them." The letters Anna wrote were a source of comfort and represented her ability to maintain her relationship with her mother in a time of upheaval. Despite the separation, the war, and the uncertainty of everything, Anna and Rebecca relied on their correspondence to continue to foster the relationship.[34]

The separation nevertheless produced great strain. Rebecca wanted her daughters to join her in New York, although she knew that staying in Philadelphia was the only way they could preserve family property—or, maybe, preserve the family and its status—during the war. Even as late as April 1781, she believed she and her daughters would remain separate, writing, "I hope you did not please yourselves with the expectation of permission to come. . . . [W]e must try to see each other in the fall." In October 1781, Anna wrote to her mother, fearing she would be "obliged to leave New York," and saying that if that were to happen, she and Peggy wanted to accompany her. Anna knew that this plan was premature, but she reassured her mother they would work out a means to dispose of their property and asked whether she and her sister might " take some steps" toward ridding themselves of property in Philadelphia. By the fall of 1781, Anna was urging her mother to allow the family to be reunited, even if it meant disposing of family property.[35]

Reunion, however, would still take several years for Anna and Rebecca. The idea of leaving for England troubled Rebecca Shoemaker, for she, too, conceived of herself as a British subject with a home in North America. The idea of exile "distressed" her, and she "pray[ed] we may not be under a necessity of leaving America. I cannot bear to think it." She could only hope for a "general peace" and reunification of family with their property.[36] But in 1783, Rebecca Shoemaker realized that occupied New York and the events of the American Revolution could not be ignored. Anna Rawle also wrote about the worsening situation in Philadelphia when some four thousand loyalists fled from that city to New York in April 1783. For weeks she "fear[ed] the destruction of property in Philadelphia" but did not mention any immediate plans to leave the city.[37] Rebecca "did not know that there [would] be any time fixed for evacuation" from New York City, but loyalists were heading for Nova Scotia and Great Britain in "droves."[38] Within weeks, on November 18, 1783, Samuel and their son Edward had left for England in one of the last ships, leaving Rebecca and her daughters behind.[39] The American Revolution meant prolonged separation for the Shoemaker-Rawle family. The separation forced the family to use correspondence to continue their relationships and ties in the absence of physical proximity.

For the Kearsley family, prolonged separation was caused by violence and imprisonment. The Philadelphia loyalist Mary Kearsley was forced take over the care of her family following the beating and imprisonment of her husband for his loyalist sympathies. John Kearsley, a medical doctor, lived with Mary and their five children in Philadelphia until September 1775, when he was beaten and arrested. Mary describes her husband as having been beaten in front of her and the children "with the butt end of firelocks" and then "dragged through the streets with blood streaming." John languished at home for nearly a month, until the Committee of Safety arrested him and he was imprisoned for a year in York, Pennsylvania. His family witnessed his near-death at the hands of the patriots, and they were now forced to deal with his absence. Mary, left with the responsibility of caring and providing for five children, moved out of Philadelphia to the country in search of safety. When the British occupied Philadelphia, Mary and her children returned, but they soon found themselves in danger again. Mary evacuated Philadelphia with the British and took only what they could carry; their ship wrecked in November 1778, and they lost everything. Penniless and exhausted, she eventually arrived in London with her children. Her separation from her husband began before the war and ultimately led to an entirely new life in Britain, with neither a male head of household nor any material possessions.[40]

The American Revolution drew clear lines between patriot and loyalist. Often these lines extended beyond the battlefield and into the home. The American Revolution represented a moment in which people could exert their political leanings—patriot or loyalist—and this extended across gender lines. Not all women shared their husbands' loyalist sympathies and used the absence of heads of households to embrace a radically different political viewpoint.[41] For example, Jane Bartram, wife of Alexander Bartram, stayed behind in Philadelphia in mid-1778, and her husband stated they did not share the same politics.[42] Jane did not uphold her husband's politics, nor did she rejoin her husband; instead, she severed her ties with Alexander and in 1785 petitioned for divorce.[43] Likewise, Elizabeth Graeme Fergusson used her husband's departure during the Revolution to embrace an independent life. In 1772, Elizabeth married Henry Hugh Fergusson, and it appears they spent much of their marriage separated. Henry Hugh left for Europe in September 1775 and stayed away until 1777. His allegiance to Britain was evident; he was one of the first to sympathize with the Crown. In 1777, he returned to Philadelphia, briefly, but evacuated again in 1778 with the British troops. Elizabeth, however, remained behind as a self-described "American."

Since Elizabeth Fergusson, the "American," stayed behind, she was able to make claims for the property in her husband's name. She began by seeking possession of goods being sold at auction following the initial acts requiring the confiscation of British property. On October 8, 1778, she petitioned the Justices of the Supreme Court of Pennsylvania for articles of furniture from her husband's estate. She made claims for furniture in the parlor, the bedchamber, and the kitchen. The Justices of the Supreme Court declared that she could possess the items until the time of the auction. One week later, a public auction was held for the sale of Henry Hugh Fergusson's household goods. Elizabeth Fergusson attended the auction and bought some of the goods that were for sale, all of which were different items from those she had previously petitioned to keep.[44]

In 1779, Fergusson made another formal appeal for some property that had her father had left to her. However, the appeal was denied because the property had passed to her husband at the time of their marriage.[45] Fergusson petitioned the Assembly of Pennsylvania once again for this lost property in 1781. She outlined her husband's fleeing America, their lengthy separation, and her husband's betrayal by joining the British troops. Her petition was quick to point out how she had previously received "no kind of Relief" under the terms of the confiscation. She begged the assembly to grant her the land that had been left by her father in "her much loved country." For Elizabeth, she and Hugh had spent the majority of their marriage apart; he had betrayed America by joining the British forces; and she felt he had no claim to the property.[46] Her petition in 1781 did garner some success; she was exempted from previous acts calling for the immediate sale of confiscated property, and future sale was avoided.[47]

Fergusson's acts of independence did not go unnoticed and faced harsh scrutiny. Across the Atlantic, Henry Hugh Fergusson knew about his wife's actions and was more than displeased with her claims. While Elizabeth petitioned for what she claimed was her property, he was in England and faced the task of putting together a claim for repayment for lost property from the British government. In 1785, nearly four years after Elizabeth petitioned the Pennsylvania Assembly, Hugh claimed she had sold his property without consent. Elizabeth asserted her authority and ability to sell property before the formal Acts of Confiscation. Hugh claimed that Elizabeth had sold some of his property in 1775, while he was abroad in England. He claimed she had sold nearly 264 acres of land that had belonged to him and realized a hefty profit of £2,000 for the land sale. Other exiled loyalists supported Hugh's claims. Daniel Coxe swore that he had heard rumors about Elizabeth selling Hugh's property in Pennsylvania. John Young, Elizabeth Fergusson's nephew, also swore that Elizabeth was zealous in the

American cause.[48] Elizabeth Fergusson successfully separated herself from her husband and showed her allegiance to the patriot cause. As a woman described as "the most devoted American," she used her husband's flight to exert her own political opinion, claim ownership of property, and, perhaps, even profit from her husband's absence.[49]

The American Revolution clearly tore families apart, and frequently left women behind while men went off to war and traversed the Atlantic world. Women responded to this challenge and used whatever means at their disposal to survive, acting independently of their husbands out of both necessity and want. Arguably, these varied reactions show a revolution of a different sort for loyalist women. They may not have revolted against the patriots in the same fashion in their husbands, but these women ignored the laws, manipulated the legal system, and seized this moment to exert a new form of independence. War shook up the existing social order and provided women with a brief moment to act independently of traditional gender restrictions. For some, this was a welcome opportunity; others hesitated. The experiences of loyalist women were vast, but women used any means necessary to care for their families. In Philadelphia and its surrounding areas some families were never reunited, and others experienced only a brief period of separation. Still other families used the Revolution to forge a permanent separation. Susanna Marshall never joined up with the British troops or saw her husband again. Yet she managed to travel across the Atlantic with her children in tow and, despite the loss of all her goods by force in St. Augustine, she still managed to provide for her children. Elizabeth Fergusson also used her husband's absence to exert her ability to petition the government for her property and managed to separate herself completely from her husband's loyalist politics. Elizabeth revealed herself as an independent American. Other women, however, sorely missed their husbands and felt profound loss in their absence. The war greatly disrupted their lives, and they had to forge ahead in the absence of their husbands during a war for independence. Letters, diaries, and claims show that the women of Philadelphia exhibited remarkable strength and character during the Revolution, even though they were left behind, and that each of their experiences was a distinctive, individual one shaped by personal choice.

Notes

1. Entries dated September 16, 1777, September 22, 1777, Sarah Logan Fisher Diaries, 1776–95, Historical Society of Pennsylvania, Philadelphia (hereafter, HSP). Sarah's husband fell prey to legislative acts passed by the Pennsylvania legislature to respond to threats of loyalism and the disaffected. The Test Act, passed

on June 13, 1777, denied citizenship to those who refused to take oaths of allegiance to the new state. The act identified rights that would be given only to those who chose the side of patriots, effectively determining who would be included in the body of citizens and those who would be excluded. The process of renouncing fidelity to King George and pledging allegiance to Pennsylvania aimed to identify and punish loyalist traitors. However, the law also succeeded in further punishing nonjurors or nonassociators, those Quakers who were still opposed to oaths of any kind. For additional information, see Anne M. Ousterhout, *A State Divided: Opposition in Pennsylvania during the American Revolution* (New York: Greenwood, 1987), 161.

2. In Pennsylvania, however, some individuals refused to side with either the patriots or the loyalists and instead chose neutrality. Those who professed neutrality, sometimes referred to as the disaffected or nonassociators, troubled the Committee of Safety. The beliefs of some groups, such as the Quakers, Mennonites, and Dunkards, forbade them from choosing a side or engaging in military action during the American Revolution. For additional information on disaffected men in Pennsylvania, see William Seibert, *The Loyalists of Pennsylvania* (Columbus: Ohio State University Press, 1920), 23–24. For more recent scholarship discussing the disaffected during the American Revolution, see Judith Van Buskirk, "They Didn't Join the Band: Disaffected Women in Revolutionary Philadelphia," *Pennsylvania History* 62, no. 3 (Summer 1995): 306–29; Anne M. Ousterhout, "Controlling the Opposition in Pennsylvania during the American Revolution," *Pennsylvania Magazine of History and Biography* 105, no.1 (January 1981): 3–34.

3. For background on the Philadelphia occupation, see Robert Calhoon, *The Loyalists in Revolutionary America, 1780–1781* (New York: Harcourt Brace, 1965), 390–94. For a general overview, see Thomas Scharf and Thompson Westcott, *History of Philadelphia, Volume I: 1609–1884* (Philadelphia: L. H. Everts, 1884). For information on social life in Philadelphia during this period, see Darlene Emmert Fisher, "Social Life in Philadelphia during the British Occupation," *Pennsylvania History* 37, no. 3 (July 1970): 237–60. For material on women in Philadelphia and their treatment, behaviors, and perspectives on occupation and the period after, see Van Buskirk, "They Didn't Join the Band," which gives space to the women's experiences during the occupation and notes their absences in the much of the literature on the disaffected and loyalist women. She writes extensively about Sarah Logan Fisher, Grace Growden Galloway, Rebecca Shoemaker, Anna Rawle, and Elizabeth Drinker. See also Linda Kerber, *Women of the Republic: Intellects and Ideology in Revolutionary America* (Chapel Hill: University of North Carolina Press, 1980); Wayne Bodle, "Jane Bartram's 'Application': Her Struggle for Survival, Stability, and Self-Determination in Revolution Pennsylvania," *Pennsylvania Magazine of History and Biography* 115 (April 1991): 185–220.

4. Laurel Thatcher Ulrich, *Goodwives: Image and Reality in the Lives of Women in Northern New England, 1650–1750* (New York: Alfred A. Knopf, 1982); Kerber, *Women of the Republic;* Mary Beth Norton, *Liberty's Daughters: The Revolutionary Experience of American Women, 1750–1800* (Boston: Little, Brown, 1980).

5. Rosemarie Zagarri, *Revolutionary Backlash: Women and Politics in the Early American Republic* (Philadelphia: University of Pennsylvania Press, 2007); Ellen Hartigan-O'Connor, *The Ties That Buy: Women and Commerce in Revolutionary America* (Philadelphia: University of Pennsylvania Press, 2009).

6. Judith Van Buskirk, *Generous Enemies: Patriots and Loyalists in Revolutionary New York* (Philadelphia: University of Pennsylvania Press, 2004); Ruma Chopra, *Unnatural Rebellion: Loyalists in New York City during the Revolution* (Charlottesville: University of Virginia Press, 2011).

7. Maya Jasanoff, *Liberty's Exiles: American Loyalists in the Revolutionary World* (New York: Alfred A. Knopf, 2011).

8. Jim Piecuch, *Three Peoples, One King: Loyalists, Indians, and Slaves in the Revolutionary South, 1775–1782* (Columbia: University of South Carolina Press, 2008).

9. Kathleen DuVal, *Independence Lost: Lives on the Edges of the American Revolution* (New York: Random House, 2015). Empire and its role on the revolution has been largely studied. See also Patrick Griffin, ed., *Experiencing Empire: Power, People, and Revolution in Early America* (Charlottesville: University of Virginia Press, 2017). Some scholars have shifted the narrative of the revolution to new spaces. Benjamin Irvin, *Clothed in Robes of Sovereignty: The Continental Congress and the People out of Doors* (New York: Oxford University Press, 2011), examines the outdoor festivals and acts that helped shape a national identity in the American Revolution. For an examination of cities and everyday actions in the Revolution, see also Benjamin L. Carp, *Rebels Rising: Cities and the American Revolution* (New York: Oxford University Press, 2007).

10. Memorial of Susanna Marshall, Audit Office Records, Series 12 (hereafter, AO 12 Series), Public Record Office, British Claims Commission, Maryland Historical Society, Baltimore.

11. Ibid.

12. The Test Act, passed in June 13, 1777 prior to the occupation, denied citizenship to those refusing to take oaths of allegiance to the new state. The process of renouncing fidelity to King George and pledging allegiance to Pennsylvania aimed to identify and punish Loyalist traitors. However, the law also succeeded in punishing nonjurors, those Quakers who were opposed to oaths of any kind. Political rights and access to the courts were decidedly stripped from those who refused to proclaim loyalty to the independent state of Pennsylvania. The Test Act began to strip men who refused to pledge allegiance access to the courts, trial by jury, and the ability to be elected or hold office. See Robert Brunhouse, *The Counter-Revolution in Pennsylvania, 1776–1790*, (Harrisburg: Pennsylvania Historical Society, 1942), 42–43; Wallace Brown, *The King's Friends: The Composition and Motives of the American Revolution Claimants* (Providence: Brown University Press, 1965), 134; Lorenzo Sabine, *Biographical Sketches of Loyalists of the American Revolution*, vol. 2 (Boston: Little, Brown, 1864), 301.

13. Entries dated September 4, 1777, September 16, 1777, September 21, 1777, Sarah Logan Fisher Diaries.

14. Entry dated November 1, 1777, in ibid. Her diary is largely empty for the next month. She resumes writing on December 5, 1777, noting that a month-long lying-in period accounted for her absence .

15. Entry dated May 29, 1778, in ibid. She notes in this diary entry an absence in writing due to fit of illness and many engagements. Her husband returned on April 29 from his period of forced exile in Virginia.

16. Calhoon, *The Loyalists of Revolutionary America*, 394; Ousterhout, *A State Divided*, 145–50.

17. Wilbur H. Siebert, *The Loyalists of Pennsylvania* (Columbus: Ohio State Univesrity, 1920), 38–55; Brown, *The King's Friends*, 130–31.

18. A number of acts punishing loyalists and nonassociators had already been passed in Pennsylvania. Beginning in 1776, the Pennsylvania legislature identified the problem of treason and stated that "high treason" was "the offense of any person owing allegiance to Pennsylvania who should levy war against the state or to be adherent to the King of Great Britain or . . . others of the enemies of the United States." Information on the legislation is in Pennsylvania Committee of Safety Records, Revolutionary War Records, Pennsylvania State Archives, Harrisburg (hereafter, PSA); Henry Young, "Treason and Its Punishment in Revolutionary Pennsylvania," *Pennsylvania Magazine of History and Biography* 90 (July 1966): 287–313. See also *Laws of the Commonwealth of Pennsylvania from the Second Day of December, One Thousand, Eight Hundred and Six, to the Twenty-Eighth Day of March, One Thousand, Eight Hundred and Eight, Both Days Inclusive*, vol. 8 (Philadelphia: John Bioren, 1808).

19. Pennsylvania Committee of Safety, October 21, 1777, broadside, Revolutionary War Records, PSA.

20. Ibid. For the city of Philadelphia, the commissioners were William Will, Sharp Delany, Jacob Shriner, Charles Wilson Peale, Robert Smith, and Samuel Massey.

21. Pennsylvania Council of Safety, *An Act for the Attainder of Diverse Traitors* (Lancaster, PA: John Dunlap, 1778), in Revolutionary War Records, PSA. This act identified treasonous individuals who varied greatly in profession and community status, and they were found throughout Pennsylvania. This legislature targeted this particular group of men because of their involvement and association with British occupation of Philadelphia. Among them were Joseph Galloway, who had aided General Howe; John Allen, who had formerly served on the Committee of Inspection; William Allen, a current British lieutenant-colonel; James Rankin, a yeoman of York County; Jacob Duche, the previous chaplain to the Continental Congress; Gilbert Hick, a yeoman from Bucks County; John Potts, a yeoman from Philadelphia County; Nathaniel Vernon, the former sheriff of Chester County; Christian Fouts, a lieutenant-colonel; Reynold Keen, a yeoman from Berks County; John Biddle, a deputy quartermaster; and Samuel Shoemaker, a former alderman and mayor of Philadelphia, as well as a prominent merchant.

22. Biographical information on Grace Growden Galloway is in Raymond Werner, "Diary of Grace Growden Galloway," *Pennsylvania Magazine of History and Biography* 55, no. 1 (1931): 32–94.

23. Ibid., 32–34. The Galloway family held a great deal of property in Pennsylvania. For information on Joseph Galloway's claims of his losses, see Loyalist Claims for Pennsylvania, British Claims Commission Records, AO 12 Series, roll 38. In his claim, Galloway notes that he sought relief from the Loyalist Claims Commission so he could reside in Nova Scotia and possibly live there with his wife and other family members. For additional information, see Thomas Balch ed., *The Examination of Joseph Galloway, Esq., by a Committee of the House of Commons* (Philadelphia: T. K. and P. G. Collins, 1855), 71. The loyalist Joseph Galloway left Philadelphia immediately after the occupation, for obvious reasons. Before Philadelphia was occupied, Galloway was a significant figure in Pennsylvania politics and government. In 1774, he was member and Speaker of the Assembly in Philadelphia. When he joined loyalist forces and aided Howe in 1778, he was immediately identified by the patriot-controlled legislature as a known loyalist. He was instrumental during the occupation of Philadelphia. During the British occupation, Galloway advised

Howe and served as the "virtual" governor of Pennsylvania. He had appointed Samuel Shoemaker, along with Daniel Coxe and John Potts, to serve as magistrates in the city, thereby solidifying his highly visible political convictions in the eyes of the Pennsylvania legislature and the Philadelphia community.

24. Entries dated June 19, 1778, July 9, 1778, in ibid.

25. Entry dated July 21, 1778, in ibid.

26. July 21, 1778, July 22, 1778, in ibid.

27. Entry dated August 20, 1778, in ibid.

28. Entry dated December 23, 1778, in ibid.

29. Claim of William Shepherd, British Claims Commission, AO 12 Series, University of Delaware Collections, Newark. For additional information, see ibid., reel 11.

30. The Humble Petition of Margaret Lock, AO 12 Series, University of Delaware Collections. Her case is found in section marked cases under the second act.

31. Introduction to Rebecca Shoemaker's Diary, Shoemaker Family Papers, HSP. Many of the offices and positions held by Samuel Shoemaker overlapped in years, and he held some in the years just before the Revolution.

32. Samuel did not maintain a neutral political stance; in fact, he actively joined the loyalist cause during the British occupation in 1777 and 1778. As noted earlier, Galloway appointed Shoemaker, Coxe, and Potts to serve as magistrates in the city; thus, they were clearly aligned with the British, and the British rewarded their break from the patriots. Shoemaker jumped on one of the first ships during the British evacuation in June 1778 and sailed north to New York. For additional information, see Shoemaker Family Papers.

33. Entry dated June 7, 1780, in ibid.

34. Anna Rawle to Rebecca Shoemaker, March 7, 1781; Rebecca Shoemaker to Anna Rawle, March 26, 1781; Anna Rawle to Rebecca Shoemaker, April 5, 1781, all in Rebecca Shoemaker Papers, 1780–86, HSP.

35. Rebecca Shoemaker to her daughters, April 11, 1781; Anna Rawle to Rebecca Shoemaker, October 26, 1781, in ibid.

36. Rebecca Shoemaker to Anna Rawle, November 3, 1781, in ibid.

37. Anna Rawle to Rebecca Shoemaker, April 26, 1781, April 28, 1781, in ibid.

38. Rebecca Shoemaker to Anna Rawle, April 13, 1783, in ibid.

39. Introduction to the collection of Rebecca Shoemaker's letters and diaries, in Shoemaker Family Papers.

40. Claims of Mary Kearsley, British Claims Commission, AO 12 Series, University of Delaware Collections. John Kearsley passed away at some point. Mary Kearsley made a claim for repayment of lost property in April 1785 as a widow. She does not mention her husband having traveled with them to London or having rejoined the family in her claim to the British Claims Commission. For information on the claim, see ibid.

41. See Van Buskirk, "They Didn't Join the Band." Van Buskirk discusses at great length how women in Philadelphia did not share the politics of the American Revolution and uses their writings to show how they became "disaffected." Her article provides a wonderful overview on the lives and daily struggles of disaffected women in Philadelphia.

42. Bodle, "Jane Bartram's 'Application,'" 195; Evidence in the Claim of Bartram, May 10, 1785, British Claims Commission, AO 12 Series, University of Delaware

Collections. For more on the confiscation of the Bartram property, Jane Bartram's claims against the property, and details on her story see Bodle, "Jane Bartram's 'Application.' " For more on women and court contests, see Linda Kerber, "The Paradox of Women's Citizenship in the Early Republic: The Case of Martin vs. Massachusetts, 1805." *American Historical Review* 91 (April 1992): 349–72.

43. Bodle, "Jane Bartram's 'Application,' " 195–203. Bodle also discusses the possible motivations for the divorce petition and the nature of divorce in Pennsylvania following the American Revolution.

44. Biographical information on Elizabeth Fergusson is in Simon Gratz, Eliza Graeme, Thomas Graeme, and John Young et al., "Some Material for a Biography of Mrs. Elizabeth Fergusson," *Pennsylvania Magazine of History and Biography* 39, no. 3 (1915): 257–321. See also Thomas Lynch Montgomery, ed., *Pennsylvania Archives Sixth Series*, vol. 12 (Harrisburg, PA: Harrisburg Publishing, 1907), 647–53. On October 8, 1778, she requested specific furniture from her parlors, bedchamber, and kitchen. They were not the same items she purchased at auction the following week. The following week, she purchased an easy chair, two sets of drawers, three bedsteads, four flower casks, two red sows and pigs, two white sows and pigs, a pair of small scales and weights, and a tablecloth. Extensive biographical details are in Anne M. Ousterhout, *The Most Learned Woman in America: A Life of Elizabeth Graeme Fergusson* (University Park: Pennsylvania State University Press, 2004).

45. Gratz et al., "Some Material for a Biography of Mrs. Elizabeth Fergusson," 305–8.

46. Ibid., 258–59, 308–11.

47. She was likely successful because a number of influential men in Pennsylvania, including James Wilson, Thomas Mifflin, George Clymer, Robert Morris, and John Dickinson, supported her petition and came to her aid: see ibid.

48. When asked by the Loyalist Claims Commission to provide documentation of the land sale in 1775, Hugh was unable to do so. He claimed, on February 3, 1785, that Elizabeth had destroyed any record of the sale and taken the profits. He also remarked, at this juncture, that he and Elizabeth were not on good terms.

49. The Philadelphian loyalist Phineas Bond was a sworn witness for Hugh Fergusson to validate his property claims and described Elizabeth Fergusson and her political opinions as the opposite of her husband's politics.

Deborah Logan's Marriage, 1781–1824

C. DALLETT HEMPHILL

The American Revolution did little to alter the legal underpinnings of women's inequality in marriage. What did this feel like for educated elite white women who were as aware as their husbands of the new thinking about equality that accompanied the Revolution? There were plenty of unhappy marriages, of course, but it appears that even the good ones were hard on women. Abigail Adams is a well-documented example. Deborah Norris Logan (1761–1836) is an interesting case because she was clearly smarter than her husband, George. She must not have been alone in that. Yet this generation of women did not protest their position as women. Other historians have suggested why they lacked the requisite feminist consciousness.[1] But we have not fully explored how women dealt with this situation. In Deborah Logan's case, a combination of avoidance, the outlet of writing, and appreciation of what her husband did offer allowed her to live with the era's constraints.

We do not have a portrait of Debby Norris as a young woman, but it is obvious that she was a catch. Educated in Anthony Benezet's school for girls, she gained polish as a young woman because her widowed mother, Mary Parker Norris, was educated herself and good at attracting company.[2] Living just down Chestnut Street from Philadelphia's State House in the beautiful Norris mansion, the teenage Debby met all sorts of people in the mid-1770s, including members of the Continental Congress and most of the signers of the Declaration of Independence. She was a vivacious young woman who enjoyed socializing with a circle of other young Quakers. She was popular and enjoyed her friends' esteem.[3]

Fortunately, we do have word portraits of Debby Norris in her correspondence with friends. Especially useful is that with Sally Wister, whose family had left town while the British occupied Philadelphia (Debby's widowed mother opted to remain in their Philadelphia home to protect it).[4] When Debby described the British occupation of Philadelphia, she did so in between reports of visits from mutual friends and of a spat between two of them, a quote from the popular British poet Alexander Pope, and her happiness at hearing that Sally's brother and sister had recovered from an illness.[5] Since both girls had been schooled by Benezet, the letters, with their scattered references to embroidery, novels, various works in Latin and French, and the *Lady's Magazine,* in addition to Pope, give us a sense of their education.[6] Not surprisingly, they reveal above all a circle of girls with an avid interest in young men.[7] Their shared Quaker pacifism notwithstanding, Sally was sure Debby would be interested in her descriptions of the American officers who were quartered near the Wisters' farm, including her admiring sketch of a non-Quaker Virginia slaveholder. The imagined responses she ascribed to Debby were not prudish, but teasing. And Debby's letters to Sally often jested. "I am amazed that Miss Stocker is called a Beauty," she wrote. "We have a chance for it now, I think."[8]

As the war continued, so did courtship as the main theme of Debby's letters to friends. At one point she apologized to Sally Fisher, writing, "I have no matrimonial intelligence to send thee."[9] Yet we do not find George Logan, because he was away in Europe, getting his medical degree. As late as May 1780, Debby confided to Sally, "Indeed my dear it seems to me that we shall neither of us marry; but for reasons rather different, thee from not having an offer thee approves, I, from having no offers to disapprove."[10] But then George appeared in her parlor that fall. Debby wrote to Sally, "We will call him Altamont" (after a young nobleman in a popular tragedy), and that he had visited for tea, was "agreeable," and had entertainingly described his recent travels in Italy.[11] By December, Debby was apparently being teased about him, and she wrote, "He is a great Beau here[.] No wonder when we have such a scarcity but seriously I think him very agreeable, And should be very much obliged to the World if it would spare its Conjectures because I should appear less Awkward."[12]

Debby's prompt assigning to George a romantic pseudonym was typical practice among educated youth.[13] She was an avid subscriber to the vogue of sensibility, or empathic feeling, encouraged by the popular new novels. She wrote that her mind was "agitated with very tender sensibilitys" over the illness of an aunt.[14] On news of the recovery of one of Sally Fisher's aunts, she gushed: "How sweetly amiable and pleasing is sensibility, how beautifully does it gild and add lustre to other accomplishments; like the sun beam to the trembling dew drop! These were my reflections when I read that part of thy letter which Concerned thy Aunt."[15]

How did this emphasis on feeling affect Debby's attitude towards courtship and marriage? Her comments about matches being made around her hint at her own views at a time of change in marriage making. Although new ideas about the importance of affection had begun to challenge purely economic criteria, the latter persisted. Debby's elite upbringing showed when a wealthy acquaintance married a man of middling rank. She noted, "Almost every body wonders at her choice." Debby thought she would be "mortified with having it Universally thought I was too good for the Gentleman." Yet, she added, "he may be a very good sort of man," thereby assuring herself and her friends of her allegiance to sensibility. When another friend had married secretly after a rapid courtship, causing concern, Debby noted, "She appears happy [and] their happiness is romantic, to one who's brain is as much turned that way as mine, it is not disagreeable."[16]

Debby and George did not tarry themselves; by February 1781, just a few months after his first appearance in her parlor, their circle learned of their engagement. Her self-deprecating comments to girlfriends notwithstanding, Debby was not acting for lack of other possibilities. One gossip commented that "Doctor Logan will have a prize in her—their intended marriage will much disappoint one of the same profession, by what I have heard."[17] Since her father was long dead and George's parents had both died while he was in Britain, the two were more or less free to make their own choice. Debby surely consulted her mother, but Mary Parker Norris could not have objected to George on either romantic or economic grounds, since, like Debby, he was descended from one of Pennsylvania's most eminent families.[18]

Debby's comments on courtship indicate that she was looking for an agreeable companion, and her friends confirmed that she and George personified the ideal mates—virtuous and moderate, tender and affectionate—extolled in sentimental literature.[19] When they announced their intention to marry at meeting on July 27, 1781, a friend remarked approvingly: "He must be entirely insensible to every delicate and refin'd sentiment if he does not feel the most tender attachment for her, she is indeed a lovely girl."[20] Debby's looks and manner were not just admired by her girlfriends. The French diplomat the Marquis de Barbé-Marbois was captivated when he met her at Anthony Benezet's and described her as "beautiful as an angel." He loved her subdued Quaker style, claiming that she was "dressed with neatness, simplicity, and . . . elegance. . . . Her hair had not been tortured by the coiffure; it was drawn back behind her head without powder and covered with a little gauze cap. . . . She wore a grey satin dress." He insisted to his correspondent, "I assure you, the charms of Mademoiselle Norris are all her own, and she owes nothing to art."[21] The pair were married at the High Street Meeting in September 1781. Forty friends and relatives gathered to celebrate afterward at her mother's home.[22]

George Logan was as much a catch as Debby was. He was the handsome grandson of William Penn's powerful secretary, James Logan, and had inherited Stenton, the house James Logan built just outside town.²³ His medical training notwithstanding, in coming home to war-battered Stenton, George became very interested in agricultural reform and soon threw himself into farming.²⁴ His new bride supported his desire for home manufactures and self-sufficiency, which was fortunate, since the paper money George had inherited was nearly worthless at war's end, and Stenton needed many repairs.²⁵ The couple set to work and apparently lived in great harmony at Stenton, where Deborah soon bore and they reared three sons with the sentimental names Albanus, Gustavus, and Algernon.²⁶

Deborah loved Stenton and did not often leave the beautiful brick home and gardens. Just as clearly, Deborah loved George. She sang his praises throughout her *Memorial of George Logan,* published after his death (and during a period of deep mourning on her part).²⁷ The challenge is to get underneath the loyal memorial and professions of marital harmony to the actual marriage. How did this bright and vivacious (Anthony Benezet and Sally Wister might have said headstrong and mischievous) young woman experience their union at this complicated time in the history of Western marriage? Deborah and George would both have imbibed the new fashion, celebrated in novels and magazines, that husbands should be sensitive and feeling companions to their wives. Yet the common-law tradition of coverture, wherein wives were safely subordinated to their husband's legal identity and authority, as well of control of property, held fast. Studies of prescriptive literature suggest that the new ideal of equality did not supersede patriarchy but accommodated it. Despite the chatter in the postwar press about equality and friendship in marriage, the small print insisted that men and women had different roles, and if there was conflict, it was up to the wife to defer to the husband.²⁸ Ideal marriage in the new republic was thus a complex mix of mutuality and wifely submission. Deborah Norris made it her business to appear to fit the mold. She was not alone. Even the most educated and politically aware women of the time, with equally good marriages—Mercy Otis Warren and Abigail Adams come to mind—did the same.²⁹

The new ideal of marriage granted some influence to the wife. Marriage was now seen as a school for the morality and virtue necessary to sustain a republic, wherein the educated and virtuous wife would have a beneficial influence on her husband's character. In a poem she wrote several years before George came on the scene, Debby had encouraged her female friends to look within for moral guidance, not to men, often "the slaves of vice." She went as far as to insist that women had "equal if not superior Qualities" to men. Perhaps these ideas, encouraged in popular literature, gave Deborah satisfaction in her role as wife.³⁰

Yet neither she nor George ever hinted that such an influence was at work in their marriage. Moreover, such an influence required a receptive husband. George was no unfaithful scoundrel like the impervious villains of seduction novels; no one questioned his virtue. But he seems to have had a deaf ear to Deborah's guidance, especially in matters political, where he sorely needed it.[31] And there was nothing she could do about that. In fact, politics might have made him impervious. Nancy Cott argues that although revolutionary-era thinking about contractual government sparked discussion of egalitarian and companionate marriage, after the Revolution there was more emphasis on the bond formed by the granting of consent. Just as citizens delegated authority to their elected representatives, so did the wife consent to that of her husband.[32] This had to have been a challenge for Deborah, given her prior conviction of women's "equal if not Superior qualities."

George's letters to Deborah reflect the mixed messages about late eighteenth-century Anglo-elite marriage. He often expressed an egalitarian affection and respect for her judgment, but he always mixed in directives that implied he maintained the upper hand. Announcing his imminent return from a trip, he declared, "I hope to have the . . . pleasure and inexpressible happiness of meeting you *my best Friend* & our dear little Son. . . . I omit giving any instructions respecting our affairs at Stenton, having great confidence in your judgment." But then he proceeded to tell her to hire some help.[33] This pattern of expressions of confidence in her judgment mixed with specific instructions continued years into their marriage.[34] From nearby Lancaster he wrote, "On receiving this Letter, if the road will admit visit Philada: spend two days with our Uncle & in visiting your friends, take our Children with you. I wish you to visit Mrs. Smith; tell them Mr. Bingham is applying to the Legislature for an act of divorce on acct: of his daughter." To be sure, George was on the legislative committee to deal with this matter and needed information, adding, "*Write to me immediately on this subject.*"[35] But did he need to specify that she was to spend two days with their uncle and in visiting her friends and should take the children with her?

Some letters were entirely solicitous. From England, he wrote, "Pray my dear Girl make use of the advantages I gave you in placing my affairs in your hands, to make yourself as happy as possible. Keep all the servants as I left them, or change them for such as may be more agreeable to yourself. . . . [N]eglect nothing or no expence that may contribute to your *own health.*"[36] Occasionally, he took pains to consult her views, as when, anticipating a Christmas recess from the state legislature in 1799, he suggested that she summon the boys home from their school in New Jersey so the family could spend a week together, but added, "I suggest this plan merely for your information & consideration should it not meet with your full approbation, it is not to be executed."[37] Yet at other times, especially early in their marriage, he could be downright preachy. George urged her to "keep good company" while he was away, for example, explaining that she was young and her manners not yet formed. He added that she should keep to her books and cultivate her mind, else on his return he would spurn her.[38] Not infrequently, George's requests come across as peremptory: "Please to send to my friend Tench Coxe *immediately* 50 copies of my last publication."[39]

How did Deborah—the spirited and charming girl who had confidently described men as "the slaves of vice"—take this instruction? In fact, she appears to have played a role in shaping the marriage through self-subordination. George's letters suggest that she did not challenge his authority and asked for his guidance. In 1802, George wrote, "I have this moment received my Dear Girls letter of Friday. I am sorry she should be perplexed a moment respecting our affairs."[40] But it also seems that, in a nonconfrontational way, Deborah did what she wanted. For example, George regularly asked her to come be with him in Lancaster or, later, in Washington, DC, but she never did. After a while, his requests on this subject became oblique, as when he wrote, "Our friends Jefferson & Madison are well, they regret very much your not coming on with me. Several Members are accompanied with their wives."[41]

Deborah preferred to remain at Stenton while George pursued his political ambitions.[42] This was not owing to a desire to remain with the children, since from an early age the boys were away at school.[43] One wonders, given the course of his political career, whether her staying at home was a means of preserving their marriage. Deborah's devotion must have been put to the test by George's political career. Time after time he engaged in projects that brought enormous criticism. Deborah always stood by him, despite some doubts about his decisions. Perhaps Stenton provided a refuge.

George's concern about what he perceived as a federalist counterrevolution in Washington's government led him into the fray. Deborah's old friends thought this development must be a trial to her, but she put up a brave front.[44] She disapproved his public opposition to President George Washington, but did not make a fuss.[45] The real challenge came when, as an avid—some would say rabid—Jeffersonian Democrat, George took it upon himself to go to France in 1798 to negotiate for peace at a time of great international tension. He was vilified by the press as presumptuous or even treasonable. Congress responded with "Logan's law," barring private citizens from entering into diplomacy with foreign powers.[46]

We get Deborah's retrospective description of all of this in her memoir of George. She describes his every step in France, including extracts from his letters, to vindicate him and his motives. But one also gets the sense that she was embarrassed by his actions. She did not hesitate to write that she had deemed the quest "romantic" or to describe her anxiety: "I could not help being appalled with a sense of the difficulties which he would have to surmount and the clamour which would be raised upon his departure. . . . I was as completely miserable as I could be. . . . I found it necessary, by a strong effort, to control my feelings."[47]

Given the newly passed Sedition Act, the threat of his being named a traitor was real, and she noted several times her doubts that he could behave so perfectly as to be free from any accusations by the other party on his return. George Logan was not a careful man, and, Deborah confessed in the memoir, "I hardly dared to hope that he, 'who certain of the weight,' often disregarded 'the impress' of what he said and did, had been so cautious that spies and enemies would not be able to pick out something to accuse him of." Deborah's defense of George revealed much about her.

This was not the last of Deborah's trials as a politician's wife, however, as George served in the Pennsylvania legislature from 1798 to 1800, followed by a term in the U.S. Senate.[48] Although no one doubted that he was a good man at heart and sincere, he generally failed to impress his peers. Abigail Adams thought, for example, that "Logan seems more fool than Knave."[49] Then, Logan's law notwithstanding, he took himself to England in 1810 to try to soothe the tensions that ultimately would lead to the War of 1812. Despite the obvious failure of this second private diplomatic mission, Deborah defended him again. But you can read her misgivings between the lines. Indeed, the memoir chapter that recounts "Dr. Logan's Peace Mission to England" opens with this: "He declined a re-election to the Senate, which he might have obtained, and which I had reason to regret he had not accepted, as it furnished reflection and employment to a mind so devoted to the best interests of his country and of society that they appeared peculiarly his province, and that mind seemed to refuse to occupy itself with interest in less important concerns."[50] If only he were safely occupied in Washington, she seemed to say, he would not have gotten involved in this second foreign mission.[51]

Fortunately, that was the last of his overseas adventures. But George, although clearly not a careful or savvy politician, continued to have an irrepressible zeal and energy to do what he thought was right. Deborah never doubted his motives, but she was by far the greater realist. The next year, for example, she wrote to her daughter-in-law, "Dr Logan has left home this afternoon upon another visit to Washington his uneasiness of mind on the prospect of Public Affairs is the inducement, I participate in his Anxieties, yet I wish he could leave things more, to this he says if it was a common time he would, but he thinks the Public good so much at stake that he makes it a matter of conscience to do what he can to save his country from an Abyss which he sees open to receive her."[52]

Soon Deborah began to keep a diary, and we get a more complete picture. Her own interest in politics is amply confirmed by a steady stream of comments on the War of 1812. Although she shared George's Democratic leanings, she did not mince words about her disappointment in the nation's Democratic leadership, referring, for example, to "the frightful imbecillity apparent in our Rulers." Soon she would refer to "the opiate besotted [last word crossed out] President" and aver that his resignation was "indispensable for the Public Good." Though always supportive of George, this was not a woman without strong opinions of her own.[53] Interestingly, "Dr. L," as she generally referred to him, is not often mentioned in the diary, even though he was now home most of the time, and when she did mention him, we see her reservations about his political behavior. When Thomas Jefferson wrote to George to complain about his publishing one of Jefferson's private letters, for example, Deborah copied the letter and added, "I must own I am of the same opinion, and told my husband so on this occasion." But she quickly backed away from criticizing George, adding that he acted "without ever deviating from his accustomed truth and sincerity."[54]

Deborah was just not inclined to criticize George—or, at least, she was not inclined to leave any such criticism for posterity. She loved him and sometimes wrote sweet vignettes indicating how much she enjoyed being at home alone with him: "At home all day and uninterrupted by company. Dr. L and myself spent it comfortably together, before a good fire in his parlour." On another occasion, she noted that after tea "we sat in the twilight meditating, as if by consent—Dr. Logan took his flute, the air he play'd was in unison with my mind."[55] He was clearly a loving husband. She was effusive in her appreciation of the tender care he took of her when she got sick and noted his "great relief" when she got better.[56]

Deborah was certainly not going to criticize George in the travel portions of her diary, written to be shared with others back home. At most she was tongue-in-cheek, as when she described meeting a lady from New York: "I saw Charlotte eyeing Dr Logan very attentively and when he left the room she observed that his Phisiognomy . . . bespoke a decided . . . character, and turning to me she said, 'Mrs Logan when your husband takes a Resolution to do anything, can he be diverted from his object?' " Winking to her niece back home about George's famous stubbornness, Deborah added, "You may guess at my reply to this question."[57] But she would not criticize him outright.

And yet one wonders what she did not say. She was so smart, so well educated, and so interested in politics, while he was clearly a bumbler, if a well-intentioned one. He somehow managed to be both rigid in pursuit of his ideals and wildly inconsistent.[58] We know that Deborah was sometimes unhappy, although she never attributes this to George. She would write things such as, "To describe what has been the state of my mind of late, is a thing I cannot undertake," followed by crossed-out words.[59]

Deborah and George were very different in her desire to stay at home and his restless adventures in the public sphere. She loved above all else to be alone at Stenton and often noted this right after he left the house.[60] One reason she relished privacy was that it enabled her to write. She found "seclusion and quiet" essential for this and complained that she could not write in the library, for "Dr. L almost continually inhabits the Library, and I hate to be asked what I am writing." She lamented one day that she had not had time to write a letter because "I cannot write agreeably to myself unless alone."[61] The next sentence was heavily crossed out.

The strikeouts in the diary, coupled with the mentions of unhappiness that are not explained, point to some sort of struggle for Deborah. It may have been about her sons, but no evidence points that way. It may have had some other cause or mix of causes. But where the strikeouts occur often points to some sort of frustration, or even conflict, with George. The cross-outs were expressions of emotion in themselves. We know Deborah objected to George's political doings. She may have expressed anger in the diary or even described expressing anger to George himself. As a Quaker wife, she would have wanted to control the expression of anger.[62] The diary allowed her to do both. In crossing out any expressions of anger, she both pointed to and erased them.[63]

Despite mixed signals during his political career, there is no doubt that the strength of Deborah's love for George only grew over the course of his final illness. It is painful to read her daily accounts of the ups and downs of his health.[64] She also noted, repeatedly, the impact of his illness on her life, especially her lack of time to write: "Constant attendance in the Chamber of my poor husband has prevented me from having much recourse to my Pen or noticing what is passing in the world around me."[65] Deborah did recognize George's appreciation of her: "Never shall I forget the kind and grateful manner in which he received our attentions and the expressions of his affectionate attachment to myself. It has left a feeling of pure and holy tenderness which can never be effaced."[66]

When the end was in sight, her anguish grew: "Oh it is utterly impossible to describe the chaos of distress and care with which I feel myself surrounded. . . . How can I part from one who loves and values me as my beloved Dr Logan does? no words can express my feelings of tenderness, respect & unutterable love towards him."[67] In addition to appreciating his love, she expressed her own, although she found it hard to put it into words. Naturally, the idea of losing him caused the outburst, but her feelings had grown in depth and complexity. Confined to his bed, he could no longer embarrass her; while he was confined to his bed, she had the chance to repay his devotion to her. Her nursing may have absolved feelings of guilt about, even in his time of need, her desire to be alone to read and write. When George died, her emotional floodgates burst: "Oh my best loved and dearest earthly treasure, in thy loss; and in the severing of a union of nearly forty years, I feel that the world has nothing more to offer me since I have lost thee!" Although she had bemoaned her lack of time to write during his long illness, now she wrote, "I never found my pen so inadequate to express what I have felt."[68]

Deborah grieved for George for a long time. She wrote that she felt lifeless, "as if 'All my pleasant days were come—and gone.' "[69] She tried to get back into her domestic work but wrote that "there is no describing how lonely and miserable I am."[70] Part of her grief seems willed, as when she noted after receiving visitors, "I reproach myself for being capable of feeling a temporary cheerfulness."[71] After a while, she claimed to be tired even of recording her grief, although she continued to do so.[72] And this is only what we can read today, for she crossed out and deleted many passages from the diary for the six months following George's death. While descendants may have been responsible for removing pages, the consistent nature of the cross-outs—in the same ink as the writing, suggest that Deborah wrote, and then heavily censored, her own thoughts. Did she erase even greater effusions of grief as excessive? Did she give voice to more complicated feelings—regrets or emotions of which she was not proud? We cannot know.

Gradually, the pain began to ease. She was helped by the project she gave herself of writing her memoir of George. This was just the ticket for her. It involved historical research and writing. It allowed her to indulge her interest in politics—difficult now since her sons were not interested. It allowed her to think about and record the story of her beloved husband. But it also allowed her to shape that story in such a way as to refute any of the criticism that had been launched against him, and even to embellish his reputation a bit. The historian Terri Premo insightfully suggests that it allowed her to create a George Logan with whom she could spend the rest of her life. It was painful at first. She said she began "without animation, without spirits

or pleasure, scarcely with sense or capability," but I have to think it contributed to her starting a new life on her own.[73] Reminiscing may even have
brought some pleasure. In November, she describes a day "alone in my
dear Dr. Logan's parlour and not without my pensive enjoyments."[74]

After several years of mourning and depression, the fog lifted. Deborah
Logan lived for eighteen years after George's death, and seemed to take a
new lease on life after 1825. She must have been interesting in old age, as
she continued to attract visitors to Stenton.[75] When not entertaining young
relations and other visitors, she pursued the history that she loved. As her
allusions to missing her writing while nursing her patients suggest, she
had discovered her true calling in 1815 when she stumbled on a cache of
manuscripts of George's grandfather James Logan, William Penn's colonial secretary, in a closet.[76] She considered the organizing and copying of
these manuscripts her most important work, although she also wrote and
published, anonymously, a number of newspaper articles, obituaries, and
poems. It is true that her work in preserving the historical manuscripts was
of incalculable value. The Historical Society of Pennsylvania, founded at
this time, made her its first honorary female member in gratitude.[77]

Visitors thus began to come to Stenton in search of historical information, especially John Fanning Watson, the Philadelphia historian, who
began to call on her in 1823.[78] The two built a strong friendship, revealed
in his constant references to her in his two volume *Annals of Philadelphia*.
Once again, however, Deborah Logan had to bite her tongue in embarrassment over the men in her life, for although she enjoyed Watson's visits,
she was mortified by the many errors she found in his history. She nevertheless remained a loyal supporter publicly, and when she died in 1839,
Watson wrote a glowing obituary.[79] But just as much as he needed her help,
she needed him as someone to talk history with—and, indeed, to get the
stories out. It is just that one wonders whether she thought she could do
a better job herself. She, who as a proper Quaker woman published work
only anonymously, would have censored the thought. She had even refused
the Historical Society's request to publish her "Memoir of George Logan"
in 1825, although she allowed it to circulate.[80] Still, it is hard not to imagine
her thinking she might have written a better book than Watson's. In the
confines of her diary, she regularly expressed pleasure when the journal
editor Robert Walsh published one of her pieces.

Unfortunately, Deborah continued to be hampered by her dependence
on men, for despite the family's former prominence, George did not leave
her very well off.[81] This came to light just a few months after his death, when
she wrote that she was "very unhappy and fatigued with a thousand cares
and distresses—among other things I doubt that my income is sufficient to

maintain this large family in the way that we have been used to live." She concluded that she knew "not what better to do than to use a decent economy, go into no new expenses that I can avoid," and trust in God.[82] As an early American woman, there was little else she could do.

Ten years later, she was still perplexed. One day, after someone had come with a bill she could not pay, she wrote, "It is a weary life that I lead now." She then linked her present situation with George: "I have walked down to the enclosure and seen the verdant turf that covers the resting place of my beloved husband, and have more satisfaction in thinking that I parted with my last ground rents and Bank shares to relieve him from such kind of embarrassment as I now feel, than I should have in their reservation for myself—I rejoice that I promptly and willingly gave them up, and made his mind easy on such a score." And yet, the next sentence, heavily inked out, does visibly begin with "But." She may have been referring to property he sold to pay for his diplomatic adventures. In any case, Deborah continued to fret when presented with bills she could not pay. But she would also urge the young women around her to take steps to protect their property before marrying.[83]

Actually, Deborah was not completely on her own at this point, as her son Algernon still lived at home and apparently did much to help manage her affairs. But when he died, she was truly alone. In October 1836, in her mid-seventies, she wrote, "I feel the loss of my beloved son in all things, and at present a kind of derangement of everything which he used wisely to control, has taken place, nothing seems to go on right."[84] Despite her intelligence, Deborah Logan felt dependent on the men in her life, especially in the male-controlled area of property, and in her old age.

Financially dependent on men, never challenging domesticity, Deborah Logan tried hard to be a submissive wife and largely succeeded in pulling off a convincing performance of that role. But her own words betray that she was more than that. Intellectually, at least, she was a full person. Her daughter-in-law Maria Dickinson Logan provided the final confirmation of this reading of Deborah Logan in her obituary in the Quaker journal *The Friend:* "Richly endowed by nature, with talents and genius of the highest order, and intellectual capacities surpassed by few, yet her well-regulated mind, conscientiously and faithfully attended to the performance of every duty, even to the minutest relations of domestic life, diligently laboring to redeem her invaluable time." But Maria Logan did not end with Deborah's adherence to duty, as she added, "Her heart was formed for love and enduring friendship. . . . [N]one more enjoyed the refin'ed & elevated companionship of congenial minds." She concludes with praise for Deborah's religiosity. What the obituary does not do, beyond mentioning in the first line that she was the "relict of the late Dr. George Logan," is say anything about her husband.[85] Of course, Deborah survived George by many years. In so doing, she showed to others, if she did not observe it for herself, that there was life for Deborah without George Logan, despite her doubts after his death. She was able to live her own life because she had already carved out a space for herself in her thirty-nine years with George. He may have been a fool in the minds of some, but she chose to dwell, not without struggle, on his idealism and love.[86] Given the circumstance, she was probably smart to do so. What would she have gained besides marital strife had she not opted for submission? George was no more likely than John Adams to have been receptive to a wife who resisted openly the gender roles of the time. Even the smartest of wives of the revolutionary era, with the most caring and well-intentioned of husbands, had to find other ways to cope with the gender limitations of their time.

Notes

1. See, e.g., Rosemarie Zagarri, *A Woman's Dilemma: Mercy Otis Warren and the American Revolution* (Wheeling, IL: Harlan Davidson, 1995), 162–67. For portraits of other elite marriages at this time, see G. J. Barker-Benfield, *Abigail and John Adams: The Americanization of Sensibility* (Chicago: University of Chicago Press, 2010); Sheila Skemp, *Judith Sargent Murray: A Brief Biography with Documents* (Boston: Bedford, 1998).

2. On Mary Parker Norris, see Deborah Norris Logan Diary, 1808–1815, vol. 35, Library Company of Philadelphia (hereafter, DNL-LCP). I thank Jim Green.

3. For a glimpse of this circle, see Kathryn Zabelle Derounian, "'A Dear, Dear Friend': Six Letters from Deborah Norris to Sarah Wister, 1778–1779," *Pennsylvania Magazine of History and Biography* 108 (October 1984). 487–516; Sally Wister, *Sally Wister's Journal*, ed. Albert Cook Myers (Philadelphia: Ferris and Leach, 1902), 203–5.

4. Barbara Jones, "Deborah Logan" (M.A. thesis, University of Delaware, Newark, 1964), 13; John T. Scharf and Thompson Westcott, *History of Philadelphia, 1609–1884, 3 vols.* (Philadelphia: L. H Everts, 1884), 1:351.

5. Wister, *Sally Wister's Journal*, 189–93.

6. Ibid., 13–14, 141.

7. Mrs. Owen J. Wister [Sarah Butler Wister] and Miss Agnes Irwin, eds., *Worthy Women of Our First Century* (Philadelphia: J. B. Lippincott, 1877), 284–87; Wister, *Sally Wister's Journal*, 15.

8. Wister, *Sally Wister's Journal*, 114–15, 123, 143, 163, 167, 175, 179–80, 194–97, 198–200.

9. John A. H. Sweeney, "Introduction," in *The Norris-Fisher Correspondence: A Circle of Friends, 1779–1782*, ed. John A. H. Sweeney (Wilmington: Historical Society of Delaware, 1955), 188, 192–93; Deborah Norris to Sally Fisher, December 1779, in ibid., 199.

10. Deborah Norris to Sally Fisher, May 6, 1780, in ibid., 203.

11. Deborah Norris to Sally Fisher, n.d., in ibid., 214–15. "*Altamont* was a young Genoese nobleman portrayed in *The Fair Penitent* by Nicholas Rowe (1674–1718), one of the . . . Augustan playwrights. A popular tragedy, *The Fair Penitent* . . . was performed in Philadelphia . . . on Apr. 15, 1754, against much opposition from the Quakers." George had traveled after completing his studies at Edinburgh: Sweeney, *The Norris-Fisher Correspondence*, 215n51, 6. Deborah and George must have known each other before George's departure for Edinburgh. The Norrises and Logans were part of a fairly self-contained Quaker social group. George's first school was in the same block as her house. His apprenticeship was also very near, and so they must have crossed paths or at least seen each other at meeting. But Deborah, only fourteen when he left, might not have caught the twenty-two-year-old's attention. She did not take long to do so at nineteen, when he returned. Jones says she did not know him before his return: Jones, "Deborah Logan," 16; Wister and Irwin said she had to have: Wister and Irwin, *Worthy Women of Our First Century*, 288. Deborah was very friendly with Mary (Molly) Pleasants, who became the wife of George's brother Charles in 1778 and maintained contact with them through 1779: Deborah Norris to Sarah Wister, April 1778 and August 6, 1779, in Derounian, "A Dear, Dear Friend," 488, 498–500, 514–15; Deborah Norris to Sally Fisher, November 16, 1779, in Sweeney, *The Norris-Fisher Correspondence*, 198. See also Deborah Norris Logan, *Memoir of Dr. George Logan*, ed. Frances A. Logan (Philadelphia: Historical Society of Pennsylvania, 1899), 31, 42; Frederick B. Tolles, *George Logan of Philadelphia* (New York: Oxford University Press, 1953), 11, 15, 18, 301. On late eighteenth-century Quaker tribalism and intermarriage, see Susan Klepp and Karin Wulf, eds., *The Diary of Hannah Callender Sansom: Sense and Sensibility in the Age of the American Revolution* (Ithaca, NY: Cornell University Press, 2010), 271–72.

12. Deborah Norris to Sarah Fisher, December 1780, in Sweeney, *The Norris-Fisher Correspondence*, 219.

13. On the common use of romantic pseudonyms among courting couples, see Mary Beth Norton, *Liberty's Daughters: The Revolutionary Experience of American Women* (Boston: Little, Brown, 1980), 52.

14. Deborah Norris to Sarah Fisher, July 4, 1779, in Sweeney, *The Norris-Fisher Correspondence*, 195.

15. Norris to Fisher, 204. That these effusions were not part of Deborah's diary writing in middle and old age are an example of the rise and fall of her generation's cultural project of sensibility, as described in Sarah Knott, *Sensibility and the American Revolution* (Chapel Hill: University of North Carolina Press, 2009).

16. Norris to Fisher, December 1780, 217, 219n6.

17. Sweeney, *The Norris-Fisher Correspondence*, 231n1.The engagement may have been the subject of a long talk between Debby and Mary Pleasants Logan, the wife of George's brother Charles, that Debby reported to Sally Fisher in late 1780. "I had a most interesting conversation with her, it was twilight when we entered upon the subject & it lasted till near 10 Oclock, reserve was banish'd we spoke our sentiments freely, and parted mutually pleas'd (I believe) with Our Conference": Deborah Norris to Sally Fisher, n.d. (1780), in Sweeney, *The Norris-Fisher Correspondence*, 209.

18. Ibid., 231n1; Jan Lewis, "The Republican Wife: Virtue and Seduction in the Early Republic," *William and Mary Quarterly* 44 (October 1987): 693–95; Norton, *Liberty's Daughters*, 58–60.

19. Lewis, "The Republican Wife," 697.

20. Sally Fisher [Dawes] to Sally Fisher [Corbit], August 1781, in Sweeney, *The Norris-Fisher Correspondence*, 224.

21. George S. Brookes, *Friend Anthony Benezet* (Philadelphia: University of Pennsylvania Press, 1937), 25. See also Wister, *Sally Wister's Journal*, fnn115–17.

22. Sweeney, *The Norris-Fisher Correspondence*, 192; Jones, "Deborah Logan," 64.

23. Logan, *Memoir of Dr. George Logan*, 121–22; Wister and Irwin, *Worthy Women of Our First Century*, 290; Tolles, *George Logan of Philadelphia*, 206.

24. Jones, "Deborah Logan," 17; Logan, *Memoir of Dr. George Logan*, 43; Tolles, *George Logan of Philadelphia*, 43, 51.

25. Wister and Irwin, *Worthy Women of Our First Century*, 294; Logan, *Memoir of Dr. George Logan*, 44, 99; Jones, "Deborah Logan," 17; Tolles, *George Logan of Philadelphia*, 53.

26. Tolles, *George Logan of Philadelphia*, 43; Wister and Irwin, *Worthy Women of Our First Century*, 296–97. It is tempting to conclude from the timing and size of their family (the three sons were born in the first ten years of the marriage, and Deborah had the last at twenty-nine) that Deborah and George were part of the Revolutionary-era vanguard of couples who cooperated to limit the size of their family: see Susan Klepp, *Revolutionary Conceptions: Women, Fertility, and Family Limitation in America, 1760–1820* (Chapel Hill: University of North Carolina Press, 2009). Both Klepp and Mary Beth Norton interpret this as a sign of greater equality for women in marriage: see also Norton, *Liberty's Daughters*, 232, 234.

27. Logan, *Memoir of Dr. George Logan*, 46–48.

28. Lewis, "The Republican Wife," 707, 712–13.

29. Zagarri, *A Woman's Dilemma*; Barker-Benfield, *Abigail and John Adams*; Skemp, *Judith Sargent Murray*.

30. Lewis, "The Republican Wife," 699–700; Rosemarie Zagarri, "Morals, Manners, and the Republican Mother," *American Quarterly* 44, no. 2 (June 1992): 192–215; Nancy Cott, *Public Vows: A History of Marriage and the Nation* (Cambridge, MA: Harvard University Press, 2000), 18–21; Deborah Norris to Sarah Wister, April 18, 1778, in Derounian, "A Dear, Dear Friend," 501–2.

31. Lewis, "The Republican Wife," 720.

32. Cott, *Public Vows*, 17.

33. George Logan to Deborah Norris Logan, September 19, 1785, Logan Family Papers, Collection 379, HSP (hereafter, LFP379), box 7, folder 8, 9.

34. Ibid., June 1798, LFP379, box 7, folder 31. In fact, George gave Debby power of attorney lest he be accused of treason on his mission to France and the property confiscated: Tolles, *George Logan of Philadelphia*, 155.

35. George Logan to Deborah Norris Logan, n.d., LFP379, box 7, folder 40.

36. Ibid., July 1798, box 7, folder 32, July 26, 1798, box 7, folder 33, July 28, 1799, box 7, folder 34, all in LFP379.

37. Ibid., December 12, 1799, LFP379, box 7, folder 39.

38. Ibid., April 5, 1783, LFP379, box 7, folder 4, p. 5; George Logan to Deborah Norris Logan, April 1783, LFP379, box 7, folder 5, 6.

39. Ibid., 1800, LFP379, box 7, folder 41. For other instructions, see ibid., February 20, 1805, box 7, folder 47, February 12, 1806[?], box 7, folder 49, in LFP379.

40. Ibid., 1802?, LFP379, box 7, folder 45.

41. Ibid., December 7, 1801, LFP379, box 7, folder 43.

42. Logan, *Memoir of Dr. George Logan*, 97–98, 101–3; Wister and Irwin, *Worthy Women of Our First Century*, 314; Jones, "Deborah Logan," 18.

43. The eldest, Albanus, accompanied George to Washington and then was sent to the College of William and Mary at the suggestion of Thomas Jefferson: George Logan to Deborah Norris Logan, December 7, 1801. That we do not have much from Deborah on the birth and raising of her children is interesting, given Linda Kerber's influential argument that the nation embraced an enhanced "Republican Mother" role for women after the Revolution to give them a quasi-political role in the new republic. Of course, for Deborah, as for other women, the periods of childbearing and childrearing were intensely busy. Deborah did not begin her diary until 1807, after her youngest son had reached sixteen; other women's diaries also show gaps or sparer entries at these times: see, e.g., Klepp and Wulf, *The Diary of Hannah Callender Sansom*, vii, 1. Yet the lack of discussion of childrearing in letters or looking back might also indicate that motherhood was not yet endowed with the importance that it would come to have in the antebellum era. The Logan boys, like others among the affluent families who were most likely to be affected by new ideas circulating in print, were sent to boarding school at fairly young ages. Jan Lewis has argued that women strove to be Republican wives before they came to focus on Republican motherhood. Perhaps this explains Deborah's lack of commentary on her sons' childhoods: see Lewis, "The Republican Wife."

44. Tolles suggests that she did not think his behavior inconsistent and supported him: Tolles, *George Logan of Philadelphia*, 129–30.

45. Ibid., 130, 146–47 (although Tolles imputes greater indifference to and ignorance of politics on Debby's part than is warranted by his own evidence of her positions and concerns). See also ibid., 171.

46. Logan, *Memoir of Dr. George Logan*, 52–60; Wister and Irwin, *Worthy Women of Our First Century*, 313; Jones, "Deborah Logan," 17, 65; Tolles, *George Logan of Philadelphia*, 154–56; Thompson Westcott, *The Historic Mansions and Buildings of Philadelphia* (Philadelphia: Porter and Coates, 1877), 152. For reaction to the venture and Logan's law, see Logan, *Memoir of Dr. George Logan*, 74–87.

47. Logan, *Memoir of Dr. George Logan*, 54; Tolles, *George Logan of Philadelphia*, 154–55; Wister and Irwin, *Worthy Women of Our First Century*, 305. Copy of George Logan to Thomas Jefferson and others (via Deborah Norris Logan), letter describing his doings, box 7, folder 35; George Logan to Deborah Norris Logan, letter, September 1798, box 7, folder 36; notes on George Logan's doings in Deborah Norris Logan's hand, box 7, folder 37, all in LFP379; Logan, *Memoir of Dr. George Logan*, 58–60.

48. Westcott, *The Historic Mansions and Buildings of Philadelphia*, 152.

49. Abigail Adams to John Adams, December 31, 1798, in *Adams Family Correspondence*, vol. 13, ed. Sara Martin et al. (Cambridge, MA: Harvard University Press, 2017), 334–36. For others' mixed reports, see Tolles, *George Logan of Philadelphia*, ix–xiii, 206–7. Tolles even quotes one of Logan's Senate colleagues, who judged that George Logan was "not a great man": Tolles, *George Logan of Philadelphia*, ix.

50. Logan, *Memoir of Dr. George Logan*, 115.

51. George Logan to Deborah Norris Logan, April 2, 1810, May 6, 1810, May 25, 1810, LFP379, box 7, folders 56–58; Wister and Irwin, *Worthy Women of Our First Century*, 314, 316–17; Logan, *Memoir of Dr. George Logan*, 116–17, 119.

52. Deborah Norris Logan to Maria D. Logan, January 20, 1801, LFP379, box 7, folder 59.

53. DNL-LCP, quotes from November 1814, January 1815.

54. Deborah Norris Logan Diaries, 1815–1839, Logan Family Papers, Collection 380, vols. 28–44, Historical Society of Pennsylvania, Philadelphia (hereafter, DNL-HSP), 2:17 (Summer 1816). That she copied letters to George from prominent political figures indicates again her continued interest in politics: see ibid., 2:27–30, 31–42.

55. Ibid., 2:108, 119–20. See also Tolles, *George Logan of Philadelphia*, 310–11.

56. DNL-HSP, 3:44, 148 (September 9, 1818), 151.

57. Ibid., 3:61. Elsewhere she addresses a reader: "You will . . . "

58. Tolles, *George Logan of Philadelphia*, ix–xiii. Tolles sums up: "George Logan . . . was not the wisest, the most prudent, the most consistent of men. He was naive, impulsive, humorless, often wrong-headed . . . but he had goodness": ibid., xiii.

59. DNL-HSP, 3:35 (September 15, 1817).

60. Ibid., 2:147 (April 21, 1817).

61. Ibid., 2:128 (March 10, 1817); Susan Stabile, *Memory's Daughters: The Material Culture of Remembrance in Eighteenth-Century America* (Ithaca, NY: Cornell University Press, 2004), 78.

62. I am indebted to Sheila Skemp for pushing me on this issue. On Quakers and anger, see Peter Stearns and Carol Z. Stearns, *Anger: The Struggle for Emotional Control in America's History* (Chicago: University of Chicago Press, 1986), 30–31. On "Quaker emotional decorum," see Kevin O'Neill, "'Pale & Dejected Exhausted by the Waste of Sorrow': Courtship and the Expression of Emotion, Mary Shackleton, 1783–1791," in *Sexed Sentiments: Interdisciplinary Perspectives on Gender and Emotion*, ed. Willemijn Ruberg and Kristine Steenbergh (Amsterdam: Rodopi, 2011), 49–56.

63. On the "constructedness" of the diary, see Terri Premo, "'Like a Being Who Does Not Belong': The Old Age of Deborah Norris Logan," *Pennsylvania Magazine of History and Biography* 107, no. 1 (January 1983): 88–89, 107–8.

64. DNL-HSP, 4:12–16 (March 20, 1819), 29–33.

65. Ibid., 4:16 (June 12, 1820). Although she claimed to be "happy if I can contribute to his welfare and comfort," she noted, "I can do very little besides waiting upon and nursing him," implying that she could imagine doing other things: ibid., 4:17; see also ibid., 4:36 (October 12, 1820), 4:38 (December 11, 1820).

66. Ibid., 4:46 (January 28, 1821).

67. Ibid., 4:61.

68. Ibid., 4:61–62: "And now that a week has elapsed since his interment . . . it seems like a frightful dream and that it cannot be that he is dead and that I shall never see him more. . . . But I have the great consolation to think that whilst he was here I made him happy, that his heart glowed with unbounded love towards me, [and that he has been saved]."

69. Ibid., 4:65, 68, 92.

70. Ibid., 4:70.

71. Ibid., 4:71.

72. Ibid., 4:79, 81–82, 102, 104 (August 1821), 107, 130 (October 1821).

73. Ibid., 4:104–5 (August 30, 1821); Jones, "Deborah Logan," 38, 112–13; Premo, "Like a Being Who Does Not Belong," 90.

74. DNL-HSP, 5:13 (November 21, 1821).

75. Jones, "Deborah Logan," 41.

76. Ibid., 20–23, 108–9.

77. Wister and Irwin, *Worthy Women of Our First Century,* 319–20; Jones, "Deborah Logan," 92; Westcott, *The Historic Mansions and Buildings of Philadelphia,* 153. On anonymous publications, see Wister and Irwin, *Worthy Women of Our First Century,* 300; Jones, "Deborah Logan," 94–95, 107. When she wrote the memoir of George after his death in 1821, the Historical Society asked whether it could publish selections, but she demurred. The manuscript was passed around and published after her death: Logan, *Memoir of Dr. George Logan,* 120–22; Jones, "Deborah Logan," 110–14.

78. Wister and Irwin, *Worthy Women of Our First Century,* 322–27; Jones, "Deborah Logan," 115, 118, 121–24.

79. Jones, "Deborah Logan," 118–19 (long quote), 121–24, 128; Wister and Irwin, *Worthy Women of Our First Century,* 322–27; John F. Watson, *Annals of Philadelphia and Pennsylvania in the Olden Time; Being a Collection of Memoirs, Anecdotes, and Incidents Concerning the City, Country, and Inhabitants, from the Days of the Founders,* 2 vols. (Philadelphia: Parry and M'Millan, 1855), 1:573–74.

80. Deborah often wrote poetry and published some anonymously in the *National Gazette:* Jones, "Deborah Logan," 94–95; Wister and Irwin, *Worthy Women of Our First Century,* 300. She also published some newspaper articles and obituaries, again anonymously: Jones, "Deborah Logan," 107. *Memoir of Dr. George Logan* was only published after her death: Jones, "Deborah Logan," 114.

81. Wister and Irwin, *Worthy Women of Our First Century,* 326; Westcott, *The Historic Mansions and Buildings of Philadelphia,* 154; Jones, "Deborah Logan," 73.

82. DNL-HSP, 4:109 (September 12, 1821).

83. Ibid., 13:11 (April 6, 1830), 13:38: "Second day was past by me without much enjoyment, I was dull and had a debt demanded of me which I could not immediately pay—a sure thing to make me fall back upon myself." See also ibid., 14:10 (March 11, 1832). On her advice to young women, see Premo, "Like a Being Who Does Not Belong," 95.

84. DNL-HSP, 13:19 (October 27, 1836), 21.

85. Maria Dickinson Logan, obituary of Deborah Norris Logan for *The Friend,* 1839, ms. 14271.Q, Library Company of Philadelphia, Logan box 8, folder 12.

86. Premo observes that Deborah's struggle to achieve a sense of resignation late in life might have served to reconcile her to the disappointments of earthly constraints as well as to prepare her for death: Premo, "Like a Being Who Does Not Belong," 99.

Afterword

SHEILA L. SKEMP

In 1989, the University Press of Virginia published what at the time was a seminal work, Ron Hoffman's and Peter Albert's *Women in the Age of the American Revolution,* an anthology devoted—as its title indicates—to an analysis of American women's position in the revolutionary age.[1] Appearing nine years after the pathbreaking work of Linda Kerber and Mary Beth Norton, the book attempted to do its part to alleviate what Norton called the "mutual neglect" that led both traditional historians and historians of women to steer clear of research on women's experience during the American Revolution. That such a project is no longer quite so necessary is in large part due to the efforts of Kerber, Norton, and the historians whose work was featured in that hefty volume.

Women in the Age of the American Revolution is something of a strange hybrid, an indication, perhaps, of the sorry state of the field at the time. Nearly half of the book is devoted to thoughtful, carefully researched analyses of the economic position of women *in* the revolutionary age, with little attention to the effect—if any—that the Revolution had on women, or that women had on the Revolution. A few other essays focus more directly on specific aspects of the relationship between women and the Revolution: two essays deal with the African American experience; one with the religious identities of white New England women; and another with the experiences of women from one elite Maryland family who saw the Revolution primarily through the lens provided by the men in their lives. An analysis of changes in the legal rights of women after the war rounds out the anthology. What binds these disparate essays into something approaching a satisfactory whole is the effort—commonplace now but much less so at the time—to view all of these subjects from the perspective of women. Instead of asking why men wrote wills in the way that they did, for instance, these historians asked how those wills affected women, and how they affected women, even in the same families, in decidedly different ways. If it did nothing more—and, of course, it did indeed do much more than that—the collection led subsequent generations of historians to rethink their approach to the study of women.

In her "Reflections" at the end of the book, Norton highlighted the contributions to the field that the volume made even as she issued the requisite call for more. She pointed, of course, to the varieties of women's experiences that remained to be studied—in terms of class, race, ethnicity, and region in particular—noting that *Women in the Age of the American Revolution* says nothing at all about Native American women, whose experience surely challenges what remains of the Whiggish view of American history. She was especially concerned about the collection's lack of attention to the lives of "ordinary women." Arguing that these women were not "inarticulate," she insisted instead that "historians are deaf"; they simply fail to hear the voices of those women who have fascinating and important stories to tell. Norton wanted more. She also wanted historians to ask different questions about their subjects, to make that imaginative leap that would allow them to enter the world of eighteenth-century women and to see the world through their eyes.

The essays in our volume are a measure of how far we have come since 1989 and how many historians have come to the fore to address at least some of the issues that Norton saw as so crucial to our understanding of American women in the mid-eighteenth century. Building on the great strides that historians have made in the past couple of decades, they both advance and broaden our understanding of women's experiences in the era of the American Revolution, even as they invite us to ask still more questions about those experiences.

As was not the case in the 1989 volume, this collection does not ignore the experiences of Native Americans. Still, much, much more needs to be done in this area. Everyone knows that Native Americans—those who supported the patriot fight for independence, as well as those who opposed it—suffered at war's end. Women in particular struggled vainly to retain their way of life, based on communitarian rather than individualistic ideals, ultimately losing control of their possessions, their bodies, their culture. Still, as Maeve Kane points out, we often find ourselves succumbing to a "narrative of decline" that fails to appreciate the complexities that characterized the lives of Native women. It seems fair to ask whether at least some of these women were able to maintain a measure of autonomy, to control some aspects of their lives, to exhibit the independence that so many other oppressed individuals have managed to achieve in the face of nearly insuperable odds.

The essays by David Waldstreicher and Sara Collini indicate that African American women often managed to do just that, contextualizing and complicating our understanding of the experience of free and enslaved African American women. More than any other historian, Waldstreicher makes Phillis Wheatley's womanhood central to her story, arguing also that her understanding of the ancient world constituted a profound and radical critique of the worldview of the slaveholding founders. Collini's essay does not dispute Jacqueline Jones's grim picture of the consequences of the Revolution for African American women that appears in the 1989 volume so much as it explores the variety of ways that the war affected those women. If Collini's Kate was a victim, she was not *just* a victim. As a midwife she was entrepreneurial and geographically mobile, a self-actualizer who demanded and received money for her services, which, paradoxically—thanks to the increased importance of slavery in the postwar world—made those services more valued than ever. Kate's story is her own, of course, but it is a prudent reminder that generalizations about "women"—or even about a particular subgroup of women—should be made with the utmost caution.

The experiences of loyalist women, as described by Kimberly Nath, are yet another reminder of the varieties of women's experiences. These women endured the same hardships that patriot women faced, but they did so in the face of social and political disapproval and ended up on the losing side. They endured hardships seemingly for nothing. They appeared to understand the arguments for independence and for loyalty and chose—at least in some cases—in a conscious way to embrace the "tory" cause. How many of these women, we need to ask, chose to remain loyal to the king simply because they remained loyal to their husbands? To what extent were their choices truly autonomous? But, then, we might ask the very same thing about those women who "chose" independence. Despite their different views of the Revolution, might loyalist and patriot women's similarities actually be more obvious than the differences?

Essays by Susan Brandt, Kaylan M. Stevenson, Serena Zabin, and Nath all introduce readers to the lived experiences of "ordinary" women in ways that force us to question many of the assumptions we make about women in the era of the Revolution. Both Stevenson's milliners and Brandt's apothecary were savvy, successful entrepreneurs long before the Revolution occurred. Thus, the Revolution did not "empower" them (in the case of the milliners, the coming of the Revolution actually destroyed their prospects for success); it did not turn them into self-confident economic actors. It is useful to ask, then, whether there might be many, many more women—some married, some not—who were involved in the day-to-day economy of the mainland British colonies and for whom the war and its aftermath actually changed very little. While Zabin brings Boston's women away from the periphery, moving them to the center, to the very heart of the revolutionary experience, her description of these women in the period leading up to the "Massacre," similarly interrogates the importance of "high politics" for women (and many men), whose primary focus was on what once would have been labeled as distinctly private concerns. These women married, socialized, bore children—but they did so at a time when marital choices bore a political meaning. What, we might well ask, was the meaning of marriage to those women who tied themselves to British officers and soldiers despite the disapproval of many of their friends and neighbors? And how, and to what extent, did their marital choices affect their political perspectives as tensions between England and its mainland colonies were exacerbated? While we know a great deal about the political views of at least some elite women, we still find it very difficult to get inside the minds of ordinary white women. Did they care about or even listen to the discussions of "taxation without representation" or the demands for independence and equality that swirled about them? Did they imagine that they could construct a new relationship to the state for themselves at war's end? Did they see themselves as rights-bearing citizens, members of the new nation?

The stories of the elite women in this volume tell us much more about the Revolution than we could even have imagined in 1989. The traditional triumvirate of Abigail Adams, Mercy Otis Warren, and Judith Sargent Murray are virtually absent from these pages. Instead, we are introduced to some women who are anything but household names, even as we come to understand women such as the iconic Martha Washington in new and significant ways. Collectively, the portraits of Washington, Mary Willing Byrd, Annis Boudinot Stockton, and Deborah Norris Logan indicate that the lives and perspectives of some elite women were profoundly affected by the vicissitudes of the American Revolution. Washington, argues Thompson, was changed by her wartime experience. She was "a very different woman" at the end of the war, no longer "the sheltered and rather fearful person" she had been in 1776. Moreover, she was something of a political being in her own right. Her duties as hostess served a valuable diplomatic function. Her active support of women such as Sarah Franklin Bache had distinct political overtones. Although we are never quite sure what Byrd believed or why, Ami Pflugrad-Jackish's essay demonstrates that Byrd consciously used the rhetoric of the Revolution to claim rights for herself and to think strategically about ways to construct a meaningful relationship to the new republican order. She paid her taxes, was virtuous, was a property owner, and provided for her children. If the state refused to grant her pleas, it did so only because American men were violating their own ideals. Martha King's Stockton was similarly astute. Her political views became more sophisticated throughout the war; she was increasingly willing to circulate— virtually to self-publish—her poems, clearly behaving as a political being, even as she feared that her views would be discounted because they came from the pen of a woman. Like Stockton, Deborah Logan used her pen to defend her husband and to proclaim her loyalty to the new nation. And like Byrd, Logan struggled with the contradictions between the ideal and the reality in the revolutionary era. As C. Dallett Hemphill points out, Deborah Logan lived in a world where the companionate marriage, bolstered by an emphasis on the power of sensibility, was becoming the ideal, even as coverture and notions of hierarchy remained solidly in place. Her own marriage, says Hemphill, was "a complex mix of mutuality and wifely submission," in which women may have exercised some influence, but never had—or even seemed to demand—real power.

As always, anthologies produce at least as many questions as they do answers, thus preparing the way for new and exciting perspectives. In broad terms, of course, we still want to know how the American Revolution affected women and how women affected the Revolution. But as these essays indicate, it is impossible—then and now—to talk about "women" in some monolithic or generic fashion. What liberated or empowered one group of women may well have enslaved or weakened another. Annis Boudinot Stockton's world was not the world of a Phillis Wheatley or a Kate. Her elite status made her wartime burdens lighter; the work of other women's unfree labor gave her the freedom to think about the meaning of the Revolution and to write about it. Martha Washington also profited from her elite status. True, her wartime experiences were hardly pleasurable, and at times she endured real hardships. But her world was markedly different from that occupied by the hundreds of women who—like Washington— followed their husbands to the battlefield. Did Washington talk to these women? Help them? Even notice their very existence? It is highly likely that neither Stockton nor Washington saw the "other women" around them as "sisters." Class and race virtually always trumped womanhood.

Indeed, if we are to take Norton's injunction to view eighteenth-century women from their own perspective, then we must do our best to avoid imposing our own ideas of what is important on women who lived in a world that is so very different from our own. How did these women identify themselves? What mattered most to them? Did they see themselves primarily in relationship to the men in their lives? Washington, Stockton, and Logan all seemed more preoccupied with their loyalty to their husbands than they did with their fealty to the new nation. Nash's loyalists were similarly focused on maintaining the strength of their families during extremely trying times. Did Wheatley and Kate think of themselves primarily as women or as African Americans? To what extent did women identify with their ethnic origin, their region, their political beliefs? How central was religion—a subject barely touched on in any of the essays in this collection—to these women?

And then there is the issue of gender identity. All of these essays at least tacitly assume that eighteenth-century women were heterosexual. Echoing—no doubt unconsciously—the binary constructions of an era that was inching ever more steadily toward the ideal (if not the reality) of separate spheres, they talk of "men" and "women" as if they were virtually opposites. They describe a world in which "men were men and women were women." This is a world, of course, that did not exist in the eighteenth century any more than it does today. Zabin's description of colonial Boston reminds us that men and women did not live in separate spheres; they occupied the same physical, cultural and emotional spaces. The divisions between men's and women's worlds were fluid and easily breached. It is also true that the eighteenth century was peopled by women who were not sure of their gender identities. In fact, both in fiction and in the "real world," examples abound indicating that people of the period were aware of, even fascinated by, women who transgressed traditional gender lines. Judith Sargent Murray wrote frequently as a man; Deborah Sampson Gannett donned men's clothing and briefly entered the field of battle as a common soldier; Charles Brockdon Brown's *Ormond* was just one of many novels that played with notions of transgressive gender identity. To discuss these realities is neither "politically correct" nor presentist. It is to address concerns and behavior of people at the time. Historians clearly need to grapple with these issues, arriving at a more nuanced and accurate understanding of the fluidity of gender identity in the revolutionary era.

Most of these essays at least gesture to a problem with which historians of the period continue to struggle: the definition of politics. They all wisely take for granted, as women did in the eighteenth century, that formal politics—voting, office holding—were not the only or even the best ways for citizens to engage in meaningful political activity. Some, such as Wheatley, Logan, and Stockton, wrote extensively on topics that were profoundly political. The marriages of women in Zabin's Boston had clear political ramifications. Washington's services as hostess were performed not just to help her husband but to support the cause that she had embraced. As historians continue to examine the stories of women, they will no doubt find even more examples of individuals who acted "politically" without even thinking about, much less demanding, the right to vote. Still, as they uncover and analyze the meaning of "the political," they need to proceed with caution. Obviously, that meaning cannot be so narrow as to preclude anything outside the realm of formal political behavior. But if we expand that definition too widely, if we assume that every power relationship takes on a broad political meaning, we risk arguing that virtually every act is "political," thus rendering the entire endeavor almost meaningless.

These essays are replete with compelling "stories" that complicate and enrich our understanding of the experience of women in the revolutionary era. Even as we continue to urge historians to uncover more such stories, adding to our fund of knowledge about the lived lives of real people, we might well ask whether the biographical approach is, indeed, the only way to help us arrive at an understanding of the general meaning of the Revolution for the women who lived through it. The more stories we have, the more difficult it becomes to make any generalization at all about *the* way in which women affected or were affected by the American Revolution. In the 1970s, colonial historians were briefly fixated on studying individual New England towns, hoping that by doing so they would be able to make some generalizations about *the* experience of seventeenth-century settlers in the region. In the end, they had to concede that no generalizations were possible; that each town had its own history, its own identity. Similarly, the analysis of individual lives allows us appreciate the variety of women's experiences in the revolutionary era, even as doing so makes it increasingly difficult to devise any generalizations about the meaning of that era for women.

In the end, we are still asking—in old ways and in new—the same basic questions. How did the Revolution affect women, and how did women affect the Revolution? And how do we go about trying to answer those questions? We know, at the very least, that the Revolution meant different things to different people. It gave some women a chance to imagine a new relationship between themselves and the state. It gave others a chance to practice their entrepreneurial skills. Many no doubt saw the war and its outcome as something of a mixed bag. They lost a great deal; they gained at least a little. Most important, the Revolution simply highlighted the contradictions between republican ideals and the reality in which women actually existed. Notions of equality and independence meant little to Kate, the African American midwife; to Wheatley; to Native American women. Indeed, for them, the Whiggish view of American history—for women *and* men—was a cruel myth. For them, as Waldstreicher argues, "history was going backward, not forward." By the turn of the century, as rights-bearing American women were increasingly marginalized and even disdained, that

254 SHEILA L. SKEMP

"backward" trajectory grew ever more palpable and disheartening. True enough, their granddaughters might rely on the rhetoric of the Revolution to demand rights for themselves, but the women of the era would not live to enjoy the true promise of the Revolution.

Note

1. Ronald Hoffman and Peter J. Albert, eds., *Women in the Age of the American Revolution* (Charlottesville: University Press of Virginia, 1989).

Contributors

SUSAN HANKET BRANDT is a Lecturer at the University of Colorado, Colorado Springs. She holds a B.S.N. from Duke University and a Ph.D. in history from Temple University. In 2016, her "Gifted Women and Skilled Practitioners: Gender and Healing Authority in the Delaware Valley , 1740–1830" won the Lerner-Scott Prize awarded by the Organization of American Historians for the best dissertation in women's history. Her article "'Getting into a Little Business': Margaret Hill Morris and Women's Medical Entrepreneurship during the American Revolution" appeared in *Early American Studies* (2015).

SARA COLLINI is a Ph.D. candidate in the Department of History at George Mason University and a Graduate Research Assistant for the Education Division at the Roy Rosenzweig Center for History and New Media. She received her bachelor's degree from the University of Texas, Austin, and her master's degree in U.S. history from George Mason University. Her dissertation explores the paradoxical work of enslaved midwives in the revolutionary and postrevolutionary eras.

C. DALLETT HEMPHILL was the heart and soul of the Early Americanist community in Philadelphia until her death in 2015. A professor at Ursinus College for twenty-eight years, she was an associate of the McNeil Center for Early American Studies and a dedicated editor of the journal *Early American Studies*. She was committed to the importance of integrating the insights of gender history into narratives of the American past. Dallett taught, guided, and mentored numerous students during her career. She was the author of two books: *Bowing to Necessities: A History of Manners in America, 1620–1860* (1999) and *Siblings: Brothers and Sisters in American History* (2011).

MAEVE KANE is an Assistant Professor in the Department of History at the University at Albany, State University of New York. She holds a Ph.D. in American history from Cornell University. Her recent publications include "Covered with Such a Cappe: The Archaeology of Seneca Clothing, 1615–1820," in *Ethnohistory*, and "For Wagrassero's Son: Colonialism and the Structure of Indigenous Women's Social Connections, 1690–1730," in *Journal of Early American History*.

MARTHA J. KING is a Senior Editor at the Papers of Thomas Jefferson at Princeton University. She holds a Ph.D. in history from the College of William and Mary. She is a recipient of the Distinguished Service Award from the Association for Documentary Editing. Among her recent publications are "Receive the Olive Branch: Benjamin Rush as Reconciler in the Early Republic," in *Early American Studies*, and "Clementina Rind: Widowed Printer of Williamsburg," in *Virginia Women: Their Lives and Times*, ed. Cynthia A. Kierner and Sandra Gioia Treadway (2015). She has a book manuscript in progress on female printers in the American Revolution.

KIMBERLY NATH is an Assistant Professor at the University of Wisconsin, Whitewater. She holds a Ph.D. from the University of Delaware. She is the author of "Loyalism, Citizenship, American Identity: The Shoemaker Family," in *The American Revolution Reborn*, ed. Patrick Spero and Michael Zuckerman (2016).

BARBARA B. OBERG is the Editor Emerita of the Papers of Thomas Jefferson and a Senior Research Scholar Emerita in the Department of History at Princeton University. She served as the editor of *The Papers of Benjamin Franklin* at Yale University before coming to Princeton. She was the co-editor (with Harry S. Stout) of *Benjamin Franklin, Jonathan Edwards, and the Representation of American Culture* (1993) and co-editor (with Doron S. Ben-Atar) of *Federalists Reconsidered* (1998).

AMI PFLUGRAD-JACKISCH is an Associate Professor of History at the University of Toledo. She holds a Ph.D. from the University of Buffalo. She is the author of *Brothers of a Vow: Secret Fraternal Organizations and the Transformation of White Male Culture in Antebellum Virginia* (2010) and is completing a book-length manuscript titled "The World of Westover: Mary Willing Byrd, Gender, Slavery, and the Economics of Citizenship in Revolutionary Virginia." She has presented her research on Byrd at a number of conferences, including the Southern Intellectual History Circle, and at annual meetings of the Southern Historical Association, the Society for

Historians of the Early American Republic, and the Southern Association of Women Historians.

SHEILA L. SKEMP is the Clare Leslie Marquette Professor Emerita of American History at the University of Mississippi. She holds a Ph.D. in history from the University of Iowa. She is the editor or author of seven books, most recently *First Lady of Letters: Judith Sargent Murray and the Struggle for Female Independence* (2009) and *The Making of a Patriot: Benjamin Franklin at the Cockpit* (2012). She has recently been recognized with the University of Montana's Distinguished Alumnae Award.

KAYLAN M. STEVENSON is a Manuscript Editor for the books program at the Omohundro Institute for Early American History and Culture. She holds an M.A. from the College of William and Mary.

MARY V. THOMPSON is the Research Historian at the Fred W. Smith National Library for the Study of George Washington. She holds an M.A. from the University of Virginia. Her book *In the Hands of a Good Providence: Religion in the Life of George Washington* (2008) received the Alexandria History Award from the Alexandria (Virginia) Historical Society in 2009 and the George Washington Memorial Award from the George Washington Masonic National Memorial Association in 2013; her new work, *"The Only Unavoidable Subject of Regret": George Washington, Slavery, and the Enslaved Community at Mount Vernon*, will be published in 2019.

DAVID WALDSTREICHER is a Distinguished Professor of History at the Graduate Center, City University of New York, and the author of *In the Midst of Perpetual Fetes: The Making of American Nationalism, 1776–1820* (1997), *Runaway America: Benjamin Franklin, Slavery, and the American Revolution* (2004), *Slavery's Constitution: From Revolution to Ratification* (2008). Most recently he was co-editor (with Matthew Mason) of *John Quincy Adams and the Politics of Slavery: Selections from the Diary* (2016) and editor of *The Diaries of John Quincy Adams, 1779–1848*.

SERENA R. ZABIN is a Professor of History and Director of American Studies at Carleton College. She holds a Ph.D. from Rutgers University. She is the author of *Dangerous Economies: Status and Commerce in British New York* (2009). Her current project is a new interpretation of the Boston Massacre of 1770 that shows the intimate connections among soldiers, their families, and Bostonians during the years immediately preceding the Revolutionary War.

ROSEMARIE ZAGARRI is a Professor of History at George Mason University. She holds a Ph.D. from Yale University. Her areas of interest are early American history, early American women, and eighteenth-century transatlantic and global history. She has served on numerous editorial boards and the Council of the Omohundro Institute of Early American Culture and been president of the Society of Historians of the Early American Republic. Her most recent book is *Revolutionary Backlash: Women and Politics in the Early American Republic* (2007).

Index